FESTO KIV

Bishop Festo Kivengere was one of the most remark-able Christians of the twentieth century. From a remote tribe, a man who never knew the day, month or year of his birth, he was probably the most famous evangelist ever to come out of Africa. He was also a teacher, pastor, aid worker, author, refugee and national hero.

As East African Team Leader of Africa Enterprise, and Bishop of Kigezi, Festo seemed destined to die at the hands of Idi Amin. The Kivengeres escaped to Rwanda hours ahead of Amin's death squads, return-ing after Amin's overthrow to play a major role in the huge task of national reconstruction. He travelled widely, preaching reconciliation in Christ. His radiant faith and tireless campaigns for justice established his reputation far beyond his own land.

This biography, the result of three years' research, was prepared with his full co-operation.

Bishop Festo died of leukaemia in 1988.

'Festo Kivengere's life and love and witness for Christ touched not only all Africa but the wider world. As an apostle of the love of God and the Cross of Christ, his story is required reading for all who wish to grow in grace, understanding and obedience to both the Great Commandment and the Great Commission.'

Michael Cassidy

'Festo Kivengere was one of those rare men with multiple gifts as an evangelist, teacher, church leader. Even more than that, I felt, as did all those who knew him, he was my friend and brother. Most important, he was like an open window through which the radiance of Jesus Christ poured. If a saint is someone who lets the light shine through, Festo was one. I thank God that believers and non-believers in most parts of the world felt the impact of this humble giant of God.'

Leighton Ford

'Whether praying with internees facing a firing squad or meeting with Presidents of east and west, Festo Kivengere's leadership touched the lives of millions. A "first generation" Christian of Uganda, his inspired preaching and leadership help to explain a Christian tide flooding across Africa that is going to be hard to stop.'

Richard Bewes

'He was an evangelist, committed to the vision of world evangelisation. He was a pastor, who cared for the people of his diocese. But above all he was a humble man of God, jealous not for his own honour but for the glory of Jesus Christ.'

John Stott

'My deepest memories of Festo Kivengere are his great sense of love, even for his enemies; his preaching, which was so anointed and enthusiastic; and his evident confidence in the living presence of the resurrected Lord Jesus Christ in his life.'

Luis Palau

'It is one of my fondest memories to have known and worked with Bishop Festo. He has to have been one of the most significant and outstanding evangelists of our time; but I loved him most for his personality—he was always warm, always humble, and laughter was never far away! I always felt I had something to learn when I was with him—and I did. His life proved, amidst all the conflicts, that love—inspired by Jesus—is the better way and the only hope in a wounded world.'

Garth Hewitt

Festo Kivengere

A Biography

ANNE COOMES

MONARCH
Eastbourne

British Library Cataloguing in Publication Data
Coomes, Anne
Festo Kivengere.
1. Africa. Christian church. Kivengere,
Festo, 1921–1988
I. Title
270.2092

ISBN 1–85424–021–8

Printed in Great Britain for
MONARCH PUBLICATIONS
1 St Anne's Road, Eastbourne, E Sussex BN21 3UN by
Richard Clay Ltd, Bungay, Suffolk
Typeset by J&L Composition Ltd, Filey, North Yorkshire

For David

CONTENTS

PREFACE

I stood beside Festo Kivengere's bed with fellow bishops and others as we prayed before anointing him during his last illness. He knew that he was dying and his family knew that he was dying and yet there were no tears, there was no gloom or sadness. No, in fact a soft light and a quiet joy suffused that room and the house. Festo smiled his gentle smile having committed himself and those very dear to him into the safekeeping of the Lord and Master in whose love he found his true security and meaning.

He had proclaimed the love of God in Jesus Christ so passionately and eloquently and was truly an ambassador of Christ in carrying out a wonderful ministry of reconciliation in his strife-torn Uganda. And when I stood beside his bed I realised that his most eloquent sermon had been his life—the manner of his living it and how he gave it up. God be praised for his faithful and dedicated servant Festo. He is now a wonderful part of the cloud of witnesses around us urging us on in the race that is set before us.

+Desmond Cape Town

Lambeth Palace London SE1 7JU

I am very glad to commend this biography of an outstanding servant of God.

Festo Kivengere was first and foremost an evangelist, with a remarkable gift for communicating the Gospel in an attractive and compelling way. His genius lay in his ability to speak with power to a nation torn apart by terrible suffering, and at the same time to point his fellow countrymen beyond their divisions to the reconciling power of Jesus Christ.

Like Christian leaders in other parts of Africa, he spoke from a situation of appalling hardship, but he spoke with a voice of joy and vitality that is uniquely African. Increasingly the African voice is being heard within our own Anglican Communion, helping us to become more catholic in the ways we express our Christian life, and more evangelical in the simplicity of our faithfulness.

African Anglicans have had few more illustrious leaders than Bishop Festo Kivengere. At his funeral, President Museveni spoke of Festo as a father of the whole nation, a tireless campaigner for justice, integrity and righteousness in Uganda. But his reputation went far beyond his own nation. We knew him as a true disciple of his Lord.

When Festo passed through London, there was always a note or a word of encouragement for me, and perhaps a meeting here with his old friend Terry Waite.

When illness suddenly struck, he was in hospital in London. It was still the same Festo - in good times or in bad he trusted in God and embraced the future in confidence and hope.

Robert Cantuar

Archbishop of Canterbury

II

ACKNOWLEDGEMENTS

In researching this book I met with goodwill and co-operation everywhere I turned. People lent me—a complete stranger—irreplaceable maps, books, photographs, private letters, transcripts of conversations, newspaper and magazine cuttings. They spent hours in writing down reminiscences, or in talking to me. They cooked me meals, gave me beds for the night, loaned me cars (in Africa) and translated for me. Without such generosity, this book could never have been written.

My very grateful thanks, then, to:

Bishop Festo and his wife, Mera, for agreeing to the project, and for squeezing precious time out of already hectic schedules to talk to me.

To their daughters Charity, in Kampala, and Peace, in Geneva. Both helped fill in the family's years in Tanganyika and the United States. Peace also read the completed manuscript and corrected some wayward spelling of Ugandan names and terms.

To the Revd Richard Bewes, Rector of All Souls' Langham Place, London, for first approaching Bishop Festo on my behalf, and for the loan of his own considerable transcripts of interviews with the Bishop, and also photographs.

To the Archbishop of Canterbury, Dr Robert Runcie, and to the Revd Dr Billy Graham, for their personal stories of Bishop Festo.

To the several hundred other clergy, missionaries, retired missionaries, friends, colleagues, and acquaintances of Bishop Festo worldwide, who responded to my letter asking for background material. It is impossible to mention everyone, but they include:

In Africa: In South Africa: Archbishop Desmond Tutu. In Kenya: Bishop David Gitari. In Tanzania: Bishop Gresford Chitemo, T. W. Edward Mwangosi, and Bishop Matt Nyagwaswa. In Rwanda: Bishop Adoniya Sebunungiri.

In Britain: My thanks especially to: Bishop Leslie Brown, who as former Archbishop of Uganda was responsible for allowing Bishop Festo to go for ordination. To the late Dr Joe Church who deluged me with stories of Festo during the revival years in Kabale. To Lilian Clarke, who worked alongside Bishop Festo off and on for thirty-five years, and knew him perhaps better than anyone else in England. To Bishop Richard Lyth, who preceded Bishop Festo as Bishop of Kigezi. To Frances Rea, a close friend since Bishop Festo's first stay in England. To the Revd Pip Tribe, who taught the young Festo, and who donated the photograph of Festo playing a drum in the Boys Brigade.

Also in Britain: To the Revd Dr Harold Adeney, the Revd Patrick Ashe, Marguerite Barley, Bishop Michael Baughen, the Revd Clive Boddington, the Revd Pat Brooks, Jean Butlin, Agnes Buxton, Canon Bill Butler, Dr Roy Billington, the Revd David Cohen, Dr Martyn Cundy, Rhoda Cutbush, the Revd Eric Delve, Dr J. D. Douglas, Margaret Ford, Dorothy Gooch, Muriel Goodchild, Roy Hession, Dr Godfrey and Phyllis Hindley, Canon A. Houghton, the Revd Frank Larkworthy, Malcolm Lea-Wilson, Gordon Landreth, the Revd Brian Macdonald-Milne, Wendy Moynagh, Cynthia Mackay, Canon Alan Neech, Margaret Orpwood, the Revd Gottfried Osei-Mensah, Ken and Margaret Patterson, Nan Read, Gwenda Sams, George Swannell, the Revd Dr John Stott, Dr Jack Symonds, Bishop David Sheppard, the Very Revd Brian de Sarum, the Revd John Selfridge, the Revd John Sentamu, and Bishop John Taylor.

In America: To Dorothy Smoker, the co-writer of all of Bishop Festo's books, who generously gave me access to many transcripts as well as extensive notes on the Kivengere's family history.

Also to: J. Duncan Brown, Sally Childs, the Revd Dr Leighton Ford, Bishop William Frey, Marti Ensign, Thomas Getman, the Revd John Guest, the Revd Richard Halverson, Revd Dr Don Jacobs, Bishop C. Shannon Mallory, the Revd Dr Stanley Mooneyham, the Revd Dr Stephen Olford, the Revd Robert Ray

Parks, the Revd Dr Luis Palau, Pat Robertson, Dr Paul Rees, and the Revd Robert Schuller.

In Europe: To Dr Sigurd Aske of Norway, Claire-Lise de Benoit of Switzerland and Wolfgang Heiner of West Germany.

In Australia: To John G. Denton, the Revd Ken Griffiths, Bishop Alfred and Marjory Stanway, Lance Shilton, and Bishop Max Wiggins.

In New Zealand: To the Revd Noel Bythell, whose records of the Alliance School were invaluable in writing the chapters based in Dodoma.

In the Solomon Islands: Especially to the Revd Jezreel Filoa.

My grateful thanks also: To the International Chairman of African Evangelistic Enterprise, Warwick Olson.

To the AEE staff in London. Jean Wilson gave me endless help in tracing people, and a great deal of background information.

To the AEE staff in Pietermaritzburg, especially to the Revd Michael Cassidy, who only found time to answer my many queries by putting his answers on tape as he drove to different engagements.

To the AEE staff in Kampala, especially Canon Ernest Shalita and the late Revd James Katarikawe.

To the AEE staff in Nairobi, especially the Revd Daniel Serwanga and Elizabeth Ferri.

To the AEE staff in Pasadena, who supplied many of the photographs for this book.

To the AEE staff in Australia, especially chairman Dr Paul White.

To the office staff of Kigezi Diocese, especially Judith Trickett, Bishop Festo's secretary, who welcomed me into her home, and gave me (at Bishop Festo's suggestion) access to his private correspondence. To many clergy and friends in Kigezi diocese, including Erica Bugaari, the Very Revd Stanley Mateeka, the Revd James and Grace Ndyabahika, Hilda Tindiwensi, Kedrace Tumwesigye, Jason Turimumahoro, Ishmael Tuzooke, and Canon Abraham Zaribugire.

To the staff of North Kigezi Diocese, especially Bishop Yustasi Ruhindi and Canon Ishmael Bugaiga, who proved an excellent translator and who has since become a friend. Also: the Revd Yosia Banyenzaki, the Revd Stanley Kashillinga,

Canon Filimon Kitaburaza (Bishop Festo's cousin), Canon Ezra Mahega, and Canon Elijah Nkundizana.

To the Archbishop of Uganda, Dr Yona Okoth, and the staff of the Provincial Office of the Church of Uganda in Kampala.

To Mid-Africa Ministry (CMS) (formerly the Ruanda Mission) in London, especially Margaret Court.

To the Church Missionary Society in London, especially Rosemary Keene.

My thanks also to the libraries and archives of the Billy Graham Center in Wheaton Colleges, Chicago, the School of Oriental and African Studies London, the Church Missionary Society, London, and Makerere University College, Kampala.

To Miss Pat Strange of AEE London, who undertook the herculean task of turning my scrawl into an immaculate manuscript.

To the Revd Richard Bewes, Lilian Clark, the Revd Michael Cassidy, Dr David Killingray, Dr Louise Pirouet, the Revd Daniel Serwanga and the Revd Dr Kevin Ward who read the manuscript and made valuable corrections and suggestions. Any fault or imbalances that remain are solely mine.

To my editors, Tony Collins and Diana Archer, for their prodigious patience and optimism as deadlines came and went, with no sign of the completed manuscript.

And finally to my husband, for his unfailing support and enthusiasm for the writing of this book.

PROLOGUE

By the late 1980s the African Church could be numbered in many millions.

Of all these Christians, the most effective, famous and best loved evangelist was a Ugandan bishop, Festo Kivengere. When he died of leukemia in May 1988, tens of thousands of people worldwide mourned his death.

*   *   *

I first met Bishop Festo at a Lambeth Palace press conference on 4th October, 1981, while working as a reporter for the *Church of England Newspaper*. The press release informed me that Dr Runcie was to welcome and formally commission a team of Ugandan evangelists to Britain, headed by Bishop Festo. Their nationwide tour was called 'From Uganda with Love'.

Most Lambeth Palace press conferences are fairly formal affairs, but not on that particular morning. For one thing, Dr Runcie arrived with a big grin on his face. A moment later the reason was apparent: three Africans bounced (there is no other word for it) into the room. Dr Runcie beamed as he introduced them: Bishop Festo Kivengere, Bishop Miseari Kauma, and Mr John Wilson, all of Africa Evangelistic Enterprise.

The Ugandans' exuberance and cheerful good humour were contagious as they shared their hopes for the coming tour. Dr Runcie then surprised the Ugandans by awarding them all with the Cross of St Augustine for their 'outstanding contribution to the worldwide Anglican Communion'.

Bishop Festo, Bishop Miseari and John Wilson had an aura about them that touched me. I felt the name of their tour well chosen: 'From Uganda with Love'.

Several years later, Tony Collins, then editor at MARC Europe, rang my office one afternoon. 'What about a biography of Bishop Festo Kivengere?'

Something clicked inside me. Suddenly this was what I desperately wanted to do. But would Bishop Festo agree? I couldn't attempt such a mammoth project without his full co-operation.

I approached Bishop Festo through a mutual friend, the Revd Richard Bewes, rector of All Souls', Langham Place, London. There was a nail-biting moment when I rang the Bishop's hotel in London (he was passing through a few weeks later) for his reply. Bishop Festo sounded friendly but cautious. 'A biography on me? I have never thought of such a thing.'

Once he had got used to the idea, he proved a model subject. He gave me (endless) lists of contacts: friends, those not-so-friendly, colleagues and relatives. Letters began arriving on my doorstep, like migrating birds, from every corner of the world: the Solomon Islands, New Zealand, Africa, North America, Europe. Bishop Festo made time to see me for interviews whenever he passed through London that autumn.

In February of 1987 I flew out to Africa for a month of research. I met up with Bishop Festo and the AEE team in Nairobi. I followed Bishop Festo on to Kampala, where he was taking a city-wide mission. Bishop Festo had a car put at my disposal as I roamed around the city, tracking down yet more people who could give me stories of the bishop: from the Archbishop of Uganda to Bishop Festo's own daughters, and many other Christians all over Kampala. In the mornings, despite his pressing schedule, he let me interview him in the guest house lounge, to the intense curiosity of several chickens who wandered in and out.

In the evenings, when all of us guests at the Namirembe Guest House tended to stay indoors (there was still a lot of gunfire after dark), I sat with Bishop Festo in the TV lounge and watched his mission advertised on the national TV news ... and asked him yet more questions. He always answered me patiently.

When Bishop Festo and his wife Mera drove back to Kabale, they took me with them in their combi van. It was a highlight of my trip: they were glad to be going home after several months of travel and laughed and joked with me. We shared roast bananas and a coke, bought at a roadside stand.

Bishop Festo had promised me some more interviews in Kabale, but he was immediately engulfed in a wave of diocesan business. Everyone begged for 'just a few minutes alone with the Bishop'—especially his hard-pressed secretary, with whom I was staying.

So I went on up to north Kigezi, and stayed with Bishop Yustasi Ruhindi at Rukingiri, at the top of the hill where Festo's conversion began. I talked to many of his former revival colleagues, as well as former classmates and pupils. Canon Ishmael Bugaiga interpreted for me, day after day. We spent an afternoon with Erica Bugaari, Bishop Festo's earliest childhood friend. Erica showed me the hill over which had come the first white person they had ever seen. He gave me on parting an exquisite carved wooden milk jug (*kyanzi*), such as Bishop Festo's parents had used for storing the milk throughout his childhood.

On my last Saturday in Uganda, I determined to make my way south again to Kabale quite early, and have one last attempt to intercept Bishop Festo. But then arose a problem: not only was the diocesan Land-rover out of petrol, the entire village was out of petrol. With dawning horror I reviewed my position: stranded in the hinterland of southwest Uganda, right on the edge of Zaire, when in forty-eight hours I was due to fly out of Nairobi for London. It would be a shame to miss the plane—I was planning to get married ten days later, in north Cambridgeshire.

All forlorn, I hovered by the village petrol pump. I confided my woes to Rosie, the petrol pump lady. When she heard Bishop Festo's name, she roared with laughter. 'He's a distant cousin of mine!' She led me out the back and there stood a jerry can of petrol. 'I've been saving it for emergencies,' she said. I evidently qualified as one.

Dear Rosie. Her petrol got me back to Kabale, where miraculously Bishop Festo *could* see me that evening. We sat in the lounge of his bungalow on Rugarama hill, and by the glare and fizz of a hurricane lamp, he told me the story of the night of his conversion. I sat spellbound for nearly two hours, as he shared the vision of the Divine Love which had engulfed and captivated him so many years ago.

He talked quietly but eagerly, his face transported with joy. It was a never-to-be-forgotten privilege to be with him that evening—to hear the story of a great love affair of the Spirit by Africa's greatest evangelist.

Back in England, and somehow married on time, I soon produced a 400-page typed transcript of all my taped interviews—and then settled down to some real work. When Bishop Festo passed through London twice again that summer, my transcript reached even more dizzy heights on my bookshelf. Our home was awash with transcripts, books, maps and a rough draft when news came late in the year that Bishop Festo was gravely ill. His remission early in 1988 was sadly brief, and his death in May a great shock and loss.

He wrote in February, before the remission, to tell me that he was dying. Part of his letter ran:

> I want you to know that the conclusion of all that you have been writing is simply that the Lord has absolutely permeated me with his peace, so that this period of grace which my Lord has allowed me to have is very sweet. In my weakness he has demonstrated his strength.
>
> Anne, the Gates of Splendour are wide open because he himself is the Door.
>
> May God bless you as you finish the book and may it be for his glory.

I pray so, too.

Anne Coomes
Peterborough
February 1990

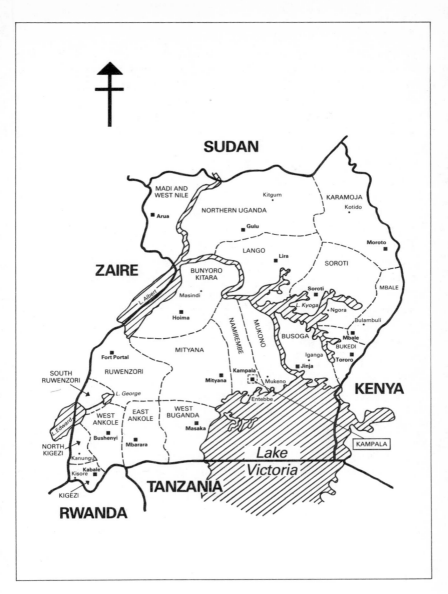

Map of Uganda
showing Anglican Dioceses (1984)

INTRODUCTION

Are great evangelists born—or called? In the case of Festo Kivengere, it is tempting to reply: a bit of both.

His ancestors wonderfully equipped him for the job of an international evangelist. His people, the Bahima, are free-spirited, semi-nomadic pastoralists, content to roam the grass-lands of southwestern Uganda as the needs of their great love in life, their cattle, dictate. As the Bahima have followed their cows for generations, Festo Kivengere followed what he believed to be God's calling for him, only trading the rolling grasslands for pulpits and conference platforms across the world.

The Bahima are self-sufficient and self-reliant. They are not acquisitive, they can carry their few skins and pots and cala-bashes (empty gourd shells) on their heads and backs. Anything that might impede their mobility would be considered a hin-drance and left behind. Home for Festo Kivengere was for many months of each year the hotel room to which he had a key for the night. He lived comfortably out of suitcases, an expert at packing only the necessities of life.

The Bahima are a gregarious people, and have an extraordi-nary gift with the spoken word. They love recitations, story telling and song composing. Oratory comes naturally to them; dramatic use of voice and gesture is practised from childhood. They use these gifts to extol the virtues of their cows, who direct the course of their lives. When Festo Kivengere became a Christian, Christ became the ruling passion of his life. He used his extraordinary talent with words, and all the dramatic persuasiveness at his command, to extol Christ, who directed the course of *his* life.

His 'spiritual ancestors' also passed on a rich tradition, that

Festo Kivengere inherited when he became a member of the Church of Uganda. That church has produced many hundreds of outstanding Christians. In the days of its earliest inception, in 1885–6, nearly 200 young page boys at the Kabaka Mwanga's court (modern day Kampala) chose to be tortured and burned to death rather than deny the Christ they had found through the first English CMS mission to the country. Later converts showed similar zeal, and by the time Uganda was made a British Protectorate in 1894, these Protestant catechumens or *basomi* (readers) were fanning out across the territory, native evangelists preaching, converting and founding many dozens of little village churches throughout Uganda. And then there was the East African revival which began in the 1930s. The extraordinary hunger for God and a daily walk with Christ, free from sin, produced Christians whose lives were turned upside down by their faith, and to whom Jesus became a dearly loved and daily talked-to friend and guide. Festo inherited the zeal and commitment for which his church was already famous.

But in Festo Kivengere's vocation as an evangelist there was one final ingredient: an unsought, even unwanted, spiritual experience that came to him one night: a towering vision of Christ and his love in suffering on the cross for the sins of mankind. It shattered Festo, upsetting all previous conceptions, much as the experience on the Damascus Road had done for St Paul. And like St Paul, having received such a revelation of Christ's love, Festo Kivengere knew there was nothing he could do for the rest of his life but share with anyone who would listen the love of God as shown through Christ.

The combination of inherited physical characteristics and spiritual riches, plus his response to a specific God-given calling, was to make Festo Kivengere the most famous and best-loved evangelist ever to come out of Africa.

But back in the remote hinterland of southwest Uganda just after the First World War, it seemed an unlikely future for a baby wrapped up snug in calf-skins ...

CHAPTER ONE

IN A BAHIMA KRAAL

1919—1929

Born a grandson of the last king of the Bahororo; brought up in the traditional ways of the Bahima; herding the calves and worshipping the spirits.

FESTO KIVENGERE WAS BORN in a beehive-shaped grass hut in a kraal full of dying cattle.

No one ever discovered the day, month or even exact year of his birth. In those days, his tribe, the Bahororo, did not measure time by the calendar. (For instance, at the time Kivengere was born, they did not yet realise it was the twentieth century.) Instead, the Bahororo kept dates by great events. For Kivengere's parents, their first-born son's arrival was always linked in their minds with the time the *omubyamo*, or *rinderpest*, a virulent cattle plague, had returned to their high grasslands, and thousands of the longhorn cows on which the people depended were dying.

The pestilence later helped Kivengere in narrowing down the year of his birth. According to government records, the *rinderpest* swept through southwest Uganda in 1919 and 1920. Kivengere therefore had a choice, and in later years usually chose 1919. As for the month and day, Kivengere always regarded the mystery with good humour: 'After all, this way I can claim anything!' He settled on 1st November, All Saints' Day, as an appropriate birthday for a Christian, and used it in passports and other documentation.

The kraal in which Kivengere was born was one of several which together made up a settlement called *Kitazigurukwa*, 'the place of the very long grass'. It was an appropriate name: in those days there was nothing else for several miles except an enormous papyrus swamp.

Kitazigurukwa was one of many such hamlets in the region known as Rujumbura, a hinterland of Kigezi district, which is tucked away in the southwestern tip of Uganda. It is a mountainous area of breath-taking beauty which deserves its nickname as 'the Switzerland' of Uganda. To the west lie the high, volcanic Bufumbira mountains and the impenetrable forest of mountain gorilla fame. To the north sprawl the great lakes of Uganda. To the east, the land falls away to the vast cattle plains of Ankole. To the south lies more mountainous terrain, scattered with deep lakes, as Kigezi stretches down towards Rwanda. Though Kigezi lies just south of the equator, the altitude keeps the climate temperate, and each morning mists lie sparkling and fresh on the shaggy green mountains.

Kitazigurukwa lay high up in Kigezi's hinterland of Rujumbura, amid a panoramic sprawl of high rolling grasslands and shallow valleys with the mighty Ruwenzori mountains a purple smudge in the distance. Here was home of the Bahororo tribe, spread out for miles and miles around Rukungiri, the main village, where the royal kraal was situated.

Kivengere was born an aristocrat of aristocrats, according to the strict tribal reckonings of the time. Not only was he of the Bahima, the ruling class of the Bahororo, but he was a member of the royal family, and grandson to the king, Makobore, whose rule extended for several hundred miles throughout Rujumbura.

Kivengere's ancestors had ruled in southwest Uganda for nearly two centuries. As a child he would hear their history from the older women round the smokey kraal fires at night. Strumming their harps of euphorbia wood, they told singsong tales of vast migrations, punctuated by battles for land and cattle. Indeed, it seems that the Bahima had been the ruling, aristocratic class throughout much of southwest Uganda and northern Rwanda since the early eighteenth century. As nomadic pastoralists, they had herded their cattle and ruled many Bantu tribes throughout the kingdoms of Bunyoro, Toro, Ankole, Rwanda, Burundi and Karagwe. The Bahima were tall and of light skins, probably descendants of invaders who had swept down from

Ethiopia and the Sudan 500–600 years ago, from somewhere between the Nile and the Red Sea.

By the 1920s, both the Bairu and the Bahima members of the Bahororo tribe lived fairly amicably together, following cultivating and herding respectively. In Rujumbura the Bahima had largely ended their nomadic ways—the grass was so rich and plentiful that pasture could be found on all sides.

Kivengere was brought up on tales of his grandfather, Makobore, who had succeeded his great-grandfather, Muhozi, in about 1885. As king, Makobore was both military leader and almost 'high priest' of the tribe. He was *Omukama was Rujumbura* (King of Rujumbura), Lion of Kagunga, and the 'One Who Cannot Be Overawed'. He had the official sceptre and spear, and held court from a three-legged stool under the sacred spreading oak of Kagunga. He was so big that he required eight men to carry him in his litter to court. He came of the ruling Bashambo clan, who had attained dominance through exceptional military prowess. Makobore had been a famous warrior in his youth, leading forays against Ntare the Fifth, the King of Ankole. He later earned a reputation as an even-handed ruler. He was also the first king of the Bahororo to have to deal with the British—signing a treaty in 1912 acknowledging their indirect rule via a Baganda adviser. About that time he cautiously welcomed a CMS missionary, who left behind a timid catechist, who founded a small church. During the early 1920s Makobore abdicated in favour of his son, Karegyesa.

All in all, therefore, Kivengere had an impressive family tree. Certainly his parents went to great trouble to drum this into their son during his childhood. But later Kivengere was to reflect on the adverse effect: 'It gave them a feeling of great superiority —which is always very unfortunate and superficial.' All the same, this sense of superiority, when later much moderated by the Christian influence, can arguably be said to help account for Kivengere's later extraordinary self-confidence and poise in the midst of western wealth and sophistication.

Kivengere's mother, Barungi, was the favourite daughter of the king. Her name was a derivative of 'Kirungi', a Ruhororo word meaning beautiful, and she was by all accounts a lovely Muhima princess with the soft and smooth skin of the milk-drinking women. She was also a strong-willed, talented lady of such individualism that she had become something of a local legend by the time Kivengere was growing up. She cultivated a garden and did her own weaving—unthinkable for the Bahima women. It is said that as the Bahima women of Rujumbura scoured their milkpots with sand, they gossiped constantly about her. Their efforts spread stories of her unconventional behaviour for miles, while Barungi tended her garden, weaved decorations for her hut, and experimented with making *nyerere* or bracelets for her ankles and arms.

Not very much is known about Ntzisira, the tall, gentle Muhima who was Kivengere's father. He was high-born—a member of the royal Kyahi clan—and rich, owning a herd of about 200 longhorn cows. (No one knew for sure how many: a Muhima would no more disclose the exact number of his cows than a westerner would advertise his bank balance.) Like all Bahima men, Ntzisira wore a long piece of barkcloth (peeled from a certain species of fig tree) wrapped round him, and carried a spear. He was fond of tobacco, which he smoked in a clay pipe with a wooden stem. He was considerably older than Barungi, having been married and then widowed, with only daughters to show for it. (This was to his constant shame. Men with no sons were considered *mucweche*—a term of contempt.)

Ntzisira had a great influence on his son. As a wealthy Muhima with a sizeable herd of cattle he could have been cruel and overbearing, but in fact he seems never to have raised his hand or voice to anyone. Though his father's face would soon be but a blurred memory, Ntzisira's personality would always stay with Kivengere, bringing back warm feelings of security, and sensible caring. If Kivengere inherited his qualities of leadership, determination and plain-speaking from Barungi, his mother, his gentleness of nature and tolerance and respect for women were those of his father.

According to Kivengere's childhood memories, Ntzisira's kindly nature was also much appreciated by Barungi. She had been married once before to a man who, though very rich in cattle, was a fighter and a drinker. In disgust, her father had finally dissolved the marriage (a kingly privilege), crying, 'No more! I won't allow my daughter to be treated like this!'

Barungi had had to leave her first baby son behind with the husband's family, but she was very glad to be rid of the husband.

For her marriage to Ntzisira, Makobore demanded a *njugano* (bride price) of twenty cows, but in turn sent with Barungi a *nshagarirano* (dowry) of forty cows, plus ten maids, five for inside work, and five for outside work.

The marriage of Kivengere's parents was surrounded by all the elaborate cow-centred rituals and taboos of the Bahima. Barungi was fattened up ahead of time (the Bahima admire fat women) by *enkwata orugo* (cows sent especially for that purpose by Ntzisira), and on the day of the wedding carried in a rough litter to Ntzisira's family kraal. It seems Barungi and Ntzisira soon settled down to a very contented married life. Certainly, Ntzisira did not bother to take any more wives, though polygamy was common. However, he did take the precaution of bringing a nephew into the household in case no son ever arrived (this would cause trouble later). He did not bring his four daughters with him; these step-sisters of Kivengere were brought up by a relative.

Kivengere was brought into the world by the hamlet's midwife. News of his birth travelled quickly beyond the kraals of Kitazigurukwa to the royal kraal at Rukungiri, several miles away. Makobore was delighted, and sent along an *obuzaire* (the traditional gift of a father-in-law to a son-in-law on the birth of a child). Ntzisira had obligations too, the chief one being the final ritual that went with a birth, that of *okuhasirira*, a purification, common in every phase of a Muhima's life. So Ntzisira crept out of his hut just before dawn to sprinkle the cows of his kraal with a mixture of herbs and leaves and chalk, all mixed up in water.

Then there only remained the question of naming his firstborn son. Ntzisira chose 'Kivengere'—the name of a former close friend of his. 'Kivengere' was such an unusual name that as far as he was ever able to determine, he was the only Kivengere in all Uganda. But Barungi hit upon a nickname that she felt summed up her small son perfectly: *akasikina*, 'Little Hiccup'. It must have been apt, as Kivengere was known as 'Little Hiccup' throughout his childhood.

Kivengere's family home was built on the typical Bahima pattern. It was a round framework of long twigs and branches pushed into the ground, bent over and tied in the centre round a tall supporting pole. Grasses were tied on the outside (they trailed down to the ground), and the finished hut resembled an enormous, dishevelled beehive. The thatching was not very secure, and leaked in heavy rain. There were no windows, just an opening for the doorway.

The back half of the hut was raised on a rough platform of dried mud about six inches off the ground. Part of this was used as the *ekitabo* (sleeping platform), covered with skins and reed mats. The other part was the *orugyegye* (dairy) where the milk pots, churn and beautiful coloured gourds were kept. Behind the hut an extension had been added to accommodate Rwabugarame, Ntzisira's nephew.

The front of the hut was also roughly divided into two, with the *amahega* (fireplace) just to the left of the entrance. The other side was used mostly to store things Barungi needed for keeping house and in caring for the milk. Chief among these were the *ebyanzi* (round conical wooden milk pots), highly prized by the Bahima. Here also was kept Kivengere's *enkongoro* or earthenware milk pot.

Outside the hut was the *ekayente* or kraal, a roughly circular fence of large branches and planted euphorbia. There were thorns facing outwards, to discourage lions. The open space in the kraal in the front of the hut was called the *ekibuga*, and here the herdsmen kept the cows at night.

*   *   *

In about 1926 Kivengere's family decided to leave the hillock above the papyrus swamp. Ntzisira chose the Buyanja area, a few miles to the east, where his own father had been born. The family settled on the tiny hamlet of Kyamakanda. Kivengere's second home was 'wilder and even dangerous' at times. 'We ran into trouble with hyenas and lions.' But Ntzisira felt that the richer grass made Kyamakanda 'ideal'.

These next three or four years were very happy ones for Kivengere. The British had been in Uganda since the 1890s. By 1920 they had introduced a new form of law and order, currency, and rudimentary system of taxation, and developed cash crops for export. However, the colonial presence barely touched Rujumbura—beyond continuing the rough agreement with Karegyesa that he acknowledge the indirect British rule through a Baganda adviser. So Kivengere was brought up wholly in the traditional ways of the Bahima. Slowly in the endless daily cycle of milking the cows in the kraal, grazing them on verdant pastures under a wide expanse of azure sky and singing of them at night under starry skies, Kivengere grew from a toddler into a sturdy little boy in calfskins. Though someday he would leave Kyamakanda far behind, much of what he learned there would always be with him.

The Hima day began just before dawn, and was entirely taken up with the care of cows. Their ceaseless day-to-day needs, plus a never-changing climate (Uganda straddles the equator and there is no summer or winter; the temperature running usually at 75°–85° in the daytime, dropping to 50° at night), added to the lack of any contact with the outside world, all helped shape life in the Bahima kraals into a slow, steady rhythm of seamless days where morning gave way to afternoon and afternoon to evening in endless succession. As through countless such days Kivengere measured his childhood as a Muhima cattle herder's son, a typical day for him and his family throughout the 1920s would have run thus:

Five–six am *AKASKESHE* (early morning) Barungi, Ntzisira and Kivengere would lay under mats on their round sleeping platforms at the back of their hut, listening drowsily until they heard the kanyonza (robin chats) begin to challenge each other. 'When they began, we knew it was time to get up.' Ntzisira dressed in a long bark cloth, Barungi in the skins they had used as blankets; and Kivengere was wrapped in a calfskin.

Six–seven am *ENTE ZAKOMOROKA* (cattle got out of the kraal) As soon as he could toddle, Kivengere followed his father into the kraal each morning to where the men gathered the cattle for milking. One of his earliest jobs in life was to gather grass to feed the small *ekomi* or fires which were kept burning at the lower end of the kraal. Kivengere loved this early time. Barefoot and barely high enough to reach the cows' long straight backs, he would scamper fearlessly among the huge horned heads and sharp hooves of the large herd. By the time he was three, he knew by name each and every cow. 'I could call them by name, and they'd reply.' He was not unusual in this: the Bahima talked endlessly to their cows, and had an impressive empathy with them. Meanwhile, his mother Barungi and her five maids would begin to churn the milk. Some was made into *eshabwe* or ghee, and rubbed onto the body and clothing. Kivengere hated the smell of it, and tried to get rid of it by rubbing his calfskin in the sand. This earned him many a spanking.

Seven–eight am *ENTE ZAZAGIRA* (cattle stand outside the kraal in the open space). As the *nyineka*, or master of the kraal, Ntzisira gave the herdsmen instructions of where to graze the cattle that day. At this point the cows were sometimes bled: either for drinking later that day, or because the cow itself looked poorly (it was thought bleeding might be a cure). Many times Kivengere helped his father and one of the herdsmen tie a thong of leather round a cow's neck, and then plunge a special arrow into the raised vein. The blood would be caught in an *eichupa* (wooden pail).

Eight–ten am *ENTE ZASETIKA* (cattle move off to pasture). The herdsmen leading, the cattle would then move lazily off to pasture, dipping their heads and enormous horns as they walked. The calves were cared for by the women and children, and as soon as Kivengere was six or seven, he joined the other children out on the hills with the calves.

It was here he made his first friend, Bugaari, a youngster of about his own age, from the next kraal. The first day the boys met, Bugaari, who was taller than Kivengere, knocked him to the ground and sat on him. Kivengere squirmed around, but could not get up, so he bit Bugaari. Bugaari burst into tears and slapped Kivengere. Kivengere sat up and burst into tears as well.

After that, the boys were inseparable, and still good friends sixty years later. Indeed, some of the happiest memories of Kivengere's childhood were of herding the calves on the hillsides with Bugaari.

It was every Muhima's dream to have a kraal full of cows, a hut, a wife and children. So the boys, out on the sunny grasslands with the calves, fashioned little kraals of their own out of twigs. Cows were made with more twigs, forked twigs used for their horns. Sticks were used for the bulls, wisps of grass for the calves. The boys would spend a long time twisting the twigs to make them resemble their favourite cows (usually the dark brown ones) in their fathers' herds. The kraals seldom lasted more than an afternoon—the boys would take their 'bulls' in hand and charge into each other's kraals, wreaking havoc. Kivengere's family were comparatively wealthy, and so he had more calves to look after than the other children, but he seems to have taken this matter-of-factly. Certainly Bugaari, to whom the issue would have been very sensitive, never remembered Kivengere boasting. He also had a sense of responsibility: duty was something to take satisfaction in, not a chore to be avoided at all costs. Bugaari found that:

> When we youngsters got into fights, Kivengere would fight as hard as anyone. When he won, and thus had 'say' over what our little group did next, he would command us to go and collect firewood and bring it home for our parents. We did it happily. Kivengere was very popular.

Ten–eleven am *ABASETUZI BAGARUKA* (the herdsmen return).

Eleven am–twelve pm *ABANTU BAZA OMU BIRAGO* (men go to their mats). The lull of the day meant time for fun, away from the calves: the boys crept into matoke plantations to steal bananas. They roasted them on little fires they made by rubbing two sticks, *oburindi*, together. 'We knew it was wrong, and felt guilty—so we just ran fast!' The hilly grasslands also provided perfect natural 'slides', and Kivengere's all-time favourite game was to slide down low, steep slopes on a thick clump of banana leaves. The only hitch was getting back up as a banana stalk is heavy to carry. (In later years he would use the game to illustrate how easy it is to fall into sin, and how hard to haul oneself out by one's own efforts.)

Twelve–one pm *ABEESHEZI BAZA AHA MAZIBA* (waterers go to the wells). This was the time of the day Kivengere hated, when the herdsmen from the various kraals fought one another for space at the watering places for their cows. 'It was very, very tough and I was always frightened.' Once a big boy lashed out at him with a stick and nearly blinded him.

One–two pm *AMASYO GATSYORA* (herds run down to water).

Two–three-thirty pm *AMASYO GAKUKA* (herds finish watering).

Three-thirty–five pm *AMASYO GAIRIRA EBIBANGA BYAMAKA* (herds come close to the vicinity of the kraals).

Five–five-thirty pm *ENYANA ZATAAHA* (calves enter). Kivengere marched his calves in past the careful scrutiny of his father. Kivengere, like all Bahima children, was called on to explain even the smallest cut and the children were taught to be very honest in this respect.

Six-thirty–seven pm *AMASYO GATAAHA* (herds enter). The sun was nearly set by now. In the brief equatorial twilight the herdsmen now marched the cows for inspection past the eagle eye of Ntzisira.

Seven–nine pm *AMASYO GAHAAFA* (herds are finished milking). It was dark as the men finished with the milking. Kivengere helped out along with the other children by holding the calves between the forelegs of the cow until the milking was finished.

Nine–eleven pm *AMASYO GAHENDA ENKOKORA* (herds kneel [literally: break joints]) or *ABANTU BATARAMA* (men visit each other). When the milking was done, and the logs piled up at the entrance to the kraal, the cattle were settled down for the night.

Inside the smokey hut Barungi would have his clay pipe (*enyungu*) ready for her husband to smoke and milk from the *kyanzi* (storage pot) to drink. Kivengere was given a small *enkongoro* or milkpot, which was refilled as many times as he liked—it and his calfskin were the only possessions he had.

Barungi also served cow's blood—such as *eith/enjuba/-y'oburingyiki*, a bowl of boiled and thickened blood, well whipped up with salt and butter, into which everyone spooned their fingers. At times Barungi would supplement the family larder with bananas and potatoes—but Kivengere was rarely given anything but milk or blood: children did not eat solids until they were about fourteen.

After supper, the comfort of the fire would be sought by the whole family. Ntzisira would settle himself on a low stool in the place of honour, and occasionally call for some strong home-made beer. Close neighbours would pay calls (no one dared wander far in such a lion infested region—especially as the only portable light was a burning reed). Much socialising went on around the fires, the smoke escaping into the vibrant African night through the chinks in the grass walls and ceilings.

In later years Kivengere would look back on these evenings with great nostalgia, when the family indulged in their favourite pastime of swapping stories of their tribe's history, telling the children fables, or singing the praises of past warriors or present cows. In fact, the Bahima never tired of praise for their cattle, and a favourite recreation during these long moonlit evenings was a recitation of one's cows' finer points. It was, by all accounts, quite a dramatic performance: the man would seize a stick or spear, and twirl it about as he strutted back and forth. He then:

> rattled his words out as fast as he could, and only paused as he made a point, which was received with approval by all the assembly grunting together. As each point was made, the spokesman empha-sised it by a sudden movement, a turn of the body or foot, a gesture with the stick or spear.

It was not uncommon for the recitation to continue at full speed for fifteen or twenty minutes.

Even the very young children were expected to memorise whole songs. In fact, it was a favourite game for youngsters to show off their memorising ability by learning a whole list of things, either about their history or the cows, and then trying to compose a song incorporating them. 'It tested your resourceful-ness and the way you handled things. It was very good education.'

Herding frisky calves in lion country and fighting to water them by day taught Kivengere self-reliance and self-confidence at a young age. It would be hard to think of anything better than these recitals around the fire at night for teaching him to think on his feet, to speak fluently in public on a theme with next to no

A village church—similar to the one in which Festo was first taught Christianity, and in which he became a Reader at ten years old.

A group of saza chiefs from the 1930s—Festo's grandfather and uncle would have looked like this.

warning ... to improvise as he went, to tell stories and use words to move an audience. ...

Here too, Kivengere would have learned to wrap up abstract ideas in concrete, everyday examples. The Bahima used fiction stories with a meaning behind them. They were exciting—about creation, about their ancestors and their tribe. Such fables included animal characters like rabbits who were the clever ones, or hyenas who were cowards, lions who were powerful, foxes who were cunning. The fables were 'wonderful', said Kivengere. He would later often use colourful stories of his own to get abstract points across.

Perhaps though, he hardly needed to *learn* all these skills. He was after all an aristocrat—a Muhima of royal blood, the grandson of a great ruler. Kivengere had eloquence, rhetoric and a gift for commanding attention in his blood. The hankering for company and conversation, finding people not a strain but a relaxation, was also to stay with Kivengere, and be a tremendous advantage in his future work and ministry.

Eleven pm–twelve am *ABANTU BATEMBA* (men climb [into bed]), though as Kivengere stresses 'there was no time keeping whatsoever!' Sometimes if lions had been heard in the area, the herdsmen would stay up two or three nights in a row to protect their herds.

Barungi unwrapped her skins and laid them over herself and Ntzisira as they stretched out on their sleeping platform of earth and mat and skins. Kivengere slept in a little cubicle next to his parents. He would fall asleep night after night, year after year, to the melody of an African night: the gentle tap-tapping of the cattle's huge horns against the croakings of hundreds of frogs, of the cows, the metallic ring of thousands of crickets, the wind stirring in the banana trees, sounding like rain, and the ceaseless rasping of cicadas.

Twelve–two am *ITUMBI RUFUZI* (dead of night) (*rufuzi*: groans and slobbering when asleep) or *Ryenda obushesha* (dawn). The family slept.

Two–three am *ENKOKO YATERA EKIKIRO* (the cock crows by night). The rooster that Barungi had placed on a small shelf inside the hut woke her up, as she intended it should.

Three–three-thirty am *ENKOKO YASHUBIRIRA* (the cock

repeats). This seems to have been a sort of early version of the repeating alarm cock. A while after the cock 'repeated', Barungi would rise quietly, and go to her milk pots ...

Three-thirty–four am *OMUSHEYE GWAJUGUTA* (first signs of dawn). It was the custom for a rich man to be awakened by his wife to drink *omurara* (milk), before going to sleep again. However, the taboos decreed that if the cock crowed a little too early or a little too late, the milk could not be given to the rich man, but would instead have to be given to the children to drink. The cocks belonging to Kivengere's family must have had a poor sense of timing, because he had vivid memories of often being awakened in the middle of the night throughout his childhood, and given milk to drink. 'Milk, milk, milk! All the time they used to wake me up in the middle of the night and make me drink milk!'

Four–five am *OBWIRE BWAYANGAYANGA* or *BWA-SHESHA* (twilight begins to see). The hour's hush before the dawn.

*   *   *

Kivengere and Bugaari quickly learned what it meant to be a Muhima. Chief among early lessons were the complex taboos which regulated every action of the Bahima, by which they sought to obey what they considered the natural laws of the universe concerning them, and as pastoralists, all taboos centred on fear for the cows. The milk was considered almost sacred, and many taboos were to prevent any stoppages in the milk flow.

Then of course, there was God, in whom the Bahima devoutly believed. They considered him to be a great creator spirit whom they called *Ruhanga*. Kivengere later explained:

Long before the missionaries came to Africa, my people knew there was a God. And we wanted him, we desired him. We knew he was the creator, and so we tried to worship him. We sacrificed to him and we believed our security came from him. Our problem was never *is* there a God, but *how* can we reach him? To us he seemed to be very far away, sitting up there, big and great, something threatening us.

The Bahima solution was to turn to spirit worship and the occult. When Kivengere was seven or eight, his father started taking him along to the little hut behind their own in the kraal, where he went to offer worship every evening on behalf of the family. As the firstborn son, Kivengere would have been expected someday to offer sacrifices and worship on behalf of his family. The family, like all Bahima, believed in the existence of a whole variety of spirits, and felt that their security depended on happy relations with the spirit world. Below Ruhanga there were believed to be the bigger, powerful spirits, called the Bachwezi, who had great power; and then there were the little spirits of their ancestors. It was to their ancestors that Ntzisira sacrificed each evening. During these twilight visits to the hut, with the nearby cows settling down for the night, Ntzisira explained to his son that these 'little' spirits 'were the ones you could actually talk to. They cared about our cows, our health, and the little things of everyday life.'

The sacrifice was simple: Ntzisira would take with him milk or a bit of dried meat, and put it in the hut. Then he would fetch some leaves and build a little fire before praying. 'I watched spellbound as he offered sacrifices for the family, the cows, our good welfare, and for that of our relatives.' Then Ntzisira would add some milk and meat to the big leaf, and he and Kivengere would withdraw.

Next day, the sacrifices were always gone. Later Kivengere was to blame 'plenty of big insects and many little rats!'—but he was always to recall with admiration his father's sincere devotion.

The Bachwezi, or bigger spirits, were believed to visit whole villages. The witchdoctor would take charge of the occult ceremonies which followed. Whereas the ancestral spirits inspired comfort, these Bachwezi inspired fear. Kivengere was once cut and bled, and his blood given to the spirit of Ahola.

Kivengere had vivid memories of a time when wave upon wave of big spirits came to Kyamakanda, sending people into a frenzy of hysterical chanting, speaking in unknown tongues, and unrestrained worship around a fire.

We children whispered about it all with bated breath, because after all, you never knew where the spirits were. I never dared ask my father anything outright, in case I brought harm to the family somehow. It left me with a haunting feeling that there was something really great out there, but as I never dared enquire exactly what it was, I was never sure, and hence never satisfied.

Witchcraft was also widely practised among the Bahororo. Whereas the spirits of the ancestors were believed to attack the wicked, witchcraft was a different matter altogether: it was believed to be worked against the virtuous. Therefore, *anyone* might become a target, at any time. Witchcraft was based on the belief that social relationships can determine natural events. Thus, the snake is poisonous, and the disease incurable, but *someone sent them your way in the first place.*

Kivengere's family used the services of an *omufumu* (or witch-doctor) when once another witchdoctor threatened Ntzisira with a curse. The whole family were in great fear for some days—not least from their own witchdoctor who loomed up out of the darkness dressed in a weird mixture of skins, feathers and cloth, his servants panting along behind under an enormous collection of mysterious bundles. He alternated between a booming voice and gibberish. At the time Kivengere was very impressed, along with all the others, at the magical tricks the *omufumu* could perform: for example, making the centre pillar of their hut burn with fire without being consumed. (Only years later did he learn about the highly flamable wax the witchdoctor smeared on the pole when no one was looking.)

When he was about ten or eleven, Kivengere joined the other youngsters in the village for the great religious ceremony which marked their 'first initiation' to God. They were taken out into the bush and left in a little hut for a day or so. Then one by one they were brought back, and led into the circle of village elders, where certain (unintelligible) words were said over them. Then each child was taught the 'words of worship', how to use the invocations, and warned to keep the secrets of the tribe. Kivengere took the whole affair very solemnly, 'but God remained far away'.

*   *   *

Visitors to Kyamakanda were sometimes alarming—and not just in the case of the stray elephant who strolled in one day and ended by killing a man. Far more terrifying was the visitor who came sometime afterwards and whose arrival signalled that the outside world was now on Rujumbura's doorstep.

Our parents told us children that morning that we had to be very, very careful that day. A *pink* lady was on her way to the village, coming along the paths like one of us! My mother warned me, 'These pink people are dangerous ... there have been stories of people disappearing and that they *eat people*.'

Barungi and the other women were all staying indoors, just in case.

Kivengere and Bugaari were jittery and immensely excited. They led their calves to the top of a small hillock, from where they could command a good view of the path from the nearest village, Kebisoni. Bugaari recalls the exact moment the two boys saw their first white person: 'Suddenly, over the brow of the hill came the *strangest* person. Her face and arms were pink—for a minute we doubted she had *any* skin. She had the strangest looking head' (she was wearing a pith helmet). Some Bahima men were carrying her along in a sling chair of bamboo. Others followed along behind, carrying all her luggage.

Slowly the little walking party wound their way down the path that led into a valley and for a moment nearly dropped out of sight. It was too much for the boys. Forgetting their calves, forgetting their parents' admonition, they tore through the high grass until they had a better view.

'She came nearer and nearer. Then she was very near ... and—we lost our nerve. We bobbed down quick in the grass (fortunately it was high because of the rainy season) and hid ... just in case she *did* eat people.' Two pairs of huge dark eyes watched as the sunburned missionary's caravan drew abreast. Then she was so close they could have touched her, and then she was past, and going on towards their village. The boys ducked away and raced towards the village.

Braver through virtue of numbers, the boys did not hide when the pink lady arrived at the village a little while later. Carefully her porters set her down near some kraals. The men came forward timidly. The women, well veiled, crept to their door-ways. The Africans stared at the woman, and the woman stared at the Africans. Her colour, her European clothes—the like of which had never been seen before—her pith helmet, were too much for the boys to take in. 'We couldn't believe she was human like us. We thought she must be some kind of strange animal.' But Karegyesa welcomed her gravely, as did Miranda, the former prime minister who had become a *gomborora* (chief under the British). Their confidence soon relieved the fears of the people.

Constance Hornby, an English woman of about forty-five, was a missionary midwife with the Ruanda Mission (now Mid-Africa Ministry [CMS]). She was on safari for the purpose of recruiting, in villages throughout Kigezi, women and girls for her reading classes back in Kabale. She had seen too much of the ignorance and poverty of the women not to want to give them a chance to learn to read for themselves. Kivengere who came to know her well, said later: 'We cannot thank God enough for what she did.'

That day in Kyamakanda she handed out little gifts and sweets, introducing herself and her idea of a school. 'It was tough for her, very tough,' Kivengere recalled. 'It took nerve.' But in the end she got her recruits. Her visit was the talk of the village for a month before gossip moved on. Unaware that he had had his first brush with Christianity, and hoping only that someday he might perhaps see another pink person, Kivengere went back to spear practice with Bugaari on the grasslands, and daydreamed of enormous kraals stuffed full of cows.

*   *   *

There is a proverb of the Bahima: '*Omwana ashukira enkongoro tashukirwa mugisha*': 'You can only pour out milk for your child, not luck.' In the few months following Miss Hornby's visit the saying might well have summed up Ntzisira's feelings towards Kivengere. For Ntzisira had contracted tuber-culosis and knew he was dying. He worried for his family's future while Barungi fought the disease with what little skill she had: mixing nourishing brews of cow's blood and milk. Kivengere, by now nearly ten years old, had little inkling that his happy childhood was nearing an abrupt end. His father's death was a great shock. The grave for Ntzisira was, as with all Bahima, the dung heap. He was probably wrapped in a cow skin before burial.

Barungi was not the type to display her sorrow before the many sympathetic relatives. She and the children left the hut. Rwabugarame, Ntzisira's nephew, built them a new one. Barungi now had to marry again, and chose Rwabugarame, as Ntzisira had planned. Her new husband gave Makobore a cow or two to formalise the marriage, and moved into the hut with her. Kivengere was sent off to stay with his grandfather, Makobore, for a while. He lived at Rukungiri, the largest village, and county seat of Rujumbura, several miles from Kyamakanda.

*   *   *

While Kivengere was growing up the missionaries of the Ruanda Mission were busy establishing themselves in Kabale, on Rugarama Hill. In view of what happened later, it is important to understand that this mission differed somewhat from the CMS. The missionaries who launched the Ruanda Mission all came from the conservative, evangelical wing of the Anglican Church. At this time, evangelicals were in a minority within the Church of England, and tended to find more in common with evangelicals from other denominations than with Anglicans of other traditions. Thus it was that the Ruanda Mission, in common with many thousands of evangelicals at this time, looked to the annual Keswick Convention, held each summer in England's rainy Lake District, as their 'spiritual home'. Here the teaching was theologically 'conservative'—the Bible was held to be the supreme authority for all matters concerning Christianity and salvation was taken as a definite turning at a specific point away from one's sins, to Christ.

Following salvation, a convert was expected to live a holy life committed to Christ. It was this tradition, with great emphasis on the Bible, rather than on church tradition or sacraments, which the missionaries would pass on when they established their mission in Kigezi. The mission had little 'clerical flavour', and never stressed the sacramental side to worship.

In 1921 Dr Algie Stanley Smith and Dr Ken Sharp had begun a small dispensary. The work grew quickly, and soon hundreds of patients were queueing in the early morning mists.

By the mid 1920s the Ruanda Mission needed—and got—more help. New faces included: Captain Geoffrey Holmes, a former soldier and international hockey player; Constance Hornby, a midwife and the Bible translator the Rev. Harold Guillebaud, and his wife. Meanwhile, back in London, tensions over theological issues between the conservative Ruanda Mission and the broader Church Missionary Society led to an agreed split; Ruanda Mission became an independent auxiliary. In Cambridge a young medical student named Joe Church survived tuberculosis and decided as way of thanks to devote his life to the mission field. He felt called to Rwanda.

*   *   *

By 1927 nearly 2,000 Bakiga (the tribe who lived in that part of Kigezi) had been baptised in Kabale. But the depth of Christian commitment throughout Uganda *was* open to question. Many still practised witchcraft and polygamy in secret. That autumn saw the arrival of Dr Joe Church. His intense, perfectionist nature was one which demanded of himself—and others—a total, unswerving commitment to Christ. In Kabale, he found much he disliked, as he felt many converts had not been properly convicted of sin.

In 1928 Dr Joe Church, the Rev. Bert Jackson and several Ugandan converts went south just over the border into Rwanda to a new mission station at Gahini to take over from Geoffrey Holmes. Gahini hill looked beautiful as it rose up beside the blue waters of Lake Mohasi, but it was a ten day march through the bush to anywhere else, and the people roundabout lived in abject poverty and disease. When a famine hit later that year Gahini became a living hell of starvation and disease that along with the spiritual struggles, nearly broke Joe and his colleagues. Yet Homesi, Jakisoni and Chacha (the missionaries' Africanised names) later believed that combating the famine prepared them for the revival. '... it played a vital part in finding that Jesus is real and satisfies in any circumstances ... It was a prelude to an outpouring of the Holy Spirit, but first we had to come to the end of ourselves.'

When the rains failed again in early 1929, Joe took action, having lost all faith in the Belgian Colonial Government. He went to Kampala and alerted the world's press to the frightful suffering of the famine. A massive relief programme was mounted, and by the summer things had greatly improved. But Joe's spiritual restlessness and dissatisfaction with his own spiritual shortcomings, as well as those of just about everybody around him continued. He did not know how to slake his thirst for God, how to find the power that the New Testament Christians seemed to have had.

Indeed, all of the missionaries were only too aware of their own powerlessness, and helplessness. The New Testament promised the fulness of the Holy Spirit would enable Christians to live a victorious Christian life. But the whole mission station lacked power. Something was missing, was wrong. The Gahini missionaries held long sessions of prayer and daily Bible study with the help of their Scofield Reference Bibles. Many converts then took an interest, hurrying to the meetings.

Then in Kampala in 1929, Joe found his breakthrough when he met by chance a convert, Simeon Nsibambi, on Namirembe Hill near the cathedral. He too felt as if he were spiritually starving. The friendship 'changed the course of my missionary career'.

It was the beginning of the East African revival, and it could not have started more humbly: Joe and Simeon spent several days together in prayer and Bible study on the power of the Holy Spirit before going their separate ways. But by then they believed they had put their finger on what was holding back the Church of Uganda: it was relying on *good works and mental assent to the Christian message*, instead of, as Joe put it, 'surrendering all to Jesus ... quitting all sin in faith, and claiming the filling of the Holy Spirit'. And Joe saw how the problem could be solved. He wrote home: 'There could be a revival in the Uganda Church if someone ... could ... point these thousands of nominal Christians to the victorious life.'

Many Christians in Kampala thought Joe was mad, and were glad to pack him off back to Gahini, but the missionaries of Kabale supported him with prayer and friendship. They were dissatisfied with the low spiritual temperature of Kabale, and watched with great interest as Gahini warmed up.

CHAPTER TWO

A READER ON THE RUJUMBURA GRASSLANDS

1929–1934

A catechist comes to Kyamakanda; Kivengere joins the 'little school' and becomes a 'reader'; is given his first Gospel; reads of Jesus while herding his calves; prepares for baptism; is baptised 'Festo' and becomes a member of the Church of Uganda; continues his mission schooling; leaves home for Uncle Karegyesa's kraal.

FROM VARIOUS FAMILY RECKONINGS it seems likely that Kivengere spent the early autumn of 1929 at his grandfather's 'royal' kraal at Rukungiri, where his uncle Karegyesa now ruled as Saza chief. Makobore's kraal was extensive with people passing through all the time, from clan relations and local lesser chiefs to visiting chiefs from further afield. But each evening at sunset the enormous aristocrat, a long piece of barkcloth wound round his waist and flung over a shoulder, pipe in one hand, spear in the other, would recline on a low wooden stool at the entrance to his kraal to wait for his cows to return from the grazing. It was a scene that would stay with Kivengere all his life: his grandfather greeting each of his cows by name. They, with their long horns dipping at each step, seemed to be nodding politely back to the proud old patriarch.

Kivengere was soon to discover that something quite un-Bahima-like had arrived in Rukungiri—a catechist from Kabale, who built a little mud and papyrus 'church' nearby. Makobore had been baptised a Christian while in Kabale on administrative business years before. He and his son, Karegyesa (also baptised) had enormous respect for (though little knowledge of) the Christian faith, and welcomed its arrival in Rukungiri. Makobore even took Kivengere to 'church' with him, where the catechist read some verses from a Gospel of St Mark in Lunyoro—a western Ugandan language only partly understood by the Bahima. Nobody minded: everyone was used to witchdoctors intoning curious, unintelligible sounds. Kivengere was left mystified by the incident, while his uncle and grandfather encouraged the catechist, but carried on peaceably with their ancestor and spirit worship. It was a small beginning, but Christianity had arrived in Rujumbura, and was there to stay. Soon reinforcements would be on the way.

Soon after this, Barungi collected her son from Makobore's kraal and they returned to Kyamakanda. Already the new marriage was floundering. Young as he was, Kivengere knew why. 'Rwabugarame was a very proud man, and a born fighter. He wanted women to keep their place, but my mother was impossible to suppress!' She was like a 'watchdog' as far as her wealth was concerned, firmly telling her new husband he could have none of it: it was being kept for her sons to inherit some day.

Rwabugarame was furious at being thus disinherited, and began to fight with Barungi, neglect the cows, and drink heavily. To do him credit, though, he was on the whole kind to the boys. But the family would never be the same again, and soon Kivengere was facing an even bigger change—one which would alter the rest of his life.

*   *   *

A man called Byensi arrived in the village one day, and set about building a large hut, which was to be a church. Everyone knew him; he had been born and brought up in Kyamakanda, but had disappeared south some time before. He gladly told his curious neighbours what he had been doing since. He had gone as far as Kabale and had there run into the thriving mission and been converted. He was baptised by the missionaries and trained to read and write. Now he was back and wanted to share what he had learned with anyone who would listen. He was there with Makobore's permission. The aristocrat had welcomed this second, more literate catechist to the region and encouraged some to send their sons along to learn from him.

Barungi immediately agreed: she wanted the best of whatever was going for Kivengere. Rwabugarame was also enthusiastic: he had heard a bit about the *Muzungu* (white men) and reasoned that the more Kivengere could learn of their ways, the better for his future.

So as soon as the little church school had been completed, Byensi, or Yacobo (Jacob), as he had been baptised, beat his big drum. Kivengere, Bugaari and several other boys were released from herding calves for the morning and joined an adult or two in making their way to the hut. There Yacobo greeted them and invited them to sit on grass mats inside. With great curiosity Kivengere entered this small, unprepossessing out-station of the Ugandan Church. Without it he would certainly have spent the rest of his childhood with the calves, and the rest of his life as an illiterate Muhima herdsman.

When Yacobo started his little church school, and turned the boys from 'herders' into 'readers', the boys had no idea that they were being caught up in a hugely successful method (unique in the history of missions) which had become the hallmark of the Ugandan Church: the evangelisation of Uganda not just by European missionaries, but by native Christians. Kivengere had now joined a tradition that went back to the first Church Missionary Society mission station at the court of the Kabaka of Buganda (now Kampala) in 1877, when the converts had then earned the title 'readers' for the simple reason that they were the only literate people in the entire territory.

Of course, in early 1930 Kivengere knew none of this. He was concentrating on learning the letters and simple words that Byensi scratched in the red earth with a sharp stick. Soon he was joining them together to make simple words: 'I thought that quite a feat!' When Byensi discovered that his youngest student, Kivengere, was also his brightest, he soon had the ten-year-old instructing youths nearly twice his age into the mysteries of how marks on the ground or a board could have meaning.

As soon as the students could read letters and simple words, they were given a little *mateka*, or primer, in Runyankole, a dialect very similar to their own Ruhororo language. It contained the alphabet, portions of Scripture, and the Ten Commandments. Kivengere poured over his for hours, 'It was the first book I had ever seen, and the smell of the glue and paper fascinated me.'

By May 1930 Kivengere had passed his first exam and earned himself a certificate that said he could read. So he was presented with a gospel and officially became a 'reader', with six months to prepare for baptism. The gospel was St Luke (St Luke came bound in black, St Mark in red). It was his second book, and he took it home 'very proudly'. He carried it everywhere, including out on the hills when he took the calves to graze. The other children were fascinated, so he began to read to them. 'There I first read the stories of Jesus. It was wonderful. And no matter how bad my reading was, in the end other children got some idea about Jesus.'

The stories soon had an effect.

Gradually I became aware that there was someone alive in those pages of St Luke. There was indeed a God, the Creator, but he was not to be reached through the ancestors of our parents, nor even through the Bachwezi. Instead, it was through his Son, Jesus Christ. And this Jesus was a human being like us—I naturally assumed he was brown, like me. My imagination did not stretch to any other colour! But the main point that kept coming across was that not only was God reachable, but he was reaching out to us! He loved us! And he was stronger than even the great evil spirits.

Rapidly the children at the little church school came to believe in the loving God of the Bible. 'The pagan beliefs we had had just fell away and faded from our minds.' Kivengere accepted 'Jesus was the Son of God and the Saviour of the world'. He was not troubled by questions. The gospels were clear enough on these essential points, and 'what I could read and understand, I believed'.

As the weeks went by, the boys were given many lessons on the New Testament, including stories of Jesus, his miracles, his parables and the words he had spoken on the cross. 'By the time I came to be baptised, I had a very thorough grounding in the basics of Christianity.' At the same time, Byensi had stressed that all pagan practices were to be left strictly behind. Kivengere responded wholeheartedly. 'When I joined the little local church my conversion from paganism to Christ was absolute. I vowed never to have anything more to do with the spirits.'

His mother was petrified when she discovered her son had discarded the lucky charms that guarded against evil spirits, but Kivengere explained that 'we boys had been taught how to pray to God on our own, and that Jesus was more powerful than any spirit'. Gradually the whole village accepted the idea that those who went to church and became 'readers' were protected by Jesus. 'People didn't quite grasp who exactly Jesus was, but they did accept that he protected us from the spirits.' As for Kivengere, 'I took his protection for granted.'

Byensi also taught his young converts that Jesus expected them to live by the highest moral standards. They learned that it was wrong for Christians to steal, tell lies, hate people, etc. The 'readers' tried their best, but inevitably ran into problems. Kivengere was soon really struggling. 'I would lose my temper and fight with the boys in the village, and then would remember I was a Christian and was not supposed to fight. I felt very guilty.'

In Kivengere's experience of Christianity, knowledge of the 'law' of God came long before knowledge of the 'grace' of God. It seems that Byensi never taught the boys much about 'grace', but Kivengere never blamed him for this as 'he himself had not experienced it'. Byensi taught the boys all he knew—how to read, and the creeds of the Christian faith, but 'we all tried to please God through our own efforts'.

From May to November of 1930, Kivengere prepared for baptism. Part of the preparation involved a certain amount of being 'discipled' by Byensi. So when Byensi made the fifty mile trip south to Kabale for more supplies from the Mission, he chose Kivengere as his 'servant boy' to accompany him and carry some of the baggage. Kivengere had never left Rujumbura before, but with his stepfather's encouragement he agreed to the trip with enthusiasm. To make his first journey partly because of his Christian faith was certainly appropriate. In later years his faith would take him tens of thousands of miles each year.

Kivengere was to be baptised in Rukungiri in November 1930. There were sixty other candidates from little local churches throughout the district. Three godparents were chosen for

Kivengere, two men and a woman. One, Hosea, was a lay reader, another, Jacob, was a young church teacher. Kivengere's godmother was called Eunice. They took the business of a godson very seriously indeed. Kivengere was summoned to their huts for talks and prayer, and also given jobs to do in order to prove 'I was a real child of theirs'.

Eunice, Jacob and Hosea had to decide on a baptismal name for Kivengere. Their search through the New Testament portions that they had, ended at Acts chapters 25 and 26. The passage tells how the Roman Governor Felix has just handed power over to the new governor, Festus, who is then faced with the problem of what to do with a certain prisoner, Paul. Festus tries to sort the matter out, and his efforts give rise to two quotes which have become famous. Paul stops Festus from handing him over to the Jews by appealing to the civil laws, and Festus acceeds to the request, 'You have appealed to Caesar; to Caesar you shall go' (Acts 25:12). When Paul then goes on to try and explain to Festus how the man Jesus Christ had risen from the dead, Festus is baffled and can only conclude, 'Your great learning is turning you mad' (Acts 26:24). Festus remained a pagan governor.

But Eunice, Jacob and Hosea wanted a biblical name. 'To them in their simple state, any name in the Bible was holy.' They liked the sound of Festus, especially when they had Ugandanised it by adding an 'o'. They informed their godson that his new name was to be Festo, Festo Kivengere.

As the baptism day approached, excitement mounted. A few days before the great event the Rev. Shemai Mogandawasula arrived. He was to carry out the baptisms, and was a very important man locally, the first in all Rujumbura to be ordained a deacon. On the Saturday night before the baptism Kivengere could scarcely sleep for excitement. A born enthusiast, he longed for the morrow when he could make a public commitment to his new way of life. His thoughts on what he was about to do verged on awe; though only eleven, he meant the vows he was to take.

My thoughts that night were very serious indeed. I thoroughly expected that from now on I would put all sin behind me and lead a good, pure, godly life. I would read the Bible, obey all the laws, and live up to the very highest of ethical standards. I wanted God, I desired God. I didn't yet realise that God never expected me to 'be a really good person' under my own steam.

The baptism service was held at the church by the school at Kinyasano in Rukungiri. It was a well-attended service, filled with the families of the sixty candidates. Kivengere's stepfather was pleased for him, and his mother 'just smiled and loved it all'.

Kivengere was dressed in the only shirt and shorts he owned and was, as always, barefoot. He watched as Mogandawasula sprinkled the other candidates after the Anglican fashion of baptism. He grew solemn as his own great moment approached. 'I expected something very radical to happen. I think I was expecting that some great power would come over me.' Mogandawasula reached Kivengere and sprinkled the water on his head. He said solemnly that with this the old man had died, and the new man had come, and baptised him Festo, Festo Kivengere. The boy waited breathlessly: 'When you are eleven years old, you desperately want things to be real.'

But Festo felt no different. Where was this new man? He had not arrived along with the new name. As Mogandawasula moved on to the next candidate, Kivengere stood feeling 'vaguely disappointed'. He could only conclude that the new man had crept in 'pretty quietly'. None of the 'great spiritual power I had longed to come upon me' had arrived. In later years he was to blame the teaching, not the baptism, for his disappointment. 'We really believed that after baptism we would be completely changed and have no trouble leading a really good life.'

Nevertheless, the boy's commitment to Christianity was real. His parents supported his first steps into the new life as a communicant member of the Anglican Church of Uganda. That same month they enrolled him in the new little school on Kinyasano hill at Rukungiri, six miles from home.

*   *   *

The school at Kinyasano was run by Ugandan Christians in close touch with the Ruanda Mission back in Kabale. It had walls of mud and branches and a roof of papyrus. Each week fresh cowdung was spread on the floor to damp down the dust. The furnishings were sparse: several rows of long hard benches for the 120 boys, and a table and bit of blackboard for each of the four teachers. There were very few books and no paper, the students shared a few slates and sticks of precious chalk. The four teachers had only very basic teacher training.

Any boy was welcomed at the school, provided there was still room in Primary One, and he could pay the two shillings a term for fees (poorer boys sometimes borrowed a chicken from someone in their village, and paid in eggs). After Primary One, there was Primary Two, Three and Four. After that the school ran out of teachers, so they gave the boys a leaving examination and a certificate. Very few made it the fifty miles south to Kabale for Primary Five and Six at the Ruanda Mission's Kigezi High School.

It was a very simple start to a formal education, but Festo was fortunate in getting it. In Rujumbura in 1931, for every boy who went to a 'bush' school, there were many tens of thousands who did not. Certainly without the little mud school on Kinyasano hill, Festo would have spent the rest of his days herding cows.

As it was, youngsters of Festo's age were already almost too old. Most of these 'readers' would return to farms and crafts. It would not be until almost another generation had passed that the students at the schools would go on into professions— invariably teaching, preaching or hospital work. There were several good reasons for this. First-generation children like Festo faced an enormous gap between their home and village life and that of the Christian mission school. For instance, even such a simple thing as homework was out of the question as there were no lights but the fire in the huts, and bugs and ants would have devoured any papers or books. On top of all that, the boys were kept busy with chores. There was also the enormous physical effort—and some danger—in getting to school on a regular basis. Like many other children, eleven-year-old Festo would rise at six am to care for the calves before gulping down some warm milk from a *kyanzi* and setting off barefoot in shirt and

Boys' Brigade at Kabale, circa 1936. Festo is in the front row,
second from the left.

shorts for the six-mile trek to Rukungiri and Kinyasano hill on
paths through lion, leopard and snake-infested bush country.
Mornings were safe enough, but the return journey at six pm
each night was a different matter, and one or two students were
killed.

Yet right from the first term of early 1931 Festo seems to have
been able to make the change to this arduous lifestyle—and stick
to it. First, Festo enjoyed excellent health and stamina—this
became a byword in later years in his international travels. He
made light of twelve miles a day barefoot plus several hours of
chores and a ten-hour school day. As well as boundless energy,
he also had limitless curiosity and a desire to learn. His mother,
Barungi, and his stepfather also fully supported him, and in a
far more informed manner than most parents. His stepfather
willingly paid the two shillings a term and encouraged Festo to
set his sights high: on a clerk's job with the British administrators
in Kabale, perhaps.

Behind this positive support from home was also the fact that home itself was an increasingly unhappy—and crowded—place. As well as Festo's younger brother Kahembera, by now a mischievous seven-year-old, there was a squalling baby, Bainamaryo, and another on the way. The bitter arguments over the management of the herd had begun to lead to considerable violence, especially when Rwabugarame got drunk, which was more and more often. Festo was anxious to avoid his stepfather, and schooling was an ideal way of doing so. Finally, and just as important, Festo wanted to stay in touch with the Christian community. His baptism had been a serious step of commitment, and it was only at the school, among the Christian teachers, that he received any encouragement in his faith.

Festo would go off to school each morning at about seven am, often with several other lads from Kyamakanda. They tried their best to arrive at school, a rambling building just below the church on Kinyasano hill in Rukungiri, by eight am each morning—in time for the compulsory daily chapel service. The headmaster, Nyabagabo, and the other three teachers took it in turns to lead the chapel services. Nyabagabo was very popular with the boys, and Festo certainly admired him (little dreaming they would one day be brothers-in-law).

After chapel, classes began. Nyabagabo and his staff followed the government syllabus and taught their young charges simple arithmetic, geography, nature study, reading, spelling, English, Swahili, physical training and, above all, Scripture. There was no lunch, 'you had drunk your milk in the morning, and then you had to wait until evening'.

Festo loved school, and was at the top of his class most of the time as 'studying was no trouble'. He especially took to geography, Swahili and the little English provided. Geography was quite a challenge to teach, as the teachers had to describe the world beyond Rujumbura 'without maps or pictures!' (Festo would learn from experience just how difficult this was.) Language study came very easily to Festo. The Elementary Leaving Examination that all fourth years would have to sit was in Swahili. (The British were trying to introduce Swahili into Uganda as the main language, not only because the territory had hundreds of dialects and languages, but also because they had discovered it was one language they could learn fairly easily.) Swahili was to be invaluable to Festo in later years, giving him access to people in Tanzania, Kenya, Burundi, Rwanda, western Zaire and southern Somalia.

By now Festo had set his ambitions even higher than his stepfather's. No clerking for him: 'I wanted to be a chief under the British! I thought that would be a terrifically interesting life.' In the meantime he studied hard, and his calm demeanour soon drew the more muddled of his fellow students to him for help. 'We nicknamed him wisdom,' an old classmate recalls, 'because to us he was as smart as the teachers. And he would never tell us not to bother him.'

Yet Festo seems to have had little patience with mischief-makers. 'Don't disobey, he would tell us,' recalls one, 'and don't steal.' His basically conservative nature and his respect for authority may have come from his belonging to the ruling family. Throughout his life he often spoke his mind, but he was never one to try to bring down authority. His tendency was rather to work within the system. There was no trace of the rebel in his make-up. In later years he would expect his own authority to be obeyed.

When classes ended at four, the games began. Festo adored football, and in due course was made captain of the little barefoot team. This first experience of leadership made a deep impression: 'It soon struck me how much more was accomplished by a group where each is responsible to the group for his part played.' Forty years later as a bishop he would tell his clergy that a diocese should be run as a football team, with everyone in his place and keen to co-operate with the others, and able to be counted on by everyone else to do his job. (He would also avidly watch football games on English TV whenever he had the chance.)

Meanwhile, at twelve, Festo's eagerness for study was catching. Bugaari recalled, 'He had so much self-confidence—we leaned on that. With Festo around, somehow we believed more in ourselves.' The teachers had confidence in the boy: he was given the prestigious job of holding the duster and chalk for the teacher.

After games, the boys would go for a quick dip in the river, and by six pm set out for the six-mile trek home. Many times Festo arrived back at the hut to find his mother sobbing. It cut the boy to the heart. 'When my stepfather started beating my mother, I started hating him.' Rwabugarame's drunken sleeps were nearly the end of him, had he known it. Festo recalls. 'I knew nothing of poison, but I did know where his spear was, and I was tempted several times to use it. I was not going to let anyone hurt my mother.' The distress brought mother and son close together—unusual among the Bahima, even though they gave women more esteem than many tribes.

These were difficult years, but Barungi proved herself to be 'an excellent mother, strong, loving and serene. She refused to be defeated by the harsh difficulties of her life. She did not indulge in bitterness or self-pity.' Festo adored her, admiring her strength of character. She became for him the 'ideal' woman: dignified, independent, outspoken, caring for her children, hard-working, not hysterical, not a gossip. Barungi's example would have an enormous influence on his future relationship with women, on the wife he would choose, on the way he would bring up his daughters, and in the opportunities he would provide for women to minister in his diocese.

The situation at home also had a more immediate effect on Festo. Former classmates recall how grave he grew. He also acquired quite a reputation among his fellow students for defending the small boys from oppression. Perhaps he was standing up to the bullies small enough for him to fight in order to relieve the guilt he felt from not being able to defend his mother. In later years the sight of helpless people being bullied made him passionately determined to uphold the cause of the underdog.

*   *   *

By early 1932 Festo had completed his first year at Kinyasano, and his uncle, Karegyesa, invited him to come and live at the kraal at Rukungiri which was by now the government head-quarters for the district, and the HQ of the Church of Uganda for all of North Kigezi. However well Festo was coping, his uncle decided that home was too far from school. He was also willing to pay Festo's fees of six shillings a year. Karegyesa lived only two miles from Kinyasano hill—in African terms a short stroll. In 1932 Karegyesa was in his early forties. Missionaries remember him, at nearly six and a half feet tall, as 'a giant of a man and very much a Saza chief. He had enormous presence and dignity.' As Saza (or county) chief under the British, Karegyesa still ruled his people, but with British support and as part of the overall British administration of Uganda. Karegyesa appears to have been very content with this arrangement.

Karegyesa had been widowed and was now married to a woman who had been converted to Christianity in the early 1920s. She had supported his decision to become a Christian. However, he retained some pagan practices and kept concubines. Both Karegyesa and his wife greatly respected the missionaries.

Karegyesa had also thrown himself wholeheartedly behind the little school on Kinyasano hill. He had collected about fifty boys from among the local Bahima families—'not without force!'—and brought them to live at his kraal so that they could attend the school. 'Uncle wanted them to have an education so badly that he even paid many of their fees to make it possible.' The kraal became so overrun with boys that at times Festo found life there 'almost like a dormitory!' Many of the boys were cousins or clan relations. Festo had a vast number of relatives. His father's side of the family tree was 'swarming with clan cousins' and through his mother's side he had 'some link with almost the whole of North Kigezi!'

Communal everything was the order of the day, from washing to meals, which were presided over by Karegyesa's wife, Faisi (Faith) Kubaga. 'She was very, very good to us,' recalls Philimon, her stepson (the one the British would eventually nominate to succeed Karegyesa). In fact, Philimon reckons, 'Faisi really brought Festo up during those years—she was very fond of him indeed, because he was so well behaved!'

As he had done at school, Festo mingled well with the boys at his uncle's kraal. He soon became close friends with his slightly older cousin, Philimon Kitaburaza; a friendship that would deepen down the years and through involvement in North

Kigezi's development. But at this point it was enough that they shared a common passion—for sliding down muddy banks on banana leaves.

Karegyesa made Festo a welcome guest in the 'inner room' of the large hut where the chief's secret councils were held. He began to confide in him, telling him about the awkward situations he faced as Saza chief under the British. Karegyesa seems to have valued Festo's responses: after all, the youngster was in a unique position as one of the very first generation ever to go to school, and whose future was obviously going to be linked somehow with the British and Christianity. It was a golden opportunity for Festo to learn of the problems and responsibilities of leadership.

Karegyesa still held court in his grandfather's old place, under the sacred oak tree of Kagunga, and was still respected as the 'Lion of Kagunga' by his people, whatever the British might say about him being merely a Saza chief. As the chief, Karegyesa had on one side the British and Baganda administrators to deal with and on the other the remnants of his father's old court. Then there was the constant problem of inter-tribal hostility, which Karegyesa perceived would only slow down the development of the country. He told Festo how his grandfather, Makobore, had become locally famous as favouring impersonal justice.

Karegyesa also shared with Festo the difference the British had made in helping Uganda fight disease: as well as curbing the rinderpest the British were also fighting the sleeping sickness, which had killed a quarter of a million people in the epidemic of 1901–1910 alone. This was Festo's first introduction to the enormous difference Western aid could make in Uganda. In later years he would help bring in hundreds of thousands of dollars and save tens of thousands of lives.

These prolonged discussions with his uncle helped Festo enormously. Had he stayed with his parents it would have taken him far longer not only to adjust to the new ways, but to reach an informed opinion about the right attitude towards the changes. It was also a great advantage that this period of readjustment should happen not only within the security of a family relationship, but with the Saza chief of the tribe.

Meanwhile, Karegyesa insisted on daily Christian worship.

Every evening the drum was beaten to summon all of us for prayers. All the men, all the servants, all the women (wife and concubines) and all we boys were expected to attend. Karegyesa was very strong on discipline. The catechist would come from nearby and conduct our prayers: this had become one of his daily duties.

Karegyesa by all accounts took it 'almost as his duty' to see that Christianity was observed in his house. Certainly such public worship was new to many and the traditional pagan worship was now carried out in a 'secretive manner', not in community.

Festo was happy to attend prayers. He had been making steady progress in his Christian life. His headmaster, Ernest Nyabagabo had helped form a small Bible reading club which met daily after school. Festo was one of the leaders.

We were very serious about our intention to read the Bible regularly. We even made a covenant with each other not to leave our homes in the morning before we had read a portion of the Bible. I had read mine as soon as it was light enough to do so. We also made a rule that you had to report to the group that you had actually done it, too!

When the missionaries were able to send in Scripture Union daily Bible reading notes, Festo began to use them—a habit that became a crucial part of his daily devotions for many years. For Festo was determined to observe his baptismal vows. 'I was determined that my prayer must not fail, my morning Bible study with SU notes should never be missed, and that I would never be late for school.' Yet in later years he was to say that even in the midst of all this devotion he had still not really discovered the true meaning of being a Christian. 'We Christians tried so hard that we turned almost everything into legalistic extremism. I was convinced that being a good Christian depended on keeping up the standard. Looking back, it was quite an astonishing regime we put ourselves through!'

At the end of 1935, Festo and his class completed Primary Four. Festo was among those who passed. His uncle was delighted. He decided that the youngster must go on to Primary Five and Six. But Karegyesa's joy in his nephew's success was tinged with sadness. He would pay Festo's fees for him, but he would lose his young confidant. The proverb *Obunuzi butsiga obusharizi* summed it up: 'Sweetness leaves bitterness' (or, 'After a man has visited, the contrast of not having him is bitter.'). Festo and Bugaari returned home to Kyamakanda to prepare for their move to Kabale. The distance would make weekend visits impossible. 'It was very hard for me to leave my mother.' In addition to his ambition to get an education another ambition was planted: to someday see his mother happy and cared for.

*   *   *

While Festo's life began to turn steadily away from that of a traditional Muhima, others were also searching for a turning point—in the life of the Ugandan Church. Dr Joe Church and his friends in Gahini were still earnestly seeking the 'secret of revival'.

By 1930 the Ruanda Mission had celebrated its first ten years. Much had been accomplished: 5,000 public baptisms, 300 village churches, two general hospitals with 200 in-patients, boys' and girls' schools, and twenty-nine missionaries divided between the two mission stations: Kabale and Gahini. The famine was now behind them, and the revival was just ahead. Prayer and Bible study increased. 'God's answer was becoming visible all over Ruanda and Uganda in two ways: a deep, divine discontent in the hearts of many Christians, and a new realisation of the meaning and power of prayer.'[1] Joe Church, Blasio Kigozi and Yosiya Kinuka continued to pray, reporting a new sense of urgency, but 'still not the spark of new life yet ...'[2]

However, the next four years saw the dawning of the revival in Gahini. By April 1931 there were early morning prayer meetings on Dr Joe Church's verandah. By the summer a vital pattern had been established: a week-long teaching convention preceding the confirmation of sixty-five candidates by Bishop Stuart from Kampala. At Christmas, 2,000 packed the new church, pouring in from bush churches from miles around.

In 1932, Dr Church hit upon the theme of 'brokenness', which made 'it possible for God in his sovereign will and time, to pour out his Holy Spirit'.[3] The teaching was to help many come to faith, and 'brokenness before God' became a byword of the revival. Otherwise Dr Church and others tried to stick to a balance of all aspects of the gospel, though Dr Church admitted, 'It was a temptation to develop some special revival message such as "brokenness", something that belongs to our mission— how terrible!—and to forget that the answer is found only in, "I, when I am lifted up ... will draw all men to myself"' (John 12:32).[4]

Then, as 1933 drew to a close, a breakthrough in true Christian fellowship occurred: two missionaries asked forgiveness of their African brethren for wrong attitudes—to the Africans' amazement. 'Never before have we heard a white man own that he was wrong!' United prayer was easier after that. Another breakthrough came over Christmas, on 27th December, at a conference of African evangelists, teachers and missionaries. The formal prayers suddenly broke down, and conviction of sin fell upon the whole assembly. Prayer became sincere, weeping confession.

Forgiveness and thanksgiving followed. Crying gave way to 'burning love' and joy. Prayer meetings flourished—some starting as early as three-thirty am. The way was now clear: 'We found that once we had repented and in some cases asked forgiveness for our prejudice and white superiority, a new realm in relationships was entered into which altered the character of all our work.'[5]

So it was no surprise to find that in early 1934 great excitement was sweeping through the Gahini station. The members of the new movement began to be called the *abaruwaka,* 'those on fire'. There was inevitably some backlash with dissensions and divisions, but the *abaruwaka* struggled on, and realised a new important lesson would always have to be borne in mind: in order for any fellowship to last, 'short accounts' would have to be kept. So at prayer meetings time was set aside for people to put things right with each other. This 'time of light' would become integral to the revival throughout East Africa.

In December 1934 a large team set out from Gahini on an evangelistic safari to Urundi. The following year would be Kabale's turn.

CHAPTER THREE

CONVERTED IN A BROOM CUPBOARD

1935–1936

Festo goes to Kigezi High School; 1935 mission to Kabale brings revival teaching from Gahini, led by Joe Church, Yosiya Kinuka and Blasio Kigozi; revival begins in Kabale; Festo makes commitment in school cupboard prayer group; joins evangelistic teams; on to Mbarara High School.

WHEN SIXTEEN-YEAR-OLD FESTO arrived in Kabale in early 1935 there were no indications that this earnest but formal Christian community was about to reel under the impact of the winds of revival. The coming spiritual storm that would soon sweep across East Africa was still gathering momentum among the Christians of Gahini. Meanwhile, the Ruanda Mission missionaries longed to see lasting changes in the lives of their converts, but did not know how to effect more than a nominal adherence to the new faith. The Bakiga, it seemed to the British, gave a mental nod in favour of Christianity coming to church when the drums summoned them to services, but never allowed it to engage their hearts. The missionaries were also well aware that their own spiritual lives lacked vigour and authority. No one dreamed that one of the most dramatic chapters of Ugandan church history was about to open. Its spiritual blessing would so thoroughly soak Ugandan hearts that it would still be a source of nourishment fifty years later.

When Festo, Bugaari and a few others set out for the school in Kabale in January 1935, that was an historic event in itself. No youngsters from Kyamakanda had ever lived as far as fifty miles from home before, let alone attend a boarding school run by Europeans. The boys' new life would be run on British lines of strict discipline and time-keeping (a most novel and difficult concept to grasp—and one which Festo took some time to get used to!).

On the morning the boys set off, Barungi gave Festo what little she could: a bit of cloth to wrap round him when the only shirt and shorts he possessed proved inadequate against the chill nights, and an extra long drink of milk from a *kyanzi*. Barefoot, the boys travelled south through the mountains and by taking short cuts through the bush, they lopped miles off the fifty mile road journey, making Kabale accessible in one day.

Kabale, at 6,200 feet above sea level the highest town in Uganda, is perched amid the beautiful Mugogo hills, which form the watershed between Lakes Edward and Victoria. The red glow of the volcanoes of Kabale's mighty neighbours, the Bufumbira mountains, sometimes shines against the night sky. South-west lies impenetrable forest, home of the mountain gorillas. Six miles away lies Lake Bunyoni, the Lake of Little Birds, sparkling clear and very deep, mountains rising straight from its serene blue surface like a postcard of Switzerland.

In 1935 it was a quiet market town, with a population of about 5,000. Even by Ugandan standards it was remote—the last town of any size before the Congo in the West and Rwanda and Burundi to the South. The town, like most of South Kigezi, was inhabited by the Bakiga tribe, whose neat terraced farms of sorghum, peas, beans, finger millet and sweet potatoes were laid out on the hillsides.The Ruanda Mission Station itself was situated on the top of Rugarama Hill. It seemed successful: hospitals, schools, the church—all were full.

This then was the setting for Festo and his teenage friends when they arrived at Kabale, footsore and hungry on that first January evening, and shyly presented themselves at Kigezi High School.

The school consisted of three semi-permanent buildings of mud and wattle with papyrus thatched roofs, one for classes, two for dormitories. It educated some 100 boys drawn from all over Kigezi, many of them sons of Saza chiefs. The school's African teachers had had the best education available in Uganda, at the CMS run King's College in Budo.

On the night the boys arrived the culture shock began. A

prefect escorted them to one of the two dormitories, where fifty simple beds stood in neat rows; though they were no more than poles with rope latticed between. Festo and his friends stuttered 'Eh-h-hs!' of surprise. None had ever seen a bed before, much less slept in one. When they went in search of a meal, there was a more severe shock—there was nothing to eat but potatoes and beans. 'To me, who had been brought up on smoked milk and warm blood, potatoes and beans were *disgusting*!'

Term and lessons got underway. Festo continued his struggle with arithmetic, and fairly danced through his lessons on geography, English, Swahili and natural science. He began to show signs of his happy gift for utter concentration on the task in hand, and had no problems studying at night by the light of kerosene lanterns. He developed methodical study habits, and was quickly discovering a love of books. Festo's ability as a teacher blossomed too. He loved to sit down with a boy and help him solve a problem. It left him with a 'warm glow of accomplishment'. Some teachers are born, and Festo was one of them; the joy of teaching coming long before he knew anything very much to teach.

A clearer picture of Festo's personality begins to emerge during these years. Though his cheerful and friendly nature made him popular, there was also a private side to him. He tended to keep his own counsel, and though he was quick in acquaintance—'I liked to be pleasant to people, and to join in what everyone else did'—he was cautious in real friendships. 'It always took me time to get to know people. I was partly shy, but it was more a hesitancy born of pride—I didn't want people to get too close because I didn't want anything to spoil my name or reputation.' This pride constantly spurred him on to do his very best in his studies—he did not want to let himself down. However, he couldn't resist some of the schoolboy hijinks, such as joining the boys who would slip out of their dormitory window at night to drink and smoke pipes. Festo was quiet and nimble, but even so he had a few tricky moments the night his shorts caught on a nail and pinned him half in and half out of a window.

In the spring of 1935, Festo joined the Boys' Brigade band of bugles and drums. He tried a bugle, but found it 'hard on the lungs' so he took to the drums instead. The Boys' Brigade, led by teacher the Revd Lawrence Barham, obviously met a great need. Though entirely voluntary, half the school had joined in its first year. And little wonder—by leaving their homes and villages and embracing a new faith and education, the boys were effectively in danger of growing up as social and cultural orphans. The BB offered an excellent opportunity of helping them to see that Christian beliefs did not exclude satisfying social contact or self-respect and achievement. The boys immensely enjoyed the occasional camps that leader Lawrence Barham took them on—marching to far-flung villages to sing and play—thus gathering entire villages together so that the missionaries could preach to them. This was Festo's first experience of peripatetic evangelism, and he thoroughly enjoyed it, though there was no inkling at the time that it would one day, minus the drum, become his vocation. He was promoted to lead a platoon and very much enjoyed the responsibility of keeping the boys 'up to scratch'. He also liked working under Barham's authority. 'I enjoyed doing what I was supposed to do.'

All in all, 1935 was a bridging year for Festo. 'My two worlds were merging. I just moved naturally from a life of fear and superstition into education, liberation and Christianity.' And more material possessions: fifteen-year-old Festo at last acquired a blanket of his very own.

When Festo and Bugaari returned from Kyamakanda for the autumn term of 1935, they soon heard about the big news: the Rev. Lawrence Barham was organising a convention in Kabale. The speakers were to come from Gahini—Dr Joe Church and a team of Africans. The Kabale Convention was booked for Sunday 22nd to Monday 30th September 1935. Festo and his fellow students watched curiously as the team of thirteen drove in from Gahini, led by Joe Church, Yosiya Kinuka and Blasio Kigozi.

Festo soon discovered that the speakers from Gahini did not actually say anything original, but that there was a difference in the way they said it.

There was power in what they said. We hadn't seen that before. Those meetings were the beginning of an incredible movement of

God. For most of us it was a remarkable and never-to-be-forgotten week. Our attention was riveted by the shining faces of these men who obviously had spiritual freedom, were in love with God, and at peace with one another. We listened, wide-eyed, to what they had to say.

Joe Church's readings from the Schofield Bible kept to one theme a day. It was an intense schedule: 'Sin' on Tuesday, 'Repentance' on Wednesday, 'the New Birth' on Thursday, 'Coming out of Egypt' (ie, separation from the world) on Friday and 'the Holy Spirit and the Victorious Life' on Saturday. A praise meeting on Sunday rounded off the week. At the end of it all nothing spectacular had taken place. People slipped away to their homes. The team returned to Gahini. Festo well understood the subdued reaction, 'It was too new and startling for most people. Yet we felt strangely restless, strangely stirred.'

Festo soon heard stories of strange happenings which began to trickle back to Kabale. 'Within a month, people began to weep unexpectedly, dream dreams of heaven, or cry out under conviction.'[1] A sense of fear of sin, and the results of sin, came upon many, sometimes upon whole gatherings, and people began 'trembling and weeping for their sins'. This was always followed by a dramatic 'breakthrough', when the person would feel himself quite definitely forgiven and 'saved' by Christ, and overwhelmed by love and joy.

Festo was intrigued. He continued with his self-imposed regime of daily Bible reading and prayer, and mulled over a parable he had heard a visiting English missionary tell earlier in the year. This told of a father and a son together making a boat for the boy to play with. One day the finished boat slipped from the boy's anguished grasp and floated away downstream. Months later the boy passed a shop window and there was his boat, for sale. The boy was so excited he wanted to grab it then and there and take it home with him. But the shopkeeper now had control of the boat, and told him curtly that if the boy really wanted it back, he would have to pay the price. The boy worked hard and finally earned enough to buy the boat. Holding it tightly and lovingly he said to the boat, 'Now you are mine twice: first because father and I made you, and then because after the river took you away, I searched for you and found you

Festo leading a brick-carrying party, 1936/37. The burned bricks were to replace the mud bricks for the floor of one of their school dormitories.

Kigezi High School, 1936.

and bought you back. You are mine twice over.' The missionary had drawn spiritual parallels for the students: 'You are Jesus' boys, twice: first he made you, you were created by him in his image. Then he bought you back after sin had taken you away. He bought you with his precious blood on the cross. So you belong to him twice.'

Festo was deeply moved by this picture of a loving God, and what it had cost to 'buy' him back. It made him yearn for a relationship with God that, if he was honest, he didn't really have. He was trying to achieve what he saw as the proper lifestyle of a Christian, but it was very hard work. Then Festo received a real shock. One day that autumn Bugaari rushed up in his boisterous way and announced, beaming with joy, that he had been 'born again'. Festo was happy for his friend, but couldn't understand the fuss; Bugaari had surely been a Christian since Byensi had started his little village church back in Kyamakanda?

That was just the start of a baffling time for Festo.

Everyone knew that God had become alive, really alive. There was a constant expectancy every day. Young people used to wake up in the middle of the night and go outside under our brilliant East African stars and wonder if they were about to see God—literally. That was the effect the Spirit of God was having on Kabale.

One morning about five am (an hour before students rose to cultivate the school fields where they grew their own food), Festo awoke to the sound of whispers. Several boys were slipping out of the dormitory and—to his astonishment—disappearing into the little storeroom at the far end of the building. It turned out they were meeting for prayer. Festo lay on his mat on the string bed and thought about it for a long time.

In the weeks that followed, the Kabale missionaries were happy men and women. Barham reported joyfully that since the Kabale Convention the surrounding district had seen:

confession of sin and restitution. Apologies followed: many had dreams, sometimes receiving a strong impression to read certain verses of the Bible which led them to put away some sin—beer drinking, for example. Preaching bands have gone out all through the district and very many are stirred ...[2]

This, in fact, was the autumn the laity of the Church of Uganda took back from the clergy the role of evangelism.

November 1935 arrived and with it a new missionary, the Revd Philip ('Pip') Tribe. He shared Festo's sympathetic but uncomprehending curiosity about the revival. A keen evangelical, who had received his 'call' to the mission field at the Keswick Convention, he was nonetheless bemused by all the repenting and weeping and talk of brokenness. As he soon found himself in charge of Festo's class, and shortly after that Headmaster of Kigezi High School, Tribe had little enough time to worry over who was 'walking in the light', and who wasn't. Festo never suspected that their strict but cheerful teacher spent his nights swotting up for the next day's lessons by lantern light, for Tribe had no experience as a teacher. He impressed Festo, however: 'He was very good to us, strong on discipline but kind. He was like a father to us.'

Tribe would come to hold an historic place in Festo's life as his was the first white man's hut Festo ever entered. (The tidiness deeply impressed him.) Tribe, in fact, established an 'open house' policy with his boys, which Festo took advantage of one day. The missionary arrived home to see the teenager slipping out by the back way, still licking his fingers. He had found Tribe's honey pot.

In January 1936 Festo was invited to join the storeroom prayer group. He readily did so. It gave him the chance to ask questions about being 'born again'. Early one morning, crouched on the floor of the storeroom with a small group of boys around him, Festo Kivengere gave his life to Jesus Christ:

> There was no weeping, no hysteria—the dormitory beyond the flimsy door was full of sleeping boys. But I knew immediately something had changed within me. What I had read about Jesus in the gospels came alive in a way it had not done before. I had suddenly caught the vision of the gracious God, the Creator, who had come in Jesus Christ to seek me.

Now he wanted to put things right, and that meant owning up to Pip Tribe about the smoking and drinking. He did so with some trepidation, convinced he would be caned. Instead, the headmaster prayed with him and encouraged him in his fresh

Christian commitment. This response made a tremendous impression. It was the only adult encouragement or special attention Festo had received since his talks with his Uncle Karegyesa. For his part, Tribe found Festo's sober confession (which even included the honey pot incident, much to Tribe's amusement) genuine and appealing. He thought the sins of smoking and drinking relatively trivial, but he realised they symbolised a real change of direction in the teenager.

Festo was soon eager to join in the weekend evangelistic teams going out from Kigezi High School. Such teamwork was becoming a hallmark of the revival: joint evangelism common to every 'revived' Christian. Festo revealed a talent for public testimony. Dressed in his KHS uniform of shirt, shorts and a little badge, which drew crowds of village boys to stare in admiration, he and another classmate, Francis Kalimuzo (later Vice Chancellor of Makerere University), would share their belief in Christ. Everywhere the boys found remarkable signs of the revival. Conversion also led to people paying off debts, paying taxes, and returning stolen cattle.

That summer of 1936, Festo went home and told his family what had happened to him. His mother was sympathetic but puzzled. 'That's strange,' was her response, 'it seems as if you have all received a vision.' She was not quite sure if such a vision was 'suitable for me in my aristocratic class', and worried that 'I might be risking my status in society', What really concerned her were the other stories—that those who had seen the vision now felt free to disregard the taboos, and eat such things as chicken, eggs or fish—unthinkable for a Muhima.

Festo then screwed up courage to tell his uncle, Karegyesa, during one of the regular times of worship at the Saza chief's kraal.

> Everyone was quite shocked. They had also heard of those who had seen the vision—*abarukwaka* they called us, a Runyankole word meaning 'to be given a vision'—because invariably our testimony was 'I have seen Jesus.' But this kind of experience and talk was strange and unknown, even among those people who had left paganism for Christianity, and had been baptised like my uncle. The difference was they had left paganism for Christianity, a religion. We had been met by and saved by a Person, by Christ.

So Karegyesa and his advisers gave Festo a mixed reception. They could not understand an experience which led to disposing with long-held customs, and asking for pardon for wrongs done. (This very practical aspect of 'revival' had greater impact than any other; the community could not but be impressed when converts began returning stolen goods, seeking and asking forgiveness, and revealing exceptional compassion and mercy.)

With thousands being converted throughout Kigezi every week from 1935 onwards, the revival was to make a shattering impact. For the pagans were never left alone; the revived, or *balokole* (singular, *mulokole*) as they became known, made them targets of loving, caring evangelism, obsessed with what they believed were their 'lost souls'. By 1941 there would be few homes in the hundreds of square miles of north Kigezi where a family, however isolated, could honestly say they had never heard of Jesus.

In the meantime, Karegyesa grew more and more concerned that his favourite nephew should have been afflicted with this new 'trouble'. As the *balokole* seemed to threaten the Bahima way of life, he came to resent them bitterly. There were also other problems, and in view of Festo's later involvement, they are worth looking at.

What Festo did not know at the time was that the revival not only healed but also ploughed up the serene meadows of established worship and belief. It had led to divisions and anger within the Ugandan Church. Joe Church, Yosiya, Blasio and the other revivalists had been surprised at first when their cries of 'awake' to the Church of Uganda had been met with irritation rather than gratitude. What the revivalists had meant as a spiritual 'fire alarm', warning of the danger of continued spiritual 'sleep', much of the church took as a jangling alarm clock going off in their unsuspecting ear. Therefore, they did not appreciate the frank challenges to their own Christian commitment, the hysterical weeping, the all-night prayer and singing meetings, the closer black–white relations, the frank public confessions of sin, the flowing testimony of 'what Jesus has done for me', and the emphasis on repenting. Irritated, the church wished it could find the 'off' button of this alarm.

At the beginning of 1935, Blasio Kigozi and his *abarukwaka* came in for severe criticism for their frank preaching during his rounds as preacher in charge of the bush churches around Gahini. Blasio was gracious and did not fight back, but neither did he stop his continual urging for all men to be born again—even those who already considered themselves Christians on the grounds that they gave mental assent to the Christian message, and were baptised and confirmed. In early 1936 he was on his way to causing even more trouble (through straightforward challenging) at the Synod which met every two years on Namirembe hill in Kampala when he died tragically of tick fever. But his challenge to the wider Uganda church remained, the catchword of which was 'Awake!' (*Zukuka!* in Luganda). The call came on three points. What is the cause of coldness and deadness in the Church of Uganda? Why are people who are living in open sin allowed to come to the Lord's Table? What must be done to bring revival to the Church of Uganda?

It must also be said that the *balokole* being only human could become divisive. Straight from paganism, the displays of emotion and hysteria to indicate genuine feeling were to some extent culturally conditioned. But some got carried away and were almost on a high of emotional exhibitionism—witness the girl who kept smearing her eyes with saliva to try and look weepy when she ran out of tears; while others became critical of those whose wailing, jumping and collapsing was not as spectacular as theirs had been.

The biggest threat, both to the movement and to the Uganda Church, was that the revival had all the force and conviction it needed to leave the Uganda Church altogether and to set up on its own as the only true Christian Church in Uganda. That the Uganda Church survived such tumultuous days with the revivalists and non-*balokole* still firmly within its fold is a tribute to the graciousness and forbearance of Bishop Stuart, who had taken over in 1934, only a year before things really heated up. Joe Church, Lawrence Barham and William Nagenda wanted to keep the revival within the church, but were involved in a situation not only beyond their control, but one which they were firmly convinced was a work of the Holy Spirit.

At the end of 1936 Festo completed his sixth year of school, Primary Six, and was encouraged by Tribe to go on to Mbarara

High School, where a scholarship awaited him. He would be among the very first handful from Kigezi to go. He shared the news with his family. His stepfather was amazed to discover that there were still *more* things a person could learn even after six whole years at school, but delighted that Festo's fees would be paid by the *Muzungu* (white men).

The holiday at Rukungiri was no happier than Festo had feared; indeed, now he was faced with the news that his mother had almost been killed. It happened one night when Rwabagarame was away on a drinking spree and Barungi had found herself practically sole guardian of the herd. Within hours a lioness arrived, leaping the ten-foot kraal in search of the cattle. Barungi attacked the huge tawny shadow with a stick. When the animal fled, Barungi found herself quite a heroine in the village. Festo would retell the story with pride for many years. 'To me, her strength of nerve, courage and independence, combined with her love for me, my brothers and sisters, made her the ideal woman.'

As January 1937 approached, Festo had conceived a new ambition: to some day go to college and become a teacher himself. For that he wanted to train at King's College, Budo. That winter, off to Mbarara on a scholarship, it seemed anything was possible.

CHAPTER FOUR

SCHOOLDAYS AND SPIRITUAL STRUGGLES

1937–1940

Guilt and frustration; forsaking Christianity; education hopes dashed; training for primary school teaching; mother dies; return to Rukungiri.

FESTO TURNED HIS BACK on Christianity within months of his arrival at Mbarara. His problem had begun while he was still in Rukungiri with his family. He felt he was being prompted by God to tell several more people at his uncle's kraal about his new-found faith, and specifically to 'put right' several things with them. But Festo ignored this urge, and left home without saying a word. He made his way to Mbarara with the belief that God had asked him to do something and that he had refused.

Mbarara, set in the wide Ankole plains, was by far the most interesting place the boys had ever seen; even in those days it was something of a crossroads for southwest Uganda. The CMS Mission Station was based two miles out of town at Ruharo. The school, of course, was also on the mission station. The boys found it nestled alongside the church, at the end of a long, softly shaded lane of eucalyptus trees. If Festo and Bugaari had to endure a term of practical jokes and bullying common to new boys at boarding schools the world over, they were also to forge life-long friendships, including one with a Zebulon Kabaza, a tall, thin lad who was outspoken to the point of bluntness.

Mbarara High School had a CMS missionary as headmaster. The staff of four Ugandans were graduates of Makerere College in Kampala. Festo's favourite subjects were English, Swahili and geography at which he again excelled. But he could not forget that he had not mended his relationships with people back in

Rukungiri. The conviction that he had done wrong and dis-obeyed God slowly increased as the weeks went by. In a couple of months he would be back in Rukungiri for holidays, but, 'I rebelled and decided I would not tell them even then.'

Soon after this Festo began to lose his 'inner peace'. A sense of coldness set in. That led to 'a kind of despair'. He could have shared it with his friends at the school's Christian meetings, but he didn't. 'All I said was that I was struggling with something and was not willing to do very much about it.'

He had been attending the regular revival meetings at the school (because of Mbarara's central position, the school easily kept in touch with the events of the revival). But he soon lost interest. The stories of many conversions at the missions held that year (1937) throughout Uganda in honour of the CMS' Diamond Jubilee in that country did not move him. A few more weeks and Festo told the revival group, 'I am no longer one of you.'

But the unease continued. Festo thrust away the thought that perhaps it wasn't *just* the other Christians who were after him. He began to cast about for a means of distraction. His attention was caught by a group of lads who seemed carefree and happy—everything he was not. 'I didn't care so much for the mischief they got up to as to the fact that they seemed so independent and contemptuous of authority. They did anything they liked and I marvelled. They gave me the impression that they were free.' Festo soon joined them in twilight escapades down the dukkas (shops), where he began to drink and smoke heavily, as well as 'falling into serious sin'. Bugaari was horrified; Zebulon contemptuous.

But to Festo's dismay, he found his new friends and ways did not take away the guilt he felt. The struggle between his will and what he believed was God's will for him continued. Even worse, he found his latest misdeeds only adding to the evidence against him. He knew there was a Law, and now discovered that breaking it did not make it go away. 'I knew what God had done for me. Now guilt at what I was doing, which I knew was sin against him, overwhelmed me.' He was no longer friendly with the other Christians among the students. He was ashamed before them. 'I timidly avoided them.' He was learning that 'guilt isolates you in your misery'. When his Christian friends tried to help him however, he grew prickly: 'I would have none of it by now.' Instead, 'The more guilty I felt, the more mischief I wanted to do.'

When term broke for holidays, Festo and Bugaari walked the seventy-five miles back to Rukungiri, spending a night with a Bahima family mid-way. Festo was a very different lad from the one that only a year before had played a drum in the Boys' Brigade band on weekend missions. The closest he and Bugaari came to talking to anyone on this trip was late in the day when, very hungry, they met a woman carrying a basket of potatoes. She churlishly refused their request for a raw potato each. Festo, impatient with hunger, moved swiftly, pushing the basket off her head, scattering potatoes everywhere. The boys helped themselves and ran off laughing, leaving an agitated woman behind.

That holiday Barungi told Festo she wanted to leave Rwabugarame. Festo would soon be old enough, according to Bahima custom, to take responsibility for his mother and his father's herd of cattle. Barungi also asked Festo to tell her more about this Jesus the Christians worshipped. Ironically, by now she was more interested in Christianity than he was, having noticed a real change in him during his last year at Kabale, and having been intrigued by the increasing number of stories coming from the revival. In later years Festo would mourn this lost opportunity. 'If I had been spiritually "right", she would have found Christ. As it was, she remained a pagan, though very warm towards Jesus.'

Back at school, Festo tried to ignore his inner misery. He began to set his sights on getting the best education Uganda had to offer: a place at King's College, Budo, followed by a diploma course at Makerere College. He and Mugimba, his English master, together planned how he could become a secondary-school teacher, for Festo had set his heart on this. He had fallen in love not only with knowledge, but also with education itself. In the Uganda of those days, teachers were desperately needed and Festo knew he had it within him to be a good teacher.

Then in September 1937 the blow fell. Pip Tribe, who as

headmaster of Kabale High School was paying Festo's fees, wrote to say that because the teenager was doing so well it had been decided to take him out of Mbarara a whole year early, and send him on to Bishop Tucker College at Mukono to take the new three-year primary teachers' course. In Festo Kivengere, they felt they had found a promising lad who could cope with the educational short-cut and still serve the mission's urgent needs. In fact, Festo was the only lad from Kabale thought capable of coping with such a demand. Festo was furious. He felt that he should have been rewarded for his hard work by a chance to improve himself further, instead of being 'exploited' for the mission's benefit. To get onto the primary teachers' course he would have to sit an examination. He immediately decided to fail it. It was typical of him to show his anger in a restrained way, rather than to rant and rave.

Festo's teachers at Mbarara were angry to learn that their star pupil was destined for nothing higher than primary teaching. Mugimba and Kapa, another teacher, even offered to somehow raise the money to pay the fees for Festo to stay on at Mbarara: that way he would no longer be dependent on the sponsorship of Kabale High School. Festo wrestled with the problem as the weeks flew by and the entrance exam loomed closer. He was tempted to accept the generous offer of help with fees but he knew his mother, brothers and sister would soon be dependent on him. Might the wisest choice be to take this course and become a primary teacher? 'In my heart of hearts I knew my mother needed me.' But he yearned to complete the promised second year at Mbarara, and then go on to Budo and Makerere. It was the only chance at further education he thought he would ever have.

So Festo still walked into the examination room determined to fail. It wasn't until the 'entrance' paper was actually in front of him that he grudgingly decided to do what he could. He was very disappointed to be told that he had passed with a good mark, and could therefore join the primary teachers' course.

So, at the end of a thoroughly miserable year, Festo packed his few possessions with a heavy heart. Bugaari would be returning in January 1938, while he would have to make his way nearly 300 miles northeast to Mukono, near Kampala. Festo felt he had lost everything. His former two major goals—perfecting his Christian walk, and getting the best education that he could—had crumbled away. Now his great love for his mother gave him the only purpose to his days. He decided he would devote himself to making her life more bearable. He did not realise how soon even that ambition would be snatched from him.

*   *   *

Back from a brief visit home Festo discovered that Rwabugarame had begun to beat Barungi savagely once again, and was threatening to take another wife. Enough was enough. Festo swiftly began plans to move Barungi and the children back to the village where his real father had been born.

The trip from Rujumbura to Mukono was nearly 300 miles. Festo packed his extra shirt and a couple of books and set off from Kyamakanda in early January 1938 to catch a lift in one of the crowded open-backed lorries that were the only means of public transport to Kampala and on to Mukono in those days. He was nineteen. Seven years of schooling were behind him, three years of professional training at college ahead.

The Bishop Tucker College at Mukono offered a course for ordinands and had only just launched the three-year course for primary school teachers. Festo's year was only the second group to be taking the course, which had been laid on because of the desperate need for qualified primary teachers. (The Government, for all its commendable progress in education, was not yet able to train students in any numbers without the help of the mission college.) Festo arrived in the back of a lorry, hot, dirty, tired and 'in a very rebellious state of mind'.

From the start of term Festo seems to have evolved a rather Jekyll and Hyde existence. During the day he was an eager trainee teacher, scrupulous in attending lectures, and always producing written work on time. His innate conservatism and respect for authority kept him up to the mark in these respects, and as he had a real talent for teaching, he was again at the top of his class in a few weeks (where he stayed without exception for the rest of the course). He and his fellow student-teachers were given a general course in the many subjects they would soon be teaching right across the protectorate: maths, history, religious knowledge, geography and English. Specialisation was out of the question as teachers were too scarce.

A CMS missionary, Reginald Hopkins taught the students the other side of the coin: *how* to teach all the knowledge they were cramming into themselves. This *how to* was vital as once back in their little villages the demand on them would be unrelenting— usually thirty lessons a week to an age-range of ten to sixteen year olds, with a dizzy variation in ability and previous schooling. Fortunately for these village schools, Mr Hopkins was, in Festo's estimation, 'a gifted, outstanding communicator'. The missionary 'really made us want to teach'. In fact, Festo reckoned that Hopkins was the major influence on his whole attitude towards his future work. 'He made me fall in love with my profession.'

So much for the calm, amenable nineteen-year-old by day. After hours, Festo changed, and continued to try and exorcise the demon of discontent and misery that pursued him. He fell in with the wilder of the students, and joined them on their drinking sprees down at the Asian-run dukkas in town. The 'serious sins' during these late-night sessions continued, but Festo would always draw a veil over exactly what he and his drinking companions got up to when the beer sank low in the mugs and the temptations of the town lay all about them. Whatever his misdeeds were, he soon discovered they did not stop the 'continual conviction and guilt' that constantly nagged him.

There were also weekly unpleasant reminders of his former spiritual commitment as the mission college required all its students to attend its church services on Sunday. Even such a nominal commitment to Christianity as this made Festo uncomfortable, as 'I was really trying to get away from God.'

The months went by and Festo found himself caught up in a vicious circle: the worse the things he did down at the dukkas, the more guilty he felt. The more guilty he felt, the further away he wanted to get from all things Christian. The further away he got, the worse the sins he committed, but the worst sins did not blot out Christianity: he only felt more guilty.

Half-term came, and Festo returned to Rukungiri. The new house and kraal were ready in Nshure. Festo broke the news of the imminent move to his stepfather, and gave Rwabugarame a young heifer as a 'thank you for being a father' to him. Custom called for this, not love, as 'he was the only man I ever completely hated'. The residents of Nshure gave Barungi and her young family a warm welcome as they had fond memories of Ntzirisa, Festo's father. Festo returned to Mukono easier in his mind for his mother than he had been for years, but still very bitter towards his stepfather.

Back in Mukono, Festo once more threw himself into his studies. The great advantage of his love for geography was that it gave him a chance to appreciate the grandeur of his country and indeed his continent. He made methodical, careful notes of all he learned, and continued to scour the library for help in how best to communicate his new-found knowledge.

It was at Mukono that Festo also made considerable progress with his English. The fascination of reading had gripped him (it became a life-long hobby) and many of the books were in English. He read everything from biography and novels to history and textbooks 'because I didn't know enough to choose between one book and another'. Again, his happy knack of utter absorption in a given task despite considerable noise and hub-bub round about came often to his aid. It was also at Mukono at this time that he began to pick up Luganda, the language of the Baganda. It came in very handy on teaching practice. From his first class, Festo realised that he had found his vocation. 'I discovered I loved communicating with students. It didn't matter whether they were ten years old or fifteen years old. Just give me a class and I was happy.' His natural leadership and calm authority ensured that the students rarely got up to mischief, while his knack of using captivating expressions meant they were fascinated by what the teacher might be going to say next.

Then, in the late summer of 1938, news reached Festo that Barungi was seriously ill. He rushed back to Nshure and sat on the floor beside her sleeping platform. Medical help was not available. It was clear she was going to die. 'Mother was not afraid, in fact, she was more worried about us than herself.' However, Festo listened to her whispered instructions with an inconsolable ache. 'I loved her so much, we were so close.'

Term began, and Festo reluctantly returned to Mukono. This time a message followed almost immediately that Barungi's death was imminent. So back he went, restless on the long journey, anxious that he should make it in time. Barungi could only have been about fifty, but she looked much older as she was frail and worn after years of brutal beatings and unremitting labour. She spoke at length to Festo about looking after his brothers and sister. 'She was very pained by the fact that she wouldn't be there to bring them up.' Festo did his best to assure his mother that he could look after the family. He had already put Kahembera to school, paying the fees with revenue from the cows' milk. Barungi also asked Festo for more news of the revival, the 'awakened ones', and this Jesus they spoke about, who somehow met people through visions. Festo tried to dodge the subject, but in later years he would never be one to accuse himself of losing his mother 'for eternity' because he had not helped her to salvation. His line would always be that God honours intentions and attitudes where action is just not possible, for whatever reason. 'She never rejected Christ, she was keen to know more. She could not help dying when she did.'

Barungi's death came quickly, and left Festo deeply grieved. The only reason he had given up his chance of a place at King's College, Budo, and Makerere was because he wanted to give her a better life. Now his last ambition was taken from him.

'I did resent the fact that she had died before I could help her.'

Immediately after the funeral, the reshuffle began. It was a case of *Otaine embwa ayebweigorere*: 'He who has no dog barks for himself' (or, with no one to help him he would have to do his own work). Festo at nineteen did his best in coping with three younger siblings and over 100 cows which had suddenly become his responsibility. He found a relative who agreed to stay on with the children. The milk from the cows would have to be enough to look after them all.

Then Festo travelled back to Mukono. He mourned deeply.'I felt Mother's death acutely—we owed her everything: our upbringing, our health, our cows. Now I would never have the chance of making it up to her, of showing our love.' But somewhere on those long miles back north across the equator he found it within himself to begin to face the future realistically.

> I reasoned with myself: 'Well, she has died. That is a fact and I can't change it. Now I must accept the sole responsibility for my sister and brothers.' In a way, it gave me even greater motivation to finish my course well, and to earn money to support us all and send them to school.

By late August 1939 everyone in Uganda who had access to a radio was tuning in daily to the news from Europe. Festo gleaned most of his news from a missionary who picked up broadcasts far and wide on a homemade set he had rigged up himself. On 3rd September, 1939 Germany marched into Poland and the Second World War began. Festo and his fellow students could not really grasp the implications; they had no idea of what Europe was like, let alone a war there. Stories of mass bombing, tanks and machine guns were 'beyond our imagination'.

Early in 1940 a letter came from Kigezi High School in Kabale appealing to Mukono for help. Teachers were so thin on the ground in Kigezi that classes were about to be closed. Couldn't even a few of the students be sent back early? The headmaster told Festo and one other student that they were the best trainee teachers of their year: would they consent to leave the course early, and go back in July? This time round, Festo did not mind having his course cut short—he was still depressed from his bereavement, and glad at the thought of being in Kigezi again and near what was left of his family.

So in June 1940 Festo left Mukono and the teachers' training college six months early, with a first-class certificate in teacher training. Young men all over Uganda were joining the British forces and preparing to leave Uganda, but Festo was content to be heading back for the hinterland. 'I was never interested in fighting; I wanted to teach.' The missionaries posted him back to the very school from which he had started: the little mud and wattle school on Kinyasano hill in Rukungiri. He was to begin the third term of 1940. Festo was delighted: he was glad to be going home.

*   *   *

Throughout 1937 and on into 1938 revival tensions had continued at every level in Uganda church life, especially among the missionaries themselves. Bishop Stuart went to heroic lengths to keep both conservative and liberal sides together in one church, but confessed to the CMS headquarters in Britain in 1937 that he did not feel he could face 'much more schism' from the revival.

Early 1939 brought a fresh wave of problems: many services were having to be abandoned because of mass hysterical weeping and praying, and Dr Joe was forced to admit that 'fires are always disturbing and sometimes difficult to control'. Throughout 1939 the revival spread: to the southern Sudan, to the north of Uganda, to the Congo and south to Tanganyika. There were thousands of conversions and undoubted spiritual blessings, as well as, sadly, many unbalanced excesses.

When the Second World War began, the missionaries were amazed to find even the government suddenly suspicious of their work. They were edgy at constant reports of preaching teams going from church to church and leaving in their wake violent hysterical conversions which disrupted village life and led to tensions between pagans and the new Christians. Revival, it seemed, could be a mixed blessing.

CHAPTER FIVE

THE FINAL BATTLE AT RUKUNGIRI
1940–1941

Back to Rukungiri; relentless revival.

AUGUST, 1940. Festo returned to the remote hinterland of
Rujumbura. He was covered in red dust and aching with
fatigue having been bounced and rolled about in the back of an
open lorry for the 300 miles from Kampala. He returned only to
have the worst possible homecoming:

> The first ugly surprise came when the truck rounded the market-
> place in Rukungiri. Some people were singing church songs right out
> in public! Imagine hearing this floating over the fruit and vegetables:
> 'Down at the cross where my Saviour ...' To me that was sheer
> fanaticism.[1]

His favourite niece, Kyabyarwa, was waiting for him. She
threw her arms around him and cried, 'Uncle Festo, welcome
home! I love Jesus now. Do you, too?'[2] Festo grunted something
and changed the subject. 'I was quite offended.'[3]

By now Festo thought he had settled his rejection of God; he had
no idea that the biggest spiritual battle of his life was just beginning. By stages he had arrived at what he later called an 'agnostic'
position (ironically only made possible by his advanced education.
No native villager would have dreamed of disbelieving in the
spirits or the creator, Ruhaga). He struggled with the problem,

> Is it possible to have sins forgiven? Having failed to get an answer, I
> assured myself that there was no answer. Therefore I tried just to
> quiet my conscience by satisfying it with other things. But God's
> finger still followed me, and my conscience was ill at ease.[4] When
> you know the truth and rebel against it, you become strangely hard.[5]

In his last few months at the teachers' training college at Mukono, he had become 'a notorious drunkard', falling into 'all the other sins that go with drinking'.[6] He wanted to prove that 'I was a free young man, and I could do what I wanted to do, and refuse what I didn't like to do.'[7] Meanwhile, in the marketplace waiting to greet him that first hot August afternoon was the headmaster of the school, Ernest Nyabagabo, a courtesy Festo found 'gratifying'. Leaving the singing balokole, Nyabagabo led Festo out of the village and up Kinyasano hill. Matoke plantations stretched away across the low green hills in every direction. The school nestled near the top of the hill, just behind the church.

Kinyasano school had changed a lot since Festo had left nine years before. First, it had a new name: Makobore Primary School, in memory of Festo's grandfather. It had become a key school in the district, the Ruanda missionaries and African teachers working hard to improve the standard of the four distinct primary years now on offer to boys throughout the countryside. Nyabagabo was proud of his hard-won resources: a few more blackboards, several maps, a cluster of simple English primers, arithmetic and basic science books. Festo discussed the coming term with great enthusiasm, 'My delight and my ambition was just to teach children and help my people.'

This was probably just as well, as there were no other rewards. At forty Ugandan shillings a month (or about £2 in 1940) the teachers were badly underpaid. But Festo as unconcerned about money then as he was in later years, 'could make it go a long way'. Poverty had developed in him simple habits, not a craving for more. Meanwhile he explored the old mud and wattle building in high spirits, memories of his childhood flooding over him. There were the same long hard benches, but now a long narrow desk as well, with holes for inkpots—some boys had pens these days.

Makobore School provided Festo with a little house deep in the middle of a banana plantation about four miles from Kinyasano. Built of the usual mud and wattle with a papyrus roof, its comforts were 'very simple'. Festo moved in at once and collected his family. He installed his stepsister, Eva, and niece, Kyabyarwa, in one bedroom, his nine-year-old stepbrother,

Jonathan, in another, and moved himself into the third. (Brother Christopher was at school in Kigezi.) He made the dining area into a sort of guest room as like all Africans, he expected guests and relatives to be passing through most of the time (and was rarely disappointed). Everyone's bed was of the 'African string' variety, a framework of four poles latticed with rope, upon which grass mats were laid. After the family and any guests went to bed at night, he used the sitting room to prepare his lessons—adjusting the kerosene lamp, sitting on one hard-backed chair and spreading his papers across the other rough chairs. Somewhere in the small house Festo also made room for two students who in return for a bed (of sorts), board and school fees acted as houseboys, cooking, cleaning and ironing the only two shirts that the young teacher possessed. Festo's herd of cows which he had inherited from his mother, were kept about a mile and a half away.

Festo had looked forward to having his family around him again, but relations within the small house in the banana plantation were strained from the start. Eva and Kyabyarwa had joined the revival, and with the raw directness of youth told Festo, and kept on telling him, that he needed Jesus. He was far better educated than they were, and moreover was a teacher, but this impressed them not one jot. To them, there was no room for argument. Without Jesus, Festo was going to hell. So they launched a campaign for his soul, which was bitterly resented by Festo. Even his youngest brother, Jonathan, at nine years old had joined the balokole, though fortunately he was young enough to leave the preaching to his elder sister and cousin.

Festo's resentment soon turned to anger, and when he drank heavily at the dukkas in town of an evening, his homecomings could be 'very harsh'. The girls grew afraid of him.

But to Festo's horror, 'as the days passed, the situation in town proved worse than I had thought. People, both young and old, were caught up in a sort of religious frenzy, doing ridiculous things. Many had been churchgoers for years, but this was something quite new.'[8] It had begun sometime during the late spring, when one Sunday a layman stood up to read the set Scripture lesson in an ordinary Anglican service. As he read, some of the congregation began to weep. More joined in, and soon even the man reading the Bible broke down. Within an hour a breakthrough had come—people felt they had found Christ in a very personal way and had been assured that their sins were indeed forgiven them. They sang, they embraced, they prayed. By the following week the congregation had doubled, and wouldn't fit into the church. They met outside under the trees. When Festo arrived a few months later, there was a burgeoning small group of fellowships in homes and communities throughout north Kigezi.

Festo was appalled. 'They would talk about Jesus in all sorts of places, and you never knew where they might burst out in song. We "enlightened" young people were angry' (Festo was not alone). 'We maintained that church people ought to confine their singing to church buildings and not spread it out on to public roads and into marketplaces. Women going to draw water were praising Jesus—how unsuitable!' Festo would drop in on former friends, only to find now 'a circle of neighbours sitting in the courtyard singing and sharing. When you tried to slip away unnoticed, they would call to you. A decent person didn't know where to hide.'[9]

One of the best things about coming back to Rukungiri had been the chance of renewing his friendship with his uncle. To Festo's relief, Karegyesa shared his resentment and alarm at the changes the revival was making. To Karegyesa, Christianity meant regular prayers and church services, but it was not something that was meant to turn your whole way of life upside down. 'This new kind of religion is dangerous,' Karegyesa confided to Festo. 'It invades your privacy. You have nothing left.'[10] For one thing; too many ancient taboos were being broken. Women who were 'saved' now refused to cover their faces before men, and even dared to speak out in public, 'as if they were set free from the ancient traditions'.[11] This was unthinkable. But even worse, the 'saved' Bahima and the 'saved' Bairu had begun to ignore the customary distinctions between their tribes. 'These extremists ... actually ate meals together, breaking the food taboos of hundreds of years! ... thereby bringing the danger of calamity upon the whole land. Church people had never done these things before. They had been as careful as anyone else not to offend the spirits of the ancestors.'[12]

Karegyesa 'took action' and told his retainers to beat up anyone who spoke of being 'saved'. Some local balokole were very badly thrashed. But the results were not what Karegyesa had expected. Festo later told of one such incident:

A court official would beat up a man because he talked about Jesus publicly, but when the beater went home he couldn't sleep. By morning he was weeping and went off to join the fanatics. Exasperated, my uncle changed his order: 'Don't beat them. That is dangerous. You might become like them.'[13]

Meanwhile, Festo was having difficulties of his own. Because his was a mission school, he was expected to attend the local church, which he would not have minded except that 'nearly everyone who was asked to speak or preach was one of the fanatics'. This meant that the sermons were always 'dangerously personal and we were constantly bombarded with talk about the cross'. Even comparatively 'safe' stories like Adam and Eve suddenly led to Calvary. It baffled Festo: 'Why did that make the cross inevitable? What was the connection? It was oppressive.'[14] Meanwhile he was discovering 'what it was to be an angry young man who was tired and lonely and finding life increasingly unmanageable and confusing. But I was ... determined never to surrender to Jesus.' He tried to ignore the fact that 'I *wasn't really free*. My cravings were too strong for me to control ... my despair led me deeper and deeper into sin.'[15]

Meanwhile, term started and with it the familiar routine of classes and prep. Like the colonials, the teachers wore shorts, high socks, a shirt and sometimes a tie and jacket. Festo was always immaculate—he was one of those fortunate mortals who just don't seem to get ruffled, scuffed and messed up, whatever they're doing. This made a great impression on boys who had come straight from pagan homes of farmers and cow herders in skins. His personal popularity soared and many dreamed of being as smart as Festo. 'He always dressed smartly; we boys really looked up to him,' recalls one former student.

Crossing the divide from pupil to teacher in a mission school brought some unexpected hazards: notably, having to share the rota for taking morning chapel. One harrowing morning early on in his teaching it was Festo's turn to speak to the entire school ...

I didn't like it at all. I knew, and the boys knew, that I had nothing to give. It was embarrassing, but somehow I ... admitted, 'Boys, I have nothing to say. Has any one of you something to tell us?' Who should stand up but my own brother! Nine years old, he came forward with his New Testament and for the next twenty-five minutes you could have heard a pin drop. He finished without calling them to make any outward sign of repentance, but about twenty boys gave their lives to the Lord. I should have got up and gone forward, but I was too proud.[16]

Instead, the embarrassment only increased Festo's fury and determination to resist this 'fanatical' Christianity.

He got his revenge in the Bible lessons which traditionally followed chapel as the first classes of the day. Though in accordance with the syllabus he did teach Scripture, there was no one to prevent him from adding his own comments to the Bible stories. 'I told the students I did not believe what we read: it was my way of trying to defend myself from the onslaught of these balokole—and my conscience.' If none of it was true, Festo reasoned, his guilt would go away.

One of his students, a former goat herder who would later become a close friend and colleague, James Katarikawe, recalled how obvious Festo's spiritual struggle was at times. 'He always sneered at "these so-called balokole" and so obviously despised us that we knew he was very bothered about us.' After this risky start to the day, Festo would get into his stride. By all accounts he was a superb teacher who knew how to grab and hold his pupils' attention. James Katarikawe recalled:

He had a great gift with talking to children. We would be so fascinated that we couldn't move when he was teaching. Even subjects which we had hated before suddenly became clear to us. He had no problem with discipline, he certainly never raised his voice— he just was in control.

Young as they were, though, the children realised that Festo led a wilder personal life than the other teachers. But in an odd way this only increased their admiration: 'Sometimes he would have spent the entire night down at the dukkas drinking and carrying on, and yet the following morning present the best lesson in the school.' Such an accomplishment, though it said a lot for his renowned stamina and energy, infuriated the more sober, God-fearing teachers and parents. But Festo usually worked very hard: he taught English with the aid of little primers full of simple stories in English based on African scenes. He taught arithmetic slowly and methodically. He taught basic hygiene and simple biology. For geography he soon outran the one or two maps of Uganda, and decided to make his own maps. Up on the blackboard would go a chalky outline of East Africa, to be filled in with mountain ranges and the giant rift valley, and other geographical features of the region. Everyone had a break at midday when the students poured out of the warm class-rooms into the sparkling fresh air. There were no feeding facilities. Some went home for lunch, some had brought a snack, some went without. Classes resumed from two till four, fol-lowed by games.

Festo and his fellow teachers were desperately short of resources, but refused to be discouraged. 'We found what we could, and gave what we had.' After all, at least the school existed—which it hadn't done fifteen years before. On the whole, relations were good with the Ruandan missionaries who supervised the school through regular visits, though at times resentment was felt when the whites became a 'bit bossy and very paternalistic'. Festo felt this keenly, and came to hold quite a grudge against one missionary in particular—Gregory Smith, who was the district's school supervisor.

Throughout the autumn of 1940 and on into the spring of 1941, the balokole drove Festo 'crazy'.

> Every one of these people never missed an opportunity to tell you with tears of your need for Jesus. It was a deep love which I rejected and resented but still it hit me hard. I was really very mad that they should feel so concerned about me in the first place. I sought comfort in heavier drinking.

But still the balokole would give him no peace. 'They were simple, very open people whose love and utter conviction that they were right made them very aggressive.' One evening Festo was humming and weaving his way home through the banana trees after drinking heavily at the dukkas. He wanted nothing more than to go to sleep. Instead, he found an uninvited guest on his doorstep, who bellowed at him out of the darkness, 'You, Festo! You are going to hell! You must repent!'

It was Jeremiah Betsimbire, a member of the local church. His evangelistic approach left everything to be desired. Festo was so incensed that he brandished his walking stick, shouting 'Now the mad man has met a lunatic!' and started for Betsimbire while three youngsters watched, wide-eyed. A furious argument followed: Betsimbire bellowed threats of future spiritual damnation if Festo did not repent, and Festo roared back threats of an immediate physical thrashing here and now if Betsimbire did not clear off. When the excitement finally ended, and Jeremiah stomped off, Festo turned on the children 'glaring in utter fury'. In later years, they felt sympathy belonged to Festo. 'The balokole could be really harsh and undiplomatic in the way they sometimes tackled people. It was almost guaranteed to drive them further away.'

Bugaari, now a keen mulokole, was also teaching at the school, and mourned the fact that his best friend was slipping ever further from him because of the revival. Bugaari took to visiting him at night, but could not hide his concern for Festo's spiritual state. At last one evening Festo angrily ordered him away, and his resentment at this revival, which was taking everyone he loved, boiled over. 'I hated being told all the time I was a perishing sinner!' Festo also found it intensely irritating that the balokole would rarely talk about anything but Jesus.

The only person who really understood Festo was another teacher, also baptised Festo—Festo Rwamunahe (whose sister Festo would one day marry). The two Festos got along fine, mainly because Rwamunahe, like Festo, was also 'always running around and trying to drink himself to death!' They found consolation in each other 'from all these Christians'. They prided themselves as being the only staff members at the school who didn't 'have a testimony'.

By March of 1941 the headmaster was about to turn Festo out of the school, he had become such a drunkard. Nyabagabo shared his problem with two women missionaries on safari to Rujumbura: the doughty Constance Hornby, and Lilian Clarke, a young woman of thirty-one, fresh from a school in Watford, England. Lilian had been sent out by the CMS to take over the Kabale Girls' Boarding School of ninety-three students, currently run by Miss Hornby. Lilian felt she should be very disapproving, but found it difficult when she finally met Festo. 'He was so clever, so attractive, so full of life.'

By early summer of 1941 both Festos were feeling quite frazzled, the weekly church services they were forced to attend becoming more and more difficult to cope with. The two young men braced themselves as week after week the people round them wept over their sins.

The new Christians would be so full of joy, 'so full of heaven, that when you heard them testifying in the market a few hours later, you'd have thought they'd been Christians for twenty years'. Even the British government officers down in Kabale got a bit rattled. So many queues of people formed outside their office, waiting to return or pay for things, that the district commissioner complained it was hard to get any work done.

One afternoon Festo was preparing a lesson in an empty classroom when he heard running footsteps. Festo Rwamunahe burst in. 'What's wrong?' Festo demanded. 'Oh,' panted Rwamunahe, 'I dropped in at the Bible study—and was nearly caught.' Festo roared with laughter. 'Didn't I tell you to keep away from those meetings? They're terrible!' To be 'caught' by Jesus was the one thing Festo was determined should not happen to him. Yet by the summer of 1941 his life 'was turning round itself like a spinning top'. The analogy was an apt one:

> A top has a big head and a thin base, so it can't stand up unless it is spinning round and round. If it slows down, it topples over. It depends on spinning to keep going. My spinning cycle was work-play-eat-drink-sleep-work-play-eat-drink, and so on, round and round. The more humdrum it became, the speedier I got. I thought that the faster I went, the livelier life would be. But I was finding out that a directionless life is difficult to live.[17]

His escapades with Festo Rwamanahe and other young men in the town gained him increasing notoriety, but no longer the happiness and distraction he so desperately sought. He still caught his niece and sister weeping over him in their prayers, and that infuriated him even more.

Autumn approached, and 'I was running headlong into self-destruction ... I considered ending my life.'[18] Term began. Festo Rwamanahe was tipped for the post of headmaster, soon to become vacant (he was more careful to maintain outward respectability than Festo). September petered out in a haze of warm sunshine and early October arrived.

On the morning of Saturday 4th October, Festo was enjoying a nice peaceful weekend when his fourteen-year-old niece ventured a piece of highly irritating information—extremely brave of her, considering Festo had smacked her for such comments in the past. She informed her uncle that God had told her and twelve-year-old Eva that their prayers for his soul would soon be answered—in fact, that weekend. Festo swore and brushed her away in disgust.

Next morning he was on duty rota to take the boys to church. Having marshalled his class outside, he reluctantly followed them into the church. Already people were singing and clapping and giving their testimonies. Festo felt very uncomfortable, and made sure 'I sat at the back!' That only gave him an even better view of what was going on, which was quite a lot, considering it was an ordinary Anglican service following the Prayer Book. 'The Holy Spirit was breathing life on the words of the Bible; it had become a speaking book. Long before any preacher came, people were standing up all over the place, repenting of their sins, and accepting the Lord.'

Festo was moodily watching the excitement increase, when suddenly to his horror he spied his own niece leap to her feet and ask for permission to share something. In a loud excited voice she piped:

> I want to praise God. The devil had been making me afraid of telling you what the Lord has done for my cousin Eva and me. On Friday night the Lord assured us that our prayers for Festo are answered. Festo is sitting in the corner right there, and we know that he is going to come back to the Lord today.[19]

Festo froze, speechless with embarrassment and fury. How dare this slip of a girl 'take the liberty of speaking about me in public like that!'[20] Later, of course, he would realise 'that in her simplicity and naivety she did not consider how I would react to such a statement—she genuinely gave it out as a promise of God, to be thankful about'. At the time, however, 'I got up and went outside, absolutely in a rage.'[21] He swore he would make her pay when he got her home alone that evening. Festo stalked off to the place where he could be assured of a crumb of comfort: his Uncle Karegyesa's kraal. The two men spent the rest of that day in the bright sunshine, drinking heavily and 'mocking the balokole'. The niece was angrily dismissed by both men as being out of her mind with religion. Karegyesa offered unlimited drink and sympathy.

By late afternoon Festo was mollified—not to say stupified—enough by the strong beer to consider making his way home. He wobbled along on his bicycle, planning a just retribution for his niece's unforgivable behaviour. By about six he had just reached the bottom of Kinyasano hill when he saw another cyclist, Festo Rwamunahe, racing towards him. He had a different expression on his face 'as if he were flying'.[22] Festo was surprised. 'I knew very well that he did not ordinarily have a glow on his face.'[23] Rwamunahe slammed on his brakes and skidded to a halt in a cloud of dust. His breathless words 'came like a thunderclap':[24] 'Festo! Three hours ago Jesus became a living reality to me. I know my sins are forgiven!'[25]

Festo stood in stunned silence. Rwamunahe continued, 'Please, I want you to forgive me, friend.' He named three specific things for which he wanted forgiveness, relating to 'some questionable things we had done together'. 'I am sorry, Festo. I will no longer live like that. Jesus has given me something much better.'[26] Festo knew 'what we had been doing together, and I knew he had never spoken like that before. So certainly something had happened, whether I liked it or not. I knew then that God was real. My friend's joy overwhelmed me. His words shook me to the core.'

The two men cycled along together quietly until they reached the mission. As they were parting, Rwamunahe asked, 'Festo where are *you*?' 'I don't know where I am,'[27] came the muttered reply. Festo cycled on to his home among the banana trees, 'utterly miserable and destitute. We had taken so much comfort in mocking the balokole together. Now he had gone to join them and I was left on my own. I began to wish I hadn't met him, he had stirred me up like mud!'

By the time he got inside the hut Festo was 'under tremendous conviction'. He tried to light his pipe, 'but my hands were shaking too much'. Then, 'I felt a whispering voice inside saying, "You go and pray."'

Festo hadn't prayed for three years, 'because of course I no longer believed in prayer'. He found doing so now most embarrassing: 'suppose somebody came in and found me?' But Festo knelt by his bed. Silence. 'I did not know what to say.' Suddenly one stark thought was before him: 'Your friend has found the reality which you have been missing all the time.'

'That's how the Holy Spirit just turned me around. I began to cry to God.' Hesitantly, he prayed: 'God, if you happen to be there, as my friends say you are, here is a life, thoroughly empty, very much in trouble, and full of guilt, because of the wrong things I have done. Do for me what you have done for my friend, Festo.'

'And that was all. I did not say amen. I just kept quiet—which meant I was challenging God to do something, though in a sense, by even saying it, I had already committed myself.'

The answer came.

'Suddenly, as if in a vision, in front of me was Jesus hanging on the cross, as clear as anything I had ever seen with my physical eyes.'[28] Festo later described it as Calvary 'almost as it were up before me on a screen'. He was shattered. 'For a time it seemed as if there was no one in the world except that man hanging on the cross.'[29] As Festo looked at him, 'I did not see just a helpless human being hanging on the cross like a criminal; I saw my God slaughtered *for my sin*.' This first impact made him reel. It was a realisation that the death of Christ 'was because of me'. It was shattering, because it was as if he was saying, 'This is how bad you are.' This realisation 'engulfed me'.

But then came the second impact. 'It was as if the Lord said, "Now that is also how much I love you."' This 'was almost overwhelming. To have the one I had done *that* to turn around and say, "That is how much I love you," was too much. I heard his voice. "While you were careless, I still loved you."[30] His eyes of infinite love ... were looking into mine.'[31]

I shook my head. Literally, I shook my head. 'Lord,' I whispered, 'you can't love me; I don't deserve it. I am your enemy. I am rebellious. I have been hating your people. How can you love me like that? I am the opposite to these Christians, in fact I hate you ...

Lord.' (Notice by now I was calling him Lord—restoration had come without my knowing it!)

Christ said; 'I love you *this* much.' And that, of course, completely melted my heart. I began to confess my sins and to seek forgiveness, only to find that forgiveness had already taken place. I was forgiven. Guilt was no longer there.[32]

He would later realise,

There is no qualification for the love of God other than that you are a sinner, completely finished. God in love has taken the initiative to meet you where you are.

A whole new world had opened before me. Love ran through me and filled me with such a sense of freedom and joy that I wondered what to do.

I got up off my knees, still crying, but now with joy. No more guilt, no more shame. God was no longer a threat. Christ was no longer an embarrassment. He loved me! I started singing and shouting. I sang all the little songs I'd thought I'd forgotten like 'Jesus loves me this I know'. They had now, for me, a new meaning! I just wanted to praise and praise.[33]

Suddenly Festo felt almost frightened.

'Lord,' I prayed, 'this is too much. I don't think I can live long like this. But give me permission to live for one week and I'll tell everybody about it. Uncles, aunts, friends.' I made plans on the spot to tell the whole area in my last week on earth. I was still expected in class on the following morning, so how I thought I was going to teach and evangelise all of north Kigezi, I can't imagine!

But Festo didn't waste time. He threw back his door and ran outside. A Christian lady who lived nearby was picking her way home in the brief dusk among the banana trees. Festo shouted to her, 'Stop, stop! Jesus has come my way!' 'Already I was out to fulfil my promise to Jesus—to tell everyone I could before I died of happiness.' However, his first ever attempt at evangelism did not go well.

The woman tossed her head and tut-tutted, thinking Festo was mocking her. She knew he had teased her husband, a fiery catechist, at times. She reproached him, and left him standing among the banana trees.

This would not do at all. He was simply bursting to tell other

Christians. He set off for the church. Though it was by now nearly dark, and his house rules forbade his sister and niece to be out this late on their own, they were still down at the church, singing and 'trusting that the Lord was going to bring me back to himself'. In the brief equatorial twilight nearly two dozen Christians who had not yet gone home were standing in an informal circle outside the mud and wattle church, their voices carrying far and wide in the evening air.

'There was tall grass shielding the narrow path,' recalled James Katarikawe thirty-six years later, 'and suddenly we saw it quiver, and out came Festo.' A few in the group feared for an instant that he had returned in fury to drag his niece and sister home. But then Eva and his niece, Kyabyarwa, spotted Festo, 'and they had no doubts as to my real reason for being there. They ran to me and embraced me, weeping, without saying anything.'

Bugaari suddenly realised, 'Festo's saved!' 'The group went mad,' recalled Festo. 'Just mad. They screamed, they clapped, they hugged each other, they nearly suffocated me. They sang.' Then Daudi, the leading church teacher, a big bear of a man, grabbed Festo, and 'literally lifted me up and put me on his shoulders and danced about with me'. Some of the group worked out their feelings on the big church drums, sending a mad beat of joy for miles across the quiet hinterland. Bugaari made himself hoarse with repeated shouts of 'Festo's saved!'

Festo did not even get a chance 'to say my little confession of sin!' No one was interested: 'I had come to the Lord Jesus, and that was what mattered!' His niece and sister wept and wept, and clung to him, uttering 'Ehs!', the Ugandan cry of rapture. They broke away only to clap and dance and sing.

Eventually, with the aid of a lamp, the group escorted Festo home. Between their singing, shrieks and the drums, it didn't take much for Rukungiri village to guess something important had happened. Soon Festo's little house was swarming with exulting friends and neighbours. Those who couldn't squeeze into the house stood about in the courtyard outside, singing, jumping and dancing.

Festo Rwamunahe heard the singing with alarm: 'The brethren have paid Festo a visit, and he'll fight them!' He rushed over and was bewildered, then delighted, then overwhelmed when he discovered that it had been his testimony which was the last straw for Festo. By now the lady and her husband next door were convinced that Festo had indeed, after all, been saved, and came to join in the celebrations. Those inside sat in a crush on the floor and prayed and sang and testified. Those outside stood as they prayed and sang. The balokole were a mixture of Bahima and Bairu, and Festo found it 'beautiful' to be 'welcomed equally' by those of both tribes. 'The cross that rescued them had rescued me and the tribal barrier was gone.'[34]

The celebrations went on and on and on. Festo, exhausted, finally excused himself and went off to bed. But the others remained in his house and little earthen courtyard all night, keeping watch over their new 'brother'. It was a demonstration of love which Festo was to treasure for the rest of his life.

CHAPTER SIX

EVANGELIST OF KINYASANO HILL
1941–1942

Brokenness; walking in the light; discovery of God's grace; early preaching on village outreach teams; engagement to Mera.

FESTO HAD BEEN CONVERTED a little over fourteen hours when he won his own first converts to Christ. It was on a Monday morning, 6th October 1941, during a geography lesson.

News travels like wildfire in African villages. 'All of us knew what had happened to our teacher,' recalls a former student. During the morning chapel assembly everyone stole frequent peeks in his direction. Festo sat quietly, but 'his face was radiant'.

Classes began. Festo entered his geography class to find forty pairs of dark eyes fixed on him with an expectancy which had nothing at all to do with geography. Festo paused, uncertain of what to say. Then,

> Somehow, the Spirit of God said to me, 'Tell them that up to now your relationship with them has been no more than that of a teacher to his boys: no real love in it. [But] they are precious boys for whom Christ died, and you are their brother ... Ask them for forgiveness!'[1]

So Festo apologised. He kept it brief and to the point: 'I didn't want to waste their time.'[2]

To his astonishment, two boys stood up, tears in their eyes. One said timidly, 'Sir, how can I find what you have found?'

Festo was momentarily speechless: he hadn't intended on evangelism in the classroom. Besides, 'I'd only come to the Lord myself the night before!' So he said, 'As he has touched you, just open your heart to him and say thank you.' 'That's all I could say, I couldn't even quote the Scriptures.'[3]

But the boys were converted. The students who were already Christians also rejoiced: 'Festo was so popular that to see *him* become a Christian was a great encouragement to us.'

The school's headmaster was delighted and sent a messenger to Kabale that day with the news. Dr Joe Church and his wife were having a quiet meal when someone burst in shouting, 'Have you heard? Festo Kivengere's been converted!' Dr Joe was overjoyed at the possibilities the news opened up. 'We missionaries had always considered Festo a cut above the rest of the young people.'

Back in Kinyasano that evening, an even larger group of Christians made their way among the banana trees to Festo's home. They prayed and sang for hours under the starry skies. When Festo finally went to bed, they stayed on, keeping watch until dawn lit up the skies. The following night, they kept a third sleepless vigil. Festo was overwhelmed 'by the love of these people'.

Festo began straightaway to put his life to rights. 'Jesus sent me to the town and out into the fields to find people I had cheated, slandered or hurt.' He asked forgiveness. He repaid debts. He went to the dukkas and broke the news to his drinking companions, who scoffed and told him he wouldn't last long.

He had a very painful interview with his uncle Karegyesa. The old Saza chief felt his 'favourite son and ally' had betrayed him. He 'froze with hostility', accusing Festo of 'catching the madness' (*eiraro*), and immediately disowned the young man, forbidding him to enter the secret council room ever again.

Still the 'tough initiating days', as Festo called them, weren't over. Soon he felt prompted by God to seek reconciliation with Rwabugarame, his stepfather. Rwabugarame lived in Nyabicence, a six-mile walk from Kinyasano through matoke plantations and grasslands. Festo wondered what he would do if Rwabugarame was drunk and became violent. At Nyabicence he found a young relative, who greeted him wide-eyed, and hastened to fetch Rwabugarame. The stepfather came out of his hut, hostile and wary.

Festo began by quietly admitting his hatred.

'I know that,' said his stepfather.

'But wait,' Festo continued. 'I have come to tell you more, which is good news: I have at last really found the God which you helped me seek after when you first sent me to the mission school.' An hour later he concluded: 'So there is no more hatred. It has been buried.'

Rwabugarame rose and put his arms around Festo. 'We stood there hugging each other. I was overcome. I never expected such a reaction.'

On Sunday, exactly one week after his conversion, Festo gave his testimony in the public marketplace. It was his first public evangelistic message ever, and one or two villagers were converted. 'Already I knew that talking about Christ was all that I wanted to do for the rest of my life.'

Soon Festo remembered there was someone else whom he had hated—the schools' supervisor for the district, a missionary, the Revd Gregory Smith. Part of the bad feeling was racial as Festo had felt that Smith acted in a very superior way. So when the missionary first came to mind, Festo argued that as he lived fifty miles away in Kabale, 'I need not do anything. But the Spirit said, "Take your bicycle and on the weekend go to see this man. Now that you are liberated, he is your brother."' Festo later wrote of the struggle that then ensued.

'My brother? An Englishman?' He nearly fell over.

'Yes, your brother. I died for him, I died for you. You have hated your brother, and made his life difficult.'

'What shall I do when I see him? You know him, Lord.'

'Yes, I know him. Tell him that you love him.'

Festo later vividly recalled that for fifty miles to Kabale 'the rivers seemed much wider than usual and the escarpment steeper than I had ever seen it. Approaching the house, I was tired and frightened and hoped he was not at home.'[4]

Festo knocked on the door and to his dismay Mr Smith opened it. Nervously he followed the missionary into his 'proper' English living room and told him that he was now a Christian. He asked for forgiveness for his hatred and 'talk against' Smith. There were tears in the Englishman's eyes, 'so I embraced him. I was African and excited because of the liberation I felt. He graciously embraced me, which I believe was harder on his side.' Gregory Smith was to be a close friend for decades to come.

Conversion was the end of a great many things for Festo, and the beginning of much that was new. He was mentally and spiritually utterly 'born again', and saw all of life from a new perspective. At last he understood why his former commitment as a Christian had not worked out. His efforts to observe the highest possible biblical morality had missed the point altogether: being a Christian was a daily relationship with God in Christ, and that only on the basis of this 'walking in the Spirit' would any consistent high standard of morality be achieved.

From the night of his 'restoration' Festo had fallen in love—and was utterly consumed—with Christ. His greatest ambition now was to follow Christ. Indeed, for the rest of his life, Christ's love was to enchant him as nothing else could, and Christ's death was to move him as nothing else could.

A close friend would recall:

> Soon after his salvation I noticed an unusual depth in Festo. While others among the balokole were satisfied with singing and praising, I could see that Festo was not. One day I came across him reading a book. On the cover was a picture of Jesus praying in the garden of Gethsemane, lying prostrate on a stone with his hands stretched out before him. Festo saw me looking at the cover and held the book out to me. He said quietly, 'To see the Son of God humbled in this way because of my sin—this hits my heart very hard.' I could see tears starting up in his eyes. It dawned on me that Festo was seeing something in Christianity which I did not see. I was still at the stage of enjoying the excitement of salvation, and all the singing and praising that went with it. But Festo was seeing beyond it to something far deeper.

Festo began to devour the Bible. He 'had a tremendous hunger for it'. He had scarcely touched it since 1936, but now he was simply responding to the love of Christ. Like the Ruandan missionaries and the balokole, he accepted the Bible as God's authoritative word (the theological labyrinths of modern biblical criticism were unknown to him). Late at night, after lessons were prepared and copybooks marked, and again at dawn he pored over the pages of his Bible. He delved into the Old Testament and found great encouragement in the stories of

God's faithfulness and love, but returned again and again to the New Testament, especially the passages about Christ. He absorbed whole passages and even chapters like blotting paper, memorising them with all the ease of one brought up in an extensive and intricate oral tradition. Other balokole did likewise, and 'very soon the extent of our biblical knowledge was to shake the missionaries!'

This immediate practical application of Bible teaching to everyday life became a hallmark of the revival, for 'people were not only feeding on the word of God, they were acting on it'. There were, inevitably, some wrong interpretations and excesses —after all, most were simple, uneducated people—but in the main, this willingness to act on what the Bible taught gave the revival tremendous power. Festo, like his neighbouring balokole, found his life turned upside down by it. When they read 'Love thy neighbour', they did not think, 'Now there's a good idea.' Instead, they thought immediately of all the neighbours they detested, and realised that God was speaking to them. They wept. Then they confessed their sin, repented and went to the neighbour to make amends.

From his Bible study, Festo turned naturally to prayer. 'I felt a great indebtedness to Christ, and wanted to give my all in return.' His actual prayers may have been 'spontaneous', but the evangelicals of that era strongly advocated daily 'quiet times', and Festo took this up wholeheartedly. Gradually he would be 'tied up in knots' over his 'QT', 'thinking God was very concerned about the exact amount of time I spent with him each day'. Only later did he learn 'to keep a balance'.

In addition to private daily Bible study and prayer, there was another immediate change in Festo: he joined the daily Fellowship meeting which met after school at the church. They formed a circle 'young and old, men and women, educated and illiterate, each one precious to all the others'.

The meeting had a definite purpose:

We were very conscious that Jesus himself was in the midst of us, and we were listening to him. We devoured his words in the Bible with full expectation that he would show us in it what he wanted us to do. It was our only book then and we came to it without preconceptions. No wonder he could speak so clearly through it.[5]

Such an atmosphere led to tremendous openness and trust,

> knowing that we were loved and instantly forgiven by the brethren
> when we were forgiven by God. It was reassuring to me, after telling
> them what God had dealt with in me, to have them celebrate the
> forgiveness by lifting a praise chorus ... the past was forgiven and
> forgotten. No one ever brought it up again. We came to know each
> other well, as sinners together at the foot of the cross. Down there
> we felt free to share anything.[6]

Some of the first things that Festo learned were what to do
about sin and failure. For he soon discovered that a 'pricking
conscience' was a sign that 'the Holy Spirit is trying to deal with
you about something'. To ignore it would leave you feeling
'utterly alone and in the cold'. Instead, 'the only thing to do was
to agree with the Holy Spirit and take that troubled conscience
back to the cross where Jesus died ... No sooner did I cry to him
than I knew I was clasped in his arms again.'[7]

Festo was so keen to live absolutely at one with Christ that he
soon determined, almost unaware, to have *no* times of failure. It
was typical of his active, practical nature that to believe something was immediately to act on it. Such spiritual enthusiasm,
though commendable, meant he was in for a rough time.

In mid November, after a month or so of 'walking on air',
Festo's spiritual euphoria began to fade. 'Temptations began to
come, things I'd thought were dead began to bother me.' That
he still desired to sin, and did sin, came as a tremendous shock.
Surely he now had a *new* nature, given him by Christ? He
determined to accept from himself nothing less than perfection.
'I was going to fight the sin in my life for all I was worth: for it to
be there at all seemed to deny my tremendous experience of
liberation.'

Festo's difficulties were compounded by his very zeal. He had
borrowed several books from the missionaries, and had been
voraciously reading Oswald Chambers, Andrew Murray, John
Wesley's Journals, etc. He wanted to be holy, he wanted to
emulate their walk with God. Unwittingly, the books confused
him: they seemed to preach that victory over sin was possible;
that the 'old man' could be crucified.

Festo began his fight. 'I nearly killed myself to be perfect. I became completely bogged down with all the Christian books which told me: if you want to crucify your old man, do one, two, three, four.' Later he understood that

> These writers were true men of God who had written their books to help other Christians. They had learned valuable lessons, but when they set them down in such a systematic manner, it became fixed. Then I, hungry and seeking, came along and said 'Aha, here is the open sesame of spiritual experience. If I only do this and that, and the other, then all will be well, and my sinful nature will be dealt with for ever.'
>
> My problem was understandable: I wanted a perfect solution for my weaknesses, I wanted to leave sin completely behind. I reasoned: sin is against my Lord; he wants me to be perfect, so I must be perfect. But in reasoning thus, I'd make a misinterpretation.

But he did not know this then. Instead, he struggled on. Temptations continued to haunt him. He was miserable. 'Anything that smacked of having failed God, or falling into temptation, to my mind was just terrible!' He found he could not share this with his fellow Christians, even at the Fellowship meetings. He did not see how they could help him. He knew they repented daily of specific failings, but his problem was deeper than that; such was his ardour to please Christ that he was not satisfied with repenting of specific sins, he wanted to deal once and for all with his whole predisposition to sin. It horrified him that it was still within him.

He read his Bible. He prayed 'almost continually'. He reread his borrowed books on holiness: 'They suggested things to do in order to be nearer to God ... but soon, what they suggested was the correct standard of life if you wanted to be perfect.' Which, of course, was what Festo wanted with his whole heart. 'I kept striving fiercely to do all these things which I believed would then make me perfect. I considered these disciplines as the key that would open the door.'

They did not work. He tried harder. 'I read more, and the clarity became less and less.' His joy in the Lord was gone. He felt spiritually dry. Temptations buzzed round his head like flies. Despair threatened. 'The devil kept pointing out my failures and urged me to forget the whole thing.'

One night, all on his own, he began to pray. Midnight came

and went and he was still praying. He felt frightened because he knew his resistance to temptation was getting weaker, and in his frustration he knew of nothing else to do other than pray. All his reading had brought no answers.

Suddenly I felt as if somebody quietly said to me, 'Festo, how did you come to me?'

'I said, "Oh, I was in bad shape, Lord."'

'And did you find me lacking to meet all your almost impossible needs?'

'No, Lord, you did it in a minute. You filled my empty heart, you lifted the burden of my sin, you changed my hostility into love, you opened a whole new world to me. It was you alone, by the Holy Spirit, but I didn't even know about the Holy Spirit when I came to you, Lord. What do you want?'

'You have done everything you can to be perfect and sinless, but you have not turned your focus on *me*. As you first received me, so, in the same way, also walk. There is no other place you can go other than to my death for you on the cross. I am always here and available to deal with anything that the devil throws at you. As long as you are in the flesh, it is at the cross where you will find my power. Where did you get your liberation?'

'At the cross.'

'Go there. Again and again.'

It was quite a shock. It was as if heaven opened that evening. I saw my struggles ending by simply turning to him who had always been right there, but whom I had been almost by-passing, as if there were another. *I wanted to find the key to perfection in order to please him; but he was the key.* My reasoning that I must be perfect because God wants me to be perfect had left out the fact that he is our perfection. In determining to present myself perfect before Jesus, I had been looking for a solution other than by Jesus ... I had got to the position where I knew Jesus had saved me, but now I wanted the secret of being perfect so I could please him. In doing this I was unconsciously saying that God is not all sufficient.

The lesson that evening brought a tremendous breakthrough. I entered a new stage of my Christian walk with God, where I was no longer working hard to make myself perfect. I was enjoying the finished perfection of someone who died for me. I had learned that a deeper relationship with Jesus Christ was all I needed. I finally realised what Paul was saying when he wrote that we had been

crucified with Christ, and that all I had to do was continually to turn
to Christ. It was almost like another salvation.

Meanwhile, Festo had continued to join the teams that went
out each weekend to testify in the villages round about. Regardless of his private ups and downs, he never missed a single
weekend: 'There was no time to waste!' They visited according
to a simple strategy: 'Is there a village we can get to where the
love of God has not been shared? We reasoned that if you don't
share what Jesus has done for you, you don't know whether
people might die before they have a chance to hear the good
news.' Such belief lent both urgency and compassion to their
work: 'I simply wanted to share what Christ had done for me.'
In fact, the indebtedness Festo felt he owed to Christ for what he
had done was a major factor in his boundless enthusiasm for the
weekend missions. 'I felt other people had a right to hear what
God had done for me. In some obscure way I felt they had a
claim on me to tell them the gospel.'

Very soon all the villages within easy distance of Rukungiri
had heard, and converts in each were founding bush churches
of their own. So the teams moved on, venturing further and
further into the hinterland hamlets and villages. Some went
by bicycle, more walked. Many times invitation to a specific
village came from a single convert in that village who had
become a Christian while visiting another village. Hundreds
were converted, drawn by the joyful spontaneous love of
the Christians who tramped miles to talk to them about
Christ.

The team weekends fell into a fairly regular pattern. Each
Friday, after classes, the teams would assemble, decide where to
go, and soon set off. Many of Festo's students, whom he had by
now led to Christ, accompanied him on the teams. The team
would walk for hours and then sleep in blankets under the stars.
By six the following morning everyone was awake, and taking
time to pray and read whatever portions of the Bible they had.
By seven they would be washed in the nearby streams and
gathering firewood for breakfast: which was invariably cooked
outside on three stones. By eight or nine am they would set
off for the market of the village to 'preach for the entire day'!

No one was exempt as an audience: chance meetings with herdsmen at wells, women in the fields, men and youngsters on the hills with their cows, or curious watchers among the matoke plantations.

Testifying was always a matter of teamwork. Often before the meetings those who felt they had something significant to say agreed to speak this time. Inevitably, with the testifying went the singing. Festo later told how, after an hour or so of singing and testimonies, 'we would often find twenty or more of our listeners had been converted'.

Festo himself was a real boost to the teams. 'Everyone, even the educated, could not help but listen to Festo—when he was there we always got a good audience,' recalls a friend. The teams in their turn gave him a great deal, and provided a valuable training for his future work. 'Through this witnessing, and through watching older Christians testifying and leading others to Christ, I grew.' A former student, Yosia, agrees. 'When Festo was first preaching on the teams, his message was, "*I* found Christ. *He* did this *for me*; he'll do it for you." But as time went on, he began to mention Christ more and himself only when he wanted to share an important lesson he had learned.'

The hundreds of new converts seriously upset the old, established ways of the villages. When the people discounted the spirits of the dead, burned their charms and ignored the threats of the witchdoctors as nonsense, the witchdoctors became furious. However, several of the witchdoctors had been converted too, which did not improve matters for the rest of them. The converts revealed their 'trade secrets' to the people and confessed to having conned them for years. This understandably caused a crisis of confidence among the remaining pagans and witchdoctors. Local chiefs were furious when the amount of beer brewed fell drastically as this had brought in revenue.

Karegyesa took action. He accused the balokole of inciting the people to be disloyal to the British, arrested them and put them in jail. Many were badly beaten. Festo haunted his uncle's kraal, begging for their release, but Karegyesa ordered him off the premises. When the Christians were finally released they marched weakly the two or three miles from the county prison up to the church.

But it was too late. One night soon after Karegyesa woke to find his wife weeping, and tugging at his arm, begging forgiveness for many things. Alone with her husband in the middle of the night she had been converted. Karegyesa was furious.

Next morning she put off her veil, and began to give her testimony in public. Kivengere recalls the reactions of her listeners: they expected her 'to collapse or faint' on the spot. News of her conversion became the talk of Rukungiri. 'My uncle was sick with anger. Whatever had happened to tradition and the ancient culture?'

*   *   *

In the summer of 1942, Festo decided he had found the girl he wanted to marry. He embarked on a curious courtship that was months in getting anywhere at all. The girl of his choice was Mera, now a young schoolteacher at Kabale Girls' Boarding School, second in command to Lilian Clarke, who had recently taken over from Constance Hornby. A Muhima from Rukungiri, Festo had known Mera all his life. That winter and spring he had come to know her better as the fellowship of the revival brought him down to Kabale for fellowship meetings or missions. In the rather formal manner of Christian African courtship in those days, he spent an evening in his chair in the little house in the banana plantation constructing a carefully-worded, polite letter proposing marriage to her, explaining, 'I want this, but I leave you free.' He did not ask for an immediate reply, but rather that she prayed about his suggestion. He would wait. Off went the letter to Kabale via the next (infrequent) bus and the wait began. Until the letter he had never spoken so much as an affectionate word to her. They had been friends, no more.

Months went by. 'She took her time, bless her!' This gave him plenty of time to reflect on his choice. He never doubted that he had made the right one. If similar backgrounds provide a good basis for marriage, he and Mera were well suited. When his grandfather had ruled as the last king of the Bahororo in the early 1900s, his second-in-command had been Miranda, Mera's father. Merabu (as she was also known) Nyiranzangye was about the same age as Festo. She was the child of Miranda's old age, and had three brothers much older than herself: William, Ernesti and Festo. When she was still only a child, William Biteyi was already a gomborora chief under the British Protectorate Government. He had been to an excellent mission school and could read and write. He persuaded Miranda to send the two younger brothers, Ernesti and Festo, to school, making them, like him, practically the first from all north Kigezi to be educated. Both went into education: Ernesti was headmaster of Kinyasano when Festo Kivengere first went there, and later transferred to Kabale in Festo's teens. Festo, of course, had started teaching at Kinyasano only just before Festo Kivengere, and the two had been partners in crime before Festo's testimony on the road had turned Festo Kivengere's life around.

Their mother, Miriam, like Barungi was a dignified, aristocratic Muhima. Miriam taught little Mera the basics of keeping the milk safe, washing the kyanzis, a bit of cultivating, and sent her out to herd the calves on the hills. But Mera had seen the books her brothers brought home and was very impressed 'by their peculiar smell'!

One day in the late 1920s, Constance Hornby wound her way up into north Kigezi on a recruiting safari for her girls' school. She visited William, whom she knew from his student days in Kabale. Playing in his kraal was Mera. When Constance went into the house for a visit, Mera crept after her, overcome with curiosity. It was to change the rest of her life.

Mera's education at Kabale Girls' Boarding School began a year or two before Festo Kivengere's. She thrived, excelling in the simple reading, writing and arithmetic. By the time Miranda died in 1931, Mera was a 'strapping lass with the dignity and self-confidence' that led the missionaries to plan an early teaching career for the girl. She was sent to the Gayaza Girls' School near Kampala for a year, and at fourteen was made a teacher. Like Festo she also resented it, wanting to continue her own education. But she understood the desperate need for teachers, and obediently returned to Kinyasano to open her own school a year or so before Festo left Kinyasano for Kabale. Many of the pupils were older than her. It was the first girls' school in the entire area for hundreds and hundreds of square miles.

By the late 1930s, an opportunity came for Mera to do another year of study herself, so she returned to Kabale Girls' Boarding School, as it was then called. There her own brother, Ernesti, now headmaster of Kigezi High School, led her to the Lord, and she joined the revival.

By 1941, after teacher training at Buloba College near Kampala, Mera was the Senior African teacher at the Kabale Girls' School (later renamed Hornby High School). She was much loved and respected by the girls, and highly thought of by Constance Hornby because of her efficiency in planning lessons, her running of classes, and her ability to maintain discipline. When Lilian Clarke arrived in the spring of 1941, she was amazed to find that this tall, good-looking Muhima girl could simply walk into assembly and 'command attention from the whole school merely by standing still in front of the assembly'. Calm, reserved self-possession was the thing people noticed first about Mera.

Lilian Clarke warmed at once to this dignified, capable girl who was to help her run the school. Together the two organised the morning porridge, shaved the children's heads to get rid of the lice, and handed out cloths so the pupils could put away their animal skins. 'I loved Mera,' says Lilian. 'I'd found an ally in a strange new world.' She talked about Mera with the missionaries: 'We always used to say that that whole family were all fifty years ahead of their time.'

Yet Festo and Mera were also quite different. Where Festo had become outgoing and effervescent with enthusiasm since his conversion, Mera remained more introverted and quiet. Self-possessed and calm are adjectives that crop up again and again in missionaries' remembrance of her. Whereas Festo lived life with more openness and freedom, and sparkled with fun and laughter, Mera's laughter was more often a twinkling in her eyes, a quiet smile. He was an activist—optimistic and impatient to get things done, but easy-going on the precise details. She was a perfectionist, concerned over details, and much more given to anxiety.

Very late in the autumn of 1942, the old bus, gasping its way up the steep hills of south Kigezi, staggered into Rukungiri with a letter for Festo Kivengere. Festo took it somewhere quiet and tore it open. Mera's reply was simple and dignified. She thanked him for his letter. She had prayed, as he had suggested (she would have done so anyway). She agreed that this did seem like God's will. Yes, she would marry him. Festo 'was thrilled'.

News of their engagement soon leaked out, and met with varying responses. Lilian Clarke was delighted, but Constance Hornby still mistrusted Festo and gathered the whole of Kabale Girls' Boarding School together to pray that God would deliver Mera 'from that bad man'! (Constance eventually changed her mind, and became very fond of Festo.) At the end of that term, Festo transferred to Kigezi High School. In some ways it was very sad—his grandfather Makobore was dying; an era was drawing to an end. He shut up the little house in the banana plantation, made provision for his young siblings, sorted out his cows, and said farewells to his fellow teachers, students and the fellowship. Then he went down to the market and said goodbye to Rukungiri as a home for ever.

CHAPTER SEVEN

'WALKING IN THE LIGHT' IN KABALE

1943–1945

Teacher at Kigezi High School; wider preaching experience; struggles with revival legalism; yearning to be full-time evangelist; marriage to Mera; call to Dodoma, Tanganyika.

KABALE IN 1943 was still a remote little town. The war made its presence felt mainly by the constant shortages of imported goods, and through crackly reports of distant battles on the missionaries' radios. The mission station on Rugarama Hill was tremendously busy, both the hospital and school were growing. Festo was given 'quite a nice little house' near Kigezi High School. In the African way of things, he did not live alone for long: James Katarikawe, a former student, was too poor to afford the boarding fees at Kabale school, and he needed a roof over his head. As the two were very nearly the same age (Festo had started school much younger), it was an altogether pleasant bachelor set-up, James doing some cooking and cleaning in return for his bed and board. Life became even more pleasant when Festo's sister, Eve, arrived to keep house and cook for both men, along with another youth who worked locally and needed a home.

Festo settled down well in Kabale, and soon made it his home. On the personal side, he saw a great deal more of Mera (or Merabu, as she was better known then) and nothing at all of Karegyesa, with whom relations were still strained. Professionally, the Kigezi High School offered him better books and resources with which to teach—and a class of teenagers that stretched him as a teacher. Finally, and most important in the long run, living in Kabale meant living at the heart of the growing revival, and at a significant time. 1942 was not only the Ruanda Mission's 'Twenty-first birthday', but also the peak of both enthusiasm for and opposition to the revival. Until now Festo's experience of revival had been parochial. Now, through his friendship with the local 'leaders' of the revival, he would see the blessing and the problems the movement had generated.

But first, term began. Kigezi High School had expanded enormously since Festo's student days in 1936. The Protectorate was developing fast, and everyone was anxious to have their sons educated in the mission schools. Festo was given Primary Five and Six to teach. His boys were in their mid- to late teens. Many would one day be professional people—and die at Amin's soldiers' hands.

Each morning, classes began in the same way, according to a former student (later an Archdeacon of Kikungiri). Festo would 'march briskly' into the classroom carrying several books. He was always 'immaculate' in his white shirt, cream shorts and long cream socks. His tie impressed the boys no end: 'He looked so smart—we all wished we had a tie!' Festo always began politely: 'Good morning, children.'

'Good morning, sir,' they would all reply.

'How are you?' came next.

'We are fine, sir, how are you?'

'I am fine.'

The greeting never varied. Once over, the lesson began. Festo's positive and enthusiastic approach to study was a great encouragement to the boys. One student was even convinced that his teacher must have read 'all the books ever written on geography'! Festo's clear, well-modulated voice could hold his pupils' attention. 'Some of us were very naughty,' recalls a former pupil, 'but none of us ever thought of disobeying *him*.'

The secret lay in the fact that he was genuinely fond of his students. 'The other teachers would tell us to read our notes or fail the exams. Not so Festo. He would teach us, but also keep reminding us why he was teaching us. He would say things like "Please listen to me carefully: you must avoid bad company, you must study your notes, don't waste your time."' Simple words, but the boys took them to heart 'because he said it with compassion'. He also gave up free time to give boys individual tuition. And he never hesitated to talk about Christ 'when the opportunity arose'.

Outside of school hours, Festo became an enthusiastic member of St Peter's Church, never missing a weekend mission. 'For me, by now all of life was what I had found in Christ.' Sometimes this led to forgetfulness: 'I was so insistent that my engagement with Mera must be kept on the highest possible spiritual level that I nearly left the romance out altogether!' Festo—on the long walks which made up much of their courtship—never tried to conceal from Mera his former 'wild ways', but made it very clear to her that their engagement 'should now glorify Christ, and never bring shame to his name'. The couple prayed together over their coming marriage and future. 'Our love was not less but more, because Christ was the controller right from the start.'

In Kabale Festo also gradually gained a new perspective on the revival, one which in Rukungiri he had never had to consider. In Rukungiri the revival had arrived through Ugandans, and had so revolutionised the churches that very soon the only real opposition had been from the expected quarter—the witch-doctors and others representing the traditional religion. The situation was very different in Kabale. Here for the first time Festo had a chance to keep in touch with the wider consequences of the revival: both on the Ruanda Mission and the CMS, as well as upon the members of the Church of Uganda throughout the rest of the country. As the months went by, Dr Joe Church, Gregory Smith, the Revd Lawrence Barham and others slowly filled Festo in on the details of what had been happening in the last few years—and why.

Several books have been written on this stormy passage of the East African revival, and this is no place to tackle such a vast and complex subject. Festo began to see that the theological tensions which lay between the very conservative 'Keswick-based' Ruanda Mission, and the 'broader' CMS and the Church of Uganda had only increased as the revival had spread. Those within the revival saw it as God's gracious blessing upon his people; those outside refused to believe that the Holy Spirit would cause—or even want—such a furore: weeping, singing, public confession of sin, etc. The revivalists defended the emotion and fervour as often the natural result when a person really encounters God. The more sceptical pooh-poohed this as excessively fanatical. Within Kabale itself, the revival was opposed by the Roman Catholics, who detested all the singing and weeping and general disruption. All in all, the revival had some years to go before it would gain any kind of acceptance and understanding within the wider church.

Festo listened with concern, but never got personally caught up in these debates. In 1942 and 43 he was still too young, and too busy teaching, to do other than be involved at a local level in 'the blessing' which was sweeping Kigezi. He simply threw himself, heart and soul, into the teams that went out each weekend from the thriving churches into every nook and cranny of the district.

These 'teamus' (teams) were more mobile than the ones in Rukungiri as the missionaries had cars. Thus the missions could be held a great distance from Kabale. Dr Joe usually taxied the preachers to and fro. In this way he, Festo, William Nagenda (another leader in the revival) and the others travelled many hundreds of miles together. The journeys themselves became events. Joe found that 'a tremendous amount of ministry was done in my car'. Sharing, or being open about their lives, became a 'key thing'. The Africans were amazed at the things he would confide to them, such as marriage and financial worries. Festo would say, 'Eh! I never thought I'd hear a white man telling us these things.' Through Dr Joe, in fact, the Ugandans felt enabled to open up on many subjects they had previously never dreamed of sharing with a missionary. 'Of course we did not become perfect together, but we were learning how to live together.' The car was also the place for deciding on the itinerary of the day. Those who felt they wanted to speak would offer, and it would be discussed and prayed over. 'Democracy by the Holy Spirit,' one called it.

Once at the village, which could be anywhere in the hills around Kabale, time ceased to have meaning. If they had agreed to start at ten am, they *might* start at eleven am. Meanwhile, for hours, hundreds of people would have been gathering on the hillside from villages round about. They settled down comfortably as the 'teamu' arrived and were refreshed with tea and bananas at the schoolteacher's house—where the final details of the mission were agreed on. Once the meetings began all eyes were 'glued' to Festo and Church and the other speakers. 'They were so hungry for the gospel.'

One day, Festo met with a recently converted witchdoctor who demonstrated just how the fake spells were done. Festo was as intrigued as the rest of the village—that day he finally knew how his parents' witchdoctor back in Kyamakanda had worked his frightening magic. Such changed lives, however, only 'greatly increased' Festo's own burden to reach more people with the love of Christ.

Not that converts had by any means an easy time of it. When women refused to make any more beer for their husbands they were severely beaten for their stand. Children were often beaten and kicked out of their homes by furious parents. Festo was undismayed by such persecutions: 'This was taken as a sure sign that those who'd experienced Christ were moving in the direction of the New Testament.' His own fourteen-year-old niece had been beaten and forced to spend dangerous nights in the bush in the early days after her conversion, 'but nobody could beat the Lord out of her'.

Early on, Dr Joe would preach in English (he had trouble with the Rukiga language) and Festo would interpret for him—into Kinyaruanda, Rukiga, Ruhororo or Luganda. Dr Joe soon discovered that 'Festo was brilliant', and the two formed a pact: when Dr Joe was preaching, if a few sentences were needed for clarification, Festo would pause and whisper, 'Bwana, may I say a word?' 'He was very bright at getting to know my way of saying things.' Festo would often add a few words of personal testimony. 'We began to have a tremendous love for each other through our preaching.' In fact, Dr Joe became immensely fond of Festo, and not only because of his genius for translation. Their personalities fitted together well: both were ardent evangelists, and Dr Joe was warmed by the younger man's 'bubbly, sparkling, warm enthusiasm'. Festo became 'like a brother' to him.

The preaching fell into a regular routine where three would preach. Nsibambi began with the sinfulness of sin, Blasio Kigozi would follow him by talking about God's judgement on sin, and Dr Joe, via Festo, would conclude by talking about how

Christ had brought salvation to man through his death on the cross.

As time went on they discovered that Festo was a 'superb preacher' in his own right. The missionaries quickly made the most of it. Lilian Clarke recalls: 'Festo nearly always spoke last when he was with us because he was by far and away the greatest preacher. Hours of study had made the Bible a part of him, and given him vision and insight.' His sermons were never thematic or exegetical, but—as they would always be—rather a series of stories or thoughts based round a Bible story. They always had one end in view: persuading his listeners to find Christ for themselves. He had the knack of picture language, and of making simple Bible stories come alive, drawing out the implications behind them. As a friend, Yosia Banyenzaki, puts it, 'Right from the start, Festo could bring people near Jesus. When he spoke, he conveyed what God's love was all about.' Another friend describes his preaching as, 'not logic on fire, but Bible pictures on fire. He was a Monet of the Gospel.'

Festo had already discovered that

> when I preached *my* thoughts, I did not enjoy it. I needed to study the Bible, and to ask the Spirit to make the word speak to me first. If I opened the Bible on which I had fed, and passed on what I had learned, then I found that it fed others.

Certainly he could establish an instant rapport with any village audience. Banyenzaki says, 'Festo's testimony always had an effect.' More than any missionary he and the other African balokole knew what fears and doubts about God the people were facing. Remembering the religion of his childhood—'always striving to appease the distant, forbidding creator from whom we sought desperately for security ... We hoped that the medium spirits would plead our cause'[1]—is it any wonder that Festo and the other Africans burned to tell the Ugandans that everything was really all right, that God loved them?

Festo's gifts as a linguist were put to good use later in the year when the Revd Godfrey Hindley and several other missionaries wanted to hold a large mission in Kampala. They urgently needed a good interpreter. The Revd Erica Sabiti, sitting in on planning meetings, suggested, 'There's a lad here who I think could do it.' Festo was the 'lad', and he joyfully made his way up to Kampala. There he translated from the English into any one of three Ugandan languages (Luganda, Swahili, Rukiga) and vice versa as was needed. 'All congratulated him on his command of each language,' Hindley recalls. 'He was very charming and gifted, but humble.'

But life still wasn't trouble free for those caught up in the revival. About this time the very enthusiasm of the balokole began to lead them into a new and subtle danger. They all wanted to live according to the 'highest', but this was becoming so associated with specific actions that the actions themselves were expected of people almost as proof that they were revived. For example, whereas people under conviction had first wept with sorrow and then leaped with joy when receiving assurance that their sins were forgiven, in many circles it now became all too easy to expect such obvious signs and to take them as proof that a person had been revived—and to doubt anyone who did not react in such a way.

It was a dangerous side-track, as Festo later realised. One day he would put it this way:

> The devil is not afraid of people singing and jumping for joy in times of revival! He doesn't say 'Stop jumping', because he knows they enjoy it. All he says is, 'Jump a little higher—and the higher you jump, the more "spiritual" you are!'
> The wind of heaven has come, and people shake. I've seen people fall down. Then the devil comes very easily, and says to the people who shook, 'Now to experience the fulness of the power of God you have to shake! If you don't shake, you haven't got it.' So you could find the brethren fighting over whether you should shake, shout, be silent or act in a particular way. But when you try and copy some kind of reaction, you produce a fake.[2]

Enthusiasm for being '100% for the Lord', as the saying went, also began to lead to the formation of many rules. The rules were petty, like not whistling Christian choruses, because in Africa one whistles to a dog, and it would seem to be a slight towards God. Or again, being careful in the way in which one sits in the fellowship meetings, because if you were sitting before an African king or chief you could not sit informally—so why do it before God? Similar petty rules evolved governing

Festo and Mera, September 1956, Dodoma, just before Festo left for England.

Festo, Mera and the girls: Peace with Festo, Joy with Mera, Hope in Mera's arms. While on a visit to Kabale, in late 1940s.

Festo, Mera, the girls, and Alice, the house girl, Kabale 1960.

hair-styles and clothes. Festo knew that 'there was piety in it', but 'nonetheless we were pushing a little bit too hard'.

This legalism would sorely beset parts of the revival movement for some years. Certainly throughout 1942 Festo struggled with the problem. He was utterly devoted to Christ, which made it hard to stand against what the brethren saw as signs of a revived person ... especially as much of it was sincere and spontaneous. He found his own solution one night at Erica Sabiti's (later the first African archbishop of Uganda) house in Kinoni, where he, William Nagenda, Simeon Nsimambi and another friend were staying after a mission. After their meal, eaten as usual sitting on mats on the floor, the friends had lingered. After a time of prayer, someone began to sing the hymn 'When I survey the wondrous cross'. The others picked it up, and sang it again. Sabiti had been quietly getting ready for bed, but he returned from his bedroom in his pyjamas and started singing with them, joining in the last verse: 'Were the whole realm of nature mine.'

The verse ended, but Sabiti sang through it again, making the last words, 'His love demands my soul, my life, my all' his own hymn of love. (In Luganda, it runs: 'It demands that I serve you and please you wholly.') Then Sabiti sang the verse through again and again. The rest were quiet and he was 'almost transformed'. Festo could not take his eyes off his friend as he suddenly realised Sabiti was expressing the deepest desire of his own heart, 'to please you and go serve you wholly'.

That sentence just captured Festo, as it had William Nagenda. When Festo went to bed that night, he didn't sleep.

> The Lord had shown me that *that* was what mattered. Not all our little ridiculous rules which we were burdening ourselves and others with. The praise and glory as reflected in Erica's face, that was what mattered. It was like a fresh revelation of Calvary.[3]

Festo would consider this the time 'when God set me free from what I call "revival rules"'.

By the time term ended in the summer of 1943, Festo decided that 'God was calling me to give up teaching and work full-time as an evangelist'. He felt attracted to Rwanda or Burundi. Furthermore, with the enthusiasm of youth, 'I wanted to know

God's exact plan for me: dates, places, everything.' He soon found that life wasn't like that.

'The Lord said to me: "No, that is not your business. Your business is simply to be available. When you're available, I know what to do with your availability. *I don't waste my people's time.*"

'So I said, "Okay Lord, I'll carry on teaching."'

So the autumn of 1943 found Festo and Mera preparing for their marriage, with no plans other than to marry and for him to continue teaching at Kigezi High School, and preach on mission weekends and school holidays.

On 30th December 1943, Festo Kivengere and Mera were married in St Peter's Church, Rugarama Hill, Kabale. Canon Ezekiel Balaba took the service. Mera wore a white dress and Festo wore a suit. It was a Christian wedding on British lines— Festo had refused on principle to pay a bride price, which would have implied that Mera was an acquisition. Certainly, carrying Mera in a basket to his house would have been 'out of the question'!

The reception was held at the home of the Revd and Mrs Gregory Smith. Festo and Gregory Smith had come a long way in fellowship since the day over two years before when Festo had cycled timidly down from Rukungiri to confess his hatred. There were one hundred guests. The war shortages meant that not only were the refreshments very simple, but also, sadly, no pictures could be taken—no film was available at any price. But there was a cake, and plenty of songs and testimonies. Both Festo and Mera gave a short testimony on 'what Christ has done for us'.

Later that evening, Festo walked Mera the few minutes back to his home. They were alone: James, the lodger, and his sister had moved out. The couple had a few 'sweet and happy' days to settle in, and then Festo went back to teaching. Mera having taught on and off since she was fourteen, decided to stay at home for a while.

Before he was married, Festo had decided that because he was such a dedicated Christian, Mera was going to be impressed no end with her 'perfect' husband. After all, everyone knew how the Ugandans traditionally treated their wives: often beating them, demanding service hand and foot, and giving them absolutely no say in the running of the family. Festo knew he was going to treat Mera better than that: with the kindness and love that the other balokole husbands gave their wives. The memory of his stepfather's brutality was an additional spur to giving Mera the consideration he had longed for his mother. Festo also anticipated absolutely no change in any of the traditions he had established in four years of living as head of a household with docile young sisters and students who were eager to please him. The home ran smoothly, he knew Mera was intelligent and an excellent cook; she would soon pick up his ways.

His early days of marriage, therefore, came as a considerable shock. The first inkling of trouble came one day after school at the very beginning of January. Festo returned home to find a small jug that was used for flowers not in its usual place. Automatically he put it back where he always kept it. An hour later he was startled to find that it had gone again, and was back in the wrong place. He decided he had better explain to Mera the mistake she was making. To his astonishment, she did not accept that it was a mistake. He was then dumbfounded when she firmly added that the jug was going to stay where she had put it. This was unbelievable!

Festo later described his reaction: 'In Africa we have an insect that is prickly, and rolls up in a tight prickly ball the minute you touch it. I am like that.' His pride was outraged, and he maintained a wounded silence for some hours. He would later say, 'I suppose my place had been the wrong place, but when she found the right place for the jug, it caused some darkness with me.' It took some time before he rallied and 'repented that I had been wanting to keep things as they were, forgetting I was no longer alone'.

I was no longer alone. As the months went by he was to discover quite what a revolutionary change this would make to his life. In his books and sermons, Festo later shared several of the lessons he began to learn throughout 1944. His anecdotes provide an interesting insight into the way the revival approached the marriage relationship—or 'revival in the bedroom', as he was later to dub it.

Above all, he and Mera came to see the marriage relationship not as a partnership of two, but of three. Jesus was always seen as the head of the family. Daily shared Bible reading and prayer were scrupulously observed. The couple took the inevitable tensions and shocks of early married life as an opportunity to let Christ reveal to each partner areas of his or her life that still needed changing: 'pockets of selfishness, pride, insensitivity'. Festo wryly admitted: 'Before marriage, when you're alone, you think how spiritually victorious you are! But there were many things God wanted to change in me: these came out as I began to do things with Mera instead of alone. I discovered that my ideas about things, my wishes, were not always the best.'

Both Festo and Mera were strong willed and very self-confident. When household decisions had to be taken, and they did not make the same one, both had to battle with the utter certainty that only he or she was right. Mera had been used to having her students 'jump' when she said so. Festo had enjoyed the same authority. No one had criticised or attempted to correct him since before his days as a student at Mbarara. So frosty silences and outraged feelings were the inevitable outcome when both refused to back down over household matters.

They also discovered that the differences in their characters, which had of course earlier seemed attractive, could be highly irritating within marriage. Mera was a perfectionist with considerable reserve. Any extrovert, over-emotional display embarrassed her. Festo was far more outgoing, with a warm, sometimes over-enthusiastic nature. He often disregarded detail in his eagerness to get things done. Exasperation on both sides was the result of some early encounters. In fact, the only solution they found was 'a constant repentance, and a putting things right before Christ'. It was very hard as

in marriage this has to be done at such a deep level. And of course the very time when you need to go to Christ quickly, is the very time you don't want to go at all. The light is a threat when something has gone wrong. But slowly we discovered that it was only when the wrong thing was out in the open, in the light of the Lord, that healing could take place.

Throughout 1944, Festo tried to understand what lay behind the painful lessons he was learning. He would later sum it up like this: 'The newly married must recognise the fact that each of them has the inherent dignity of having been created in the image of God. When either does something that denies their spouse that dignity, it is self-centredness, and forgiveness is needed. It's never easy—it caused Mera and me big problems.'

By the early spring of 1944, Mera became pregnant. Both she and Festo loved children and looked forward to parenthood as 'wonderful'. Their excitement renewed their determination that their love for each other would be protected by a proper, Christ-based foundation for their marriage. They patiently continued to stress openness, repentance, forgiveness and trust.

In fact, in several other ways, 1944 was a year of hope. By the summer even the outlook for the revival had picked up. In August the bishop arranged a convention at Namirembe, on the subject 'Christ and him crucified'. The balokole—Festo among them—preached and sang their hearts out, and though there was little reaction from CMS, at least the missionaries were not hostile. Some even joined in the worship.

Late in the autumn Mera gave birth to a daughter at the mission hospital on Rugarama hill in Kabale. In traditional African homes girls were unwelcome, but Festo and Mera were delighted. They baptised her 'Peace' at St Peter's. 'Her name was our testimony: we called her Peace because God had given us peace in our home.' Ironically, Peace screamed the house down each and every night for months.

1945 came, and with it news of Hitler's suicide. But the war in Asia dragged on. Meanwhile in Kabale opportunities for work and ministry presented themselves at every turn. The school was growing—throughout East Africa the desire for education was increasing at a terrific pace. Festo had gone obediently back to school at the beginning of another year, when once again his prayers for guidance to become a full-time evangelist were met with the impression of 'Yes—but not yet!' But evangelism had long since taken over from education as his life's vocation, and in Kigezi though not yet nationally, he was regarded as one of the leaders of the revival.

Thus he was in on the talks when the idea of holding a

convention to mark the tenth anniversary of the revival coming to Kabale was first mooted. It would give the balokole throughout the district a chance to celebrate, but more importantly a chance to have some sound biblical teaching. This was always a great concern of the missionaries and leading African brethren. Dr Joe began to cast about for a suitable place to sit several thousands of people. He found it in a grassy hollow on Rugarama Hill itself, just below the church. It was a natural amphitheatre, and as Festo went back and forth to school each day, he watched Dr Joe's progress at directing several African volunteers as they gave nature a little help: marking out seating and aisle spaces in the grass. They also built a wide wooden platform down at the front where the preaching would take place.

The summer of 1945 arrived. New beginnings seemed just around the corner. News of the end of the war was greeted by Christians with praise, prayer and all-night singing. (The economic bite of the war had had its effect on Ugandan stability, however: riots broke out that year in Kampala. They were but a foretaste of the coming struggle for power as the end of the British Protectorate loomed.) Everything seemed set for a celebration not only of the past ten years of revival, but for the coming ten years of growth. The fellowship that Dr Joe and the other missionaries had established with their African colleagues, especially men like William, Nsibmabi, Shalita, Balaba and Festo was practically unique in the history of the Ugandan church. The lessons they had learned were a rock-solid basis from which the work could continue to expand.

Then one Sunday, 5th August, Canon Ralph Banks, the commissary of Bishop Chambers of Tanganyika, and the CMS Education Secretary, arrived in Kabale. He was in Uganda on leave, and very much enjoying his holiday. He therefore hastily declined Ezekiel Balaba's invitation to preach. So Dr Joe 'pressed him to give us five minutes from the chancel steps at the big morning service because we knew so little about Tanganyika'.[4] Canon Banks stood up and sought inspiration. None came. So he explained in a straightforward manner the rather dull condition of the church in Tanganyika. He described it as 'fairly sleepy and stuck'. He said that even from the little he had seen in

Kabale, much more was happening here. These two observations seemed to give him an idea, and he warmed up, 'God has given you revival in Uganda. Have you forgotten all about us in Tanganyika? Can't you come and help us?'

He sat down and the service carried on. When it was over, Dr Joe went home for a late Sunday lunch. His thoughts were back on the coming convention when Festo banged on the door. From his face, Dr Joe could see at once it was not a casual call for Festo looked tremendously pleased and excited about something. Then Festo dropped his bomb. 'God has called me to Tanganyika. Erisa Wakabi is coming with me.' Erisa was a teacher at the Bible College in Kabale and a close friend of Festo's. Wakabi would later describe their deep camaraderie as, 'I was to him as Jonathan was to David.'

Dr Joe was horrified. 'My first reaction was "We can't possibly spare them! Why should God call away our very best people?"' His dismay was shared by many people throughout Kabale—not least, Mera. No one could—or wanted to—believe the news. Festo and Wakabi's decision seemed so abrupt; few knew of the years of preparation and eagerness that lay behind their 'call'.

Yet one African argued with Dr Joe, 'Why can't Tanganyika have the best?' So Joe reluctantly resisted the temptation to dissuade them. 'But we were staggered at our loss—they had become such leaders.'

There was an urgent need in Tanganyika for Christian teachers to join a mission high school that had just been launched by the CMS and some other missions. It was to be called the 'Alliance School' after the alliance of its founders: the Anglicans, Moravians, Lutherans, and Africa Inland Church. Erisa Wakabi had no trouble with his application: he held a Makerere College certificate for teaching. But Festo had problems; all he had was a primary teacher's certificate. Would this qualify him to teach at high school level? He very much doubted it. Indeed, he was not even keen to go as a teacher. 'I wanted to go as a full-time evangelist.' But the only opening was for teachers, and Festo was at least that. He sent off his application with a prayer: 'Lord, I'll go if they say yes.' Mera's prayer was more along the lines: 'I'll go if you insist.'

Meanwhile, the convention was booked to begin in December. 'By the afternoon of the 19th December, people were arriving from all four points of the compass: from Uganda, Rwanda, Burundi, Kenya and Tanganyika, and even a small group from the Congo.'[5] There were about 15,000 people in all. The Kivengeres, like all the other local Christians, soon had a houseful of guests.

Dr Church's message was followed by William Nagenda's testimony. Festo also spoke—it was the largest crowd he had ever yet addressed. For Festo, the convention was an ideal way of commemorating the first ten years since he had been touched by the revival. Then a letter arrived from Tanganyika and he learned that ten years to the month since he had been converted in the closet at the end of the dormitory (January 1946), he would be off to take the gospel to other boys in a school in Dodoma, central Tanganyika.

After the convention, Festo and Mera, Erisa and Apofia, his wife, sat down to finalise their plans in earnest. Everything was difficult. The journey would be exhausting and hazardous: the post-war lorries were appallingly overcrowded. They had little money; Erisa's wife Apofia had four small children, Mera had Peace, and was heavily pregnant again. But the missionaries in Dodoma had said 'come', so Festo and Erisa prepared for the trip.

Festo and Mera visited Rukungiri for final farewells. They did not know when they would see their friends or family again. Karegyesa had softened considerably in the last two years (he now offered Lilian Clarke milk when she visited the district) and bade them a fond farewell. Jonathan and Eva were well looked after. Erica Bugaari had recently married Faith, one of Festo's distant cousins. Miriam wept to have her daughter Mera and the grandchildren so impossibly far away—Tanganyika seemed like another planet. Kitaburaza was dismayed at his cousin's departure; he had just become a gombolola chief under the government administration in Kabale.

The Festo who now took his leave of them all was much more mature than the one they had welcomed to Kabale three years previously. His testimony was now backed up with considerable biblical knowledge and practical experience in the teaching of the gospel. Three years was also long enough to make mistakes in: 'I learned that a testimony should be taken as a sharing of one's experience, but no more. It was wrong to tell people, "God did this for me, therefore he should do it for you in exactly the same way. If he doesn't there must be something wrong with you"!'

The 'teamus' also had given Festo valuable practical lessons in just what it meant to be 'transparent' with other people. By nature a somewhat private person, Festo would find 'walking in the light' with others at times as rewarding as it was also costly.

At the end of term, December 1945, Festo and Mera packed the few possessions they were taking with them. The luggage was no more than Festo himself could carry; Mera was nearly full-term in her pregnancy, and had to watch Peace as well. The two couples were guests of honour at a special commissioning service held at St Peter's. The brethren at Kabale might be saying 'farewell', but they were in no sense saying 'good-bye'. If Festo and Erisa must go off to the wilds of Tanganyika they should go as Kabale's 'teacher missionaries to central Tanganyika at Dodoma', a land which nobody knew much about except that it was 'arid, both physically and spiritually'.

The brethren assured Festo, Mera, Erisa and Apofia that 'in our struggle against the hostilities of the Enemy, we would be empowered by the Holy Spirit, who would keep our eyes turned towards the Lord Jesus. They said that, in seeing him, the weakest believer is able to cope with the shocks of life.'[6]

Perhaps it was still just as well that none of the four dreamed of the shocks in store for them.

CHAPTER EIGHT

DISCOURAGEMENT IN DODOMA
1946–1949

Revival feared and misunderstood; banished from preaching.

IT WAS 1946. The war was over at last. The East African
territories were eagerly launching a ten-year plan for
economic development. Education was a key factor in this, and
Tanganyika aimed not only to extend its primary education, but
to lay the foundations of a secondary education.

The war had had a tremendous economic and social impact
on the cultures of the East African people. In the decade to come
Africans would aim for political independence. This meant that
Festo and his colleagues in the very few secondary schools in
Tanganyika in the mid-1940s were training not just those who
would hold key positions in Tanganyika, but those upon whose
shoulders would fall the burden of actually creating a modern
self-governing nation out of 200 miscellaneous, non-literate
ethnic groups.

The Protestant missions had founded the Alliance Secondary
School in 1943. 'They recognised the great and fleeting opportunity that existed to train future Christian leaders not only for
the church but also for the community,' as Noel Bythell, a
former headmaster of the school, put it. The Revd George
Pearson, the founding headmaster of the ASS (and later an
Archdeacon in Tanzania), had enthusiastically shared this vision
with Festo and Wakabi by letter. But neither did he make a
secret of the fact that as well as a home, a secure job, a minute
salary and a chance to teach and even evangelise the boys at the
school, there would be constant stress, overwork and few
resources—all inevitable in building a school from scratch in
parched and desolate central Tanganyika.

Festo and Wakabi eagerly accepted the offer, including the difficulties, 'with enthusiasm and thankfulness', as Noel Bythell put it. However, things did not begin smoothly between Festo and the CMS missionaries who ran the school. The cause, sadly, was the journey itself, made in early January 1946. For although Festo and Wakabi were coming as missionary teachers, in reality they were culturally very little different from the Wagogo of Dodoma who were pastoralists. 'Our lives had been very sheltered,' Festo said later, recalling the misery his family had suffered on the trip. The Ugandans needed *more*, not less, guidance than that which was carefully given to any white missionary arriving in Dodoma. Festo and Wakabi were to reach their own conclusions as to the reason behind what they saw as thoughtlessness.

But as for the journey, Festo, Mera and little Peace joined up with Wakabi, Apofia and their four little ones. They covered the miles to the port of Bukoba on Lake Victoria, standing in the back of an open lorry. Covered in red dust from the road, the little party then made their way to the steamer at the dock. They bought their third-class tickets, as the missionaries had told them to do (Africans were not allowed to travel first or second class). What the missionaries hadn't explained was what third-class steamer travel meant: spending the night on deck, come rain or shine. As the Europeans swept inside for dinners and cosy berths, the Kivengeres and Wakabis were herded up onto the open decks with hundreds of boisterous, drunken soldiers returning from the war zones of Egypt and Burma. And, to make matters worse, it rained. With four little ones, a baby in nappies and Mera pregnant, the night was 'an absolute nightmare'.

Next morning they huddled together on deck and watched as their first view of Tanganyika came into sight: the thriving commercial port of Mwanza. Not until after the First World War had Britain taken Tanganyika under her wing, and the territory was the most backward in East Africa. Festo and the group had a day's wait before the train left for Tabora. It was jammed with soldiers, but Festo managed to grab a seat for Mera (third class, of course). An instant later he realised that she was in real danger as frustrated soldiers had begun heaving their heavy wooden boxes up and through the window of the train, completely disregarding her. Festo quickly shielded her and Peace with his body, as box after box rained in on his back.

The train journey lasted two days and two nights. With the little children, the baby, and toilet facilities best left unimagined, Festo's description of the trip as 'terrible' seems an understatement. In later years Mera confided to Peace that she had spent much of the journey wondering if her husband was utterly mad. When he kept up a facade of quiet cheerfulness she knew beyond doubt that at any rate he was 'a very determined man'.

Tabora was once a station of the old slave caravan route. It was from here that Livingstone had set out on his last journey. When the Kivengeres and Wakabis reached Tabora, they felt that they themselves would not survive more than one more journey.

Finally, they reached Dodoma—an arid town in the central province of Tanganyika—a few dusty streets and shabby buildings in a wilderness of blazing sun, sand, thorn bushes and scrub. They felt they had reached the end of the world. Nobody visited Dodoma or its surrounding district, Ugogo, out of interest in the 1940s. The whole place was covered in grit and sand, and could be crossed in less than ten minutes on foot, even taking the time to avoid potholes. The biggest building was the 'Cathedral of the Holy Spirit' (built by past CMS missionaries and their converts). It seated 300—at least Dodoma did have an established Christian community among the nomadic Wagogo.

The Alliance Secondary School consisted of a few mud-brick buildings two miles south of Dodoma on the Cape to Cairo highway at Kikuyu, the CMS mission station. All around was dangerous hyena and lion infested bush. Fortunately, the missionaries were at the station and this welcome was 'the only comfort we had' for some time. Festo was rallying himself silently to forgive his new friends' 'thoughtlessness', when they arrived at the school itself, and discovered their little concrete and corrugated iron bungalows were not ready. The families were taken out behind one missionary's house and shown a shabby mud-brick hut, originally built as houseboys' quarters. This was to be the home for all nine of them for some weeks. Festo felt completely disillusioned.

We did not complain because we felt God had called us and we knew he would look after us. But we were very disappointed that the Christian brothers whom we had come to help had made so little preparation for us—especially when we later saw what enormous lengths they would go to for any arriving white missionary.

White feelings of superiority had been met head on and dealt with in Kigezi; here it looked as if they were back to square one.

One thing that the hut did have in plenty was ticks—hundreds of them. They were the source of spiral parasites which could enter the blood stream and cause a virulent fever known as 'tick' or 'relapsing' fever from its recurring onsets. The Ugandans were horrified, but the missionaries indifferent. Sadly, it was only the first of many instances which led Festo to believe that although the white CMS missionaries said the African teachers who had joined them at the school were their fellow workers in Christ, in practice they treated them as anything but 'fellows'. He found that 'the missionary allowances and standard of living was miles ahead of us, but we were never expected to challenge why this should be'. In truth, the missionaries were almost certainly completely unaware of how the discrepancy looked to the Africans: they were leading extremely deprived lives compared to what they could have enjoyed back in Australia. But Festo, not realising what the whites had given up, would find it hard to stomach that 'if we as Africans objected to the discrimination, we were branded as political. If we objected to the appallingly low wages, we were told we mustn't be worldly.'

That first afternoon, however, Festo 'swallowed my pride and did not argue. I reasoned that my Lord had it far rougher than this—ticks are not worth spoiling my ministry for.'

Soon, however, when he had settled in, Festo would object— and often. Though his objections were always polite, they were also very forthright and over the years he became quite a headache to the CMS missionaries. He would explain that this self-confidence and boldness, extraordinary in an African in those days, sprang from the effects of the revival:

> Erisa and I did not consider the missionaries vastly superior, but as our brothers in Christ. As Africans we had always felt before that we were only number twos. Now we had become proud of who we were, because we were that way by the grace of God. We felt it only

right to demand that other human beings, especially Christians, treated us like children of God.

Some of the missionaries would be 'very shaken and resentful' at such straight talk. Meanwhile, within days, all of the Ugandans had succumbed to tick fever. To make matters worse the whole area was also a malarial one, unlike Kigezi, and 'so we then all had malaria'. Festo managed to catch malaria before he was over the tick fever and nearly died. But Mera had sized up her husband well. He lay recuperating on his string bed in the hut and prayed and never dreamed of going home. 'In all this I knew the presence of the Lord Jesus was with us.'

All the same, term was well underway by the time Festo and Erisa were strong enough to make it across the compound and into the classroom. By then, the little bungalows had at last had their corrugated iron roofs put on and the two teachers were able to leave their wives determinedly sweeping out the sand and checking everything from bedclothes to shoes for scorpions. There was maize for breakfast, lunch and dinner each and every day. The odd sweet potatoes, sorghum or plaintain were sometimes thrown in, but on the salary the school gave, the prices in the market had made maize the only choice. Mera cooked everything in a pot balanced on three stones over a small fire— later she had a cooking hut. At least they had an electric light, run off the generator. Having light so accessible was the only improvement on Kigezi, but when the hyenas laughed outside the house at night, and lions roared not so far in the distance, Mera wanted only to go home.

The arrival of Festo and Wakabi doubled the number of African staff at the Alliance Secondary School in 1946. There were two CMS missionaries from CMS' Australian branch: the founding Head, George Pearson, and Noel Bythell, a New Zealander with an MSc in science and maths and a teaching certificate. Together the six planned the coming year with enthusiasm. Festo was given geography and English to teach. (The missionaries were delighted at how well he spoke English.) Chapel and scripture were a 'must' each morning, and Bythell found Festo's spiritual input into the scripture lessons and chapel services was of the highest order. 'He was an evangelist "incognito" and must have led many to a Christian commitment.'

As George Pearson had promised, the pace was killing. Academically, the teaching was at a far higher level than Festo had been trained for. So every night when he wasn't 'very busy marking papers', he was studying in order to keep ahead of his class. He also drew maps, dictated notes, gave out subjects for essays—and 'enjoyed every bit of it'. 'Many times I was tired, but being tired was not the same as being fed up or bored. I never felt bored! I loved the students and they loved me.'

But the academic work was not all. In games Festo proved 'the best football referee', according to old friends. The boys were all boarders, so the staff had to draw up a rota system of responsibility to see that the boys were constantly supervised, and that they had the necessary food, bedding, clothing, text-books, stationery and even health care. If the staff were some-times in doubt as to whether it was all worth it, the future rewards were to be great. The influence of the ASS in Tanganyika was enormous; both from among the students and the African teachers themselves would emerge bishops, cabinet ministers and other political and church leaders. Within days of getting out of their sick beds, Festo and Erisa began open-air evangelism in Dodoma, fretting that time had been passing all too quickly while they had lain ill. 'We had a clear vision that God had called us to Tanganyika to witness for Jesus!'

So they walked through the scorching heat, took up a prominent position in the market, simply opened their mouths and began giving their testimony to a few passing Wagogo, the nearby nomadic tribe who occasionally made forays into Dodoma for supplies. Festo's Swahili had come back to him quickly. It was the language used at the school, and after *jambo* (hello) and *habari*? (what news?) he gave his testimony and then set about translating for Erisa.

Open-air preaching caused no embarrassment in Dodoma, and within a very little while the two Ugandans had attracted a motley but intrigued collection of Wagogo who had come to town for supplies. (From them Festo rapidly began to learn to speak Chigago.) There was no hostility on the part of these men and within a few weeks Festo and Wakabi found, to their delight, that they had some young fledgling converts on their hands. One convert recalls, 'Festo got along very well with us.

Alliance Secondary School staff, 1955. Festo is second from left.

Even though he wasn't of our tribe, we loved him.' When they saw him speaking in the market, they would head for him *upesi* (quickly), and leave only *pole pole* (slowly), their soft *'asante sana'* (thank you very much) lingering in the dry air.

Then the troubles began. To their utter astonishment, Festo and Wakabi discovered they had indeed a powerful opposition, but from a totally unexpected source: the local, doctrinally correct, devout evangelical church and especially its leaders. It wasn't the converts the church objected to, it was the message that Festo and Wakabi were giving; for not only had some wandering Wagogo been converted through these street meetings, *but some members of the church itself*. Their overwhelming conviction of sins forgiven was very emphatically rejected by the church in Dodoma.

At first the church leaders in Dodoma were fairly polite about it. 'We don't like that sort of thing in our church. We don't think that kind of testimony is scriptural. We don't want you to bring in some strange doctrine to disturb our people.'[1]

The word 'testimony' was a partial clue to what lay behind the reluctance in Dodoma. When Festo said he knew Christ personally, and that Christ had saved him from sins, the church leaders believed he was saying that he was holier than everyone else in the church, that he was a special kind of Christian; 'Our testimony revealed their own spiritual deadness, so they fought back by calling us self-righteous, extreme, mad men.'

Festo and Mera, Wakabi and Apofia were puzzled and distressed. 'We had come thinking that we were going to see the whole country come under the fire of the Spirit of God. Isn't that what had happened in Kigezi, and in many other places we had heard of? But here the doors kept shutting in our faces.'[2]

There was another reason. The church in Tanganyika had already tasted revival, but unfortunately the taste had soured. This had happened in 1939, when the revival was actually brought in by invitation from Bishop Chambers, then Bishop of Tanganyika. He invited Dr Joe Church to bring a team to a mission station in western Tanganyika as he was 'so keen' for the people to 'be filled with an evangelistic spirit'.[3] Unfortunately, the bishop got more than he bargained for. The team preached the need for conviction, repentance and new life, and seem in the process to have worked the people up into a considerable state of emotion. Throughout the months that followed hysteria and chaos grew. There was fainting, weeping and uncontrollable praying in the services. Bishop Chambers was greatly alarmed, and withdrew his invitation for Dr Joe and his team to visit Tanganyika ever again. By then, of course, news had got around. Little wonder, then, that the Dodoma congregation were alarmed at Festo and Erisa's preaching. They had heard enough to want to stick to their respectable, orthodox, non-emotional Christianity.

At first, the four Ugandans 'were completely taken aback and confused' by the lack of response.[4] They 'pushed' a little harder, insistent that they knew what they were talking about. The church leaders felt antagonised and were soon much franker in what they thought of these revival testimonies, accusing them of proclaiming themselves instead of proclaiming Christ. 'Actually, the fact was that we were confessing our sins, giving our testimonies without any mincing of words that we were no better than the rest of the people. We were saved by grace.' But word began to spread that Festo and Wakabi were fanatics.

Festo's frustration increased. In Dodoma he had found not heresy, but 'a good ground laid biblically, but without the spiritual insight to make the Bible teaching come alive. We'd needed the divine fire, and they did too.' Pointing this out only made him more unpopular. It earned him and Wakabi nicknames of 'the pious ones', the 'saved ones'.

As the months wore on, Festo and Wakabi began to feel anything but pious. 'We began to resent the criticism because we were sure we knew that revival was the right way to start. Naturally, then, we called those who had closed the doors to us "enemies of the blessing".'[5] Even worse, Festo and Wakabi 'treated them like that'.[6]

> That put us in the wrong place. We were no longer sitting low at Jesus' feet, receiving his grace. We were judges on a high pedestal, pointing fingers. And of course, as soon as you become judgmental, you become as cold as ice. You cannot judge and bless anyone at the same time.[7]

As Festo and Erisa and their wives had supported each other in their witnessing and ministry, they now sought comfort in the fact that they seemed to be the only four true Christians in all Dodoma.

Soon the school staff found themselves inevitably drawn into the issue. George Pearson convened a series of meetings with the best of intentions and on planned, pre-announced topics to discuss what the CMS missionaries meant by Assurance, Witness, Confession of Sin, and Fellowship. 'The discussions were full and fair, though unco-ordinated and inconclusive, leaving us much as we were before,' found Noel Bythell. 'Festo seemed to sum up by saying that these things are not something we all agree to, but which spring up out of loyalty to Christ.'

The missionaries established a clear position early on and stuck to it. They were the representatives of solid, orthodox, zealous, evangelical Christianity to which heresy or unbiblical teaching was anathema. On doctrine and Bible teaching they were strong. They had given their lives to bring the Gospel to the people of central Tanganyika and that was what they had been doing for years, and would continue to do. This put their problem with Festo in an awkward light. They had no theological quibble with him; they too believed in a turning and commitment to Christ. But they had heard enough stories of the revival to frighten them. They wanted no hysteria, no excessive emotion, and no confessions of personal sins in public.

The missionaries had become very fond of the two Ugandans, and were the first to praise the work they were doing in the school, their preaching in chapel and their pastoral help for the boys. But even the missionaries closest to Festo and Wakabi finally dissociated themselves from the revival meetings. Festo felt bitterly hurt. However, the missionary families were always on 'cordial speaking terms' with the African families and Mera was soon a frequent visitor in Mavis Bythell's kitchen. Mavis liked Mera very much, but at times was at a loss to know how to respond to Mera's continual testifying. Outside the compound, Mera was lost: she spoke little Swahili, and her 'jambo's ('hello'), 'habari's (what news?) and 'kwaheri's' (goodbye) with the locals did not help her extreme loneliness.

In the summer of 1946 Mera gave birth to their second daughter, whom they named Lydia. She was a sickly baby, and soon the whole family joined her. An era of malarial attacks began, when Festo would put his daughter in a box tied to the back of his bike, or balance Mera on the bike and wheel the cycle carefully into the hospital a few miles away. The loose shifting sand made cycling very hard indeed, and there were many scorpions. Family visits to the hospital became so common that Festo became friends with the staff. On the occasions when he wasn't the patient, he would preach in the ward while Mera or the girls were undergoing treatment. In this way he caught the attention of a young medical assistant, Sebastian, who was attracted by Festo's 'quiet joy'. Sebastian soon agreed to go along to the small weekly group Festo and Mera had started in their home. He didn't mind risking a fall by sitting on their only bit of furniture—a wobbly bench, and was careful not to drink beforehand 'for fear they'd smell it on me'. Festo and Mera read the Bible to the group, and then shared their testimony. 'You could see how happy they were.'

Shortly afterwards, Sebastian got drunk one evening and decided to kill an enemy with poisoned arrows. As he crouched in the bushes Sebastian suddenly recalled all that Festo had told him about Christ. 'I suddenly realised that I could follow Christ too, and how terrible it would be to do what I was planning—to murder someone.' At home, Sebastian knelt by his bed. 'I knew who to cry to—Festo had told us all about Christ at the weekly meeting.'

Back on the compound, it was soon clear that even the school had picked up the prevailing wind against Festo. Gresford Chitemo, one of his pupils, later the Bishop of Morogoro, recalls that year:

> Festo was one of the first people we had met who testified to knowing Jesus personally, and making him Lord of his life. We found that very hard to take—we thought he was pretending to be better than us. One time we purposely spilled ink on Festo's trousers and he got angry and then we said, 'Now we have got him; see, he is a sinner like us.' But that afternoon, before teaching us, he started by repenting to us for having become angry with us!

This left the boys in confusion for a while. But the temptation of trying to make Festo, whom they acknowledged to be a 'nice man', angry, was too much. They would snatch his trousers off the drying line, rub one leg in the dirty sand, pin them back up, and lie in wait to see the reaction. Exasperation was the most they ever got. Comforting Mera's indignation, Festo would say 'I love them still.'

In 1947 Festo, Mera, Wakabi and Apofia were 'spiritually dry' and 'puzzled'. 'What had God called us to? Only to teach geography and science and never to preach?'[8] This soon seemed to be literally the case, for that year the two men were hauled before the church council—a nasty experience. They were accused of upsetting the Christian community. They were told to stop being fanatics. That the missionaries were sitting in as arbitrators at the stormy meeting really hurt Festo, as he considered them friends.

Festo found his opposers 'staunch evangelical watchdogs guarding against anything which did not toe the line of evangelical understanding'. The church leaders could not understand that the people they had baptised, 'when they are hit by the power of this new thing, this so-called revival, stand up to confess conversion, as it were, for the first time'. They were disturbed by the 'inevitable excesses of joy a person feels when God deals with him'. The church leaders even suspected Festo and Wakabi of wanting to steal the congregation away.

Festo remained silent as long as he could, but finally burst out: 'You can't uproot what you did not plant. The revival is of

God, and if you want to stop it, you had better ask his permission.' Erisa and the two wives began to sing *'Tukutendereza
Jesu'* (Luganda for 'We praise you Jesus'). Festo joined in.

Steaming with anger, the council threw them out, but not
before officially removing Festo's status as one of the lay
preachers of the church, and forbidding him to preach in
Dodoma ever again. The ban would continue for several years.
Festo and Wakabi were too upset to understand that they were
really facing two forms of opposition. Whereas the Dodoma
Christians were, from their own later accounts, for the main
part spiritually cold, with their faith largely a matter of outward
respectability, the missionaries were very different. Their opposition was to Festo and Wakabi's insistence that until they had
come to God in the way that the Ugandans had come to God,
then they were failures. The missionaries would have argued
that they had known and followed God for years and did not
need a Ugandan to arrive and insist that they have their eyes
opened before they could be accepted as committed Christians.

So that year Festo was to begin to learn a lesson that would be
invaluable to him if his ministry was ever to stretch beyond the
revival areas of East Africa: that in Christianity it isn't a case of
whoever is not for you is against you, but of whoever isn't
against you is with you. If he was ever to have a worldwide
ministry among many denominations and traditions, he had to
leave the rigid revival delineation of who was 'in' and who was
'out' behind. Here, surely, can be found the first step in his later
attitude of sharing Christ's love, and letting the Holy Spirit's
entry into other people's lives change them as he will. But
learning not to fuss about other people's spiritual condition
must have been the hardest thing of all. Festo and Mera gained
just as much in Dodoma as they ever gave.

In the meantime, Festo, Mera, Wakabi and Apofia spent
hours agonising in prayer over those 'enemies of the blessing'
two miles down the road in Dodoma town. Festo later wrote
about the answer they got.

> As we were praying, God said to us: 'Ah, dear ones, you are suffer-
> ing from . . . success.'
> 'What do you mean, Lord?'
> 'You came from an area where everything was easy; meetings

were warm, people were being saved, many were rejoicing. Now you have to change. You are feeding on successes instead of feeding on me. I want you to learn a new lesson.'

'What is it, Lord?'

'Please learn patience that does not demand experiences. You will find me alone as the One who can satisfy you, direct you, and make you love the unlovable.'

So we repented. We did not repent of our testimony, but of our attitude—a kind of holier-than-thou-spirit that was hard and critical.[9]

Festo and Wakabi began a new tack: learning how to 'follow the Lord and be at peace even during a time of great misunderstanding. It was a tough lesson.' They visited the people whom they had resented 'to apologise and to ask forgiveness. Some didn't make it easy for us, but we began to be happy again. It cleared the air.' Others were touched at the Ugandans' approach. 'Then the Lord set us free to show our love in little ways to our former "enemies". We found God brought us all kinds of opportunities to speak for him along the path in our work and in our homes.'[10] Festo was learning that in 'spiritual warfare', love and a quiet spirit were the most effective weapons.

Festo and Mera, following the custom back in Kigezi, had begun to hold regular meetings in their home for anyone who wanted to come and talk about Christian things. They attracted a motley crowd: several humble Wagogo converts straight off the streets, some boys from the school and even Christians from the cathedral in Dodoma who had been touched by Festo's message and wanted a deeper spiritual quality to their own lives. As one later put it: 'Before Festo and Mera came, we Africans had decided it was good to adopt the white man's faith. It meant we were more "advanced". For many of us our commitment to Christ went no further. We had no love for Jesus.'

The meetings were very informal: it would have been hard to be anything else in a small room containing a single bench. Most sat on the floor. A few ended up on the floor without intending to: if they sat on one end, the bench reared up like a bucking horse and dumped its guest, arms and legs flailing about in undignified surprise.

Though such domestic difficulties were laughed off (Noel

Bythell found 'their sense of humour often saved them trouble'),
on at least one occasion a missionary's attempt to thwart
frustration with humour missed the point. One evening Bythell
was attending a fellowship meeting at the Kivengeres' when the
baby cried at length. Just when she was really getting on
people's nerves, Bythell quipped, 'She's only giving her testimony.' His joke fell flat. 'Nobody laughed, least of all Festo and
Mera. Afterwards they approached me solemnly to say I was
ridiculing "testimony"!' Bythell explains, 'We *all* took ourselves rather seriously in those days.'

The home meetings grew in numbers and caught the attention
of the canon of the cathedral, Canon Yonathani Songoro and
Mama Mariana (the 'Bible woman'). When they discovered that
banning Festo and Wakabi from preaching in church had not
put an end to their talking, and that they were still actually
managing to talk to members of the cathedral—and indeed 'the
Holy Spirit was continuing to save people'—they were beside
themselves with anger. Drastic steps were called for, but unfortunately they couldn't actually silence Festo in his own sitting
room. So instead they stood up in church the following Sunday
and announced that anyone going to Festo's home meetings was
going to be excommunicated from the church for six months.

It was a blow, but Festo and Wakabi were on their spiritual
mettle now, and did not try to retaliate. Instead, they prayed for
humility and grace to maintain a quiet spirit. If it hurt them to
hear that Canon Songoro at the cathedral was calling them
wolves in sheep's clothing, and accusing them falsely of refusing
even to eat with less pious folk than themselves, his words
certainly had a different effect on the cathedral caretaker, a
young man and former witchdoctor, named Zachariah Msonga.
For he decided to put the rumours to the test. One morning he
arrived on their doorstep and announced, 'I've heard you are
too righteous to eat with some people, and I've come to find out
if this is true.' So Mera and Festo had lunch with him.

As the three ate, Mera and Festo gave their testimonies,
sharing 'what God had been teaching us about the ways of a
truly Christian marriage'—the importance of repenting, and
asking forgiveness. By the time Msonga left, he was wondering
if it would work with his wife, whom he described as 'very

difficult'. 'Could I speak like this to her?' Festo doubted whether he was serious, but said he could try if he liked. Msonga began that night. His wife was so dumbfounded to have him apologise that it began a chain of events that led to their conversions within a few days. Festo and Mera were delighted. The young couple joined the group with complete disregard for threatened excommunication. Msonga went on to evangelise with Festo for years to come.

The hostility of the church in Dodoma led Festo and Wakabi to contact Christians in other parts of the territory. They burned to 'awaken the churches to the love of Christ'. So they packed their bags and were off—first to answer an invitation from the Lutherans to hold a mission in Dar es Salaam, then the political and administrative centre of the territory. Its palm trees and sea breezes were a welcome respite from the desert.

Then they were invited to conduct a series of meetings at a Lutheran Theological school in eastern Tanganyika—the back of beyond. The train ran to the end of the track, where heavy rains had washed away the roads, so they simply walked the next fifty miles, carrying their bags on their shoulders, with hardly a bite to eat between them.

They arrived at the house of the missionary in charge, Dr Daniel Friberg, soaked their badly blistered feet in hot water for an hour, and then limped over to the church and preached. The Lutherans had not had any contact with the revival at all, and Festo and Wakabi were determined to get it off on the right lines. They seem to have been very successful. 'A number of important people responded, including senior ministers in the Lutheran church in eastern Tanganyika.' Then Festo and Wakabi walked the fifty miles to the station, caught the train back to Dodoma, had two days with their wives, and were back on the train again for western Tanganyika, 700 miles away, where several other clergy wanted them to come and talk about the revival. They paid for the tickets out of their own meagre wages, and with the few shillings local people who had become converted were able to spare them. It was the beginning of a way of life that was to last for the next fourteen years. 'Soon everywhere we went we found God was working. The church was coming alive, pastors were experiencing new life.'

Gradually many of the Lutheran and Moravian churches throughout Tanganyika were touched by the revival. Teofilo Kisanji, who later became the first African bishop of the Moravian Church, was converted through the preaching of Festo and Wakabi. Over the years, hundreds and eventually thousands of 'bush' churches would spring up all over the territory.

Festo and Wakabi were eventually joined by Yohana Omari (later Assistant Bishop of Central Tanganyika) and others. During school terms the team adopted the Kigezi practice of going out to nearby nomadic villages around Dodoma. They encouraged the bush churches that already existed there, and indeed helped 'found' many more—the pagans and the Muslims never opposed them.

Festo now had two vocations: his teaching and his evangelism.

Back in Dodoma that autumn, several more cracks in the wall of opposition opened up. At school several boys, led by Gresford Chitemo, took to hiding outside Festo and Mera's house at night. The Ugandans' notoriety had made them objects of great curiosity to the boys. The ridicule died on their lips after they had spent a couple of evenings eavesdropping. Chitemo recalls: 'We found they were still talking about Jesus! This was all a great challenge to us.' The boys began to listen more carefully when Festo spoke in chapel. 'Our hearts were always touched by his message, even though we were resisting it.'

Further encouragement was the conversion of another local young man, Matt Nyagwaswa, at the cathedral. He would one day be the first African bishop of the Africa Inland Church in Tanzania but at the time his friendship with the Ugandans led to his excommunication from the church. Several others were excommunicated. Festo and Wakabi could have set up a rival church. But 'God had taught us that if the eyes of those who are blessed just remain fixed on Jesus, and if we were always willing to be challenged by his Holy Spirit, then revival would continue'. The problems hindering the work, he discovered, came not from outside opposition, but when those who claimed new experiences turned them into the central point of their faith. 'No one experience, or even several can be the centre of the faith; there is only one centre: Jesus.' Therefore, Festo had no desire to set up a 'revival' congregation.

In practice, this refusal to push the revival experience to the point of setting up a rival church made the revival unstoppable. It would go on to touch all the Protestant churches in Tanganyika: the Lutherans, Anglicans, Mennonites, Africa Inland Church, and Moravians.

At the end of 1947 Festo and Mera, Wakabi and Apofia went home on leave for the school holiday. They eagerly caught up with all the news of the past two years. Post-war progress had put a strain on Uganda. There was 'the constant pull of the old ways, and now ... new attractions—money-making, political agitation, the glitter of superficial civilisation'.[11] A portent of problems to come.

Festo and Mera had glorious reunions with special friends. In his letters Festo had mentioned problems vaguely or not at all. 'He spoke instead of the beauty of the Lord, of the new converts in Dodoma.' Safely at home, in privacy, Festo and Mera shared the trials and heartbreak of the last two years. Some friends, like Stanley Kashillingi, were indignant on his behalf. 'Come back home then to us,' they argued. But Festo would smile and say, 'No, the Lord has work for me to do in Tanganyika.'

James and the others also noticed a change in Festo and Mera: 'They had definitely matured; they seemed "bigger" than they had been. Their world view, which had been like ours, had changed. The people they had met, the places they had seen and the secondary-school teaching had enlarged his outlook while we were still parochial.' As the missionaries Phyllis and Dr Geoffrey Hindley noticed: 'Kivengere's social acceptability had greatly increased—he could relate well to the very educated, and yet still to the uneducated.'

Festo and Mera, Wakabi and Apofia returned to Dodoma by early 1948, in time to see the Assistant Bishop, the Rt Rev. William Wynne Jones from CMS, Australia, enthroned as the second Bishop of Central Tanganyika.

That year there were several changes at the Alliance Secondary School. Two more African teachers arrived. George Pearson left and Noel Bythell became the new headmaster, with the Rev. Max Wiggins (later Bishop of Victoria Nyanza) and the Rev. R. M. Connor as two assistant teachers.

The expatriate newcomers tended to adopt the attitude that

Festo and Wakabi's hearts 'were in the right place', but that the revival teaching was not necessarily something they could take on board and push because of their position and the fact that the missions had sent them out to work with the established church. This detached tolerance was all right on good days: on bad days there were inevitable tensions. In all, Noel Bythell found, 'Festo caused us probably more headaches than all the rest of the African staff put together.'

But exasperations aside, Festo spent more time with the white expatriates than any other of the African staff would have dreamed of doing. His self-confidence with the whites had developed over the years in Kabale and those many miles in the car with Dr Joe and Lawrence Barham and Algie Stanley Smith. His English was already excellent, and Noel noticed with amusement that as the years went by Australian and New Zealand idioms began to creep into his speech.

Meanwhile, Festo and Mera continued their ministry. The home groups became more popular and firmly established, despite the fact that the members had been excommunicated by the Dodoma Church. Some of the remaining congregation in Dodoma became very curious. They quizzed their former friends as to just what went on. They were told among other things that Festo and Mera were sharing what a true Christian marriage should mean: mutual love, kindness and respect. This enraged several young men at the church more than any doctrinal questions, which they left to their leaders. An African husband treating his wife as more than a kind of slave was unthinkable. Festo had to be lying. The young men deputised one of their members to creep up to the bungalow one night when the Kivengeres were alone, and eavesdrop for a few hours. The poor wretch they 'volunteered' demurred because of the hyenas and lions, but he finally hid in the mango tree by their house for three very uncomfortable hours listening through the shuttered windows.

He soon forgot even the mosquitoes in his amazement at hearing Kivengere apologise to Mera for something, and then, even more astounding, offering to put the girls to bed for her as she was busy doing something else. After three hours, he had heard enough. He slid down the tree and pounded on their front door. Startled, Festo opened it to a dishevelled young man who announced without further ado: 'I now believe that what you are teaching about Christian marriage is quite true: I've been listening here for hours. I would not have believed it possible that a man would help his wife around the house.' He came in for something to eat, and was converted.

Titus Lwebandiza, the local vet, was part of the group who had sent out the 'spy'. He recalls: 'When we heard the news we were all shaken. We no longer queried that everything Festo said was true—but the men did not necessarily want such an arrangement for their own families!'

But 1948 was for ever to stand out in Festo and Mera's minds for quite a different—and tragic—reason. It happened when Mera went into the mission hospital thirty miles away to have their third child, leaving four-year-old Peace and two-year-old Lydia with Festo.

Peace had never been much trouble and Lydia was well now, so Festo was sure he could cope. But within a day of Mera leaving, Lydia suddenly developed a raging fever and convulsions. His hands shaking with fear, Festo tied the familiar wooden box to the back of his bike, placed his unconscious baby girl inside, and set off at a breakneck pace through the hot and shifting sands, skidding along, praying he would make the hospital in time. He arrived dripping with sweat and speechless, and spent anxious hours while the doctors battled for Lydia's life. But his 'beautiful child' died. She had cerebral malaria. In his book, *Revolutionary Love*, he told the story:

'Jesus had taken our little girl to himself. It was a shock and I wondered if it would kill me and my wife, when she heard about it.'

In the hospital in Dodoma, Festo was surrounded by Muslims but as he stood by the bed,

I uttered a desperate little prayer and the Holy Spirit, the Dove of Heaven, was there to answer. I had hardly finished the little cry of pain when Heaven opened. I had been looking at my little girl, who was gone, with the most empty feeling you can have, when un-expectedly the Comforter brought in the Lord Jesus. He was my Saviour, I knew that, but at that moment he brought Heaven down and my heart was filled. Heaven became so close that it was as if the child had not died.[12]

Festo turned round and shared this with the Muslim staff, and some of them wept. Festo then, 'with some trembling', sent a messenger to tell Mera the news. 'I knew how she loved the little girl and I couldn't see how she could cope.'[13]

What happened he only learned later, but he has described it in this way: 'Mera loves Jesus, and the Comforter went immediately, before the runner got there.' Their new baby, Joy, had been born that very day, and when Mera received the message of Lydia's death, 'the unexpected took place. What my wife could never have done, she did. She got up and praised the Lord and even told the other patients. Some have never forgotten that, specially those who knew our Lydia.'[14]

Festo contended that 'for a mother to lose a daughter with a heart comforted and released was far beyond their ability to understand. But she was able. God blessed her soul, and heaven came near her, too.' Festo and a friend went to fetch Mera in a car. 'I had not seen her so free in the Lord. It was as if the Holy Spirit had taken the death of our child and turned it into a blessing for us.'[15] Back in Dodoma, they made their way to the cathedral to pray with 'our hearts overflowing'. They softly sang in Swahili the hymn: 'Loved with everlasting love'. Then they sent the sad news back to granny Miriam in Rukungiri, but along with it the news that gives a hint of their feeling at this time: they had named the new baby Joy Ntengwa 'because we had joy in the Lord'.

As the year drew to a close, they began to find joy in the fruits of their labours at long last. Festo found that 'opposition began to die down through the positive working of the Holy Spirit. People suddenly said: "Who are we opposing? Festo is nothing —he is just giving his testimony. We are opposing the Lord!"' Slowly, those very people who had most opposed the teaching, weakened in opposition, until a time came when they counted Festo and Wakabi among their best friends.

One morning in the cathedral in Dodoma the assistant pastor under Canon Songoro stood up and said solemnly, 'Didn't I tell you that if anyone here became one of the "saved" I would excommunicate you?' The congregation pricked up their ears and looked round guiltily. Who was for it now? The pastor slowly continued, 'Well ... I want to tell you,' and a smile broke across his face, '*I* have now been saved. If you like, you can excommunicate me!' Several other church leaders, severely shaken by his news, soon followed his example and made a real commitment.

The ban on Festo's preaching was never formally lifted—everyone just forgot about it—and soon he was once again 'an outstanding lay preacher' and 'leading church elder', according to one former colleague, Edward Mwangosi.

Festo was loved by his new friends for his humility and his ability to teach them things through mistakes he frankly admitted making. A good example of this soon took place. It happened one evening just before the high school boys arrived for their weekly Bible study. Festo knew 'they looked up to me as their teacher'. But that day he and Mera had had a 'misunderstanding' and

> A fog settled between us. I had nothing to say, but the silence was hypocritical. Inside I was saying a lot and of course God knew it. I had forgotten the Bible study group, when I heard the voices of the boys coming up the path to our house.
>
> 'Lord,' I cried, 'what shall I do? They're arriving and I have nothing to say to them. I'm in a mess. Help!'
>
> Quietly the Lord said, 'Don't try to give them a message. Just tell them who you are. It is time for them to find you in a mess. They will know you better.'
>
> I didn't like it at all, but there was nothing else for me to do. In the telling, I repented and God forgave me. When Mera came in, I asked her in front of them to forgive me too. For the boys that was a time of new insights, and from that day some of them began to walk with Jesus.[16]

1949 arrived. It was a hectically busy year. Festo would be up at daybreak to gather firewood and carry water. After the chores he read his Bible and prayed. Then it was time for a bowl of maize before going off to school for the day, engrossed in grammar, maps and games.

Many evenings were spent in study and marking papers by the light of a single bulb. Other evenings Festo and Mera would sweep the room clear to make room for the Bible study group. At weekends he and the converts from the church took the boys from the school on weekend missions to small villages and nomadic camping sites nearby. Sometimes they went by train, sometimes they walked. Once out in the bush Festo misjudged the width of a deep gully of rushing water and didn't jump far enough: his companions pulled him out to safety.

When Mera and Festo's fourth daughter was born late that year, they named her appropriately, Hope Kishande. 'Hope' well summed up their feelings as the decade came to a close. 'In Dodoma we had learned how to praise God despite hardships, sickness, opposition, even bereavement. These years had become a real blessing to us.'

Now instead of returning to Kabale, as had been their intention after three or four years, they felt they could not possibly leave. Too many opportunities lay open before them here in Tanganyika. It was becoming home. Festo's Swahili was so fluent that people assumed he was a born Tanganyikan and even Mera could now speak it. It had become second nature to look out for scorpions in the bed, and to learn that after all, the hyenas' wails and laughs couldn't really harm anybody. And so their return that year to Kabale was no more than a holiday.

CHAPTER NINE

TRAVELS IN TANGANYIKA
1950–1956

Revival accepted; constant missions; becomes an acknowledged leader in Tanganyika church circles.

BY THE TIME Festo turned thirty in 1950 he had been married six years and had four (three still living) daughters. He had been a schoolteacher for ten years, an evangelist for nine years, and by all accounts had 'led' hundreds of people to Christ through this own testimony. He had also been among those who introduced the Tanganyikan church to the principles of 'repentance', 'fellowship' and 'walking in the light' rediscovered by the revival—travelling several thousands of miles in the process.

Festo thrived on all the work. An activist and enthusiast, his was a personality which functioned best in motion. In 1950, there was no lack of opportunity. The most serious opposition to the revival was fading, and Festo was keen to continue his missions and do all he could to help the church in Tanganyika wake up to the tremendous spiritual riches it possessed in Christ.

This was a task demanding extensive travel in rough conditions, little privacy, and new names and faces at every turn. Temperamentally, Festo was well suited to the challenge. His equable nature and enormous natural self-confidence protected him from dissipating his energy with nerves or worry. He was also highly indifferent to his surroundings: travel and new places and hard beds caused him little stress. Neither did he require a great amount of solitude—he thrived on company. He was more himself with people than without them.

During these next seven years, Festo's life would follow a

busy but established pattern: term time meant classwork during the day and preparation at night, plus home meetings within the Kikuyu mission community, frequent duty as a lay preacher at Dodoma Cathedral, and regular attendance at the cathedral's English services on Sunday evenings. Weekends and school holidays meant missions to any number of far-flung places throughout Uganda, Tanganyika and even Kenya, as well as the yearly trips home to Kabale. From 1950–56 Festo's ministry would not only place him among the leaders of those establishing the revival in Tanganyika, but the experience would in its turn help prepare him for his future work. It was, however, to be at a cost: he would find his family growing up without him.

The Kivengeres and Wakabis returned to Dodoma in early January of 1950. Term began. Each morning before dawn the girls would wake to hear their daddy quietly slipping out of the house into the hushed half light to go in search of firewood. In the dry season he could be gone for up to two hours. Collecting firewood near the Kikuyu compound was an uncomfortable and even dangerous business: the brush had thorns like small daggers, and often sheltered scorpions.

Once the fire was made, water was needed. One evening Mera remembered she had left the water bucket outside and went to fetch it. When she did not return, Festo strolled out after her, and found her standing stock still in the garden—while a huge lioness eyed her with great interest from a few yards away. Festo eased his very frightened wife slowly back into the house, and quickly closed the shutters.

Once the water was collected, Mera made breakfast. Almost always it was maize porridge. After family morning prayers, Festo walked off to the school, sometimes not to return until early evening.

By 1950 the school was firmly established with all classes held in English. East Africa having been gripped by a 'thirst to know ... to learn', Western education was seen as 'the shining symbol of progress'. Tanganyika was still desperate to expand its educational system: the census of 1948 had badly startled it by revealing there were far more children out there than anyone had suspected. Though this craving for education, irrespective of a child's abilities or interests, would lead to enormous social problems in the years to come, it did mean that in 1950 the Tanganyikan government's subsidy enabled the Alliance School to expand. Festo took up his geography and English class once again under the headship of Noel Bythell. Though the two did not always see eye to eye on the revival, within school they worked together extremely well.

It was through Bythell, in fact, that Festo picked up some valuable non-academic skills. He learned to drive—Bythell gave him lessons in the school's pick-up van. Soon Festo was thundering in and out of Dodoma in clouds of dust, collecting school supplies from the railway station and food from the market. His driving was 'quite reliable' according to Mr Bythell, though others in later years would shake their heads over the speed at which he went.

Secondly, Bythell taught Festo the rudiments of administration and finance. Bythell knew that 'African casualties in the area of finance were legion, especially in Government service', but 'Festo was always scrupulously honest, and this was the first step'. Soon Festo was in charge of the school shop, which sold food and personal items such as soap, stationery, cloth and blankets. When he did an 'efficient' job with the shop, Bythell began to introduce him to the mysteries of keeping the school's accounts. The New Zealander was glad to introduce Festo to 'this necessary area of our culture, and help him to a Christian insight into the meaning of stewardship which must have been quite important to him in later life'.

While Festo's days were spent at the school, Mera was left, day after day, week after week, at home with the girls. As they grew older she spent her mornings teaching them their letters and simple arithmetic. Peace also picked up a great deal of schooling from Mavis Bythell's home classes held for her daughters Elsie and Grace. The girls went barefoot; the Kivengeres simply could not afford more than one pair of shoes for each daughter, and these were kept for church and travel. In the long evenings when Festo was away, Mera would put the girls to bed with stories of Uganda, their clan and family. When she sang some of the sad old Bahima songs, 'she could make us cry', recalls Peace. Other nights, when Festo was home, the girls remember waking up very late and seeing him doing the family ironing with a heavy iron full of glowing charcoal.

Meanwhile, the weeks sped by, and Festo and his team began to prepare for yet another preaching trip during the coming school holiday. These trips of his were not popular with the school, where the other staff found his constant evangelising activities a real headache at times. 'Festo was always an evangelist, and this was often disconcerting to us in administering school affairs, as he so often requested leave to go off to conventions and missions in the school holidays,' recalls Bythell. The other staff found this extremely annoying, as even out of term time the school had to be kept going. But Festo 'left the mundane duties to others—such as maintenance of buildings, food and clothing supplies, stationery, finance, curriculas, ground or sports materials'.

On the other hand, Bythell would come to view the missionaries' frustrations as 'a human reaction'—like Martha and Mary. 'Those who felt they were left "carrying the baby" should have been more conscious of serving God in an equal capacity.'

Though Bythell tended to be closer to Wakabi, who was quieter than Festo, nevertheless, he saw that Festo 'gave good value in all he did at the school—he was a first-class teacher and his spiritual and moral influence for good was beyond human criticism'. However, human depression and strain crept in, and years later, the then headmaster, when considering Festo's replacement, was quite emphatic that 'he did not want any more evangelists on the teaching staff'.

This was certainly an understandable reaction. Though Festo enjoyed his teaching at Dodoma, his only reason for being there in the first place was his continuing urgency to preach the gospel to those who were not yet Christians, and to pass on the spiritual lessons those caught up in the revival had rediscovered. From 1950–56 this was precisely what he did, using his few spare evenings from schoolwork for prayer and Bible study in the small home fellowship groups, and organising team missions nearby (most weekends) and far away (all school holidays).

In fact, during these years Festo's love of joining the revival teams sometimes led him astray from his other, just as important, commitments. For example, in February 1950, soon after the family had returned to Dodoma, came news of a great convention being planned in Kako, Uganda. Festo was desperately eager to go. He asked Bythell for permission to leave his class, but was told no, as it was now term time. Festo seems to have found this hard to accept, for he then approached the Bishop for permission to attend (the Bishop was the chairman of the Board of Governors of the school). The Bishop said only that as Bythell was headmaster, it was his decision. Festo then approached Archdeacon Banks who was the Education Secretary. Banks gave the same decision as Bythell had done: during term time Festo was needed in the classroom. Another missionary, Max Warren (later General Secretary of the CMS), heard of the incident. He also stressed in a letter that even those caught up in revival had 'to get on with the business of living'.

Another time Festo fell into the hands of a revival team when there was no constraining influence on his enthusiasm to remind him of other responsibilities. He was taking Mera and the girls back to Uganda for the long school holidays, and they had got as far as Mwanza when they ran into a revival team of African evangelists led by a missionary, Captain McKemey. They were on their way to a convention in Dodoma. These men prevailed upon Festo to let Mera struggle home to Uganda alone with the girls and only a schoolboy named Hosea to help her, while he returned with the team to preach in Dodoma.

By the early 1950s the church in East Africa was still burgeoning (one million Christians in Uganda, seven hundred thousand in Tanganyika), and had changed its attitude towards the revival. The movement was no longer seen as the ravings of extremists, and indeed interest in its emphases of a daily 'walk' with Christ and a transparent lifestyle was growing rapidly. The favourite Ugandan revival hymn, '*Tukutendereza Jesu*', was resounding from bush churches all the way from Southwest Uganda and northern Rwanda to central Kenya and Tanzania.

This growing enthusiasm was now familiar in Dodoma, where the missionaries as well as the local Christians had been touched by the revival. The missionaries, who were spread between Dodoma and the Kikuyu mission station, had become, according to one, 'fairly evenly distributed between those who participated enthusiastically in the fellowship and conventions, and those who affirmed this expression of witness and evangelism but who were not themselves wholly given to the revival movement as the mode of missions'.

During these years several missionaries were very sympathetic to what Festo was trying to achieve. They would include Bishop Alfred Stanway (who arrived in 1951), the Rev. Gordon Chittleborough, Jack and Flo Shellard (in fact, the missionary fellowship often met in their home) and Miss Beryl Long, another teacher now engaged in literacy work among the Wagogo. But Festo's vision was for Tanganyika, not just Dodoma. During these seven years he answered invitations from churches of many denominations from Dar es Salaam, on Africa's East Coast, to Gahini in northern Rwanda. Highlights in 1950 included the great convention among the Kikuyu in Kenya.

Festo, although still cautious in deep friendships, made many countless acquaintances with Christians in Tanganyika. They represented a wide range of denominations, from African and expatriate Lutherans to the Moravians. One name that crops up in these years is that of Matt Nyagwaswa, later Bishop of the African Inland Church of Tanganyika. Festo met him in 1950 during a mission to Mwanza, where Matt was just completing a teachers' training course. He went along to hear Festo and Nagenda preach:

> My heart was very much touched, and my Christian life established by their testimony and message. I noticed that Jesus was very real in their lives. Festo and William were very transparent in their walk with Jesus, and in their testimony, and in their fellowship with one another.

Festo met up with other old friends from other missions including Dr Joe Church and Yosiya Kinuka. Then former student, Gresford Chitemo (later Bishop of Morogoro), joined the missions that went out. Then there was Yohana (John) Madinda who became the Assistant Bishop of Central Tanganyika in 1964 (and fourth bishop of that diocese in 1971); Zachariah Msonga of Dodoma, already mentioned; and Edward Mwangosi, a long-serving and senior civil servant.

Festo's circle of acquaintance with the whites also increased. Dodoma was the headquarters of the diocese and CMS, so all visitors who passed came there, as well as a constant stream of delegates, representatives and members of various missionary or church committees, boards, conferences, conventions, etc. Soon several English Christians, excited by the revival, also made their way out to East Africa to see the revival for themselves. Among these was the son-in-law of C. T. Studd, Norman Grubb (author of *Continuous Renewal*), Roy Hession, author of *The Calvary Road* and Dr Paul White, later chairman of AEE in Australia). Dr White met Festo in Dodoma when he was part of a mission team in the town. He had served at the CMS hospital, Mvumi, thirty miles away from Dodoma during 1938–1941. Then he was the only doctor to 200,000 Wagogo, and hence 'The Jungle Doctor' of later literary fame. By the time White met Festo he had learned the tribal language, Chigogo, but his Swahili 'was only sketchy'. He lacked fluency, and needed an interpreter. He was given Festo, who 'expertly moulded my Australian-accented English into colourful Swahili. I told a story, and he brilliantly interpreted the punchline.'

In fact, Festo as part of the Dodoma set-up made a deep impression on Dr White. 'He was always utterly willing to do more than requested, and was always asked to do more than was a reasonable amount.' (And so also was the hard-pressed school staff in giving Festo the time off.)

January 1951 saw the arrival of a new bishop for Central Tanganyika, Alfred Stanway; his wife; and a new headmaster, Max Wiggins, who took over from Bythell. There was also a new teacher, one of Festo's own former naughty students, Gresford Chitemo. (He had in fact been converted through Festo's testimony.) The two now began a life-long friendship and were later close colleagues. It was a hectic year for team missions, during one of which Festo heard the news that away up in Kigezi the Rev. Jim Brazier had just been made the first Bishop of Kigezi, Rwanda and Burundi.

Festo listened with care to Max Wiggins' well prepared Bible expository sermons. (Just how good they were is reflected in the fact that Max Wiggins in due course became Principal of Kongwas Theological College and later the first Bishop of the new diocese of Victoria Nyanza.) Festo began to borrow Max Wiggins' books. 'It was then he really began to take hold of biblical exposition and theology,' recalls Margaret Wiggins.

The two men remained friends for life. Festo would later endeavour to have Bishop Wiggins preach at his consecration as Bishop of Kigezi. Regretfully it did not prove possible.

At the end of the year Apofia Wakabi persuaded Erisa that it was time for them to return to Uganda. The Wakabis had eight children by now, and life in Dodoma was very difficult.

1952 arrived—the year of the Gahini Jubilee Convention. Several thousands of balokole flocked to northern Rwanda from right across East Africa to visit the 'birthplace' of the East African Revival. It was a jubilant reunion: the Kivengeres rejoiced to see so many well-loved friends from Kabale, who brought them news of home. Sharing in huts went on late into each night: Nagenda and Joe full of stories of their trips to Angola and India, and their planned trip to North America in 1953.

But the news from Kenya was most decidedly not good. The Kikuyu Christians brought gravely disquieting stories of a new, evil force abroad in their land: Mau Mau—an African resistance movement aiming to drive the Europeans out of Kenya altogether.

By very early in 1952 there had been considerable violence: arson in Nyeri district and raids on Europeans on isolated farms which ended in hideous deaths. A state of emergency was called. Kikuyu Christians were in an impossible position: they *were* Kikuyu, and knew only too painfully the wrongs done to their people. So their natural sympathies lay with the national freedom Mau Mau wanted. But on the other hand, how could they, as Christians, dream of taking the obscene blood oaths and agree to participate in the murder of people?

It was the beginning of eight years of life on a razor's edge for the Christian Kikuyu: refusing arms from the authorities because they could not bear to kill fellow Kikuyu, but also refusing to join Mau Mau—and often facing torture and death for their stand. Festo heard the stories with horror and was deeply impressed by the Kikuyu bravery. He retold the stories in his preaching, praising the Kikuyu's devotion to Christ, and their determination to love: 'How do you destroy Christians like that?' Festo was later even to preach alongside a converted Mau

Mau, who had come to Christ by what Festo called the 'invincibility ... about God's people living in the power of Calvary by the presence of the Holy Spirit'.[1]

Sad news filtered through from Rukungiri: Makobore, Festo's grandfather, was dead. Festo hurried home for the funeral, which was attended by representatives of the British administration as well as by hundreds of former sub-chiefs, rich Bahima and well-wishers through north Kigezi. When an opportunity came to preach at the graveside, Festo seized it.

'Where is Makobore now?' his clear voice rang out over the grief of the crowd. 'Makobore was a big, important man, but now he is dead and gone. Jesus died, but he is now alive, and will never die again. He is bigger than any other king.'

Karegyesa pulled Festo to one side afterwards: 'Is this *really* true? Is Jesus really bigger than my father?' Karegyesa knew only too well the power Makobore had wielded in his day.

'Yes!' said Festo.

Karegyesa said little more, but turned away 'much impressed'. Then there was only time for a brief visit with his brothers and sister, whom Festo was putting through school in Kabale ('we did what we could for them'—mostly with the revenues from his cows) before it was time to catch the cramped steamer back to Mwanza and thence to Dodoma.

About this time Festo and Mera faced a new problem— Peace's education. Sadly, they decided that she must be sent back to boarding school in Uganda. 'Such scenes we then had!' recalled her sisters. 'Peace did not want to go—and could she scream!'

Nevertheless, the day of departure came, and Festo and Peace (still screaming) boarded the train for the four-day journey to Port Bell. It took two days to reach Mwanza, and one and a half more days to cross Lake Victoria (which is, after all, the size of Ireland).

The steamer had not improved. Peace hated the deck passage with the lack of privacy, and makeshift camp beds, but did not realise that as Africans they were not allowed to travel any higher, and that even had they been, her father could not have afforded it. Indeed, Festo kept up a calm cheerfulness that so completely fooled Peace that she decided he must actually like travelling third class. 'I said to myself I would get Mummy to take me next time because she would make sure we had nice bedrooms.'

They docked at Port Bell, near Kampala. Festo and Peace were met by Yona Mondo, one of the balokole in Kampala (at this time, a good friend of Festo's). For the next few years he and his wife took care of Peace on her way back and forth from Dodoma to the girls' school in Gayaza, near Kampala. Only at Christmas did Peace go home to Dodoma; in the holidays she stayed with William and Sara Nagenda and their children who became her 'second family'. Some years she would see her own parents for less than two weeks.

Back at Dodoma, Festo was himself progressing in his Christian pilgrimage, and finding that in such simple matters as everyday domestic life there were profound spiritual lessons to be learned. He continued to find that walking with Christ at times like this was 'revival in the home'.

In his book *Revolutionary Love* he gives several fascinating—and humorous—glimpses into the effect this had on his private life. For instance:

Too often, when something goes wrong at home, I turn in on myself and keep quiet, hoping that my wife will not detect it. But she does. Thank God, she does.

We both know that we are grieving the Holy Spirit when we sit on something that is unforgiven. My wife's ministry is a gentle word that turns my eyes away from my misery to see again the pure light of Jesus' face and to kneel down at his cross.

She knows when I have a problem. She knows when I am hard. She knows when I am depressed and she knows how to help me. Sometimes when I preach she afterwards takes me aside and says, 'Festo, as you were preaching today, you made too much noise. People could not get all the words.'

Or another day she might say, 'Festo, you are wearing a frown. Is there something wrong? Let us go to Jesus together.' I sometimes thank God and am healed. Other times I pull back, swell up and begin thinking, 'Am I not the head of this house? Why should she speak to me like that? She is just impossible.'

When that happens, I get more and more puffed up until finally I am like a big balloon. A balloon's emptiness of all but air reminds me of the New Testament word that means 'empty glory'. I am inflated with myself, thinking that the bigger I am the better I act as if I am saying, 'Now everyone bow down to me!'

I get fussy with the children. They bump into my balloon and it bounces them away. Of course, when the children bounce away they become like balloons too and soon the whole home is full of inflated human beings. In the evening I take my Bible, while I am still inflated, and call the family together for prayers. My wife comes, poor thing; she has been bounced off and is becoming inflated. My children come, resenting me. In that condition, is there any fellowship in our home?

How in the world is the Holy Spirit going to draw this family together? It isn't easy. But in one way or another, using the sharp point of his Word, the Saviour gets ready to prick one of the balloons. My problem is that I think my wife ought to be deflated first, but the Holy Spirit knows better. He is just and good and will deal only with me concerning what is wrong with *me*, not on what I think is wrong with someone else.

When he pricks a balloon . . . whooooosh! One of us truly asks for forgiveness and that balloon is limp, and then others also get tender and approachable and we can relate, communicate, and understand each other again.

You know how the hinges of a door can get rusty, and when someone opens the door, it squeaks loudly? In our home, when patience or flexibility is growing thin, we squeak. I hear my voice going up and up. This makes the children squeak too. We need oil. When the Spirit of Christ puts his oil on the hinges, our voices are natural again, hearts beating in tune.[2]

Festo took these, and many other examples of lessons learned, with him into the pulpit. He was never one to preach only from head experience of Christ. Instead, he shared with others the love of Christ as he had found it: a love which seeped down into every corner of his life, soothing, challenging and transforming. He lived out what he preached, and it was this which gave such power to his message.

Bishop Alfred Stanway warmed to Festo, and by the mid-1950s even tried to persuade him to offer for ordination. It was obvious that his was an outstanding personality marked out for great things for God. He knew that the church in East Africa would need such leaders. However, Festo politely declined. Although he yearned to be a full-time evangelist, he was wary of ordination, still influenced by the Ruanda Mission's emphasis on the laity. It was not clear to him yet how big a change was on the way: with the days of colonialism and missionaries passing, a national native church would have urgent need of all the gifted leaders it could find.

Instead, Festo continued as he was: 'One of the line of the testifying revivalists,' as a colleague summed it up. This was where 'you simply pass on what has happened to you'. Festo was by all accounts a gifted testifier, 'dynamic and fiery'. So vivid, in fact, was his account of finding Christ that, according to others at Dodoma, 'although he also preached, what most impressed people about him in those days was his testimony'.

Although he testified constantly, Festo admittedly had 'no formal theology'. All the same he did claim to have a 'biblical message'. Certainly his preaching, as far as anyone recalls, was free from the defects of peculiar interpretation. In fact, during these years, the missionaries were inadvertently forcing him to build some sort of theology by often challenging him to explain in a logical way what he meant by some of his statements. Festo's response was biblical and orthodox, due in no small measure to the immense amount of Christian reading he did, but also, in part, felt the missionaries, 'it was a gift of God'.

In the meantime, life went on. At the beginning of 1953 the Alliance School acquired the highest qualified teacher it ever had: Jack Shellard, a CMS missionary with an MEd (Aust.) degree. He would be Headmaster and Joint Headmaster at Dodoma for several years, and a great supporter of Festo and the revival.

May 1954 saw the birth of Mera and Festo's fifth (and final) baby; yet again a girl. They christened her Charity after 'the binding cord in family relationships' and Charis, after a Greek godmother living in Dodoma. Again, the name was chosen as 'simply our expression of what Christ had done for us'. Four daughters and no sons would normally have been a sore trial to an African, but Festo always insisted he missed none of the kudos of having a son. 'I love my girls—I would never exchange them.' He was horrified to discover that some village women, feeling sorry over his lack of sons, were trying to get Mera to drink evil potions they had brewed up which guaranteed that the next baby would be a son. Gently he explained to them: 'We want only what heaven sends us.'

1955 arrived, and with it another landmark in the revival: the second great Kabale convention, ten years on from the first. Mera and Festo journeyed back to Kabale, arriving with thousands of others to celebrate the past ten years of the Holy Spirit working among them. There was abundant spiritual vitality throughout East Africa at this time: 'communities of fellowship' in hundreds of hamlets, villages, towns and cities kept in touch with each other through letters, travellers or small gatherings. When that summer many overseas visitors arrived in Kabale and marvelled at the exuberance of the convention, some mistakenly referred to it as 'the East African revival'. They did not realise that the convention was just, as Festo described it, 'an overflow from the daily discipline of the fellowship going on in hundreds of places'.

But Festo was profoundly disturbed to learn of another trend going on in the churches of Kigezi. On a subsequent visit to Kabale he confronted the brethren over their relationship with East African Protestants' traditional enemy: the Roman Catholics. Much of the hostility would later seep into politics (Roman Catholics would be members of the Democratic party or DP, Protestants would be Uganda People's Congress), but even by now the mistrust had deepened to real bitterness since the revival had arrived in the 1930s. The Roman Catholics labelled the revival as fanatical and even demon-inspired. In their turn, the balokole took up a position that was almost martyrdom. They considered the Roman Catholics as evil, worse enemies even than the pagans (as the Roman Catholics claimed to be Christians, but did not preach, in balokole eyes, the true Gospel).

James Katarikawe, who lived in Kabale at this time, was honest about it: 'We hated them, and they hated us.' Canon Balaba and the CMS missionaries were counted as the Protestant leaders, and the RC missionaries 'led' the Catholics. Such was the tense situation when Festo arrived for a visit. James later realised: 'Festo came. He saw. He preached.'

They all sat in Kabale Cathedral one Sunday morning and listened wide-eyed as Festo preached in a way he had never done before. He suddenly announced: 'I have noticed there is terrific hatred between you all and the Roman Catholics. But I want to tell you that you can't be a man of God and nourish hatred.' He went on to tell his astounded congregation: 'You should *love* the Roman Catholics. Christ died for them as well.' The most hated local RC was a Mr G. Festo named him that morning and added, 'If I met Mr G., I would embrace him because Christ has died for him.' Most of the congregation reeled out after the service, 'deeply offended'. In a flurry of whispers in the sunshine the most charitable comments were 'Festo simply doesn't understand. If he did, he would not be talking like this. He has been in Tanganyika too long.'

It was to take several years before many balokole realised 'we were so blind', and accepted what Festo was saying. 'We'd felt our hatred was justified—we argued that the Roman Catholics were trying to destroy the word of God, so hatred was our only possible response.'

Festo's sermon lingered as a baffling irritant long after he returned to Tanganyika. The brethren at Kabale felt he had badly let them down and resented it. Only 'gradually did we realise how wrong we were', according to Katarikawe. 'Not in our understanding of the Gospel, but in our reaction to the Catholics.' But even a few years later when Festo stressed he would vote RC Democrat if the candidate was good, and not along party political lines, he appalled the local brethren.

In 1956 Festo and Mera celebrated the start of their tenth year in Dodoma. Tanganyika was home now, though daily life was as difficult as ever. Hardest of all, perhaps, was the constant illness. Despite mosquito nets the whole family succumbed to malaria again and again. When both the little girls had it at once, Festo tied one to the seat at the back of his bike and, with Charity falling out of the box on the front, he ferried them in and out of Dodoma. Mera's cupboard had become a small dispensary all on its own, and she learned how to give the necessary injections.

It was soon evident that 1956 was to be a memorable year. First came news that Karegyesa, Festo's uncle, had finally decided to wholeheartedly 'surrender to Jesus' after fifteen years of struggle. There was a staggering change in him:

He returned thousands of shillings to people he had falsely fined. People he had oppressed he summoned and asked to forgive him. He emptied his bank account and gave back many head of cattle. All knew that the chief had changed, and his enemies became his friends.[3]

Shortly after this came more news, this time sad: Karegyesa had been taken ill and died. At his funeral, Festo preached by popular demand. It was a great gathering, with Christians 'singing "Hallelujah" and speaking the praises of the Saviour. The occasion became a resurrection as well as a burial because a number of people came to the Lord, including his own elder brother, another uncle of mine who had been a staunch pagan.'

Festo saw his cousin, Philemon, at the funeral. With Karegyesa dead, the British had plans to make his son Secretary General of the whole of Kigezi district—directly responsible to the English for all the Saza chiefs.

Festo and Mera returned happily to Dodoma where, shortly afterwards, yet another piece of unexpected news broke—this time most definitely good. Bishop Stanway, at this time the Education Secretary, and with whom they had become close friends, had discovered that Festo would be able to obtain a bursary from the Tanganyika Government to go to London for a year and do a diploma in education. Free education in England! At first the Kivengeres were astounded at the idea, but with Stanway's encouragement Festo soon agreed. He was as keen as any East African to get all the education he could. Plans were swiftly made and it was agreed that Festo would take Mera and the girls back to Kabale in August, and then fly on to London for the beginning of term in September.

Ten years is a long time in a developing territory and much had changed in Uganda. The route home had been better for some time: a network of 3,000 miles of all-weather roads had been built. Another sign of the times: near where Festo's grandfather had once ruled, dangerous for its many predatory beasts, the Government had recently set a national park—to preserve the wildlife for the benefit of tourists from Europe.

The family arrived in Kabale, dirty and exhausted as always

after such trips, to find Lilian Clarke had swept out and aired her little guest house in preparation. Mera and the girls moved in, while Festo went on to Kampala, and then on to Entebbe Airport (built only five years before). At thirty-six he was about to leave Africa for the very first time.

CHAPTER TEN

FIRST TRIPS TO AUSTRALIA AND BRITAIN

1957–1959

To London University; early English revival contacts; tour with William Nagenda; return to Dodoma; decision to return to Uganda; Bishop Stanway offers trip to Australia; and so on to the Aborigines; Solomon Islands; New Guinea.

FROM ENTEBBE IT WAS a sixteen hour plane trip to London. Festo took his first ever international flight with his usual aplomb: 'It didn't bother me.' He was keen to become an associate of London University's Institute of Education.

Two of the early pioneers of the Ruanda Mission, the Barhams (now retired), met Festo at Heathrow Airport in London. Lawrence Barham drove them home to Herne Hill— the first home in England that Festo ever entered. He stayed with the Barhams for his first three months of study at London University, until the hour-long bus rides each way persuaded him to seek a room at the Alliance Club, a hotel at 2 Bedford Square, London, run by the Evangelical Alliance for overseas students. Those long bus rides had only two advantages: they gave Festo some idea of the 'bewildering vastness of London', with its bombed buildings under dirty snow; and also the endless waiting in the chill for a bus gave him a chance to chat with other passengers at the bus-stops. Later, English friends would always marvel at how Festo could turn even a casual conversation with total strangers around to Christ.

Once very early on, it was two strangers who approached Festo first, in order to help him out of a difficult spot. He had taken an underground train 'with great apprehension' and when he reached his station and got off, he was bewildered.

How could I get out? A mass of humanity was passing me. It seemed to know where it was going, but I was too proud to ask. Then I saw two wonderful words written in electric lights: 'WAY OUT'. My, that was good news! I followed the arrows ... they led me to a moving staircase. For a while I watched other people get onto it and go up. Finally my need to get out began to overcome my fear of the moving stairway. Slowly ... I put one foot on the escalator.

Of course, the escalator, being automatic ... didn't wait for me to get more courage ... it took the leg![1]

Festo was toppling backwards when two Englishmen grabbed him—realising 'I was a stranger, in trouble ... They put what I call "gentle pressure". Firmly, but without embarrassing me, they got me onto the staircase with both feet.'

Festo later put the experience to good use by adding it to his collection of homely examples to illustrate truths of the Christian life. For example: 'God, in Christ, has provided a beautiful, gracious escalator to him. Just step on by faith, with both feet (!) and Jesus Christ takes all that you are and all that you have and before you know it, you are on the way—with praise!'

Festo worked hard. Weekdays were spent at London University's huge Institute of Education, where he attended lectures and seminars in education and methods of teaching in Africa, as well as geography. He was given a report to write in order to gain his associateship (AULIE), and tackled 'On the Development of the Teaching of Regional Geography in Secondary Schools in England in Relation to Her Educational System Compared with that of Tanganyika.' It ran to 110 pages and was written mainly in the Institute's library.

In the preface he mentions London itself.

To the writer, London gallaries, concert halls, and Christian churches have been a means of enlightenment in many ways ... The opportunities of travelling ... meeting people in trains, in their homes, in tea-rooms and in parks, and in places of worship, has itself been a valuable experience.

Festo suffered comparatively little culture shock in London. The English reserve did not baffle him: 'I'd learned the quickest way to know people is to open your heart to them.' Another great advantage he had over many foreign students was the amount of contacts he had in London the minute he arrived—mostly ex-missionaries.

Then there was the outspoken English evangelist, Roy Hession. Hession had been deeply involved in the Ugandan revival for some years now, and introduced Festo from many a church pulpit. Many English Christians were deeply interested in the lessons Kabale had learned about revival.

There were also the families of old friends. One was a young Cambridge University student, Richard Bewes. His father, Canon Cecil Bewes, had been Canon of Mt Kenya. Canon Cecil had known 'and loved' Festo from the day the Ugandan had begun to appear at revival conventions in Kenya.

Soon after this, William Nagenda came to England, and the two Ugandans were invited to Cambridge University to speak to the Cambridge University Intercollegiate Christian Union (CICCU). Richard Bewes went along. He sat on the floor (Festo and William had attracted a huge crowd) and warmed to the merry way in which Festo spoke of the Kabale revival. 'He said things like, "Oh, we used to just preach our heads off!" This impressed me—I'd grown up in Kenya, and yet had never heard Africans preach so casually, so freely before.' Nagenda, on the other hand, Bewes found 'unfathomable', 'intense', even 'unsettling'. 'But Festo couldn't read people's thoughts ... and he seemed so much more like one of the boys, with his irrepressible, infectious high spirits and joy in his faith.'

Certainly, Festo had great cultural mobility. His twenty years at mission school had given him not only fluency in English, but familiarity with western idiom and ways. While remaining African to the Africans, Festo was already English among the English, and in years to come would always slide easily back and forth between the two cultures. (Though, at Namirembe Guest House in Kampala, where he always stayed when fresh off the plane from abroad, the staff referred to him affectionately as the 'black white man'.) Yet Richard found Festo's ability to acclimatise 'an utter amazement. He'd been a spirit worshipper in skins looking after calves in the hinterland, and now he was preaching in fluent English, and brilliantly, at Cambridge University! It was astounding!'

Festo made several more friends at the Alliance Club itself,

which in those days provided a bedsit home for about thirty
students at any one time. One special friend was the warden, Mr
Leslie Thompson. He was a West Indian Christian who as a jazz
trumpeter, had played with Louis Armstrong and also Edmundo
Ros for many years. At the meal-table one night, Festo discovered his name was already well known to another resident
who was passing through on holiday from Birmingham University. He was an engineering student, Gottfried Osei-Mensah.
Osei-Mensah was from Ghana, where 'Festo in those days was
one of the three young African leaders of the revival known to
us in West Africa'. (The others 'known' were John Mpaayei and
John Gatu of Kenya.) Osei-Mensah found Festo stimulating but
at times faintly alarming. 'He could suddenly ask you such
penetrating spiritual questions.' Along with a senior medical
student from the Westminster Hospital, a Dr Felix Konetey
Ahulu, the three formed an occasional but warm friendship that
was resumed whenever they could spare time to be together.
Konetey Ahulu was no stranger to revival: his father was the
minister of the largest Presbyterian Church in Accra, Ghana.

In the 1950s the evangelical wing of the Anglican Church
often felt more at home with Free Church evangelicals than with
Anglicans of other traditions. In addition to making friends with
many Baptists, Festo began going along to hear the famous
Welsh Independent Free Churchman, Dr Martyn Lloyd-Jones,
at Westminster Chapel every Sunday evening. He found the fiery
Welshman 'very impressive'. Dr Lloyd-Jones, in his turn was a
firm supporter of the revival, and helped Festo where he could—
which included lending him Christian classics from his own
library. Festo devoured the books: reading was his favourite
pastime.

But as far as Sunday worship went, Festo had settled at All
Souls', Langham Place, which was not only the mecca for
evangelical Anglicanism, but had the additional merit of being
near his hostel. The rector was then the Revd John Stott, later
to become an 'unthroned bishop' of evangelical Anglicanism.
Unaware that one of the greatest spiritual crises of his life would
someday take place within that All Souls' sanctuary, Festo went
enthusiastically along each Sunday. His African mind decided
that All Souls' and Westminster Chapel held 'very tidy' services

with 'time-conscious' people in mind, and that the general tone was very 'reserved' in comparison to the cheery, effervescent swing of a service back home. However, he accepted that this was worship English style, and heartily joined in. His enjoyment of these straightforward Anglican evangelical services was a measure of just how far he had 'broadened' from the balokole stress on public confession, public repentance and public weeping. (Some brethren dropping into All Souls' from Kabale would have wondered if there was truly 'a saved man' among them.)

But Festo wanted to do more than just attend services; he wanted to share his testimony whenever and wherever he could. And there was no shortage of chances. In addition to the Sunday afternoon fellowship meetings held at the Alliance Club itself, one early opportunity came when he was invited to be one of the special guest speakers at a Missionary Convention held at London's Central Hall, Westminster. Other opportunities would include being a regular speaker at 'The King's Own Bible Class' at Holy Trinity, Aldershot. Then there was the large Christian Union at Guys' Hospital where 'Festo spoke in his own very gentle, inimitable way: with his unpretentious, warm sense of humour'.

Other Christian Unions heard about Festo's testimony by word of mouth, and also invited him—again and again. One was the Tate and Lyle Christian Union. Another was the House of Commons' Christian Union. A friend found the politicians 'loved Festo for his simplicity and directness'. Another opportunity arose with the 300–400 West Indians of the 'West Indian International Christian Fellowship', and Festo, Dr Felix Konetey-Ahulu and Martyn Lloyd-Jones were among the many regular speakers.

By the end of that first year, Festo had contacts with Christians right across England. He loved the English Christians he met, but felt sad that 'many didn't take the Bible as seriously as they ought to have done'. Gottfried Osei-Mensah sensed Festo's spiritual seriousness.

When he spoke, he was so clear and penetrating that you realised you were being searched by the Holy Spirit. Yet Festo was not a critical person—of others or of their traditions. I realised he was truly a very godly man, and knew then he would make an impact wherever he went.

But not through sheer force of personality. 'Though Festo was outgoing, he was not an extrovert. When with a group he never hammed it up or chased the limelight.'

Festo's preaching, of course, had to be fitted in around a heavy academic workload. It was a demanding schedule, but Festo never considered lightening it. A clue to his urgency in preaching is found in a letter he wrote to Frances Rea, a close English friend, in late May of 1957, from Bedford Place. She had shared with him her shyness about talking over her faith with some friends and he replied:

> It is not easy for me to give you advice on what you can do, for I am no expert myself. But Frances, supposing you had cancer (very crude example!) and then luckily you met a specialist who knew how to treat that cancer—and you got well again. Then one day you noticed that the people you live with show signs of the same disease— perhaps in a smaller way than yours—what would be your natural reaction to such a situation? Say nothing and let them go on, lest by telling them of your problem and how it was met, you make them uncomfortable? The latter would be the most unusual attitude, wouldn't it? And supposing one day they discover the specialist themselves, and then later discover that you too had suffered from the same disease and had found that same physician—and yet all these years you never told them what had happened! They would certainly think you had behaved in an unusual way, wouldn't they? So, my dear Frances ... it is not the technique that our Lord wants of us, but a spontaneous testimony of his goodness and mercy—and that should be natural to you and me ... Tell him you want to do what he has saved you for and he will give you grace.

* * *

Meanwhile Mera lived with the girls in Lilian Clarke's guest house until a little house on Rugarama hill was found. Though she and Festo kept in regular touch with warm, affectionate letters, the burden of raising four lively daughters by herself was a heavy one, especially as money was short. At times she struggled against loneliness and resentment that she should be left on her own for months on end. Yet she always fully supported Festo in his ministry. She never complained to Festo during his brief stops at home. She never complained to her daughters. 'Mummy always seemed calm and in control. When we were young she only ever spoke of Daddy's preaching with enthusiasm.'

Festo returned to Kabale in August of 1957, collected his family and they all returned to Dodoma without delay, where Festo was urgently needed. Noel Bythell, headmaster once again, was having difficulty keeping the school running smoothly with several new staff and other changes. 'I knew I was much better at teaching geography now, but in the depth of my heart, I was also increasingly aware that God was calling me for full-time service. But I didn't know how this was to be.' He began to pray about his next move.

Meanwhile, there was a new and irresistible force abroad in Tanganyika: nationalistic politics. Independence was pencilled in for December 1961. Festo was a Ugandan, and his own country was also approaching independence. As all the secondary schools in the territory had become the centres for political enthusiasm and debate, his colleagues at the ASS certainly provided any amount of discussion he could possibly have desired.

But all the political turmoil affected Festo very little. He never entertained any illusions as to the future: he never expected paradise to be ushered in with independence—not even under the popular TANU (Tanganyika African National Union) led by Julius Nyerere. In this respect he had a practically identical attitude to that of Assistant Bishop Yohana Omari, whom the missionaries all considered 'a very sane' revivalist. For when Omari went on visitation and was greeted with an excited crowd yelling '*uhuru*' (freedom) he would calm them all down, say he didn't want to hear 'uhuru' just then, and talk about another sort of 'uhuru': 'If the Son makes you free, you will be free indeed' (John 8:36).

Festo followed Omari's example, capitalising on the all-pervading nationalism to remind his hearers that they could be

now 'citizens of heaven'. Not that he didn't sympathise with
their desire to be masters of their own country, as one incident
that happened about this time reveals. Festo and a friend, Daniel
Manase Kija, were in Mwanza and went down to the station,
from where Festo was going to travel to Dodoma. Festo had
booked a berth in a mail-train coach well beforehand, but the
station master came and told him he could not have it. The
reason? An Asian gentleman had booked the other berth in it
and the station master was sure the Asian would not be willing
to travel with an African in the same compartment.

Festo was not pleased. 'Why should you not ask him?' he said
firmly. 'Let the Asian come and I will travel with him down to
Dodoma. If he refuses, let him find another seat.'

Although the station master objected, Festo was adamant.
'The Asian will either have to travel with me, or make other
arrangements.'

In the end, when the Asian arrived, he was very amenable to
travelling down to Dodoma with Festo. Festo left Mwanza still
angry with the station master. The humiliation lingered.

However, Festo's 'sense of call by Christ to his service', as a
friend put it, took away any ambition whatsoever for political
advancement. There were certainly opportunities for literate
men to rise to prominent political leadership in the new African
governments which were on the eve of appearing, and many of
Festo's contemporaries took this course. But political power was
never a temptation to Festo. Although he was never one to say,
as some revivalists did, that Christians had no proper part in
national politics, Festo believed that God had quite another
course for him to follow. A friend later believed 'he sought and
found God's perfect will for him. As with the Apostle Paul,
"what has happened to me has really served to advance the
gospel" (Phil 1:12). So it was with Festo.'

But soon the Kivengeres began to question their future in
Dodoma. It was one thing to send Peace home to Uganda, but
all the girls? Then, too, the coming national upheavals in
Tanganyika would involve many changes in the schools under
the new government. This was a time for long-term workers
(and Festo, with thirteen years behind him at ASS, was by
now the longest serving African teacher there) to take stock,

to consider bringing this phase of their life's work to a conclusion.

Then came news from the Ruanda Mission in Kabale that there was a vacancy coming up as assistant schools' supervisor for Kigezi District. It was offered to Festo on the off-chance that he might be interested. Festo prayed as to what he should do. He wanted to return to Kabale, but 'at forty, I began to feel I was getting on in years. I wanted to be in full-time evangelism. I did not want to be an assistant schools' supervisor: I felt it would be just a waste of time for me.' He felt frustrated.

From here, events moved quickly to bring him to a decision to accept the job all the same. For that summer Bishop Stanway told him it was time that a team of 'revival brethren' visited Australia. Bishop Stanway wanted the revival to be shared with Australian churches so faithfully supporting this work in Tanzania, but not yet benefiting from it themselves. Also, he wanted the Australians to meet his new assistant bishop, Yohana Omari, the first Tanganyikan in the job. Most of the CMS in Tanganyika were from Australia, and Stanway had decided that Omari should widen his contacts to include the CMS home team.

But a problem arose: Omari had little formal education, and his English was poor. However Festo, Stanway knew, taught English at the ASS and was fluent in the language. Soon a plan was agreed: Omari and Festo would go together to Australia, following an itinerary that the CMS would set up right across the continent. They would leave in December: Omari to preach in Swahili and Festo to translate into English—and also to give his own testimony.

But such a lengthy tour would be impossible if Festo stayed on the staff at ASS. So he swiftly arranged that on his return from Australia he would take up his new job in schools supervision for Kigezi District. His resignation from the Alliance School would be effective as from the end of 1958.

Ironically, it was Mera who found it most difficult to leave Dodoma—she had put such a terrific effort into making it her home. 'The fellowship is going wonderfully, but shouldn't we give it another two years?' Such questioning as hers was common between many mission couples at this time. With

Independence coming, 'the firm ground on which we stood was shaking and we were seeking God's guidance with regard to the future well in advance,' Bythell later explained.

But Festo's intention had not been to *lead* anything: 'I knew any signs of revival had never come through me. It had come through Christ. All I had done was to share the great joy of Christ with the Tanganyikans.' Of course,

> because we were human, we'd be proud when certain things happened. We would be tempted to say: 'Look, look what we've done.' But we knew that to take any credit was spiritual pride, and we had to repent of this. Whatever happened was the result of God working in people's hearts. Our testimony was only given because he'd sent us to give it. In Kabale we had also learned that in revival God uses *all* his people, and you never really know anyone who is particularly being used.

Perhaps Festo's assessment of what he had accomplished during those thirteen years reveals just what God had accomplished in him. 'I didn't think I had accomplished much other than to share my great joy in Christ with the Tanganyikan people.' Yet in humbly doing so, he had helped start the trickle of revival which, by 1958, had swelled to a great flood through central and eastern Tanganyika in the Anglican, Lutheran, Mennonite and Moravian churches.

In fact in later years, Festo and Mera would always speak of their years in Tanganyika as nothing but a time of 'great blessing' for themselves. 'It was thirteen years of real joy! We later praised God for our time there: we learned to rely on him, and to appreciate the beauty of a very simple lifestyle.' As for the problems? 'They gave us an opportunity to learn that the "joy" spoken of in the New Testament means the ability to take adverse circumstances and turn them into chances to see the creative hand of God. This was life indeed!'

Festo's last month in Tanganyika was spent conducting evangelistic missions across the territory. He travelled from Arusha to Morogoro. As people heard the news of his impending return to Uganda at the end of 1958, the meetings became a series of fond farewells, or more accurately, 'till we meet again's. The Tanganyikans, in fact, insisted he was one of them now, and that they were letting him go to Uganda only as one of their missionaries. Even Festo, in a rare moment of introspection, found the thought of returning to Uganda strange: 'I was a Tanganyikan by now!' He spoke Swahili so like a native that everyone always assumed he was a Tanganyikan.

Mera prepared to go in a more practical way: she packed up the household. After final farewell services in December 1958, the day of leaving dawned. The girls found it all 'terribly exciting, though we found it very sad as well—it was our home by now'. Festo and Mera could still carry all their worldly possessions, with a little help now from the girls. They left the wobbly bench behind for the next unsuspecting inhabitants.

Back in Kabale, they moved into the little three-room house that Mera had used during her time as matron. Festo helped the family to settle in, including Mera's ailing mother, Miriam, a shining Christian, who was now weakened by arthritis. Mera was offered work as a matron at the Hornby High School and the girls were enrolled in school. Then Festo caught a lift to Kampala and thence to Entebbe to catch a plane for Nairobi, where he met up with Bishop Yohana Omari. Together the two caught the flight for Bombay and on to Singapore. There they changed for Australia, landing at Perth.

The CMS home officer had worked out a very busy itinerary for them as the Australians were very eager to welcome the first-ever Africans to come on an evangelistic tour of their country. In friendly laid-back Aussie fashion, they opened their homes and hearts to the two visitors.

For the next six months in car after car, interspersed by occasional flights, Omari and Festo worked their way from the care of one CMS regional secretary to the next, right across the country. They spoke at churches, youth rallies, summer schools and all manner of conferences.

After Adelaide around the turn of the year, late January found them staying near the cathedral precinct in Melbourne. Festo wrote to Lilian: 'Time has been so hectic. The Lord has indeed answered your prayers in the salvation of many here ... The hunger among the youth is staggering.'

Despite the excitement of his new lifestyle, Festo kept himself in firm check. He knew the dangers. In a letter to Lilian he admitted: 'We continually have to repent of self-congratulation in these things—how subtle is our sinful nature! Praise the Lord, Jesus is able to subdue it, and to him we continually look for grace.'

In fact, they were kept so busy in Melbourne that in the end they spent nearly a month visiting churches and groups around the city. Then it was off to Sydney and following that to Canberra, before catching a plane for Tasmania.

The meetings were a great success. At the first one Omari had preached in Swahili, with Festo translating and then giving his own testimony. But then Omari decided he wanted to piece together the bits of English he had and preach his own sermons. The Australians listened carefully to the result, which was 'quite beautiful' according to Festo.

So, after that first meeting, Omari and Festo devised a new pattern which suited them well. East African style, they 'shared' the pulpit at every meeting. Omari would begin, and after ten or fifteen minutes simply run out of English and have to sit down. Then Festo would stand up, with all the English of eighteen years in the classroom at his command, all the poise of a royal Muhima, the clear speech of a trained teacher, the oratorial skills of a Muhima fireside childhood, the passion and conviction of a deep devotion to Christ, and the persuasiveness of a born evangelist. His stories and deceptively simple Bible exposition held his audiences in thrall. He gripped their interest with his experience-oriented approach, he won their sympathy, made them chuckle, cry and think about their souls. Dozens upon dozens were converted. The Australians took the two African to their hearts, and as their popularity spread, more and more invitations flowed in.

One Australian Christian described Festo's preaching as that 'of a very creative mind which, with revival brethren pre-suppositions, dealt very imaginatively with the Bible. It was a unique, very Christo-centric appeal to Scripture: East Africa's special contribution to the world church's understanding of the gospel.'

In fact, so popular were the two, that as early as the end of January it had been decided that when Omari returned to Tanganyika (after all, he did have a diocese to attend to), Festo should stay on. Bishop Stanway arranged for Festo's visit to be extended (the missionaries were happy for him) until November, and the Australians got busy planning the best itinerary for him. 'I felt my dream of full-time ministry was at last coming true.'

It was decided that the Rev. Lance Shilton (later Dean of St Andrew's Cathedral, Sydney) should accompany Festo on a mission among the Aborigines. By 1959 there had been Christians ministering among the Aborigines for many years with hardly a conversion: those on the mission stations obediently attended the services, but that was as far as anyone got with them.

So in May Lance Shilton and Festo set off for the Northern Territory and spent a month touring the Aboriginal mission stations in Arnhem Land, North Australia. Having wanted full-time evangelistic work for twelve years in Tanzania, to begin it among the Australians was unexpected!

It was the first time Festo had met an Aborigine, but it was also the first time the Aborigines had ever even imagined an African. 'I created a sensation!' recalled Festo, albeit an un-demonstrative one: the Aborigines stared and stared for all they were worth. Festo just smiled at them.

Shilton and Festo were booked to visit five mission stations, meeting several hundred full-blooded Aboriginal people of many different tribes, each with a different language. At each place Festo was to follow a simple routine: he would give a simple gospel address and wait for audience reaction. Had this been Africa the room would have been vibrant with emotion. But at the first station 'I may as well have addressed stones. There was no reaction whatever, not even in their eyes!' Thoroughly shaken by such a non-experience, Festo prayed long that night. He reasoned that the missionaries had, after all, warned him. 'I began to wonder why I had come.' He even chatted with Shilton about it, saying, 'I think we made a mistake in coming here.' For Festo, it was the response to the message which was all important: though so indifferent to hardship that he could walk fifty miles through bush to preach back home, and count the effort well worth it when people responded, here a couple of 'dead' meetings shook him so badly that he thought of going back.

It was something of a crisis. For the first time in his life here was the opportunity to be a full-time preacher, and his first service on his own, and—nothing. And all this in the outback of northern Australia. But as he prayed again the following night, searching his heart and asking for wisdom, 'the Spirit began to convict me. "The problem is not with the Aborigines," he said. "It is with you. You had already made up your mind about them when you got here. You did not pour out your heart to them. You were speaking to yourself, so of course they could not hear."' Festo realised then that he'd been preaching with a bias; 'I had created my own barriers.'

His response was simple. 'I knelt down and asked forgiveness for my cold attitude. The Lord said, "All right. You just speak to them as my precious people for whom I died and forget everything you heard about them."'

'We had a small group of about twenty that evening, and I don't know what happened. I couldn't stop, and they responded. I saw one girl with tears streaming down her face. From then on it was quite different. God did a work.'[2]

It was the first time the Aborigines at that mission station had responded in such a way and the missionaries were 'quite shocked'. Festo pondered the lesson. 'God had taught me something crucial: that the key to communication with people was not words, but love. When once you love people, then you will find ways and means of putting it across.'

Sometimes Festo's honesty amused Shilton, especially on the day the two had to catch a small boat to get from Groote Eylandt to Rose River on the Australian mainland. The forty-eight mile journey across open sea lasted a miserable eight hours. Festo sat near the edge of the small boat, and Shilton in the middle. Shilton recalls:

With the constant tossing of the heavy waves, my face became the colour of light green and Festo's a dark green. He kept looking over to me. That night before we retired, he came to me and said: 'I want to walk in the light with you. I have to confess to the sin of jealousy. When we were on that boat today I knew it would be easier if I could make my way to the middle of the boat, but it was impossible. That's when jealousy filled my heart because you were there!' We laughed together.

Word travelled fast among the Aborigines, and from being shy and distant, Festo found everywhere 'the people became so friendly' that it began to embarrass him. They followed him around the compounds, watched the way he ate, stared at his clothes, his hair, his skin. At the mission station called Oenpelli, a missionary teacher was intrigued when one boy came to class with a handkerchief across his head with a knot at each corner. The boy was too shy to explain, but one of the other boys solved the mystery: he had tried to cut his hair like Festo, but had made a mess of it.

There came a moving glimpse into just why the Aborigines were struck by Festo. One Aboriginal man stood up in a meeting and said,

> We are so glad that a brother in Christ has come here. He speaks of the same Jesus we know; he speaks of the same love of God we know. He tells us these things which the missionaries have told us for years, but now we can see clearly that Jesus Christ is also the Saviour of the black people.

And yet it was more than skin colour. Shilton was impressed by how 'Festo spoke to them about their tribal customs and how some customs in his land were similar to theirs. He talked about sacred mountains, rocks and creeks.'

Festo was so popular that some of the Aborigines wanted to take him on a 'walkabout' deep in the bush. 'There we will prepare a great delicacy for you to eat,' they enthused, 'a kangaroo tail.' Festo, who had grown up drinking cows' blood, was appalled. 'Eating a kangaroo tail in the bush sounded very primitive. I was terrified.' He politely backed out.

News of his successful mission reached government ears. One bright government official asked, 'Please would Mr Kivengere consider becoming a government officer in the Northern Territory and working with the Aborigines, as, sir, they listen to you more than they listen to us!' Festo toyed with the idea. He wrote to Mera and asked how she would like to live in the Australian outback. Mera replied briefly: absolutely not. So Festo dropped the idea.

Yet the work he left behind him that month went on to bear fruit. Shilton testifies to this: 'Twenty-seven years after Festo's visit, my wife visited the same Aborigine communities ... Many who are now Christian leaders remember with deep gratitude the ministry of Festo who inspired them to give Christian leadership to their own people.'

At the end of June Festo returned South, where CMS told him that he had an invitation to spend July in the South Sea, or Solomon Islands. It had come from Ken Griffiths, then chairman of the board of directors of the South Sea Evangelical Mission, who had heard Festo and Omari preach one morning in an Anglican church in Sydney. Mr Griffiths knew of the East African Revival, and already had a real burden 'for a deepening work of the Holy Spirit on the national churches in the Solomons'. Festo gladly accepted the invitation and it was decided that Mr Griffiths and he should make a tour of the islands, visiting six main centres.

It was a long journey. The Solomon Islands are situated to the south-east of Papua New Guinea, 1,000 miles from the coast of northern Queensland. Mr Griffiths and Festo did not waste a moment. They spoke in their first meeting less than two hours after stepping off the plane. Hundreds came. They then set off for the island of Malaita on the mission yacht 'Evangel', which became 'home' for the next three weeks as it slipped along the coastline of Malaita.

From the very first day, the tour of the main stations of Guadalcanal and Malaita was an immense success, and an encouragement to all. Festo thoroughly enjoyed the love and joy of an already vibrant church (a few of whom had been cannibals) who were eager to hear insights into how the East Africans had deepened their walk with Christ. He simply shared the blessings and lessons hammered out in nearly thirty years of continuous revival. The Revd Jay Filva, later Superintendent of the South Sea Evangelical Church, recalls, 'The non-Christians in our villages responded very well. They were impressed to hear one of their own skin colour able to speak good English, and to expound the word of God challengingly and convincingly.'

Several centres had been chosen on Malaita for the convention's gatherings, including Aukiloina, Afio, Nafinua and Honiara. Each time 'Evangel' moored, there were at least 1,000 Christians eager to greet them. They came from every part of the islands, some by road, others by canoe, from up to three days' journey away. By now a few from Guadalcanal, Makira and Rennell had joined the ship and were part of the tour. It all added up to a 'time of joyous fellowship with the Lord and each other'.

Festo often had four meetings a day to address, generally through one interpreter and sometimes two. He was 'wonderfully sustained in health and spiritual vigour with such a big demand on him', said Mr Griffiths. (Festo, a poor sailor, had heartfelt 'gratitude to the Lord for quiet seas'.)

At the end of July 'Evangel' sailed back to Honiara, where the Christians gave them a rapturous welcome. They presented Festo with the nicest thing they could imagine and a great delicacy: a large green sea turtle, alive and kicking for all it was worth. 'You eat it,' they told Festo, dumping it in his arms. 'It's delicious as a soup.' Festo stammered out his thanks and struggled to hold on to the turtle. If the delegation had only stayed a little longer, they would have seen him slowly turning as green as the turtle. He later gave it to members of the crew, 'who would enjoy it very much indeed'.

When they flew out the following morning, Festo found that he might have 'left the dear brethren of the Solomons in the body, but I was still with them in spirit'.

He stopped off briefly at a mission station in Papua New Guinea to preach to the missionaries. He would one day return for a much longer visit.

The rest of the summer was spent on mainland Australia, preaching in churches, at youth rallies and conferences. All too soon it was over. Festo, who had made friends throughout the continent, had no way of knowing that he would ever see them again.

Throughout the several legs of the long journey home to East Africa, Festo prayed and pondered his future as schools' supervisor in Kigezi—a job for which he had no real experience and which did not really attract him. In a moment of self-revelation, he was utterly certain now that evangelism was what God had called him to do. 'These strangers on the other side of the world had been used to confirm the calling, revealing that in evangelism, culture and language did not matter as long as there was love.' He now knew 'that I could reach any kind of person, not just Africans'.

But as Africa drew nearer, so did the supervisory job. 'I began to feel confused. I did not want to be schools' supervisor. For me it was a waste of time. I had always enjoyed teaching, and felt I had a vocation for it, but now I knew evangelism had replaced it completely.'

Festo was nearly forty and badly baffled. 'If God wanted me to be an evangelist, why had I already spent twenty years in a classroom? And now that I was doubly confirmed in evangelism, I was returning to only more education. What was God trying to say to me?'

All the same, at the end of 1959, fresh beginnings lay ahead for him: a new decade, his fortieth birthday, and Uganda's independence.

CHAPTER ELEVEN

WINDS OF CHANGE
1960–1961

Schools supervisor of Kigezi district; schools work with Lilian Clarke; translating for Billy Graham; to Switzerland for church leaders' conference; cripple healed; calls from Zambia, Tanganyika; feels call to full-time evangelism.

JANUARY 1960. The British and French were busy winding up what remained of their empire in Africa. And none too soon. The British Prime Minister, Harold Macmillan, described the strength of African national consciousness as 'the wind of change, blowing through the continent'.[1]

The wind was blowing strongly through Uganda. Everywhere there was a mood of vibrant expectancy. Uganda had never been in better shape as the date of independence—1962—approached.

But a wind, however refreshing, also blows up a lot of dirt and debris, as Festo found to his cost before he even stepped foot back in Uganda. While still abroad in December he heard from one or two friends that tongues were wagging about his new job. Why, people demanded, was he having to work as Lilian Clarke's assistant? Why should an African still need a white woman as boss?

Thirteen years before, when the Kivengeres had left Uganda, such a question would never have arisen. The 1940s had been the heyday of colonialism, and so far from resenting a white woman's leadership, most African men would have felt it a privilege to have been given the chance of assisting her. But now there was widespread bitterness and determination that Africa must unite, be black and independent if it ever were to take its proper place on the world stage.

Festo was African and felt the force of the argument. But his faith led him to adopt a different view of things. He took swift action. He wrote first to Lilian, 'When I come back to Kabale and onto the supervisory team, I will come only as your assistant. I have no intention of pushing you out!' He also wrote to his friends, explaining,

> If I can't rejoice in the Lord and have fellowship with Lilian when working under her, then when am I likely to learn the lesson that God's grace is sufficient? If we run into trouble, that is an opportunity for us to go to the cross together, and then we can say, 'Praise God, she's the boss, I'm her assistant. I have a contribution to make to her, and she has one towards me. We will work together as a body.'

Nonetheless, the incident put Festo on his guard. He arrived back in Kabale, alert for other changes brought on by impending independence. It was certainly not difficult to hear about them. Festo's cousin, Philemon, was now Secretary General of Kigezi, and 'warmly welcomed' Festo back to Kabale: 'I often used to drop in to get Festo's advice over problems in running the district.' Certainly things had changed since the war: there were hard roads, swamp drainage, and even a safari lodge for tourists in Kabale!

Lilian Clarke again lent the Kivengeres her guest house until the house that went with the school job was ready. Festo and Mera had hardly unpacked their boxes before the next jolt came: one Sunday morning worship service in Kabale revealed that the brethren had become caught up in some rather vicious religious politics.

What had happened was this. The ancient hostility between Roman Catholics and Protestants had not died down with the approach of Independence. Instead, national party politics had emerged along old bitter dividing lines, with the result that by 1960 the Archbishop of Uganda, the Rt Revd Leslie Brown, found that in Kigezi 'intimidation and violence were extremely serious'. Festo stepped into the breach in Kabale. It was a brave thing to do. One Sunday morning soon after his return, he again stood in the pulpit of St Peter's Cathedral and pointed out that the balokole were wrong to hate the Catholics. 'A true Christian can't love God and not offer his brothers a forgiving spirit.' He said that it was 'wrong to bring party politics into Christianity', and he added that he would vote for a Roman Catholic if he were the best man for the job. 'We were appalled,' recalled James Katarikawe, who was in church that morning. The most charitable thing the balokole said about him was that he'd been away too long. The Catholics were surprised and confused. Some good came of it: several Catholic clergy became friendly towards this unusual Tanzanian/Ugandan Protestant who didn't hate Catholics, and invited him to take Bible studies for small groups at their churches. When soon after Bishop Brown and the French Roman Catholic Bishop of Mbarara, Bishop Ogez, ordered that a joint letter by them calling for peace be read in all churches in Kigezi and the southwest, it had a considerable effect. It certainly protected Festo from too much criticism.

Meanwhile, the first day of term of January 1960 arrived. Festo resignedly returned to education. His new base was the small Education Office in the Church of Uganda compound on Rugarama hill, next door to Kigezi High School where he had been converted twenty-four years before. He and Lilian Clarke would spend the next two years together ensuring that all of the 150 schools the government had 'selected' in their Kigezi area would be kept up to scratch, that the financial affairs of each school would be kept straight, and that books and other meagre supplies would get through to the teachers.

Festo and Lilian soon agreed on a supervisory strategy. Theirs was obviously a two-fold job: the standard of teaching, with the proper books and facilities for the children must be maintained; and the teachers themselves must be given constant care, advice and encouragement in their isolation. Lilian had left Hornby School in 1946 to found a teachers' training college in Kabale. Festo had a gift for communicating a vision, and the patience to help others see it. The answer was simple: Lilian would concentrate on keeping the teaching up to scratch, and Festo would make sure the teachers stayed up to scratch. Together they would encourage more parents to follow the government guidelines in improving mission 'bush schools' and so qualify to become grant-in-aid government selected schools.

Lilian and Festo's schools were spread out over a couple of thousand square miles of mountainous terrain serviced by poor dirt roads, and often by no roads at all. There were not even tracks to some of the more remote villages. For most of the schools, fortunately, they could use Lilian's car. When Festo politely asked her on their first day out 'on safari' if she would like him to take the wheel, her surprise that he could drive turned quickly to delight. 'After that I had a nice restful time.' A surprising phrase, as Festo was known for his fast driving over rough dirt roads around sharp bends. Lilian's nerves were clearly as steely as his.

Their arrival at a school was an event of great importance. The teachers had no more than to hear the roar of the car engine coming than to be galvanised into action. The conscientious ones cut short the morning break time to summon their pupils back to their desks in order to be seen working hard when Lilian and Festo arrived. While Lilian made sure the teacher had whatever textbooks she could get for him, and enough chalk to last him on a quota of two sticks a day, Festo would run a practised eye over each teacher's lesson book. 'We watched him write things in their books and thought he was reprimanding the teachers. We thought then he was a very big boss indeed!' recalled a former student. If only two lessons had been prepared instead of the five required, Festo had a disconcerting way of immediately wanting to know why!

Festo's talent for motivating others with his cheery, calm self-confidence came into its own. 'We discovered we had nothing to fear if we'd been doing our best,' recalls one. His compassion when they fell into difficulties was obvious—he never lost his temper or threatened; his approach was always one of 'sweet, reasonable' talking. 'He longed to help us recognise our temptations (drinking and smoking were big ones) and learn the best ways of overcoming our weaknesses,' says another. Only persistent and wilful failure evoked a strong warning.

Festo had one message he stressed again and again with teachers throughout Kigezi: the need for self-discipline in order to achieve anything. 'Discipline starts with the teacher,' was his motto. 'The children learn by example.' He also passed on teaching tips learned in Dodoma and London, and would even take classes himself to demonstrate better ways in which certain subjects (especially English and geography) could be taught. A former teacher recalls enjoying these lessons as much as the pupils: 'It was wonderful!'

Festo could be very direct on occasions. When a school in a remote forest region of Kigezi was languishing for lack of a teacher, he insisted: 'One of the teachers in this district *must* go up to that valley. Remember, those children whom you think of as "primitive" are the children of God, and need education like any other child.' 'He finally inspired one of us to volunteer to "go",' recalls a former teacher.

Other times Festo would assign a particular man to a particular job. One day Ezra Mahega was summoned from Kigezi Primary School. He was appalled when Festo announced, 'Look here, brother Ezra, the Holy Spirit has guided us to choose you to become the Head of Bukinda Primary School for Girls.' (It was a school deep in debt, with a wreck of a building.) 'Don't fear, we are behind you, and the Holy Spirit is with you. You are not alone.' Trembling, Mahega could only reply, 'Yes, brother, then I must go.' Festo stood by him, talking the parents into giving Ezra more money to get the school out of its difficulties.

In the course of his travels, Festo made many friendships that would last for the rest of his life. When one young teacher, Ishmael Bugaiga, was getting married to his fiancée, Nora, Festo offered the use of the education car and his own services as chauffeur to drive them the fifty miles from Kinyasano to Kabale after the wedding. Ishmael would later become one of his archdeacons. Other friends at this time were John Bagorogoza (later national head of the Boys' Brigade) and Ernest Shalita, who would one day be his diocesan secretary and later a leader in AEE. Festo also met up again with his friend James Katarikawe, who had shared his home before his marriage in 1943, and was now a teacher.

They all endured one particular crisis together, when some teachers felt driven by poverty to strike over pay. Soon many others thought about joining the strike. Festo got in his car and moved swiftly. He visited the striking teachers and 'talked to us calmly'. His argument was that 'it is not good for a teacher or a medical worker ever to strike: our responsibility is too great'. Yet he did not argue with the teachers. 'He came to us in love, smiling,' one recalls. Most went back to work and the strike quickly collapsed. But Festo argued the teachers' case with the government. He had a strong point: with the children lay the future of independent Uganda. Within a couple of months the wages went up.

Festo also urged his teachers to apply his methods of calm reasoning and talking with regard to their students. 'Don't just beat them,' he said. 'Talk to the naughty student and find out the reason for his behaviour. Then put your point of view to him.' This 'love approach' 'helped the pupils increase their confidence and love for us, and we got excellent results—much better than by anger and beating' found Kashillinga. For this reason the children came to love Festo. But he had other attractions as well, it seems. 'We greatly admired his tie and long socks,' remembers one. 'I wanted my hair to be like Festo's,' remarks another. In the meantime, Festo urged the children to 'put into practice what your teacher tells you', and told them that when he had been young he had done 'many wrong things', but that 'Jesus had forgiven me—and would forgive you too'.

The long hours in the car 'on safari' gave Lilian and Festo time to become great friends. 'He'd regale me with stories of his past: herding the calves as a child.' He once pointed to some cows on a hillside and told Lilian they belonged to his cousin. 'I was incredulous as to how he could know. All the cattle looked the same to me.' Festo just laughed. 'All we Bahima know our cows,' he said. Other missionaries also felt drawn to Festo. 'Many missionaries with difficulties fell into the habit in those years of going to Festo with their problems,' says Lilian. 'He had great discretion, and no one ever felt he was judging them.' This quality had already been recognised by the Ugandans, and that year as he rejoined church life in Kabale 'he was always surrounded by several Ugandans at any one time, all wanting to talk to him'.

Soon Festo had so many opportunities to preach on different missions that he never had a free weekend. Dr Joe Church and the other missionaries welcomed him back on the 'teamus' with great delight. In all, these were tremendously satisfying months for Festo. 'I just wanted with all my heart to communicate the Gospel'—and communicate it he did. In one village a little boy herding calves crept up to the bush church where Festo was preaching. By the time he had finished speaking, the boy's heart was 'bursting'. The boys thought such understanding from such an important person was wonderful, not realising that in their faces Festo was looking at his former self.

However, Festo continued to struggle with personal failures. He would later readily admit that he could be proud, stubborn and thoughtless at times. He did not like to have his decisions interfered with. He and Mera still clashed many times. Festo, though outraged at such a strong-willed wife, was always learning a lot. Afterwards he would sometimes humorously pass the story on:

When you point an accusing finger at your partner, watch out! Three fingers of that hand will be pointing back at you! ... One day my wife and I were preparing for a weekend spiritual conference. In the evening we sat discussing the things we were going to take in the car. It went well until she suggested one thing, and I said, 'No, I don't think we need that, dear.'

I thought she would say, 'Fine darling.' Instead, she explained why we needed it. I explained why we didn't. The more we talked, the farther apart we got. Finally it got late. I stacked my guns and she stacked hers. Our brief prayers were meaningless and we went to bed.

She slept, bless her, but I didn't sleep.

About midnight, the Holy Spirit called me: 'Festo!'

And I said, 'Yes Lord?'

'You aren't sleeping.'

'No, Lord.'

'And of course you are very holy and your wife is a sinner. Does that mean when people are holy they don't sleep? Or is it because you have a burden for your wife? Aren't you really accusing her? And aren't you wasting your time? You wasted the prayer time, you put your wife in the cold, and you are just miserable. You were unnecessarily hard. Now no more talk.'

I said, 'Yes Lord. What shall I do?'

'You must ask for forgiveness.'

'*Now*, Lord?'

'No, no! In the morning.'

So in the morning I said, 'Dear, I'm sorry. It was I who caused that terrible patch of darkness. Please forgive me.'

Bless her, she forgave me, and said: 'No, it was my fault. I was unnecessarily fussy.'

Light came into our darkness and peace came back. We embraced and sang in the bedroom and then went outside to put things in the car. When she put that thing in, I wondered why I had argued over it, and we both went rejoicing in the Lord.

At the conference, the Spirit said, 'Tell the people about it.' I did, and he broke into lives, and mended some nearly broken homes that day.[2]

But Festo did not turn all his failures into success stories from the pulpit. For months at a time he would simply attend the bi-weekly fellowship meetings at Kabale, and quietly 'share with us ways in which he had failed his Lord, and of which he had been forgiven'.

* * *

Soon after Festo's return, exciting news reached Kabale: the American evangelist, Billy Graham, was about to pay his first visit to Africa. His tour of East Africa would include crusades in Moshi (Tanganyika), Kisumu and Nairobi (Kenya). Festo was interested, but also somewhat wary at the news. He had heard rumours that the American evangelist used such a device as 'altar calls' and even let specially prepared choirs sing at the rallies. These things were unknown in East African evangelism, and to Festo sounded quite bizarre. 'These methods were not our methods. All this talk of "going forward", "follow-up paperwork" ... The organisation! The efficiency! This seemed very strange to us. We even wondered how valid the conversions would be: would they "stick"?'

Nevertheless, Festo decided to give Billy Graham the benefit of the doubt, and joined in with national church leaders who were helping with the preparations for the visit. He soon discovered he was going to get a better view of the evangelist than he had anticipated: Billy Graham was speaking at a series of meetings at the foot of Mount Kilimanjaro in Kenya and an interpreter with fluent English and Swahili was urgently needed. Would Festo consider the job? Everyone agreed he had not only the fluency and poise needed to translate before thousands and

Lilian Clarke, circa 1948.

thousands of people, but also the evangelist's urgency to put across the message. Festo readily agreed, and flew to Kenya for the meetings at the end of February.

100,000 people turned out for the crusade meetings at the foot of Mt Kilimanjaro. As Festo joined Dr Graham on the platform before the meeting on that first night, Dr Graham, who knew Festo's reputation as a formidable evangelist of the revival, whispered, 'Don't bother to translate literally. You know what I mean—get that across.' Such a vote of confidence warmed Festo's heart.

So the two preached; Dr Graham in English, Festo repeating his message in Swahili. By the end of the evening, altar call, choir and paperwork notwithstanding, 'Both Billy's preaching and the effect it had on people convinced me that this was indeed a man of God. I realised I had a lot to learn about how God could use different methods and gifts—all to his glory. Even PA systems!'

In addition to the nightly meetings at the huge stadium, Dr Graham also visited a village or two nearby. Several of his team, including Festo, accompanied him. In one of the villages most of the inhabitants were quite obviously under the influence of drink. Dr Graham felt momentarily at a loss. 'What can I possibly say to them?'

'Just talk to them about John 3:16 and trust the Lord,' murmured Festo.

Dr Graham did so, and several were converted. Some weeks later, when he was in England speaking to Cambridge University students at Great St Mary's Church, he gave exactly the same message as he had given to that African village, and many students were converted. 'I learned then something of the power of the simplicity of the gospel of Christ,' Dr Graham said. 'An evangelist is a communicator of a powerful and simple message, and what Festo had said and how he lived brought that fact home to me.'

Soon after, Festo interpreted for Cliff Barrows, Dr Graham's Programme and Music Director, at a Sunday afternoon rally in the stadium at Mombasa. Barrows remembers feeling 'greatly encouraged by the fact that if my message didn't quite fit the situation or didn't make sense in their language or culture, Festo was able to transform it on the spot and preach his own—and certainly the audience wouldn't know the difference!'

What impressed Cliff Barrows most about Festo was 'his radiant smile and his buoyant spirit and personality—evidences of the joy of the Lord, and the Holy Spirit filling his life'.

Festo stayed with the Billy Graham team throughout the three week tour. After Kilimanjaro, they flew south to Burundi, where he translated for Dr Graham in a stadium in the capital of Usumbura. The African Christians loved Billy Graham, and also greatly admired the Ugandan who had been chosen to translate the American's message so 'dynamically, simply and clearly'. A missionary explains Festo's impact on the Africans: 'He was considered to be very good looking, smartly dressed and radiating enthusiasm for God.'

By the end of the East African tour, Dr Graham and Festo were firm friends. Festo was struck by Dr Graham's love and humility: 'When you were with him, his humility gave you the feeling that you were very important, which you knew you were not! ... He was a deeply spiritual man—a very open man.' It seems that the regard was mutual, as Dr Graham was moved by Festo's 'humility and deep spirituality'. In future years he would come to consider Festo as 'one of the most spiritual men I've ever known'.

Festo returned to Kabale exhilarated by what he had seen. He later confided to Dr Graham that the crusade had strengthened his resolve that despite school supervisory jobs, full-time evangelism must also be his goal. In the meantime, he treasured his contact with a man who so obviously shared his passion for saving souls. He never dreamed that it was but the beginning of a lifelong friendship.

*   *   *

Back in Kabale Festo divided his time between his schools supervisory work and helping to prepare for a great convention to be held one weekend in Rugarama hill. Christians from all over Uganda were to come, especially from Kampala and Ankole. Festo was asked to translate the notices into seven different languages, as well as to preach. Another preacher was Matt Nyagwaswa, a Tanganyikan who had heard Festo testify in Mwanza ten years before. Festo eagerly invited him home:

> The warmth with which Festo and Mera received me was very welcoming. I was very much surprised at the way they accepted me just as I was, even though I viewed them at that time as Christian 'giants' and myself as a mere Christian 'baby'. I was impressed by their simplicity and genuine humility.

Festo had another friend for life. (Nyagwaswa later became Bishop of the Africa Inland Church of Tanzania and a leader in AEE in East Africa.)

The convention itself went wonderfully. On the plus side, the Archdeacon of Kigezi suddenly saw the point of what Festo had been saying about the Roman Catholics. He publicly repented, with deep sorrow, of the hatred he had felt towards them. 'From that time on, a friendship of sorts began between us and the

Roman Catholics,' says one Kabale Christian, though others have described it as more of an unarmed truce.

Then disturbing news began to filter through from Kampala. Brother Mondo, with whom Peace had stayed in her schooldays in Kampala, and several other Christians were calling the Church of Uganda to a 'reawakening'. His message was: 'The things we did, ten, twenty years ago, were marks of true spirituality. If we are to be truly spiritual, we must recapture them.' He said it was time for the Christians to 'awake out of sleep' and repent of their incipient worldliness. As 'worldliness' included long hair on women, guitars and insurance policies, it seems really to have been the fear of an older generation of too many changes in too short a time. But the 'reawakened' were very militant, soon insisting that any who did not follow them were not truly saved. 'Reawakening,' Mondo said, 'was the final stage of salvation. You get saved, but it's of no avail if you're not reawakened.'

Festo was alarmed at this new teaching called the 'reawakening' as it seemed a blend of spiritual pride and jealousy. He warned publicly against its dangers, urging Christians not to concentrate on this word 'reawakening' when they were already committed. He and William Nagenda remonstrated with the 'reawakening' —and were furiously criticised. Still, Festo and Nagenda did what they could to 'keep the fellowship', little knowing there would be eleven years of near schism ahead of them. Throughout this difficult time, Festo's line would be: 'The revival has been built on Jesus alone. If we divert, we will go astray.'

Meanwhile, a letter arrived for Festo in the early summer of 1960. It was from Billy Graham. Would Festo like to come to Montreux, Switzerland, in August to attend a short, private conference which Dr Graham was convening for a select group of forty world church leaders: teachers, theologians, and evangelists? The purpose would be to discuss effective evangelism. Also, several of the leaders had been deeply touched by the East African Revival, and wanted an opportunity to meet someone closely involved in it. Festo eagerly accepted, and flew to Geneva, catching the train for Montreux.

For everyone at the conference, it was 'a precious time of fellowship and enriching ministry; but more than this, it was a searching and disturbing week as we gave ourselves to prayer, self-examination and a serious survey of world events and trends', as Revd Dr Stephen Olford of New York later explained:

> As one after another disclosed the startling facts concerning the spread of Communism, Romanism and Islam, we were forced to our knees and to our Bibles for an answer. We were made aware that local church life, itinerant evangelism, and overseas missions played a relevant part in reaching men and women for Jesus Christ.

But the conference was then forced to ask itself some hard questions. 'Had we lost the anointing of the Holy Spirit? Were our methods obsolete? Had we become so absorbed with secondary issues that we had lost sight of priorities?' As usual, position papers were read, addresses given, and discussion, 'sometimes heated', followed. One afternoon in particular, several men almost lost their tempers 'in an attempt to sustain their positions'. Dr Billy Graham in the chair, sought to moderate the debate that was going on, but arguments for and against had reached an impasse. There seemed to be very little hope of harmony, let alone progress.

At this point, Festo stood to his feet. 'There was absolute silence. Up to this point I don't believe he had said a word.' Appealing to the chair, Festo looked around and said very simply,

> Brothers and sisters, I am not a theologian, and I don't pretend to have the training and experience of these great men around me, but I believe there is a solution to the world's problems and, indeed, to every discussion we are having right now.

And then he paused and with 'exquisite reverence' said one word: 'Jesus.' What followed will live in Dr Olford's memory for ever.

> Every person in that room was smitten with conviction and a spirit of brokenness. With a word from Billy Graham we were all on our knees, and for hours prayers of repentance, brokenness, confession and restoration poured forth from every person in the room. God had met us under the spell and power of one word: 'Jesus'.

After such a contribution, no one was surprised when at a later meeting Billy Graham introduced Festo with the words:

'Now we are going to sit at the feet of our African brother, and learn from him!'

*   *   *

Back in Kabale, early in 1961, it was decided that Lilian and Festo should swop jobs: he became the schools' supervisor for Kigezi district and she became his assistant, in charge of all girls' schools. After all, independence was right round the corner. 'But it made no difference,' said Lilian and Festo. 'We carried on just the same way as before.' Both were delighted as more and more parents decided to push their schools forward to qualify for the government's grant-in-aid. More buildings were put up, and money found for qualified teachers.

Another highlight—totally unexpected—of the year took place at the end of one such safari in a village called Nyakageme, where Festo and Lilian found themselves at the end of the school week. On the Sunday Festo was leading the service of about twenty-five worshippers, when a well-known local cripple, a man of about forty, who had crawled into the service, began to weep at Festo's sermon. He said, 'I want to accept the Lord Jesus.' One of the leaders said, 'Well, get up and accept him then.' And the cripple got up, healed. The whole church was electrified, especially the man who had told him to rise. The cripple testified to having found Christ, adding 'And as if that were not enough, he has straightened my legs!'

Festo and Lilian gave him a lift part of the way home after the service, and watched while he walked away into the bush. 'It was a real New Testament miracle, but our joy was not for his straightened legs. He was bound to die one day. We were rejoicing over the miracle of the new life,' said Festo. 'That is the greatest miracle.'

As Uganda approached independence that autumn, the Church of Uganda, knowing the halcyon days of mission society leadership and support were nearly over, faced an enormous problem. There was an extremely small ordained native leadership. 'In many a case when the missionary Mother Hubbard eventually went to her cupboard to get "a black bishop", the cupboard would prove all too bare of men with experience and education.'[3]

Though he was not ordained, Festo was considerably concerned about the problem. With his close contacts with missionaries and church leaders, he could anticipate just how serious it would become in a few years. He and Lilian wrote to four of their outstanding teachers: Ishmael Bugaiga, Stanley Kashillingi, William Rukirande and Ezra Bigaruka. Ishmael recalls the letter: 'Festo said he felt we should all be ordained. He said the future church and also the leaders of the country really needed to be trained and able.' It is indicative of how high the four held Festo in esteem that 'when he explained to us what his vision for the future Church of Uganda was, we felt the Lord was speaking to us through him'.

Festo's vision was of a future church run by well trained, able and mature Christian men who would not only give leadership to the Christians, but also act as a guiding moral support to the nation's leaders as they struggled to develop a national consciousness out of dozens of tribes. It was a measure of Festo's ability to spot talent that later these four became canons, archdeacons and one, William, was made his own assistant bishop in later years.

Meanwhile, Festo's own ministry, at weekends, weekday nights and holidays had grown so fast that he was always fully booked. 'At any big meeting, people pressed for him to be one of the speakers,' according to a friend. Memories of missionaries and fellow Ugandans provide revealing snapshots of Festo that year. These include a youth camp on the island of Lake Bunyonyi near Kabale for young secondary schoolboys of Rwanda and Burundi, led by a missionary the Revd Pat Brooks. In the early evening, Festo—wearing his University of London blazer—and James Katarikawe came over by boat to share the story of Joseph. 'The boys were riveted,' according to Mr Brooks.

A geography student from St Andrew's University, Elizabeth Traill, was in Kabale that summer, and wrote a diary in which Festo kept making appearances:

Kabale, Sunday 6th August: After arrival, bath and tea, 'there was a wonderful time of Christian fellowship. Festo

Kivengere was there, a deeply spiritual man ... He said many helpful things. We finished with open prayer.'

A week or so later, Festo and Nagenda spoke at the Butere Convention in Kenya attended by 8,000–9,000 people. Elizabeth wrote in her diary: 'Festo gave a masterly exposition of the story of Jesus at Bethany with Lazarus ...' When Festo had to leave the convention early next day, the 9,000 bade him regretful farewells: 'Ooh Festo! Oh! Oh!' She went on to note:

> Festo is a well-known and well-liked speaker at services and conventions. He is very lively and makes the Bible stories come alive. His talk on the raising of Lazarus is told quite vividly. He knows how to build up the suspense of the crowd: 'There will be a stench after three days' ... His use of English is excellent.

Elizabeth was also amused to hear the missionaries call him 'the squire' because of his fondness for the tweed jacket he had picked up in London. (Thirty years later he was still fond of tweed jackets.)

Also that year, Festo and William Nagenda, and a missionary, the Revd John Selfridge, spoke at a conference for missionaries and African ministers in the Copper Belt of Zambia (then northern Rhodesia.) Selfridge was delighted when 'Festo brought out some wonderful thoughts from Scripture at the fellowship and in the conference session. He was specially used among students at a large teacher training college nearby. The students gave him rapt attention.'

In the summer of 1961, Festo was conducting a mission with William Nagenda down in Tanganyika (very soon to become Tanzania) when horrific news arrived from home: massacres and the burning of villages had heralded the start of an inter-tribal war in Rwanda and Burundi, just across the border from Kabale. For various reasons the Hutu tribe, which made up eighty-five per cent of the population, turned on their Tutsi overlords. Tens of thousands would die in the coming years. Of course, the Christians were caught up in it. Christian Tutsi and even Christian Hutu were massacred, despite their refusal to take political action.

Festo rushed back to Kabale and wrote to his friends among the leaders of the Rwanda Church: 'The theme of our prayers [for you] was in the words of our Lord, "I do not pray that Thou shouldst take them out of the world (or out of Rwanda) but that Thou shouldst keep them from the evil" (John 17:15). Keep a positive testimony ... Use only one weapon, that of Calvary love for all, particularly those that are persecuting you.'

Festo well knew that political struggles were a part of modern African life. But he was convinced that the love of God was the only ultimate solution to the hate which lay behind the conflicts. For example, a Tutsi friend of Festo's, Yona Kanamuzeyi, was seized by Hutu soldiers. Festo learned afterwards:

> He said to the gunmen, 'Before you kill me, may I have permission to say a few things?'
> 'Say them quickly.'
> 'First,' he said, 'I love you, second, I love my country. Third, I will sing a song.' In their mother tongue he sang all four verses of the hymn which starts: 'Out of my bondage, sorrow and night, Jesus I come.' When he finished, they shot him.[4]

Festo went on: 'But he has not died, he is still speaking. One of the messages which is being passed on from country to country is that "death is not defeat. It is a glorious arrival".' Another message is: 'Our one only weapon is love.'[5]

Throughout much of that summer of 1961, Festo and William Nagenda travelled far and wide, answering invitations to preach throughout East Africa. Then came autumn. Festo had to return to school supervision. He struggled to continue his evangelism with Nagenda in his 'spare' time. The contrast between what he could achieve when not involved in the supervisory job really hit him that year. 'It was clearer than ever before that I simply could not do my job without refusing many, many calls to preach.'

The weeks went by and Festo began to feel 'more and more pulled apart'. He was thoroughly settled into his supervisory job, and 'enjoyed it so completely that I had no desire whatever to leave'. But also, 'The calls were coming in and my ministry was growing.' The realisation quickly grew that God was telling him it was time to leave teaching. 'I was shocked—very shocked —at the idea! For twenty years I had yearly been expecting to resign, and only recently had finally become content in teaching. And now God was telling me to leave!' But the 'call' still made excellent sense. 'When God calls you to something specific, you have normally already been going in the direction of his call, discovering things in yourself he wants you to use.'

Nonetheless, there was one major hurdle to be faced: if Festo gave up his supervisory job, it would also mean giving up his salary and his house. The family would have to 'live by faith', as the saying goes, trusting God for literally every need. The local church certainly didn't have the means to support them. Festo, to whom money was never an issue, was not at all perturbed by such a prospect for himself. But he took his responsibility for his family very seriously indeed, and was determined that if he did give up his job to follow God's calling, then it should not mean his family having to go without necessities, especially school fees. He told Lilian, 'I never want my daughters to have suffered because I became a freelance evangelist.'

Festo and Mera prayed. Both quickly decided that Festo's call was so strong that they must 'step out in faith, trusting the Lord who had called us to meet our needs. How, we didn't know!'

Having made up their own minds, they shared their tentative plans with some of the missionaries and other Christians at Kabale. 'Yes, you must leave teaching,' was the general reaction. 'Your time has come. We have faith that God is indeed calling you to be a full-time preacher.'

So Festo decided he would resign and go at the end of 1961. There only remained the choice of a suitable successor. James Katarikawe was chosen.

Resigning was, in fact, the wisest move Festo could have made, though this would only become apparent in later years. Had he stayed on into 1962 he would have been caught up in the affairs of the new Uganda. This almost certainly meant that he would have been appointed a government officer for education—a job that 'would have demanded all my time'—and in the developing politics of the country, from which it would have been 'very difficult indeed' to resign.

So Festo always believed that for these reasons, 'God said, "That's enough!"—and I think he timed it right.'

On Festo's last day at the schools office on Rugarama hill, Lilian came across a note he had scrawled to himself and left with his Bible on his desk. It read: 'Praise the Lord, at last I am free!'

CHAPTER TWELVE

FREE AT LAST

1962–1963

Preaching tour of United States; preaches with Billy Graham; Stephen Olford; British tour; Switzerland and India; Independence for Uganda; seeks to go for ordination.

IN THE END, Uganda and Festo became independent in the same year. Uganda began fairly prosperously, but Festo in debt. It wasn't his own debt, but expenses he had incurred by using the school's car and hence the school's petrol for weekend missions. Most of his fellow Christians had come to take it for granted that Festo had the car, and it never occurred to them to make any contribution towards petrol.

Festo could not possibly pay it off himself: 'Mera and I had perhaps £2 worth of savings in the whole world.' They still had a roof over their heads only because the schools' board had allowed them to stay on in the schools' supervisor's house until James Katarikawe took up the appointment. There was also the big problem of how to meet the girls' school fees. Yet Festo and Mera took the financial problems of those early weeks of January 1962 very calmly. Their faith that God would somehow meet their financial needs was undoubtedly based on their certainty that he had called Festo into full-time evangelistic work in the first place. 'Mum would worry sometimes,' observed the girls, 'but tried to keep it to herself. Dad was utterly calm and self-possessed.' They grew up 'thinking there weren't any problems'.

Then a letter arrived from America for Festo. It was from the planners of the Sixth International Student Missionary Convention to be held at the University of Illinois. Would he

come and be one of their speakers? They would pay his fares
and a small honorarium. Festo and Mera praised God for the
opportunity, and Festo got ready to leave at once. Mera was
happy to let him go, though it meant leaving her in debt and
soon to be homeless.

The very week he was due to fly out, they woke up to find
someone had pushed an envelope under their front door. Inside
was a gift of 4,000 Uganda shillings—a fortune in those days.
Later they discovered it had been sent by the parents of one of
the missionaries in Kabale. Rejoicing, Festo paid off the petrol
debt and left for his first trip to America, secure in the
knowledge that Mera had money to live on and could rent a
house when the time came to move.

Chicago in mid-winter was bitterly cold. The wind howled
around the university campus. Festo practically lived in his
tweed 'squire' jacket. When the convention began he found he
was sharing a platform with Billy Graham. It was a cordial
reunion. From this time on, firm links between the two evangelists were forged, for soon Dr Graham had discovered Festo's
concern for his girls' education, and the Billy Graham Association
helped out with grants for the school fees.

Festo's preaching at the convention was unlike anything many
of the students had ever heard before. He spoke in vivid picture
language, a truly African tradition. As a missionary once put it:
'African preachers are not like European preachers. It's not a
matter of three points. They make Bible stories come to life, and
Festo was the master of this style which is common in many
African countries.'

The sermon was later described (rather too lavishly) as 'one of
the most moving sermons of our century' by *Decision*, the Billy
Graham Association's monthly evangelistic magazine. But it
reveals how Festo introduced the 'revival' of East Africa of the
1930s to the educated and affluent America of the 1960s.
Telling the story of Jacob, Festo went on to say that to have
'revival' 'requires honesty'. Jacob tried to be someone else—
Esau—in order to qualify for the blessing, and:

> many of us ... try to appear to be wonderful Christians, victorious
> outwardly, without acknowledging that we are sinners. But God
> cannot bless until we, pastors or laymen, are willing to acknowledge

Festo and Billy shared many platforms throughout
Europe and the States.

our conditions and our need. So Jacob makes the mistake—'I am not Jacob, I am Esau'. What a terrible assertion, but we hear it echoed so often: 'I am not Jacob, I am not defeated. I am a victorious Christian. I have had a wonderful upbringing and belong to a very evangelical church. I am Esau.' And then we wonder why the blessing has not come ... We are Jacobs pretending to be Esaus. We are not willing for the skins to be taken off. Personal revival is always near. It is as close as our honest recognition of who and what we are and a longing look to the Lord who has chosen us as his 'lot'.[1]

Such a winsome call to holiness and greater Christian commitment touched the hearts of many. Festo's preaching began to be talked about. In the American way of things, friendly invitations to speak soon poured in. So he decided to stay on and join up with his close friend, William Nagenda, who had also responded to invitations to preach in the States.

Festo's early impressions of the United States, and his own new ministry, are glimpsed in a letter he wrote to a friend from Glendale, California, in early February. His enthusiasm shines through—every sentence bears an exclamation mark:

The Lord is abundantly answering all your prayers! There have been many wet eyes every night here as grace has melted hearts.... Oh, what a havoc sin has made in many lives and homes in this great land of America! But there are triumphs of grace, too! So we praise him to see couples reconciled, broken relationships healed! It is the wonder of Calvary alone!

Festo had been especially touched by 'a dear saintly lady of about seventy-nine' whose few words warmed the Ugandan's heart: 'I have been praying that the Lord would send us men who would preach the simple gospel, and he has sent you.'

Other American Christians obviously felt the same. One was the Revd Dr Stephen Olford, the Baptist pastor of a large church in New York City—Calvary Baptist Church—who had met Festo before at Dr Graham's conference in 1960. Olford invited Nagenda and Festo to 'bring a report' to his Wednesday night Bible study and prayer meeting. Olford, 'as a student of revival', was 'hungry for what was going on in East Africa'.

Olford was careful to publicise the meeting well, and 'a very impressive' number of people turned up. After a brief opening and introduction, Olford simply handed the meeting over to Festo and Nagenda. He would 'never forget' what followed.

> These two dear servants of God approached the pulpit together, and in tandem fashion taught and testified concerning the work of the Holy Spirit in revival, illustrating lucidly what was taking place in Rwanda and Uganda. The power of the Holy Spirit was so evident in the hour that followed that there was hardly a dry eye in the congregation, as the great themes of brokenness, confession of sin, walking in the light, being filled with the Spirit, and living out the glories of the blessed Saviour were emphasised and applied. My own heart was deeply moved in repentance and response to the call of Christ to another quality of life.

When Festo and Nagenda finished, Olford found himself in a quandary—there was an important church meeting following, 'with matters awaiting immediate action'—and the mood of the service had been 'contrary to anything like a business meeting'. Olford decided to ask all non-members 'to leave the sanctuary and meet with Festo and William on the sidewalk outside the church while I conducted the order of business as quickly as possible. If there were those who wanted to hear more we would invite them back inside at the conclusion of the business meeting.' That was precisely what happened. 'Rarely had an important meeting been finished with greater dispatch!'

After a brief prayer,

> Festo and William came to the pulpit once again, and for nearly another hour they opened their hearts to our people. There was a spirit of revival pervading the entire church and lives were touched and transformed in a living and lasting manner. That is a memory I will always treasure.

This was just one of dozens of similar meetings held in churches throughout America that spring. Throughout the tour, and indeed many times in the years to come, Festo and Nagenda preached together. They were 'like brothers' and 'made a great team', a friend recalls. 'Festo was supremely the evangelist, while William had some of the quieter, pastoral gifts that Festo lacked.' Nagenda was quiet and often described as 'intense' whereas Festo was warm, 'bubbling' and outgoing. They also had their similarities. Both had a great gift for loving people, with no strings attached. According to those who heard them, they were both 'great preachers and expositors of Scripture, had tremendous insights and could make the Bible speak'.

Nagenda was a man 'with an open heart', who 'never spared himself' when sharing a lesson he had learned—even when it meant 'humiliating himself to the dust'. Festo by nature more proud, found this quality of Nagenda's immensely challenging. His natural desire was always to be correct—not in keeping with 'dropping bricks'.

> One day we were together on a mission. I had a burden on my soul and wanted to share it. But I was afraid to share it with William. While I was refusing to open my mouth, William came and shared with me exactly the same temptations which had defiled his heart— and shared them openly. The Lord used that to cut my chains of pride as with a knife. William was absolutely in love with Jesus Christ.

Festo's deep friendship with Nagenda was also the stage for other battles with his own personal pride. As time went on, and the preaching itinerary grew more and more hectic but successful, Nagenda's skill as an evangelist, though outwardly applauded by Festo, began to niggle.

> I became jealous of the success of my brother. I became critical of everything he said. Each sentence was wrong or ungrammatical or unscriptural. His gestures were hypocritical. Everything about my brother was wrong, wrong, wrong. The more I criticised, the colder I became. I was icy and lonely and homesick. Then the Holy Spirit intervened. I didn't invite him, but he has a lovely way of coming anyhow. He said quietly, 'Festo, you are suffering.'
> 'No, no. It is his fault.' I had worked out carefully how to defend my case and expose my brother.
> But he turned the whole thing around, saying, 'You are not right! Whatever you see in your brother, your attitude is dry—dry as a bone. You are pushing him away.'

When Festo finally admitted his sin, he next found that God was saying, 'Go tell your brother why you were so cold.'

Festo hesitated and hesitated, but when he finally approached Nagenda and admitted his jealousy,

That dear brother got up and hugged me and we both shed tears of reconciliation. My heart was warm, and when he preached, the message spoke to me deeply. One thing he said was: 'St Paul didn't think that to admit failure was a blot on the gospel.'

Festo would add:

When we are taken into the triumphal procession of the crucified risen Christ, we are *not* saying we are perfect. What we *do* say is, 'Hallelujah! I am weak and sometimes fail, but thank God, he has made a perfect provision for me. The perfume of his grace.'[2]

If many American Christians found themselves encouraged by Festo and Nagenda's tour, the same was certainly true for Festo. 'It was a marvellous year. It ushered me into the great arena of full-time evangelism, and confirmed my determination to share my faith.' The tour also confirmed for him 'the vitality of the message God had given me'.

Festo's preparation for the many meetings was done with an open Bible, a looseleaf notebook (Lilian Clarke had introduced him to these, and soon he had filled dozens with his notes), and plenty of prayer. He would spend hours in meditation, but never write out a structured message, preferring rather to note down his thoughts on the subject and relevant verses.

Yet these were still early days, and often when Festo was finally seated on the platform before several thousand sophisticated people, and the programme was underway, he would have a brief moment of panic: 'I'd pray and tell the Lord: "My notes and my thoughts on this text are still not quite co-ordinated!" Then the Devil would step in and accuse me: "Is it going to make sense? Haven't you been lazy? You didn't pray properly. You were careless!"'

Yet when he finally stood up to preach, no trace of this uncertainty showed. Festo would plunge into his message—described by one hearer as like 'a garden crowded with wild flowers—a beautiful profusion of insights. When he'd done, you felt Jesus really understood you and loved you so much better than you did yourself.' Festo desperately wanted to get exactly that message across: he once told a friend he felt that Western Christians needed most of all 'a fresh presence of *the love* of the risen Christ.' One ex-missionary, the Revd Pat Brooks described it 'as the gift God gave him of ability to communicate with practically everybody. He had a word for rulers, for church leaders, for ordinary Christians.'

Paradoxically, Festo found that his being a black African was actually a great advantage in worldwide ministry. He confided to friends that on one hand he 'was more acceptable and gave less offence' in the things he said than if he had been a white American or Briton; and on the other hand, he was not in 'competition' or up for comparison with the great number of gifted white evangelists and expository speakers.

Festo also rejoiced in the many new people he met, revelling in 'the fellowship of those who love Jesus'. Many of the Americans he met were very well off, and soon plied him with presents. While Festo was touched by such generosity, the wealth that he saw did not make him jealous. 'I never felt attracted by it. Money seemed to me to be superficial to meet human needs. I found families with the most beautiful homes—but full of problems.' Many times the Ugandan, much poorer in material possessions, would be up awake past midnight counselling troubled hosts and hostesses, often 'simply sharing my testimony'.

Invitations to speak in other countries also came in—including to the Leysin, later Les Diablerets, Revival Conference in Switzerland—an annual international conference that had begun with Leonard Brechet and Roy Hession. Then on to England, where on one of his engagements Festo forgot he wasn't in Africa. It was an area missionary meeting and a good number of church people had come from far and near. Festo, as the main speaker, gave 'a moving account' of his testimony. But after the usual questioning and discussion, those organising the meeting began—'in the English manner!'—to glance at one another and look at their watches. The chairman began: 'Well—time is getting on. Several have long distances to go—perhaps buses to catch—so we are very grateful to Mr Kivengere for his stimulating talk.'

One lady there that night said,

> I shall never forget the almost stunned look of astonishment on Festo's face—he who had just been telling of his own long bicycle rides on unmade-up roads, and of his long days of evangelism.

'What?' he cried involuntarily. 'But there is so much *more* to tell of the Lord's great work among us—surely we cannot *stop* talking of it?'

I remember there was an uncomfortable silence, and a great sense of incompatibility, as it were, of two completely different cultures within the Christian church!

But Festo seems to have controlled himself quickly, for the meeting was brought to a close 'with traditional English restraint'.

Then an invitation to speak came from India. Festo went with his close friend and colleague from Kabale, Yosiya Kinuka who, with Dr Joe Church had been used in launching the revival in the early 1930s. If the Indian churches were blessed by the message, Festo's ruthlessly honest self-portrait of himself on the trip reveals that he was learning a lot from Kinuka, who rarely overstepped his allotted twenty minutes as a speaker. 'I would speak for thirty or forty-five minutes,' admitted Festo later. 'Then Yosiya would get up, take a little expression and use it to great effect, and then sit down. You saw people getting blessing, and I began to feel jealous.' He was disarmed, however, by Kinuka, 'who loved me ... he was really like a father—a lovely man, very open-hearted'. Festo used the time in India to continue to come to terms with one of the temptations of all preachers: professional pride in speaking.

*   *   *

By October Festo was back in Uganda: it was the eve of the long-awaited Independence Day and excitement was running high for Milton Obote of the United People's Congress to become Prime Minister (having ousted the Democratic Party's Benedict Kiwanuka, who had become the first Prime Minister of Uganda that March). Festo's cousin, now head of Kigezi district under Obote, dropped in on him to discuss the big day. 'We were both keen for it,' he remembered later, 'but Festo reminded me that even independence in itself won't bring peace or happiness to the world. There will still be problems and fighting in Uganda.' Festo felt the best way forward was for the Africans to take over, but to continue to consult the British. Such a conservative view would be given little heed by the many pressing for nationalism. Like most of Uganda at the time, Festo agreed with Philemon that Obote seemed 'a good man'.

Independence Day was 9th October. Uganda became an independent state within the Commonwealth, governed by a coalition of the UPC and the *Kabaka Vekka* ('Kabaka alone') party. Dick Lyth, later the first Bishop of Kigezi diocese, having succeeded Bishop Kosiya Shalita who had been Bishop of Ankole and Kigezi, drove Lilian Clarke and Festo up to Kampala for the celebrations. They stayed in the Anglican Guest House on Namirembe Hill, but spent the day in town, watching the floats and parades march past. The Duke of Kent, representing Her Majesty's Government, handed over the instruments of Independence in great pomp and ceremony, followed by prayers led by the two Archbishops and the chief Muslim leaders.

Certainly Obote had a tough job ahead of him: he and his ministers had no experience of government. They had inherited power from the colonials, but not the authority to go with the power. (So while there was great respect for the Kabaka, Obote would soon have to pass a law making it an offence to throw tomatoes at him.) Plus, under British colonial rule, Uganda had been unevenly integrated into the capitalist world market. The areas of the East and South had been favoured, leaving the North and West Nile regions poor and backward. The people had been used as a labour reservoir for the plantations or the army. An army made up of such poor, disaffected soldiers would one day take a devastating revenge upon their wealthier fellow citizens.

Meanwhile, Obote relied on Britain and Israel to support newly independent Uganda. They gave military supplies, trade and aid. But by the end of the decade, relations would have gone very sour.

That day, at least, was one of joy. Lyth and his wife Nora, Lilian and Festo made their way to the big stadium in the evening for a spectacular fireworks display. Festo joined in the joy and optimism of a free independent Uganda. 'He was a Ugandan at heart, and was very optimistic,' recalls Lilian. As for the people's former mode of dress, 'Festo would never have thought of despising the wearing of hides and skins. "That was our custom!" and he was proud of it.' In all his efforts to improve and modernise his country, denegration of the past had no place.

The celebrations were still going strong a couple of days later, by which time Lilian Clarke and Festo had decided they should return to Kabale. They caught the bus back to Kabale, wondering about the implications of freedom for the future of their church. The old rivalry between the Roman Catholics and Anglicans was being heightened by politics. Certainly, the Christian leadership was strained to deal with the problems facing it: the continuing Roman Catholic/Protestant rivalry, and the pastoral problems the terrible Rwanda massacres had produced. Festo's main concern was for the missionaries to continue their work under the new government. 'We did not know if the change to independence was going to cause them to be creative or destructive.'

By early 1963 Festo had joined up with a mission team including Kinuka and some American missionaries on its way south to Burundi. The country was in upheaval, like Rwanda, since the civil war of the late 1950s. Two ports of call were the Kivimba Teacher Training School and the Kweya Bible School where two American missionaries, Marti and Leonard Engstrom, acted as his chauffeurs and soon became his friends. Marti delighted in Festo's

> marvellous gift of dramatisation and story telling. He told the story of the treasure hidden in the field in a way no one could ever forget it. With this as with other Bible passages, he made the setting and circumstances wholly African. For example, the man was hoeing in someone else's field, and he painted a whole scenario of his financial status, family and temperament. Nearly 200 students and faculty stayed spellbound on the edge of their seats while he made application of the greater treasure we have in Christ, who is worth more than anything we might give up.

As for the trip to the Bible school, 'he was a great model for these "preachers in training"'.

A missionary lecturer at the Bible school, the Rev Pat Brooks, was astonished by the way in which Festo could make the Bible stories so vivid.

> Festo was preaching on Noah and the ark, and when he got to the part where Noah steps out of the ark after the flood, he made us *see*

the expanse of total desolation, everything covered with mud. This wet wilderness came to life.

Then it was on to a boys' secondary school, where Festo had no illusions as to the sort of things the boys might get up to. 'He spoke to them at their level—mimicking a probably callous reaction if they got a girl into trouble and she came to them for help. He had the boys helpless with laughter, he was so natural, not in the least priggish.'

Out of meetings, the Engstroms soon grew very fond indeed of their bright, sunny-natured Ugandan guest:

> His good nature and humour never seemed to diminish, no matter how late he was kept counselling or praying, or what difficult experiences we had on the road. Often when situations got tense in traffic jams or airport waits, he would diffuse the arguments with a joke and we could carry on.

In April of 1963 the All African Conference of Churches was established. The Church of Uganda hosted the inaugural assembly at Makerere University College in Kampala, where delegates from churches in thirty different African countries discussed everything from 'Economic, Social, National and International Responsibilities of the Church' to 'Christian Education and Youth', before drafting a constitution and deciding to set up their headquarters in Nairobi. Festo was among those who attended on behalf of the Church of Uganda, and the conference was described by Archbishop Brown as 'the most representative gathering of Christians ever to meet in Africa'.[3] It gave Festo an invaluable chance to meet and talk with Christians from all over Africa, and beyond. Not the least valuable contact he made was a Norwegian, Dr Sigurd Aske, a missionary and later Director Emeritus of the International Mass Media Institute at Konggard in Norway. Aske's first glimpse of Festo was of 'a young man (Festo at forty-three looked in his mid-thirties) walking briskly up to the entrance of Makerere University College'. The two would later be close colleagues.

1963 was as busy as '62 had been. But such a fruitful ministry was achieved only at tremendous personal cost. Family life had become fragmented, with little time for fun and homely routines. One daughter remembers: 'The few times Daddy was with us were wonderful. He played games and even took us on picnics. But then he would go away again.' These long absences hit Mera and the girls much harder than Festo, whose compelling desire to evangelise was a constant draw. Over the years Mera endured great loneliness and later acknowledged a real struggle against hardship and some bitterness that her husband's ministry should mean her being left alone so much. Yet she won her personal battles, for close friends found the Kivengere household 'happy', with an atmosphere of 'love and peace'. The daughters grew up 'knowing that even if Daddy was always away, yet he and Mummy were "together" and loved us'. They followed Mera's lead: 'We grew to accept Daddy's absences. We knew he had to go. Preaching was his life. He was born to preach.'

But Festo was to state no more than the simple truth when he later said that without Mera's full co-operation down the lonely years, he could never have had the ministry he did. 'May the Lord bless Mera indeed. She had a lot to go through for the Master.' It was also entirely to her credit that the girls grew up with a strong and stable sense of 'family'. Meanwhile, family life adapted itself to Festo's comings and goings. Mera and the girls 'counted the days' until each return. On the morning Festo was due at the airport, Mera would pile all the girls into a missionary's car and drive ten miles or so to meet him on the road. Festo, though a faster driver than ever, could hardly have rushed past the little 'welcome' car. His daughters were hanging out of various windows and waving furiously.

Back home, the girls had quickly discovered that their father found 'his time with us so precious that he wanted to make the most of it'. They shamelessly exploited this: 'We knew Daddy would give in to us, so we begged him to let us do things Mum had forbidden.' When the occasional real discipline problem arose, however, Festo always backed Mera, though 'he never smacked us'!

Prayer was always a major part of family life. On top of daily devotions, whenever a specific need presented itself, 'Mummy and Daddy would get down on their knees and pray together.' Over the coming years Festo and Mera would spend a lot of time praying over the educational needs of their daughters. Festo, however, never stepped into the pulpit at home. He gave his daughters room to grow and make their own choices. 'Never did he try to push anything on any of us.' As they grew older he would sometimes chat over various decisions with them, and give his own opinion, but 'whatever choice we finally made was ours'. He never even urged them to go to church on Sundays. When in their teens they would occasionally skip a service, 'Dad never said a word.' His approach, one daughter says, 'was a wise move because none of us turned anti-religion'—which can easily happen to the children of high-powered Christian leaders.

The way eventually opened for both Peace and Joy to go to England for further study. Peace wanted to be a secretary and Joy wanted to be a nurse. As Festo wrote about this time to Lilian: 'Let us look to God about Peace's future—money is no obstacle to our God! While Festo's poor bag may be empty, our God is never empty!' Indeed, one excellent strength that Festo possessed, on which many people would comment over the years, was his total lack of interest in money. 'Festo never cared a button about getting rich!' recalled a colleague. As the Revd Richard Bewes, Rector of All Souls', Langham Place in London, put it,

> This is one of the great lessons that evangelists have to learn (if they need to learn it, which Festo apparently didn't)—that the temptations for an evangelist always include that relating to money.
>
> It was very wonderful that Festo did not succumb to this temptation —because coming from a rural background straight into Western sophistication it might have been tough for him. It seems that all the *great* evangelists of the world have had a good record on this matter—Moody, Billy Graham, John Wesley, Festo.

The rest of 1963 was as heavily booked as 1962 had been, both inside Africa as well as in the United States and Britain. By now, Festo was well used to western congregations and audiences and had benefited enormously from his travels among them. He was slowing down what had sometimes been too rapid a delivery, and his accent was improving. His vocabulary continued to expand—'like elastic!'—according to a friend, who was astonished at the American slang Festo could use when talking to young people.

But preaching alongside 'top' American preachers had also led Festo to do some very critical self-assessment. Their preaching methods were vastly different from his:

> Their messages were so clear, usually reduced to three simple points. I appreciated the discipline needed to achieve that. I began to think that maybe I should preach that way as well. It was *such a discipline* to one's thinking! It stopped you from wandering—in Africa our approach was always 'the sky's the limit!'
>
> So, gradually, I decided I would try and conform.

In the months to come Festo made many fumbling attempts to deliver 'tidy' preaching. Any success seems very uncertain: there is no record of any three-point sermons from him! But his colourful messages still deeply touched people, and demands for his preaching grew.

Just one example was when in August of 1963 Dick Lyth, then completing a four-year stint as Headmaster of Kigezi High School, and Festo went to Addis Ababa, the capital of Ethiopia, to speak to the American Presbyterian Mission missionaries' conference. The two shared a room, where the preparation for their sermons had to be done as well as sleeping. Lyth discovered that

> Festo prepared his talks sitting in an upright chair, writing nothing, but with legs crossed, endlessly swinging one of his feet. I had to face the other way as I made notes for my talks. At the end of the conference one of the missionaries said to me, 'Dick, don't think that we didn't appreciate your messages as well.' That said it all!

As the 'first generation' of revival speakers, such as Nagenda and Kinuka, grew older, Festo, at forty-three, had become the acknowledged leader of the 'second generation' to emerge from the Kabale revival. The balokole in Uganda could have paid him no higher compliment than when they openly expected that one day he would step into Nagenda's shoes as the leading itinerant evangelist in the revival. But, unknown to the Christians at Kabale, Festo had been making other plans concerning his future. It had not taken him many months of worldwide travel in Christian circles to see that there was a real difference between lay Christians and those who were ordained when it came to influence. That clerical collar was magic when it came to opening 'doors' that no layman could have passed through, especially when getting access to preach at semi-Christian/semi-social functions.

Festo pondered this for some months. He kept coming back to the simple, pragmatic premise: 'I wanted to use what I was in the best possible way.' If, as he knew now, his itinerant evangelism would be the rest of his life's work, would not the best possible way of achieving this be by way of ordination? Gradually, by mid-1963, his mind was made up.

As always, once he had reached a conclusion, he was quick to take decisive action. The offer of a three year scholarship to the Pittsburgh Seminary had been made to him during a United Presbyterian Missionary Conference at New Wilmington, Pennsylvania, in 1964. He would be admitted for a degree course in theology, leading to his ordination. Though at forty-three it would be tough to go back to college and leave his family back in Kabale, he began seriously to consider the matter in prayer. Soon he startled several of his closest friends by revealing his intentions. Dr Joe Church was appalled. 'He was doing perfectly well without ordination; what more could he achieve by wearing a dog collar?' As for Lilian Clarke, she dismissed it as 'his wanting promotion, and therefore unnecessary'. She in the end proved far easier to convince than Dr Joe. 'When Festo came round and talked through his reasons with me, I saw at once that he was absolutely right.'

The Christians in Kabale gave Festo's plan a very mixed reception. The Christians in Tanzania wrote protesting at the very idea.

> In those days we believed a good revivalist would be hindered by becoming a pastor. Testimony was telling exactly what God had done for you. If you'd been mischievous and then he'd helped you, you said so. But pastors are honourable people: they would not like to say this.

They begged Festo to forget ordination, but he did not write back. Certainly many just could not understand that if Festo wanted to be ordained, why couldn't he just be ordained? Why go for more study? Festo explained time and again that to be ordained, as he was, into the Church of Uganda would defeat his purpose. He was called to a worldwide ministry, so his credentials as a clergyman must be on a par with the clergy he would meet. 'If I'm not properly theologically trained, my fellow clergy will soon know it.'

Lilian was encouraging him by now, though Dr Joe was still uncertain of the wisdom of further training. Many balokole in Kabale were very worried. 'We thought we would lose Festo for ever if he went to study in the States; that he would come back a "white" man!' But the person who really mattered now was Archbishop Leslie Brown. So off Festo went to Kampala to ask him for permission to be ordained.

Archbishop Brown had known Festo slightly during his time as Schools' Supervisor, and more recently as an evangelist alongside Billy Graham. 'I knew through various friends that Festo had been greatly used.' But this did not convince Archbishop Brown as to Festo's call to ordination. In his study on Namirembe Hill, he put it to Festo:

> But why ordination? The ministry of a pastor is different from the ministry of an evangelist. The pastor must also be an evangelist; the bishop must be an evangelist; but some people are called primarily to work in evangelism, as are you. It doesn't seem to me that you need to be ordained. Because otherwise you turn ordination into a sort of mark of status in the church. I really don't think your ordination is a good idea.

Thus ended the first interview. But Festo persisted. He went back to talk it over with Archbishop Brown again. 'So finally he gave in, and said, "Well I must arrange for your training."' Back came the prompt response: 'I've already arranged it: I'm going to the Presbyterian Seminary in Pittsburgh.' Archbishop Brown was taken aback—though he would later admit: 'I don't know quite how Festo conned me into it, but I found myself agreeing to him going away and then later, found myself writing to the Bishop of Chicago on his behalf, asking if he would ordain Festo a deacon.' In the end, it wasn't a hard decision for Archbishop Brown to make: 'I knew Festo to be the most intellectually able African I had ever met, and I knew he was of a fine Christian character, with remarkable gifts, especially in evangelism. So there was no doubt about his suitability.'

That settled, Festo arranged to go to Pittsburgh the following autumn, September 1964 (the month Archbishop Leslie Brown would announce his retirement). The interregnum was filled with constant preaching engagements throughout East Africa and further afield. One Sunday Festo was asked to translate for missionary Pat Brooks, who had just returned from his honeymoon. Brooks gave his testimony rather nervously, and then marvelled at how 'Festo took my words and seemed to make them 300 per cent better.' But afterwards, Festo congratulated Brooks: 'That was just what was needed.' Brooks wasn't so sure, only convinced that 'his message was far better than mine'!

Festo had developed a gift for translating to the extent that 'if a speaker was not on the ball, he would make sure in his translation that they would get on the ball'! Brooks saw this happen on several occasions, and found that the original speaker 'would usually end up feeling better and more blessed than when he started'! Another friend found Festo's 'gift par excellence' to be 'speaking to a crowd of people, whether evangelistically, or speaking to convict or encourage. He was less at ease with an individual because he had little "small talk", and people could feel shy or scared.'

That year also saw the completion of a bungalow he and Mera had at last been able to build with the financial help of many Christian friends. Frances Rea, his nursing friend from London, came for a visit about the time that the electricians had arrived, and everyone tripped over yards and yards of wiring until the electricity was properly installed, making an enormous difference to daily life. Mera, a superb cook, still cooked on an outdoor oven, but once the bungalow had been plastered and whitewashed, Frances found it looked 'almost English', with its tidy doors and windows. Inside, Festo and Mera adopted the very English habit of listening to the BBC on their radio—only this was the World Service. The family had a crowd over to listen on the day Obote got married in Kampala. When the radio informed them of President Kennedy's assassination it sent shock waves even through Kabale.

Frances found Festo's private home life to be sometimes a puzzling blend of pure African—haggling over the price of bananas with poor peasants, and Christian compassion—

spending days driving an alcoholic church leader back and forth to Kampala for medical help, when everyone else wanted him sacked.

While Festo during these months welcomed English speakers to conventions in Uganda, including the English evangelist Roy Hession, and an American missionary to Tanzania, Dorothy Smoker, who later helped him on several of his books, he also rejoiced that Mera—following a trip to England—was beginning to testify in English with some confidence. 'This thrilled me!'

In early 1964, at a conference in Leysin, Switzerland, Festo ran into two missionary friends from Uganda, Dr Kenneth and Agnes Buxton. (Dr Buxton was now working in London with the Mildmay Mission Hospital.) One morning Festo got up early to pray on the terrace. He was concerned about what would happen to his daughter Joy when she went off alone to London that autumn. While he was praying he suddenly heard a soft movement further down the verandah—it was Agnes Buxton, praying over a decision she and her husband had made that morning: to offer to be Joy Kivengere's legal guardians in England.

By the summer of 1964 the bungalow was finished, Mera had found a part-time job at Hornby High School, Peace and Joy were in England, Hope was at Gayeza Girls' School near Kampala, and only Charity was left at home. So it was a sad and diminished family farewell the day Festo finally left for Pittsburgh.

CHAPTER THIRTEEN

GOING FOR ORDINATION
1964–1967

Studies in Pittsburgh; 1965 Kabale Convention; ordained deacon; ordained priest.

'THE CHURCH OF ENGLAND is not the best for giving elbow-room to a layman, therefore I am determined, if God spares me ... to go up for ordination by the Church of England.'[1] One of the earliest missionaries to Uganda, Alexander Mackay, wrote these words last century. For exactly the same reason, Festo arrived in Pittsburgh in the early summer of 1964.

Festo moved into a small brick house often used by students, and near the seminary. He made contact with the local church, Calvary Episcopal Church, in due time taking part charge of their Christian education classes. The rector, the Revd John Baiz, found Festo 'the most mature and convinced Christian man, let alone seminarian, whom I had ever met. His faith and witness were delightfully contagious. He served with grace and influence in the life of the parish and won many dear friends.' Calvary was a 'fairly sophisticated parish', and so 'it was fascinating' to see in a time of 'some racial turmoil' that the parish 'opened its arms wide to receive this beautiful black Christian'.

Throughout July and August Festo preached. After three weeks at a lively youth camp, he went on to be one of the guest speakers at the Annual Presbyterian Missionary Conference. He found it daunting, and wrote to a friend, 'I am due to speak at eleven am each day. We are five hours behind you, so whenever you can remember, a word to the Throne of Grace for this un-worthy and often wobbly servant will always be appreciated!'

Term began in September and within days Festo was engulfed

in a wave of reading, term papers and essays. His weekdays and most evenings for the next few months were spent in lectures, the library, or his little sitting room, pouring over theological tomes of varying size and difficulty. In a letter home to Kabale he confessed he found returning to study at forty-four had been more difficult than he had anticipated. However, he doggedly persevered.

Weekends and even some weekday evenings were set aside for preaching at a wide variety of Christian meetings, from church services to evangelistic rallies to holiday or retreat camps. Festo had no trouble adapting to the luxurious pulpits and sophisticated PA equipment of many American churches, but a picnic table was his undoing on one informal occasion. It was at an outdoor Christian get-together held near some woods, and light tables had been set up, laden with food. When Festo, as the guest, stood up to speak, he leant against the end of one of these tables. The other end promptly shot up into the air, and then the whole table collapsed, strewing food everywhere. Not in the least unnerved, Festo helped clean up the mess before continuing 'unperturbed to preach the Gospel'.

Festo's diary was soon solidly booked, and he became adept at reaching churches far and near by means of the not very brilliant American public transport system. Festo loved America, often referring to it in his letters home as 'this great country'. Much of his fondness for the country was based on the immediate rapport which he had established with the American Christians, whom he found open, friendly, loving and generous. They in turn were delighted to have stories of the now world-famous East African revival from someone who had been converted and brought up in it.

However, Festo was not happy preaching 'revival', and instead would stress that he wanted to preach about Christ. As he said,

> Many people have asked me to speak about revival and I have never really felt comfortable—because then you get into giving people *well-worked techniques* of how you get a church or community revived: 'What do you do, etc.' That has never been what I call the key to revival.
> To me, as I look back on the team which was used to bring revival

to Kabale in the 1930s, what did they teach? They taught us nothing about techniques, they just stood there like the apostles in Jerusalem and proclaimed *the gospel*. The facts of sinning, of judgement, of redemption. It just poured out of their burning hearts.

Now they didn't meet with tremendous success immediately—in fact, far from it. But I shall never forget what they left behind–Jesus Christ. They preached *Jesus Christ and him crucified*. Sin was made sinful, judgement was made inevitable, and redemption was the only door.

They went, but we were left with something unshakable, and they didn't once mention the word revival to us. Just that the Holy Spirit was with us ... many of us really didn't understand but *everybody* in the church felt God was there.

Festo was touched by the problems of many Christian people he met. 'The needs in the lives of Christians are simply overwhelming,' he wrote to a friend. But he was not dismayed. 'The resources to meet those needs are ample in him.' Not that he always felt up to the opportunities for ministry that lay everywhere around him. 'Often the hands that dispense these ample provisions of grace are far from being pure—and need to be cleaned. Thank God, however, that one can say: "I know a fount where sins are washed away."'

Festo's sermons crackled with God's love towards sinners. For example, when telling of Jesus' reaction when Peter denied him, 'Jesus was saying, "No Peter, you are not out ... when you were denying me, I still loved you more ... you need me desperately."'

He would often urge Christians to show love towards each other: 'Let us be patient with one another, shall we? ... until the presence of the risen Christ renews us completely.' Many times he saw people give way to temptation to do the opposite:

You meet another Christian who is struggling, and you look down on him ... It is possible to use your blessings as a hindrance ... Sometimes a husband wants to put something right, but his wife is so self-conscious of her spiritual gifts that he is scared. Sometimes a wife wants to mumble a few words of repentance, but her husband is so high and holy that there is a barrier and she goes into the dumps.

So often did Festo go out preaching that first term that by Christmas one of the families in his congregation at the church in Pittsburgh had hit upon the ideal gift for him. Audrey Brown had become very fond of 'this very special seminary student', and told her husband Duncan: 'For *my* Christmas present I want you to buy Festo a car.' They gave him the keys to a second-hand car quite matter-of-factly: 'We simply want you to be mobile in our big city,' but Festo was overcome. This practical example of love and fellowship in his ministry served him well. Over the next three years he would clock up many thousands of miles in it.

By early 1965 there was a glimmer of a possibility that Mera, Hope and Charity might be able to join Festo in Pittsburgh. Peace was in London at secretarial college, and Joy was training as a nurse, also in England. Festo asked Frances Rea and other close friends to pray about it: 'It is a big thing to take up.'

Meanwhile, No 616 Highland Avenue, Pittsburgh had become the scene of much personal blessing. He confided to friends in letters: 'The sense of his love and care over me sometimes overwhelms me!' He felt very humbled by it: 'For my unfaithfulness he ... should have thrown me out ... if it were not for his everlasting mercy.'

Studies were progressing 'slowly but steadily. All I desire is his peace as I work.' Unfortunately, there was little other peace. Festo had overcommitted himself: 'Many doors for preaching have opened round about ... I am so fully booked for meetings that I sometimes wish no one knew about me!' For that year Festo was preaching from Pasadena, California, to Canada. The invitations came from Episcopalian churches and also from any number of free and independent churches and communities. Festo had St Paul's ability to 'be all things to all men' when it came to the practicalities: he was not fussy about where he ate or slept, and he blended in with whatever company he joined: among the Anglicans he wore a surplice, among the Baptists a business suit, while among the Pentecostalists, bright, casual clothes: 'I felt right at home!' One invitation came from the Amish of Pennsylvania. On that afternoon Festo parked the car some distance away and removed his tie so as not to offend their own very simple way of living.

Meanwhile, the studies continued, though when a friend, Daniel Kijo from Tanzania, paid a visit to Festo in Pittsburgh about this time, he remarked: 'I was astonished at how he did it, because during the days I was there, there was phone call after phone call inviting him to come and preach.' The strain sometimes showed through: 'Often I go with an awareness that all is not well in my spirit. But time and again, I have found my Lord extra-gracious at times like these!'

That spring plans to bring the rest of the family over to the States developed fast. Mera, Hope and Charity began taking English lessons from Lilian Clarke in Kabale, carefully mimicking not only her grammar but her English accent. (They got quite a shock when later they heard English spoken Pittsburgh style.) Neither Mera nor Hope wanted to leave Uganda, but if that were the price of being near Festo, then so be it.

In the summer of 1965 Festo went home for the third ten-yearly Kabale Convention. Thousands came from all over East Africa and beyond. 'Some people had grown cold, new people had been saved ... We sat at Kabale with open hearts ... things which had become old, tired, broken, were all made new.'[2] Certainly, there was need for a unified church: national politics were still turbulent. The year before (1964) Obote and the Kabaka Yekka Party had split. By 1965 the politicians had stopped even pretending that they were 'appealing to the electorate'. Instead, the army 'was now decisive in the power struggle that was waging within the ruling party'.[3]

It is worth noting that the growing worldwide charismatic movement, with its emphasis on baptism in the Holy Spirit and speaking in tongues, had not affected the revival. Festo always maintained that while the revivalists did not 'despise the manifestations God has sent to shake people up, real revival is Jesus Christ himself'. His line in talking to people involved in the movement's extraordinary experiences and unusual manifestations would be: 'Don't think the manifestations are going to feed you. They shook you up so that you may go to the Lord for the bread of life.' Later he would decide that perhaps the only contribution he had made to some of these groups was that 'I have reminded them not to overlook the fundamental issues'.

Back in Pittsburgh later that summer Festo joyfully collected his family from the airport and took them home to a little flat he had rented near the city centre. Friends from the church had provided furniture, a fridge, a television set, and did their best to make Festo's family feel welcome. Sally Childs, the only other Anglican student at the seminary, secured scholarships for Charity and Hope at the nearby exclusive private Ellis school which could give the girls the individual tutoring they would need in order to adjust to a new syllabus in a new language.

The family settled down with varying degrees of difficulty: Mera was shy and stayed in the flat much of the time. Charity discovered American ice cream and television and did little else but eat and watch TV for the rest of the year: 'I don't remember doing any work, because most of the time I could not write down my thoughts in English!' Hope had it very tough. She had to learn a new language if she were to get through tenth grade.

Festo spent as much time with Mera and the girls as he could find away from preaching. Fortunately his stamina seems to have stuck with him, as the girls remember him sometimes staying up all night at his desk and going everywhere with little cards with Greek words printed on one side and English on the other.

About this time, Festo had an opportunity to do some more evangelistic preaching with a former student from Dodoma days, Matt Nyagwaswa, who was now studying in Arizona and California. Together they took on speaking engagements at Christian camp-out retreats and conferences held that summer throughout the mountains of California.

At first Nyagwaswa was uncomfortable: 'Every time I was asked to speak together with Festo, I felt so inferior ... I wished I could just keep quiet and let him speak.' Several weeks of mountain retreats later, Matt, feeling miserable, finally summoned up courage to admit his feelings to Festo. To his immense surprise and encouragement, Festo 'simply laughed' and gave Nyagwaswa the same advice that Nagenda had once given him:

Matt, remember I am just as much a sinner as you are, God has given each of us gifts for his glory. Please do not try to be Festo. Be just Matt. Preach like Matt, testify like Matt. God wants you to be Matt all the time while imitating and following Jesus Christ, our Model. Then you will have no cause to feel inferior or even superior to this person or that person.

Festo went on to share his own past jealousy of Nagenda, and how his very feelings of inferiority had become 'a sort of hidden pride, which seeks for reputation'. As far as Matt was concerned, 'That did it. Since then I have always enjoyed simply preaching and sharing what the Lord wants me to say.' (He was later made Bishop of Askofu of the Africa Inland Church of Tanzania.)

When Festo later flew out to California to preach at the wedding of Matt Nyagwaswa and Josephine Mwambi, held at the Lake Avenue Congregational Church in Pasadena, he began by reading the passage in Deuteronomy concerning the Mercy Seat in the Tabernacle. Matt and his bride exchanged glances of alarm: they couldn't see how such a passage could suitably relate to a marriage occasion! But Festo went on to draw an analogy between the young couple and the two cherubim that stood facing above the Mercy Seat, 'facing each other, but not looking at each other; but rather fixing their eyes and focusing on the Mercy Seat'.

Festo urged the young couple to face each other in harmony, fellowship and service, always remembering to focus their eyes and attention on the Lord Jesus, our 'Mercy Seat', where God has promised to meet us. Festo warned:

> If you make the mistake of focusing on each other, you will be greatly disappointed, and your marriage will end up in ruins ... Please fix your eyes ... where all failures and shortcomings and sins are forgiven. That's where you will learn to forgive and encourage each other.

* * *

By autumn Festo was back in Pittsburgh for his second year at the seminary. Again he plunged into a maze of essays, reading and examinations. Yet his increasing theological knowledge did not alter his style of preaching. His sermons were still never hung on a carefully balanced three-point structure, instead the message 'came at you rather like a child throwing paints with his fingers all at once on to a canvas in great excitement', according to the Revd Richard Bewes, now Rector of All Souls', Langham Place in London.

Festo was encouraged in this while in Uganda, when he had an unpleasant shock. After all the American influence on his preaching, 'I discovered I was losing my freshness in communicating with my African brethren.' This was ludicrous: 'I was after all going to college to prepare myself for ministry in Africa!' So he decided forthwith 'I must be careful not to lose my understanding of the African way of communicating. I made up my mind that Western influence should help to clarify my thoughts, but not force me into a set mould.'

It was a very liberating moment. From now on 'I would learn from my brethren in the West and use it in the relaxed atmosphere of the African approach'.

This done, Festo found it easier to relax before meetings almost anywhere. His message would be the best he could make it, but it would be *his*. And he made a conscious effort to participate in the service:

> After all, I loved being with the people. I loved the singing. So I asked the Lord to give me peace and bless *my* soul. 'Lord,' I'd say, 'I'm here now, and I've done my little bit. Let me not spoil this experience now of being with your people.'

Dr Paul Rees, an American, found that:

> Festo saw with double vision as William Blake, that strange dazzling genius of English literature, once wrote: 'What, it will be questioned, when the sun rises, do you see? Do you not see a round disc of fire, somewhat like a guinea? Oh no, no, no, I see an innumerable company of the heavenly host crying, 'Holy, holy, holy is the Lord God Almighty.'
>
> That is what I mean by double vision ... To a degree seldom appreciated by prosaic minds, the Bible is a pictorial book. Its abstract content is minimal. Its concrete, colourful components are everywhere. No one is more at home with such material than Festo Kivengere.[4]

Festo also read many Christian books, of which a vast variety were available in the States. He especially wanted ones with the subject on how to find a deeper spiritual walk with God. In the end, however, he decided that in the main 'these books did not warm my heart'. Each book, it seemed to him, gave a *method* of how to get God to give blessing. 'They seemed to be whispering between the lines that we were really bargaining with an unwilling God.' But Festo knew from experience 'that God is more willing to bless us than we are to pray for the blessing'!

Festo also read widely in theology—'some of which did not agree with my evangelical stand at all! Those books educated me—helping me to get out of my cosy evangelical little shelter and be exposed to what other people have seriously thought.'

As for books on how to receive God's guidance, 'Those of us who read the good evangelical books on this subject, got tied up in knots!' Festo decided it wasn't such a complicated series of manoeuvres, and preferred to stick to basic principles: 'I knew the Holy Spirit had been given to guide me. He would not leave me in confusion if I was walking in brokenness.' By this he meant an attitude of meekness and humility, willing to repent of wrong, and to be instructed. This brought him tremendous liberty.

Then there were the numerous enthralling testimonies of God's work in someone's life. Festo found many of these books excellent for directing a confused or closed mind to God's love and presence. The problem arose when the reader wanted to copy such experiences. Festo was certain that

> Testimonies are never meant to be copied. They are only meant to encourage, challenge, whet another's appetite for God. But when we hear a brother or sister telling us what God has done for them, we often think: 'I'd like to imitate that.' But usually this is not at all what the Holy Spirit intends! He wants to wake you up and get you to seek after God, not the spiritual experience—however exciting—of someone else!

As exams approached in the spring of 1966, Archbishop Leslie Brown wrote to Bishop William Thomas, then suffragan bishop of Pittsburgh, to ask if he would ordain Festo deacon. It was one of the steps of major importance which Archbishop Leslie Brown did before Sabiti's enthronement as the first Archbishop of Uganda.

As Festo left the examination room after his final paper he found a letter with some weighty news waiting for him. It was from Richard Lyth—he had been asked to become the very first

Bishop of the newly formed diocese of Kigezi. 'We need your advice and help,' Lyth said, and then explained how the offer had come about. Kigezi had long been waiting for its own bishop,

> and, though of course they have always had you ultimately in mind, they thought that Balaba would be able to do the job for a few years. And then, when the Lord took him, they thought that Lawrence Barham might do it ... and then he had his heart attack ... And so they began to look round again.

The bishop's advisory commission had made many enquiries and concluded that the first bishop should be a European: this would avoid tribal tensions and set a good standard of impartiality in leadership. While Lyth saw their point, 'This is the last thing I personally want to do.' But everyone's reply was, 'It is no use my (or the mission's) pretending to be the servant of the church and then making my own decision about the way in which I intend to serve ... We should so much value your thoughts and advice.'

Festo replied at once, admitting Lyth's name had been mentioned to him already by other friends at Kabale. He encouraged Lyth, who had been a district commissioner in the Sudan, to accept: 'We both have always felt that the new diocese would need someone of your calibre with your gifts of organisation ... A young diocese is not an easy project to launch but it is not you launching it. It is the Lord.' Encouraged by Festo and others, Lyth reluctantly decided to accept the job.

The girls' term broke up about the same time as their father's. The school asked Festo to be guest speaker on graduation day.

Then it was Festo's turn. He graduated from Pittsburgh Theological Seminary with a Master of Divinity degree. His ordination to the sacred order of deacons took place at ten-thirty am on 11th June, 1966, at St Stephen's Church, Sewickley, Pennsylvania. The rector, the Revd Benedict Williams, presented the two candidates, Mr Robert Hetherington and Mr Festo Kivengere, to be ordained by the suffragen bishop of Pittsburgh, the Rt Revd William Thomas. The church was full, and many of Festo's Presbyterian friends attended. The service followed the Book of Common Prayer and included a prelude fugue and choral by Honegger, the kyrie eleison by Willan, and the gloria tibi (traditional).

The day, of course, was a landmark in Festo's ministry. He had left behind his itinerant preaching days and was now ministering within the Anglican communion. Looking back, he could see ten-year landmarks: thirty years since his first conversion and meeting with the revival (1936), twenty years since he had left Uganda to be an evangelist in Tanganyika (1946), ten years since he had left Africa for the first time to go to London (1956). He was the only African of his generation to have changed from being a popular evangelist of the revival to an international evangelist in his own right. He had friends and contacts from Papua New Guinea to Pittsburgh. Perhaps therefore it was both symbolic and suitable that he was ordained in the USA and not Uganda—from now on his ministry would belong to the world church. In the coming years America and Britain would become a second home to him.

After his ordination, the Kivengeres did not return straightaway to Uganda. Festo and Mera had both spent a lot of time praying for guidance as to what their next step should be, and within a month or so they were sharing their hopes for their future with several American churches. A photocopied two-page typed letter which he and Mera released in October of that year complete with a photograph of the family on the front, puts succinctly the vision Festo now had before him:

> While at Pittsburgh Theological Seminary, my wife and I have been laying before the Lord, who called us into his blessed service more than twenty years ago, the fact of where in his great vineyard back in Africa he wants us to serve, and in which way.
>
> It is through these times of heart-searchings, desiring to know his will for us, that the idea of WORKING ON AN INTER-DENOMINATIONAL BASIS FOR THE MOBILISATION OF AFRICAN EVANGELISTS INTO A UNITED FORCE FOR GOD WHEREVER THEY ARE began taking shape in our hearts.

Festo spells out what he means: bringing existing evangelists together

> for encouraging each other in Christ. There are many lives which God has changed and called in Africa, but isolation has done much

harm in keeping the fire of God's love from spreading. We have seen things happen when groups of men and women whose hearts God's Spirit has touched and changed got together and moved under one vision of spreading the goodness of our risen Saviour. But such efforts lacked the needed support of God's people, both in prayer and finances.

Festo went on to pinpoint what he called 'our field' with the certainty of one who has seen what education can achieve; running conferences for evangelists and pastors in different parts of the continent according to where the need is. These conferences would be held within interested evangelical churches. The expected outcome of such conferences should be a united vision for reaching out to the masses both in and outside the churches with the good news of the Lord Jesus Christ.

Having shared his vision, Festo sets out exactly what he expected. Perhaps he had fallen under the influence of Americans who were not shy in asking for help.

A home: Festo had received a gift of $3,000 in 1965 and had immediately bought a piece of land in Kabale as prices were rising rapidly. In order to complete this home he still needed between $6,000 and $7,000.

A car: A new five-seater saloon as a used car is usually a more expensive item in Africa because of the condition of the roads.

Living: In the States the family had managed to get by on $250 a month. In Africa they could do it on $2,400 a year— because of the tremendous travelling expenses. This would meet the necessities of life.

Festo explained why he would prefer a fixed salary: 'In living by faith the Lord has been very faithful in meeting our daily needs, but ... an unfixed income might breed suspicion in the community.'

Under the 'needs' that Festo lists in order to get his ministry off the ground, he includes: 'Simplified literature to equip the evangelists', adding: 'The need here is simply staggering and your fellowship in meeting it is essential.'

Office: He needed no more than a room to begin with, but an equipped room would certainly cost something, as would a Christian secretary to work in that room.

Finally, finances would be required to help meet the needs of conferences, plus travelling expenses for those too poor to afford them, the occasional hiring of rooms in town for an evangelist or two, and a bicycle or motor bike for a God-provided servant in a needy place.

He concludes: 'There is no limit to what you can do with what God has blessed you with to enable others to hear what God has done in Christ for their eternal salvation!'

But there was no direct demand for money. Festo closes with dignity: 'Waiting to hear your word of encouragement in the Lord and your loving advice over this whole vision.'

Several churches responded to the appeal most generously, but it would be several years, and in a different way, before his vision was realised.

1967 arrived, and with it the consecration at Namirembe on 8th January of the first Bishop of the newly formed Kigezi diocese: Richard Lyth (who was the son-in-law of Dr Stanley Smith, a founder of the Ruanda Mission). By 21st January Archbishop Sabiti had arrived in Kabale for the following day's official inauguration of the diocese of Kigezi, the installation of Bishop Lyth, and the convening of the first diocesan council.

Festo was still in Pittsburgh, but Lilian Clarke wrote with all the news. He replied:

We read the news of Dick's reception by the Kigezians, and our hearts were greatly thrilled. In fact, we were jealous of those who took part! We would have liked to join in the throngs and express our joy to Dick and Nora as representing a new stage in what the Lord has done for Kigezi through the Ruanda Mission.

That last spring in the USA Festo had never been so busy. Engagements included preaching in Cleveland, Ohio, before flying to New York for a day's meeting, and then returning to do some preaching at St Stephen's Episcopal Church near Pittsburgh. In March there was the Christian Life Convention, a form of Keswick, at the Calvary Baptist Church in New York, where his friend, Dr Stephen Olford, was still the pastor.

Olford always found Festo's visits a channel of the 'blessed

Holy Spirit'. As Festo put it: 'No one went away without being profoundly affected.'

One sermon was on the subject of unity and harmony, a sensitive issue during this era of the civil rights movement in America. Speaking from John chapter seventeen, Festo pleaded for the oneness in Christ that makes the world believe that Christ truly came 'to seek and to save that which was lost'. To illustrate the point, he turned to the Steinway piano where Olford's wife, Heather, had just been playing. In his typical way he said: 'You know, Heather, you would have never produced that beautiful music tonight if you had not used both white and black keys.' The national tension between whites and blacks made his message 'prophetic and powerful'.

By April Festo was finishing off the two last papers of his final exam, and was able to encourage Hope, who was in the thick of her final exams. He graduated on 9th May, 1967 (and Hope on 16th June). One week after his graduation he teamed up again with Dr Stephen Olford and another clergyman, the Revd Ernie Wilson, for a series of meetings in Harlem, New York, where a large black community lived. Then it was on to Montreal to preach at the United Church of Canada on 'Man and his world', an apt subject considering that year was the centenary of the World Fair.

In July the Kivengeres caught the ocean liner, the 'Queen Elizabeth', for England where Festo did some further studying, sponsored by his affiliation with the Evangelical Fellowship of the Anglican Communion. He also headed for Cambridge, where he was booked to give a Bible Reading to the CICCU, and also preach on a Sunday morning at the Round Church.

By late October the family arrived back in Kabale, laden with presents for their fellow Christians. Their household possessions, which had been stored in a little crooked, disused house, were unpacked, and not an item was missing—for which Mera was very grateful. A crowded fellowship meeting was held at the cathedral to welcome them, followed by a noisy tea party.

The Kivengeres soon discovered that they had returned to a much changed Uganda, and indeed Africa. The previous year, 1966, had marked a watershed with the granting of independence to Botswana and Lesotho. The independence of African nations, which had begun with Ghana in 1957, was now proceeding at a tremendous pace. But the nature of that independence was also changing. Throughout the continent 'a certain semi-democratic optimism was being replaced in country after country by military or dictatorial governments—frequently the only apparent alternative to political chaos'.[5]

May 1966 had been a critical time: that month a building block of future doom fell into place. Obote had again clashed with the Kabaka, and feared Buganda might secede and claim independence. So he called on the help of a soldier with whom he had worked in the early 1960s in aiding the rebels in the civil war next door in Zaire. This 'ally' was Idi Amin, a member of the small and insignificant Kakwa tribe from the underdeveloped West Nile scrub country near the Sudanese border. Amin was a vast hulk of a man, and all but illiterate. But he wasn't squeamish when it came to violence, and so that month came willingly to Obote's aid. He and his troops stormed the Kabaka's palace, looting and killing. The Kabaka fled to Britain (where he would die three years later). Buganda was quelled by force. The constitution for all Uganda had already been suspended. Hundreds of prominent citizens were detained without trial.

At this time it seemed to Obote safe enough to trust Amin. He showed as yet no signs of political ambition. So Obote reappointed him Deputy Commander of the powerful Uganda Army. From now on Amin would be Obote's principal means of discouraging any more unrest. He was needed, for by now there was little civilian support for Obote.

By 1967 and the time the Kivengeres returned, Uganda had been made a republic, with Dr Milton Obote as the first Executive President. There was also a new constitution, and the abolition of several traditional kingdoms was underway. As the national lines of power were shifting, so the old Protestant/ Roman Catholic rivalry was fading.

There had been major changes in the Church of Uganda, too. For one thing, Archbishop Leslie Brown had retired in November 1965, leaving the way open for Erica Sabiti to become the first African Archbishop of Uganda, Rwanda and Burundi in 1966. Sabiti had appealed to the missionaries to stay on in a new role:

working under the African church, which they were happy to do. Relations between the church and the state were still fairly good, with no great outward change in the religious influences surrounding the government. Festo was due to be ordained priest into the Church of Uganda on 17th December, along with six other deacons: O. Tibemanya, J. Kahigwa, E. Shalita, J. Busingye, W. Rukirande and A. Bamweine. Their ordination retreat, planned for the week before, was to be taken by Bishop Amos Betungura. But as the weeks drew nearer, an unusual, if not unique, problem arose: Festo's diary was so booked up with evangelistic commitments that it looked as if he was going to have to turn down some very key preaching opportunities abroad if he were to be in Kabale for 17th December.

Rather embarrassed (not many deacons have such a demanding international ministry that they can't even make their own ordination!), Festo took his problem to Bishop Lyth. Lyth could have been adamant that Festo attend the ordination, but instead, with his great understanding and support for Festo's ministry, he soon hit upon a solution. Bishop Lyth would simply ordain Festo priest a week earlier—on 10th December. (There was never any question of giving Festo a parish to care for in Kigezi—his gifts as an evangelist were recognised and it was accepted that, under the bishop, he would be free to pursue his own ministry as a 'free evangelist'.)

So Festo was ordained priest on Sunday 10th December in a two-hour service. The Cathedral at Kabale was packed with clergy and Christians. Bishop Lyth began: 'This service is going to be special. We are ordaining Festo Kivengere a week earlier than the other deacons because he is needed to go and preach.' The theme of the service was Jesus' first and last command to his disciples: 'Come and see', and, 'Go and preach'. They well summed up the essence of Festo's spiritual experience. Afterwards everyone crowded into the long, narrow dining room at Kigezi High School for another tea party.

Festo was now an ordained clergyman in the Church of Uganda Dick Lyth was his bishop, and Erica Sabiti his Archbishop. A clergyman from the North of the country, the Revd Janani Luwum, was the Provincial Secretary. Little did Festo dream what lay in store for himself and Luwum one day in confronting Idi Amin. In the meantime, Festo was eager to start on the rest of his life's ministry. It was as simple as Jesus' last command 'Go and preach.' Festo hastily packed a suitcase—and went.

CHAPTER FOURTEEN

THE 'BILLY GRAHAM' OF AFRICA
1968–1970

Festo's fame as evangelist grows; travels worldwide; meets Michael Cassidy; accepts challenge to launch African Evangelistic Enterprise in East Africa.

B Y EARLY 1968 'everybody was talking about Festo', according to Christians in Uganda at the time. 'People had begun calling him "the Billy Graham of Africa".' If evangelists are fishers of men's souls, then 'the whole world had become his lake', says Misaeri Kauma, later Bishop of Namirembe. No other African at that time 'fished' such a wide expanse.

Certainly by early 1968 Festo was at the brink of being recognised as an evangelist of truly international standing. He was becoming known as a superlatively gifted evangelist and communicator. Many people found him personally very attractive. He was good-looking and poised. 'His presence commanded attention. When he came into a room he became the centre.' He dressed immaculately—when not in a dog collar, he always wore a shirt and tie, never a pullover. He was meticulous about his hair. He had a pleasing, melodious voice, and a merry laugh, which he used a lot: time and again his sense of humour and fun is remembered. Such basic personal advantages became invaluable when he spoke before thousands of non-Christians: the African young people, preoccupied with their own appearance, admired him tremendously. They copied his hair style and bought shirts similar to his. 'He is a *modern* saved man', the saying went among many of them. Festo was a good advertisement for Christianity in another way: he appealed both to the upper-class Africans, who assumed anyone with such poise must be a Muganda, and to those from humble tribes who loved him because, though he was of the ruling Bahima class, still he showed courtesy to people from any tribe or background.

His story-telling was becoming legendary too—he would often begin with a deceptively simple story from the Bible which everybody knew. Then, in unconscious, vivid gestures using his hands and facial expressions, he would fill it in with splashes of humour, a stroke of pathos, cheery touches of the everyday. As he progressed, his listeners would quite suddenly see their own reflection coming into focus on his canvas and beyond that, the love of Christ reaching out to them. Evidence of his gift is that over twenty years on, people can still remember the story Festo told them and the impact it made. For example, 'When he talked about the disciples in the storm at sea, I saw it so clearly that I felt seasick!'

The Revd Dr Stanley Mooneyham of World Vision had by now offered him a place on his team of international evangelists. Mooneyham later explained:

> Festo's deep spirituality, his sensitive insights, his loving spirit and his exposition of the Scriptures made him a favourite speaker in World Vision pastors' conferences. His empathy with pastors and church leaders in Third World countries was felt by all as soon as he stepped onto the grounds. I offered him a position 'at large' which would have put no constraints on his time or travel. He would have been free to accept any invitation which seemed of God and go anywhere he could render spiritual service. Recognising his multiple and abundant gifts, I simply wanted to help make those gifts available to the church around the world.

But after much prayer and discussion, Festo told Mooneyham he felt:

> it was God's will for him to stay with his diocese and use that as his home base, ministering abroad as much as the constraints on his time allowed. I admired and greatly respected his decision and we continued to invite him to join our speaking team as often as he was able.

Festo's return from America and the family's resettling in Kabale had been greeted with warm approval by the brethren. It would take some time for him to get used to a clerical collar and his new status as a 'Rev'. He was pleasantly surprised at how many doors were opening to him now that he was ordained. He joked with friends that as far as evangelism in international church circles was concerned, a clerical collar was 'good for fishing'.

Similar light-hearted comments reveal the fairly pragmatic way in which Festo viewed his ordination. Both the strong emphasis on lay ministry in his revivalist background, and becoming ordained so late in life tended to make him take it in one way less seriously than do many young men: as the seal that their life is to be devoted to Christian ministry. After all, as far as Festo was concerned, he had been completely at God's disposal for the past twenty-eight years, since the night of his restoration at the little house in the banana plantation at Rukungiri. For him, a dog collar was the means to the end for which he had longed for nearly thirty years: full-time evangelism.

As 1968 began, 'People were calling for him to come and speak here, there and everywhere,' adds another clergyman. During these next three years Festo would eagerly seize every opportunity he could, responding to invitations to preach at a wide variety of missions, conferences, retreats, rallies, services, for any number of denominations in a bewildering span of venues: from New Guinea to Israel to Switzerland to New York, to little bush churches in the villages of his own beloved Kigezi.

His preoccupation always seemed to be entirely with the ministry itself: he was burning with what he felt God would have him say. The different countries, continents and churches were taken matter of factly. The romance of travel never affected him: he was not one to be easily influenced by his surroundings. In no letter does he delight in the place or the travel: it is always the work. Whether the postmark is Israel, Pittsburgh, London or Africa, the news is only of the Holy Spirit working in people's lives.

Festo's great enthusiasm for this often hid the fact that life as an itinerant preacher could be very arduous. It might look to some as no more than ascending pulpit after pulpit sharing 'spiritual blessings' with fellow Christians, but this was far from the truth. Indeed, at times the host Christians contrived, usually by sheer thoughtlessness, to create endless obstacles for their guest preacher.

There were the ones whose invitation was so couched in spiritual language as to be an earthly disaster. Thus 'share some messages of God's love with us' became, on arrival at one week-long convention: 'We want you to take every two-hour morning Bible reading, the pastors' seminars on three afternoons, as well as, of course, the main evangelistic address every evening—but please have the rest of the time off to enjoy yourself!' Festo found such schedules would 'almost kill you', as 'because your name is known, you are expected to speak, prophet-like, any-time, without fumbling'!

Or there were the organisers who were so excited to have Festo as their 'star' attraction that they concocted a programme to try and do him justice, and only succeeded in nearly eclipsing him altogether. Festo would ponder this tendency with friends.

> Sometimes I find they've got two—three—or even *four* choirs laid on! For what reason? Then someone gets up and gives a commentary on the song! Then somebody else tells at length of his experiences. I end up with five to ten minutes to speak to a congregation already *over-heard*—and then the service is swept to a close.

He wondered at times like these why on earth they had flown him in from thousands of miles away.

Then again there were the organisers who tried to lure in 'the young people' by tempting them over the threshold of the church or conference centre with rock music. Many a time Festo sat through an hour of crashing drums and screaming electric guitars. 'Now that is a killer! The noise gets into my head, and my ears are popping ... By the time I'm asked to preach, I really am in another heaven! It takes grace to orientate to the people after that kind of music.'

Then there was the time (Festo never forgot it) when an American church insisted he fly all the way over from other engagements in Uganda to speak to them. It was quite a trek: via Entebbe, Nairobi, London, New York and on out west ... he finally arrived and was ushered (exhausted) into the pastor's study with a casual 'so glad you could make it ... now our sermons in this church never last longer than twelve minutes ...'

This was more than Festo could bear, and once firmly lodged in the pulpit, he appealed direct to the congregation for a bit more time. It was given rapturously, and he was overwhelmed with good wishers an hour later.

So, whenever possible, Festo asked his hosts to brief him as to the *reason* they were holding the meeting.

I always said, 'If you have got something as your concern, please share it with me, because it will help me, as I pray and read, to work better.' But most people don't do it. Though I tell them 'We would have done a better job in fellowship if you *had* shared with me your burden at this particular stage.'

The craving for 'success statistics' was another headache that Festo found in America. He pitied Billy Graham for the pressure this put on him, pointing out to friends that 'there has never been a Billy Graham crusade which is reported as being less successful than the one before it . . . each crusade must be bigger with more responses'. Festo would fight this approach, insisting he had to 'minister according to the way the Lord has really given me ability'.

Another minefield was what to do at the end of services: should he invite the people to come forward? He had many reservations about this, for: 'Just the fact of calling the people forward has become a sign of the "success" of the *evangelist*.'

His inclination was rather to 'preach the Word, and close with a prayer and say "Brethren, now go home and think about this."' But he was often not able to do this. Many of his hosts, especially American Christian journalists writing for American Christian publications, did not like this one bit: 'What are we going to report? It was very good and we all went home? You are covering your failure. Were you afraid of calling them forward? Maybe you know no one will come forward . . .' Festo struggled a lot with the problem.

Of course, Festo had his 'off' days in the pulpit, usually due to overwork and fatigue. A friend describes it, 'Sometimes he wasn't just being African—he was just plain *rambling*.'

Festo felt the strain at times:

Once your name becomes well-known, Christians can *kill* you! You must speak on the dot, or if it isn't 'one, two, three', it must be one of those profound statements . . . Well, if you don't have it, the pressure to strive for it and never waffle can take away the freshness of being you.

Yet for all this, Festo had conquered pre-meeting nerves, and pitied those who hadn't.

> I have sat with some preachers before a meeting and they are almost killing themselves with worry. Will the meeting be a success? Will many come forward? ... By the time they get to the meeting they feel jaded, and afterwards 'punctured!'

Festo never felt 'punctured'—a fact remarked upon often by friends and envious colleagues. He was philosophical: 'God gives me the words to say, and I say them.'

Even when meetings ended, often at a late hour, Festo's 'day' was far from over. Literally scores of people would beat a trail to the platform to greet him, to seek counselling or to try and engage him in all manner of conversation. Festo was courteous, for 'it was a joy to meet them', but when dozens upon dozens were queueing up and the hour was approaching midnight, it could be 'very taxing'.

Festo also rapidly established a firm rule of staying in a hotel rather than with local Christians. He had learned the lesson the hard way: having arrived at numerous Christian homes at midnight to discover that *they* had been waiting all day for this chance to have him to themselves, for some in-depth counselling—perhaps until three am in the morning. And Festo loved people too much not to succumb: 'I can't be in someone's home and *not* stay up late and share many things with them.' So, 'to keep on top', he sought the solitude of impersonal hotels: 'I feel no responsibility to talk to the room!'

And in between all the conventions, conferences, youth meetings, church services, rallies, etc, were the many plane flights. Festo took great delight in these, confiding to friends that they were 'wonderful times when you can be quiet'. For 'when God blesses the messages you have, people hardly ever give you time to think or to be on your own ...'.

So he came to savour the anonymity and the solitude of the journeys, using the time for prayer ('drawing strength from the HQ' as he put it). 'Prayer for me became just a talking to my heavenly Father. If sometimes I fell asleep I wasn't wracked with guilt ... I had been in the presence of one who loved me more than I loved him.'

Although he had several African languages at his command, and preferred to get along whenever possible without a translator, the scope of his travels in Africa inevitably meant that local Christians or missionaries would find themselves interpreting for him at times. 'It was like being caught in the slipstream of a jet plane!' found one. When Festo used an interpreter, he made full use of him: the Revd Pat Brooks in Usumbura was translating for him one day at a school and suddenly found Festo was using him as an impromptu visual aid as well. The sermon was on loving one's brother, and putting things right, so Festo, to illustrate his point, suddenly reached out and grabbed Brooks around the waist and gave him a little hug. 'One had to be prepared to be an Aunt Sally for him! But it was nice to be given the chance to be involved in the message.' He was also invaluable at conventions in Uganda as he would translate in up to five languages, effortlessly slipping from one to another without a moment's thought. 'He was known among us as "the man of many languages",' recalls a distant admirer.

As for his own preaching, 'Everyone knew that he was the strongest preacher in Uganda,' according to Ugandan Christians. 'Back in the 1950s and 60s, it had been William Nagenda. We all thought that there would never be another preacher as loving and convincing as him. But then came Festo. ... He would talk about the old truths of Christianity, but in words that nobody else had used.' Almost invariably these were his picture words. For example, Festo pictured a person as a squeaky hinge, and conversion as a time when Christ came into one's life like soothing oil: 'Then life begins to feel the ease of Jesus,' for 'the love of Christ is our spiritual shock absorber.' His gift with words made him extremely popular, and with good reason, as one clergyman has explained:

> By the time Festo returned from Pittsburgh in 1967, the balokole were in a curious position. Though they still loved their fellowship meetings, they had all read the Bible so much that they honestly did not expect to get much more from the preaching at those meetings. And then here came Festo, who could open the Bible and make you feel as if you had never really read that particular passage before.

Festo never considered his enormous success to be of his own doing. Indeed, he made very clear: 'Without Christ, preaching is a dry exercise. The Bible does not speak, and words don't come.'[1] He explained what he did, along with the work of other Christians, by means of yet another picture:

> Take a piece of metal: it is colourless, dull, cold, nothing attractive about it. But put it into the fire. Let the fire run through it. It will get warm. It loses its rough surface, its hardness, its colourlessness. It begins to flow. You begin to see glory, not the glory of the metal, but of the fire in the metal.

Festo knew that there was a high personal price to be paid for anyone willing to be such a conductor of Christ's love, and Festo testified to this at a conference in Montreux in Switzerland: 'Jesus began to break me in 1941, and he has done so ever since.'

His spiritual walk was as difficult as anyone else's, as he made clear time and time again. He would be quite honest that:

> I am not always full of love, not always seeing him clearly. Self-indulgence has a way of creeping in. Sometimes I am thoroughly empty and have to say so in public. But what I have discovered is that JESUS LOVES TO FILL EMPTIES! All I need to do is to keep open to him and to admit frankly what's wrong. He does the rest.
>
> This is where 'respectable' Christianity fails. God does not deal with respectability; he deals only with reality.
>
> Sometimes I make the mistake that Moses made when he disobeyed the Lord in the desert and struck the rock with his staff instead of speaking to it. In his anger at the people he disobeyed God, but he probably rationalised it, saying the water came out and ... so I must be all right spiritually. The results prove it.
>
> But the water came because the Lord is merciful and had compassion on his people.
>
> Sometimes I see people responding to the word of the Lord which I have preached, even if my heart is not quite right. But I don't get away with self-congratulation, and neither did Moses. God took Moses aside as a friend, had some fellowship with him, and told him a few things that had gone wrong between them. He loves me that way too.
>
> No matter what grace has done for me in the past, I still need to experience daily the power of the cleansing blood of Jesus ... And that is not easy.[2]

Festo's total honesty about his own failings, even his honesty about his lack of honesty at times, and how it worked out in his home life and among the brethren, was in fact his great strength. As a fellow clergyman once put it: 'Festo was a repentant sinner. That is why you can't find weakness in him: he already admits it, and is always willing and ready to make amends.'

He loved the verse Isaiah 57:15, which, translated directly from the Kiswahili, runs:

God, whose name is Holy, says, 'I dwell in the high and holy place, with him also who is of a humble, broken spirit, to revive the spirit of the humble, and to revive the heart of the repenting ones.'

Festo always stressed his own need for continuous repentance:

In and of myself, I can't be real. It frightens me. It embarrasses me. But when I go down to the foot of the cross and meet Jesus there, his grace covers my sins, forgives my weaknesses, and allows me to be what I am—a forgiven man.[3]

Once, having preached on spiritual warfare in London, Festo was discussing the paradox of repentance being the way forward with George Swannell, then a member of the staff of All Souls' Langham Place. Both agreed that repentance did not, on the face of it, seem a particularly victorious attitude. Then Festo added a remark which stuck in Swannell's mind 'like a burr'! 'George, we don't repent in circles, but at a deeper and deeper level!'

And in all his preaching about repentance and forgiveness, Festo had no illusions as to the difficulty of it.

It is easy to cause a wound, but hard to heal it. If God did not intervene, with grace, we would all be reckoned as murderers. One day I used an expression that cut the heart of my dear wife and caused a wound there.

In the atmosphere of mutual forgiveness, and in the provision that Jesus Christ has made for us, Mera and I have discovered that through self-forgetting and self-sacrificing is born a truly creative love. Instead of one emptying the other person for one's own need, each fulfils the other, making him or her more of a person, having more dignity. It brings out the latent qualities in the other, and it partakes somewhat of the love of Christ, who loves his Bride into perfection.[4]

Meanwhile, that spring of 1968 the assassination of Dr Martin Luther King made world headlines. Festo was angry and deeply saddened at the American civil rights leader's tragic death. From his own experience of even petty malice (for example, being given the change for a meal in hundreds of pennies instead of pound notes at a London restaurant), he knew the sting of racial discrimination. Yet from the Bible and his own Christian experience, he knew all men are equal before God: 'Colour disappears at the cross. At Calvary the hearts we present are all alike. When Jesus came down from the Mount of Transfiguration, he stepped on level ground. We are all on level ground before him.'

In a more light-hearted vein, Festo had by now learned to turn the tables on those American pastors who welcomed him into their pulpits with the best of intentions but the still patronising introduction of 'our coloured brother'. With a twinkle in his eye, Festo would politely respond: 'I'm so pleased to have an opportunity to speak to you, my colourless brethren!' When 'black' came into fashion in describing those with dark skins, he would tease his American or European friends, 'You're the *pink* people,' with a chuckle.

An observation made by a missionary friend during these years summed Festo up well: 'His preaching helped hearts turn from doubt to faith, unbelief to trust, nominal assent to commitment.' And, believing he had been called to his ministry by God, 'Festo preached his heart out.'

In May 1968 Festo was one of the main speakers at an international congress on evangelism, held at the University of Ibadan in Nigeria. In a letter to a friend, he had referred to it as a 'stop-off' on the way home, and arrived with no idea that a major turning point in his life had arrived. For one of the other delegates at the congress was a young South African Christian, Michael Cassidy. Since admiring Festo Kivengere's preaching when Festo had visited Fuller Seminary in 1962, where Cassidy was, in his own words, 'a very insignificant little student', Cassidy had gone on to become a dedicated and successful evangelist himself.

Cassidy was born in Johannesburg in the mid 1930s, and grew up in middle-class circles: educated at Michaelhouse in Natal and going faithfully—if dully—to an Anglican church. It was not until he was studying at Cambridge in the mid 1950s that he had been really touched by the gospel, and become personally committed to Christ. By the time he left Cambridge, the seed of an idea for evangelistic teams in Africa had been planted, though the name and structures of his future ministry remained hazy.

At Fuller his vision had come into focus based on the fact that Africa was swiftly changing from a continent of rural villages to one of burgeoning cities. A burden for the often lonely and dispossessed people of those cities and their leaders fell on him: there was a crying need for a ministry specifically geared to reaching them with the gospel. The vision would combine with his growing ministry of preaching worldwide, wherever opportunities presented themselves.

Cassidy had not waited to return to Africa to get started. By the time he left Fuller he had the beginnings of African Evangelistic Enterprise in place: with four years of Prayer Partners and financial support behind him, as well as a Board and office in Pasadena to which he was accountable. Soon there were also representatives in Europe: Claire-Lise de Benoit in Switzerland, Wolfgang Heiner in West Germany. 'The ripples were already spreading across the world.'

During the 1960s he had founded and nurtured his team (international, inter-racial, inter-denominational, non-political) of mainly South African Christians dedicated to the evangelism and spiritual renewal of their vast continent. They travelled far and wide, and had met with considerable success. They developed a strategy of targeting leadership in towns, cities and colleges, always working alongside already established churches. In South Africa they were also deeply committed to the work of reconciliation among polarised groups. In fact, until Ibadan in May 1968, Cassidy had assumed that African Evangelistic Enterprise 'would always be just our team'.

But after a session in the big conference hall, Cassidy returned to his room with 'the whole of the African burden very much on my heart'. Even the roadblocks caused by the Biafran war which he had encountered on the way to Ibadan served to heighten for him Africa's need for peace. He knelt to pray. 'Suddenly I had one of those extraordinary experiences where the room seemed pregnant with the presence of Jesus Christ. The word I seemed to get was: "Move out and build another team around Festo."'

Cassidy was 'electrified at the idea! Festo was a rising star and international spokesman for the revival.' With his support, Cassidy felt that African Enterprise could have great impact on East Africa as well. 'I was so excited and convinced about this that I rushed downstairs and into Festo's bedroom without even knocking. I cried: "Brother, I want to share a word from the Lord with you: God says I'm to help build a second team around you!"'

Festo sat back from his table in astonishment and stared at 'this wild young man with his wild idea'. If Cassidy had expected to begin arranging things there on the spot, he would have been disappointed. Festo, 'startled no end', responded politely, but with no encouragement whatsoever. He was very silent and reserved as Michael Cassidy eagerly expounded his idea for a second African Enterprise team to be founded and built up around Festo's ministry.

It is easy to understand Festo's lack of enthusiasm. To begin with, he already had an extensive ministry, with more invitations than he could possibly answer. He preached constantly throughout Africa as well as in countries worldwide. No organisation could possibly facilitate his ministry, already at world level, to which he believed God had called him. So what was the good of him beginning an African Enterprise in East Africa? Another major sticking point was that Michael Cassidy and AEE were South African. Apartheid was deeply resented in all independent African countries, and South African whites were anathema. 'I feared that to work with *that* man could jeopardise my own ministry in independent Africa too easily.' And Festo's ministry, his evangelism, had become his life's blood.

But as Michael Cassidy talked, Festo began to realise he could not just dismiss him as a misguided enthusiast. Cassidy's vision of the need of Africa and his determination to respond were too clear.

'I'll pray about it,' Festo ventured at last.

That was not enough for Cassidy. 'Well, won't you come and preach with me early next year at the Nairobi City Mission? It would be tremendous if we could work together.'

'Well, I'll pray about it,' was the hesitant answer.

Cassidy left, 'puzzled, excited, and on tenterhooks. I knew Festo was big game!'

1968: Festo and Michael Cassidy, together for the Nairobi Mission.

Festo was puzzled as well. Immediately he wrote off to Nairobi to investigate this mission. Was it a cowboy outfit? Who was involved? When he learned that the Revd Tom Houston (later head of World Vision), then a Baptist minister of a large Nairobi church, had instigated it, and that John Mpaayei of the Kenyan Bible Society was chairman of the mission, he was 'pleasantly surprised'. But then he realised he had to fulfil his promise to 'pray about' an African Enterprise set up in East Africa. He was deeply concerned about the risk.

But as he prayed, a thought kept recurring: 'If I really do fear this, then it may well be a barrier worth breaking.' He knew that Michael Cassidy's position was: 'I am a South African and here is a Ugandan brother and we are both against things which dehumanise black Africans in South Africa.'

Festo had got this far when he decided to take at least one step. He wrote to Michael Cassidy: 'I'm happy to come and preach with you in Nairobi early next year.' But he gave no indication as to his feeling for AEE in East Africa.

Commitments were pressing, and the rest of 1968 was just as

full of conferences, conventions, retreats and rallies. At one, the first ever Keswick Convention in Kampala, Canon T. Houghton, chairman of the English convention council, and Festo were among the main speakers. Houghton was attracted to Festo, and 'despite the great difficulty' which Festo had developed in keeping to time ('he was always bursting with things to say'), decided then and there that he must come and speak at the English Keswick as soon as possible. (In the end, this would not be until 1972.)

More and more preachers kept referring to 'what Festo said', recalls another friend from those years. 'His gift for apt summations was made much of, and he was widely quoted.' For example, 'Repentance is never action—it is re-action,' or 'We don't preach a Gospel of grace, we preach a Gospel by grace.' Certainly his 'unusual turn of phrase' caught the imagination of the Revd Stanley Voke, visiting Kabale to attend the Ruanda missionary conference that spring. After a final meeting when the sense of God's presence was so great that the testifying and repentance went on despite the chairman's efforts to close the meeting five times, Festo said joyfully to Voke afterwards: 'Did we not feel the heavy glory of God?!'

Festo's vitality, stamina and singlemindedness over evangelism during these years was legendary. He did not know the meaning of the word 'slow'. One of his favourite expressions was: 'Time is against us' or 'Time is not on our side.' He often repeated it—and 'Festo seldom repeated himself', according to Pat Brooks. Even in daily life, such as driving in or out of Kabale, he would drive so fast and be so lost in thought that he would speed by his own daughter Peace frantically waving to him for a lift home. When she would puff in half an hour later, he would be contrite but truly innocent: 'Where were you? I didn't see you!' When it came to ministry, nothing was allowed to get in the way. After speaking at a big school in Usumbura, the Belgian headmaster invited him back to his office for a drink. Festo had downed his coca cola and was counselling the troubled man before the accompanying missionary even had a chance to start on his drink.

On another afternoon he was due to preach at the cathedral in Mbarara, eighty miles from Kabale. He took Hope and Charity and two Christians with him in the Peugeot. Miles out from Mbarara the car went out of control and turned over twice. Charity was badly bruised and cut. Festo got a taxi and dropped her off at the hospital and then went on to the cathedral. The delay meant that someone else had taken his place in preaching, and the service had reached its final prayer. Every eye in the place was closed as Festo came through the door. He walked quietly down to the front, and by the time the congregation opened their eyes he seemed to have materialised out of nowhere. He began preaching his sermon to the startled congregation.

Once preaching, 'he just went on—not aware of anything else', according to his daughters. During their teenage years they went through a period where they were convinced that people did not want him to preach so long, usually over an hour at a time. The girls used to 'get very worked up' about this. One daughter began to sit down at the front near the pulpit so that she could give him a look which meant 'try to finish now!' In service after service she wore herself out with stern looks, which gave way as the minutes passed to anguished looks, but after-wards Festo's reply was always, 'I'm sorry, but I didn't even see where you were sitting!'

As for the rest of the family, Festo's fame began to rub off on the girls about this time. As soon as people heard that Peace (in London working at the Uganda High Commission), Hope (studying in the States), Joy (nursing in London) and especially Charity (as she was still in Uganda at Gayeza High School near Kampala) had the last name of Kivengere and that yes, it *was that Kivengere*, they were besieged by Christians. Would they join this that and the other church committee? Why not lead the coming project at church? Or—'even worse!'—why not stand up and preach? 'Everyone else had a choice as to the sort of person they would become, but not us. We were always expected to be "four star" Christians, able to preach like Dad, and be keen evangelists ready to lead any mission on the spot!' The girls found this notoriety deeply embarrassing at times. One took refuge for a time in a false last name. All felt thankful that 'at least Dad had been an obscure school teacher during our childhood'!

Their big consolation was that 'Dad never, ever tried to pressurise us into being anything we weren't. He loved us for our own personalities and did everything to help us achieve our own, different ambitions' (from advanced study to particular careers). Even when it came to Christianity, 'Dad encouraged us to be Christians, but he accepted us always as we were. We never had the feeling he was pushing us to be Christians.' With hindsight, the daughters believe this 'space' was the thing which drew them also to Christ. And Festo was overjoyed the day one daughter shyly admitted that she had made a personal commitment to Christ at one of his own meetings.

Along with the speed, however, there was always control and poise: it was the speed of determination, not of nerves. Festo, in fact, had an amazing ability to relax while in full flight. He would arrive at a crowded service or rally, 'not knowing the programme or what was expected of him. Yet far from fidgeting in the lobby or vestry beforehand, he would chat to the organisers, hum a little, and patiently await developments.'

But however far he went, for however long, the Christians of Kigezi always greeted his return with joy. Thousands of them travelled for miles over mountainous terrain to be at conventions and missions where he was due to preach. His 'fellow Kigezians' (as he called them) listened wide-eyed as 'Festo filled us in on what God was doing around the world'. They loved him because he never set himself up as an evangelist *from* Kigezi, but as an evangelist *of* Kigezi. 'He always made us feel involved in his ministry, and he was eager to share with us, as his friends, news of what God, not he, was doing.' When he was away, the diocesan council passed on news of his latest engagements, and prayed for him and his coming missions.

A friend explained: 'We'd known Festo all our lives. We'd preached with him on missions to little bush churches throughout Kigezi and beyond. If nowadays he had to catch an international flight to get to where he was to preach, rather than walk, we reasoned it just meant that on his return he'd have all the more thrilling stories to tell of God's work.'

The new year, 1969, found Festo in the States, but it was soon back to Africa for the mission with Michael Cassidy in Nairobi. 'Crossroads Mission to Kenya', or *Njia Ipi* (Swahili for 'Which

Way?'), had the backing of nearly all the churches in this sprawling, hustling city of nearly half a million people.

Festo was still concerned as the time approached. He shared his worries with Michael Cassidy—both frankly expected a great protest at the fact than an African of independent Uganda should be willing to share even the same platform as a white person from apartheid South Africa. 'It was quite a risk. We both did not know what to expect.' Festo even feared he might be about to jeopardise the ministry he had built up over the last ten years. But after prayer, both decided: 'Okay, let the protest come. We are going to proclaim the gospel.'

The meetings began at five pm each day. The two preached in turn. Festo spoke in Swahili, with an American Mennonite Bishop, Don Jacobs, interpreting for him. Michael spoke in English with a Swahili interpreter. And in all the weeks that followed, 'We didn't have a ripple of protest.' Perhaps because 'Michael did not stand there as a South African of apartheid. He had a message which could heal the rifts between our peoples.' Hundreds came forward as 'seekers'; hundreds were converted. John Mpaayei, for one, was delighted: 'This is going to have repercussions for all of Africa!'

Soon Festo and Michael began preaching in the revivalist style: in tandem. For example, Festo would take the Prodigal Son to the far country and put him in the pig sty; and Michael would fetch him home again. Or they would share the text of Mark 1:15, 16: 'Repent and believe the Gospel.' Michael would do 'repent' and Festo would then come in with 'and believe the Gospel'. On reconciliation, one would tackle the vertical relationship between God and man, the other would dwell on the horizontal—between man and man. Cassidy soon decided 'it was best to defer the climax to Festo, so I would go first'. He found the end of such sermons 'very exciting', watching from the platform as Festo's words wooed many to Christ.

The Nairobi mission was concluded in April. Festo returned to Kampala. Michael Cassidy decided to follow. Not only did he want a 'post-mortem' on a most remarkable mission, but he just had to know whether Festo had made any decision with regards to an East African team of African Enterprise.

An American colleague, Chris Smith, accompanied Cassidy to

Kampala where they booked into the Equatoria Hotel and spent a very restless night listening to gunfire out in the streets. (Though Obote was still in charge of Uganda, the political situation was fast destabilising.) But Michael Cassidy wouldn't have slept even had there been peace and quiet:

> Everyone who was anyone seemed to be after Festo. We were just a funny little baby outfit—of white South Africans! What made us even think we could hook in this giant of the faith? I knew that Billy Graham and World Vision had both tried to persuade Festo to sign on as their full-time associates—and failed.

Festo had excused himself on the grounds that his 'base' was the revival Christians in Kabale.

Next day Festo came to lunch at the Equatoria. The mission to Nairobi was discussed, and then the delicate subject of the future lay before them. Festo did not waste time: 'I have thought and prayed about your offer to become part of African Enterprise. I feel I should accept. I feel this is something the Lord requires of me.' The Nairobi mission had shown him, he continued, that 'here is a pattern God can use'.

'I'll never forget getting goose pimples and shivers down my spine and a sense of ecstatic delight when Festo said yes,' said Cassidy. 'This was titanic!'

After the meal, Cassidy and Smith went back to Cassidy's room, where they fell on their knees by the bed in 'prayers of joy to God in his goodness. Festo was to be my brother and partner in ministry across the continent!' Tears of joy streamed down Cassidy's cheeks.

As for Festo, there were good reasons why in the end he felt he could commit himself more easily to African Enterprise than to the huge American outfits, with all their resources. To begin with, he was proud to be African, proud to be part of the revival. He had therefore no desire whatever to become merely what would be seen as the African arm of an American overseas aid ministry. If he was going to team up with *anyone* on a more formal basis than that which he had had over the years with numerous revival Christians, it should at least bear the stamp 'made in Africa' on it. African Enterprise had overseas links, but was still African at grassroots.

His comment to Cassidy: 'This is something the Lord requires of me,' is also interesting. He had never worked with a South African before, and it would not have been easy to envisage a future teamed with a citizen of the most hated regime in Africa. It could conceivably bring nothing but trouble and disruption to his own ministry. But for a preacher of reconciliation, it was also a poignant 'visual aid'.

So plans went swiftly ahead for the founding of the team. Archbishop Erica Sabiti agreed to chair a board for the East African team, and the US Board welcomed Festo by letter to the team. Don Jacobs would soon join as well, and gradually the team would prepare for action. Before Cassidy returned to South Africa, he met a wealthy young businessman and good friend of Festo's, John Wilson, a warm, stately, devout Christian. Cassidy immediately coveted him as a future member of the East African team—but it would be years before this came about.

In the meantime, both Cassidy and Festo had to move on: their diaries were heavily booked. In fact, to make Festo's life easier, Bishop Lyth had arranged for him to move to Kampala for a time where he would become assistant chaplain of All Saints, Kampala, that August. It was a secure base, allowed great flexibility—and quick access to an international airport. This settled, in late May Festo and Zeb Kabaza (who until that month had been Headmaster of Kigezi High School) were on their way to the Leysin Conference in Switzerland, and then on to the States for the Billy Graham Great New York Crusade.

By early June Festo was preaching to hippies on the streets in New York City as part of the open-air ministry of the Crusade. He found the hippies very 'interesting' in that they were 'dead in earnest in seeking after reality. They hate convention and long for a "communication by contact".' All the same, Festo was startled when one listener turned up with a great snake wrapped round his shoulders and cuddled close to his chest. 'This was indeed communication by contact!'

After one meeting Festo was approached by an enormous militant Afro-American who said, 'I hate Christ. What are you going to do about it?' Festo looked up and up and up and was for a moment at a loss for words. Then he said simply, 'Well, I love him. May I take five minutes of your time to tell you why?'

'You do that, man.'

Festo then simply told the young hostile American about the night Christ had revealed himself to him in his hut in the banana plantation in Rukungiri. Five minutes later the young black had tears in his eyes. 'Maybe I need him too.' Again Festo had found that no one has ever been converted by mere theological arguments: they respond to a vision of Christ's love.

In July 1969, while Festo was still in America, which was about to put its first man on the moon, Uganda welcomed an important visitor: the Pope. His visit to Namugongo, the site of the martyrdoms of both Roman Catholic and Anglican 'pages' of Mwanga's court in 1886, and his welcome there in a service with Anglican clergy aroused the fury of the 'awakened'. (This was the legalistic faction of the revival who by now had been at variance with the rest of the Church of Uganda for nearly ten years.)

Mr Mondo, the leader of the 'awakened', made a variety of wild public accusations, among them that the Church of Uganda leaders now accepted the Pope as their ruler. His anger provoked others, and in a short time a heated public row was well underway. Within weeks it shifted back to the ten-year-old dispute over who was truly Christian: the brethren and the Church of Uganda, or only the 'awakened' ones.

The awakened had by now become exclusivist to a startling degree. For example, they held that *no* 'muzungu' or white missionary was really a Christian and any African who travelled to Europe or the States inevitably lost their faith, because there were no Christians in those countries. This was partly because they insisted that one had to wear shabby and old-fashioned clothes. Women had to have their hair short, men were not to wear beards or moustaches. Nobody was to comb their hair often. In reality, the awakened wanted a return to the ways of perhaps fifty years before.

Festo was gradually drawn into the row. (The awakened had dismissed him years before as worldly: not least for his international travels and fastidious appearance.) He had returned from the States in early August, spent a week preaching in Kinshasa, the Congo, and arrived in Kampala by the last week in August for the second ever Uganda 'Keswick' convention, which was being held at Namirembe synod hall. Festo was one of the convention's main speakers. Here he was told about the latest troubles with the awakened.

When he heard how Mondo had publicly equated true godliness with hatred of Catholicism he was furious. As well as a large group of enthusiastic Roman Catholic schoolgirls from Rubaga school, a group of nuns from the local Roman Catholic convent had happily attended the Keswick meetings, enjoying themselves so much that they invited him back to their convent to hear more—and to learn the revival songs. Such concentration on Christ and his saving love was, felt Festo, the true business of the revival: not seeking to offend others. He had been a friend of Mondo's but a chasm now yawned between the two: for years Festo had travelled the world, delighting in the work of the Holy Spirit in lives everywhere, while Mondo had stayed in Kampala, defining true spirituality in ever-decreasing, but always self-congratulatory terms.

When the Keswick convention was over, Festo had to take a series of meetings in Addis Ababa, the capital of Ethiopia, among them guiding Ethiopian Christians already caught up in revival, and also speaking at a studio director's conference of several hundred for Radio Voice of the Gospel, then headed by a Norwegian, Dr Sigurd Aske.

Back in Kampala in late September, Festo was still concerned about the Mondo row. By early November he had put pen to paper, and was writing in the Ugandan newspaper *New Day* as well, angry over the 'unwarranted ... confusing ... irresponsible public statements' that 'Brother Mondo' was making. Festo was given the front page to state his case.

> Each individual Christian may hold his own private views on non-essential points in the Christian life on such things as food and drink, and hair fashions and the like ... When any Christian brother or sister makes his or her private views on certain things 'the standard or rule of Christian living for all brethren', then his or her private views have replaced God's standard ... Our Lord Jesus forbids us to judge by mere outward appearance.

Festo, in fact, was far from ascetic. In a letter to Lilian he had once commented on his daughter Peace's new hairstyle with great approval: 'I really enjoy seeing pretty things. And I hate seeing shaggily dressed or badly made-up girls.' In the newspaper Festo continued:

> When any group of Christians rest their security on the views of certain individuals, their faith rests on 'sinking sand'. Many of our leaders ... develop a system of patterns of behaviour with special rules to guard these patterns; and then conclude that as long as the patterns are kept, spiritual life is secure among the members of the group. It was heresy when ruling elders taught that to disagree with them was to fight God.

Referring to the Kawempe incident, he said that Mondo was becoming 'a spiritual pope'. Festo then chivvied the Christians who hadn't stood up against this faction: 'Failing to speak against wrong views expressed publicly is to assent to them.'[5]

Other commitments forced Festo to drop out of the debate at this point, but he took the problem seriously enough to begin a very public, if mute, protest—he grew a moustache. He startled some European friends with it, but gravely explained it was his 'testimony to the freedom we have in Christ'.

November 1969 was filled with a pastors' conference in India, and a large mission back at Makerere University in Kampala, and commitments at All Saints Church, Kampala. In December Peace returned from London on leave, Joy's finals in nursing were well and truly over, and Festo went on home to Kabale to be with the family.

Like all Ugandan families, the Kivengeres were growing very concerned for the future of their country. Obote's continuing quasi-military rule, and several very unpopular decisions had served further to erode any remaining shreds of popular support. Most crucial had been his announcement that autumn of the Common Man's Charter, which set out his decision to move the country politically to the left, into socialism.

To add to the mounting tension, Obote was now having his doubts as to Amin's complete loyalty. He did little, however, as Amin had become indispensable to him in holding on to power. But Obote was right to worry: Amin was quietly recruiting more and more of the rurally poor from among the Nubians and southern Sudanese, with whom the giant Kakwa had ethnic links. They in return gave him their loyalty; a time bomb was ticking away under Obote.

The Mbarara Convention in mid-December was crowded and merry with old friends meeting up once again. The English revivalist, Roy Hession, gave the Bible readings, which Festo interpreted into Runyankole and Matt Nyagwaswa put into Swahili. Hession wrote afterwards: 'All the three of us caught fire.'[6]

Then it was on to Kabale for another brief convention with Roy Hession and Dr Joe Church before Festo packed—three days before Christmas—and left for a preaching tour of Australia, where he 'fired over 1000 people with enthusiasm for Jesus' at Sydney Town Hall, according to a former medical missionary to Tanzania.

Days later, in Uganda, Obote was shot leaving a party delegates' conference. Festo heard the news over the radio in the States, where he was fulfilling yet more speaking engagements. The bullet injured Obote only slightly, but heightened his suspicion of Amin. The 1970s reign of terror was drawing closer to an unsuspecting Uganda.

1970 opened with Festo's diary again booked up with speaking engagements at churches, rallies, youth and pastors' conferences and conventions from southern California to Malawi. He spent the first few months of the year mainly in the USA and Europe, where an issue that came up time and again was that of the baptism in the Holy Spirit, or the charismatic movement. This was spreading as fast—and causing as much divisiveness—as the revival itself had once done in Uganda. Festo's general conclusion to the squabbling and often arrogant bickering over who had had what experience and was operating with which spiritual gifts, was brief: 'We take our blessings to hit each other with. We make them a battlefield.'

Festo was not afraid of or averse to the movement: 'With Jesus, there is no tradition ... If we build walls of traditions, his life comes in like a river.' He was also concerned that in this rediscovery of the immanence of the Holy Spirit, the enthusiasm should not lead to an imbalance: 'Christ is the source of all gifts. The Holy Spirit does not speak of his own authority. He does not open his own storehouse. He takes what belongs to Christ and glorifies him.'

When the Revd Richard Bewes, then vicar of an Anglican church near Romford in Essex, ran into Festo in London about this time, he invited him out to his church. The interview with Festo in the hall after the service that evening soon veered to the Holy Spirit and the question of speaking in tongues. Everyone knew that Festo had come out of the great East African revival, and revival was also always credited with the coming of the Holy Spirit. So what did Festo think of the manifestations of tongues and the like? (At this time, *glossolalia* and other gifts were causing great concern in some circles.)

Festo explained that in the early days of the Ugandan revival: 'Oh yes, yes, we also had people who could speak in another language.' And it had startled them at first. 'So we said, "Is there anywhere in the Bible that mentions this?"' And we checked.' Using his hands as a visual aid, Festo flicked busily through an imaginary Bible until he came to rest his finger on a page. 'Oh yes, here it is: in Acts. It is in the Bible. So that's fine.' And with a great smile, he happily shut the imaginary Bible. 'Once we knew that, we just continued with our fellowship. Some people spoke in tongues, which was fine, and others didn't, which was also fine.' He went on to stress that he believed that the key to really renewing the church spiritually was not the charismatic movement, or any other movement as such, but the centrality of the crucified, glorified Jesus. Then the spiritual gifts and experiences would find their proper place.

Divine healing was another subject under considerable debate at the time. Festo often shared simply what had happened in the revival:

> We came to realise that Jesus could do anything. In our fellowship meetings we had seen epilepsy and TB cured. But such miracles were spontaneous and we never asked specifically for them. There was among us the feeling that 'Jesus is here and if you believe, he is able to do for you what he will, as he did with people in the New Testament'.

What made Festo very wary indeed were the 'healers' at this time who held meetings and 'practically banged people over the head' in an effort to heal them. His query to such practices was a cautious: 'Do you have to grip people so? Are you trying to imply that the power is in your hands?'

By the early summer of 1970 Festo returned to find Uganda in a considerably aggrieved state. Armed robbery was rampant, with thugs preying in force on shops, offices, houses—even ambushing people in the street in many big towns and small villages throughout the country. When the nation's security officers did not come to their aid, some citizens had begun to take the law into their own hands.

People were losing the last of their confidence in Obote. It began to look like there would be a slide into anarchy. In May Obote went ahead and began nationalising the economy. Trouble lay ahead.

Meanwhile, Festo and Michael Cassidy began drawing up plans for founding the East African arm of AEE. They decided, after prayer, that they needed to go public with their vision to get support for it. A tour of the United States was therefore put in their diaries for November to December. Cassidy had no doubts that this was the right way forward: he had had a very clear impression all throughout 1969 that he should make this tour of America in the latter half of 1970.

While the Pasadena staff of AEE got together with Michael, to draw up a tour incorporating both their own contacts as well as Festo's throughout the States, Festo continued his own busy set of preaching engagements. Just one example took place that summer in Blantyre, Malawi, in July. It was the launching of the 'New Life for All' programme, 'an interchurch, nationwide programme of evangelism' led by a well-known American minister, Dr Paul Rees, and Festo. It included a retreat for church leaders, and an outreach to students at the Chancellor College, part of the University of Malawi. The student rally would in fact be quite an historical event: the Student Christian Organisation had never before organised a definite evangelistic event. The Professor of Mathematics at the university, Dr Martyn Cundy, believed 'I would date the renewal of the SCO to this occasion—it was really the first time they were made to realise what being a Christian was all about.' Festo, 'full of joy, and confident of what he was talking about', spoke of his joy in sharing Christ with educated young people, saying, 'A change for the better for the continent of Africa has to begin with God's people.' One convert at his meetings was Malawi's first woman lawyer.

Back in Uganda, tensions reached snapping point in June when another attempt was made on Obote's life. When Amin went to Cairo in September, Obote began moves to outflank him. These failed, as Amin's Secret Services contacts warned him in time. There was now open enmity between the two leaders.

One highlight of the autumn was when Festo and Mera flew to Britain for the Jubilee Convention of the Ruanda Mission, held in Derbyshire's Swanwick convention centre. Over 300 came, including many old friends from the revival. Festo and Yosiya Kinuka (Dr Joe's former hospital dresser before the revival had begun, and now an international evangelist with fourteen grandchildren) were the main speakers.

Festo's standing with the Ruanda Mission and wider CMS is glimpsed in a letter written later that month, when the then CMS representative of the Ruanda Mission put forward Festo's name as:

> the one African from this District whom I would highly recommend for the honour of becoming a Vice-President and Honorary Governor for Life of the CMS ... Throughout the world he is known and loved as a member of the Ruanda Mission of the CMS, and the aim of the Missionary society, to preach the gospel and evangelise is, by the Lord's grace, materialised to a maximum degree by Festo's life and witness.

After the convention at Swanwick, Festo and Mera flew on to the States. In Boston, they joined Michael Cassidy and his wife, Carol, in final preparations for the AEE tour. The tour, in fact, had become a difficult thing for the Cassidys: they had only recently discovered that Carol was three months pregnant— hardly a good condition to be in when faced with irregular living and constant travel and stress. The four had long talks with members of the Pasadena Board, including Keith Jesson, who would become a close friend and colleague of Festo's in the years to come. Several last minute hitches in just how an East African arm would work did not rattle Festo. He took the attitude: 'We must learn to wait for the vision when it delays ... to come into effect.'

Festo and Cassidy spent a great deal of time in prayer together before sorting out the content of the tour. They decided to call it 'Mission 70' after a campaign Michael Cassidy had held earlier that year in Johannesburg. Both then received the impression that their theme should be taken from 2 Corinthians 5: that God had committed to them both the message and the ministry of reconciliation.

Both evangelists were agreed that the Holy Spirit

> was telling us that we had been brought together for a ministry of reconciliation—both vertical and horizontal. We prayed that between us, a white South African from apartheid South Africa, and a black Ugandan from independent Africa, we would in ourselves be almost a sort of living audio-visual aid to the Gospel and reconciliation.

Festo came up with a nickname for them: 'the miracle brothers', reflecting as they did the 'miracle' of fellowship across almost impossible divides of background, age and above all, race.

The tour began on the East coast and headed West, touching down along the way at a dizzying variety of churches and Christian groups in all sizes of towns and cities. It was interdenominational from Episcopalian to Presbyterian to Baptist to Independent. The unifying factor was only that all were Christians who knew of African Enterprise's work in South Africa, and were also interested in learning what needed to be done—urgently—with regard to the evangelism of East Africa. Festo laid before them time after time the vision of what a team could achieve in these developing countries.

The tour, lasting a few weeks, was a success—both on the public (prayer and financial support was promised) and personal side. Certainly the Americans responded well to the theme of reconciliation which Festo and Michael Cassidy presented. In this, the 'transparent' unity the two men had achieved was a great help. For example, Ted Engstrom, President of World Vision, was Master of Ceremonies at a Christian banquet for them in southern California, and had already introduced Festo when Festo leaned over and quietly asked Cassidy something. 'Festo's water glass was empty and Michael's was two-thirds full. Festo asked Michael if he might drink from his glass before he spoke, which he did.' That simple act seemed to Engstrom 'so

symbolic of the oneness of these black and white Christian
brothers. I remarked about this in introducing Festo, and it
made a considerable impact on the audience.'

On the personal side, the tour gave the two men a chance to
learn how well they as personalities would actually be able to
minister together. Michael Cassidy soon decided Festo 'was a
man of one passion—to convey the gospel of Christ to others,
and especially to convey the message of the East African revival,
in terms of focus on the cross and Calvary love'. He also
discovered that Festo did not give his friendship easily, and
though cordial, was more independent and reserved than his
rvival past might have led Cassidy to expect.

For though the unity in ministry was there, such teamwork
did require a conscious act of will on Festo's side. Since his tours
with Nagenda in the 1960s, with whom he was already very
close, he had not worked so closely 'yoked' to anyone, and
despite his occasional comments to friends in Kabale in the past
couple of years: 'We must get ourselves a team again,' he had
not actually taken any steps to create one. With his passion for
evangelism and the constant opportunities for international
preaching engagements, he had concentrated on simply
responding. But in the process he had gradually become something of a lone ranger—his self-confidence, determination, and
single-mindedness made it easily done. By now he was such a
high flier, not very many could have hoped to keep up with him.

Yet Festo would come to realise on this tour, and on later
ones, that being a law unto himself was not personally good for
him. In later times he would tell Cassidy that the AEE yoke,
though irksome at times, would be in fact vital for him. Though
never the introspective type, 'he had enough insight to sense that
being a lone ranger could have come to so dominate his life as to
be destructive'. Festo really did need a fellowship again, and as
far as his ministry went, an organisation of team framework
within which the financial and administrative side of things
would be cared for. African Enterprise would provide that:
though South Africa and East Africa would each have its own
indigenous African boards, they would also be answerable to
the Pasadena Board, as the parent body—not always an easy
thing for Festo to accept in the years to come.

Tragedy struck near the end of the tour. In Pasadena, Carol suddenly haemorrhaged and was put to bed by the doctor. Michael Cassidy and Festo reluctantly flew on to Seattle, Washington, and were preaching in a Presbyterian church on the 'fellowship of suffering' when a message came through: Carol had been taken into hospital. By the time the two men got back to Pasadena she had miscarried and lost the baby.

Here was suffering indeed. Cassidy and Carol struggled to make sense of their loss, finding firm ground only in their continuing certainty that they had been meant to make the tour at this time, and that Christ was with them in their sorrow. Festo and Mera were deeply moved by the loss of the little girl, and indeed the grief seemed to open Festo up more on a personal level than any other time on the entire trip. He told Cassidy of his own Lydia, who had died so many years before of cerebral malaria—brought on by the harsh climate Festo had imposed on her by his ministry to the Tanganyikans. More than anything, the bereavement cemented Festo's determination that his and Cassidy's future ministry of AEE should be at least in some small measure worth the appalling loss the Cassidys had suffered in bringing the East African team to birth.

The tour drew to a close. The Pasadena Board got down to work on setting up an East African administration. The Cassidys flew back to South Africa, and the Kivengeres flew home to Uganda. It was to be but a brief stop at home for Festo: in early January he was due in New Guinea.

CHAPTER FIFTEEN

CONSECRATED AMID VIOLENCE

1971–1972

Obote's government falls to Amin; Festo launches AEE in Kampala; teething problems; the Amin violence begins; Festo's reaction to state brutality; Indonesian revival problems; nominated for bishop; consecrated and enthroned.

LATE JANUARY 1971 found Festo in Papua New Guinea, guest speaker at a pastors' conference. The pastors had a problem: in 1975 Papua New Guinea would gain its independence. What role should the Christians in the country take in such a maelstrom of change and conflicting self-interests?

The pastors lingered long with Festo over meals and throughout the afternoons, 'devouring his every word', according to a World Vision leader there at the time. Uganda was just coming up to its tenth year of independence, but the story Festo had to share with them was certainly not encouraging: the Ugandan Church in fact had been all but helpless to stem the chaos which Obote's regime had caused. Mismanagement and corruption at every level of government had eroded public support for the government. The unrest had been held in abeyance by sheer oppression for several years now. (There were thousands of political prisoners.) Increasingly Obote had had to rely on his army and Idi Amin to keep him in power. But as the two assassination attempts on Obote in December 1969 and June 1970 were widely suspected as being Amin's work, by early 1971 Obote's unpopularity and (rather understandable by now) paranoia had Uganda in a most tense and unhappy state.

Festo had no sophisticated political solution to his country's problems. He was an evangelist, not a political scientist. Beyond believing that the church *did* have a duty to speak as the conscience of the nation, and applauding the attempts of several bishops and of Uganda's church newspaper to do so in recent years, he could only apply broad principles based on one simple premise: that the only ultimate solution for any nation's welfare was when its citizens' individual spiritual welfare was looked after. He argued that this was not a pie-in-the-sky solution—the Ruanda Mission and CMS had made enormous progress in development once the Africans had made a Christian commitment.

As Sunday 25th January approached, he prepared his sermon. Whatever lay in store for the Christians of Papua New Guinea in the future they would surely need to remember the 'low place at the foot of the cross', where bitterness could be turned to forgiveness through the blood of Christ.

As Festo prepared, little did he dream that in the years ahead, he, perhaps more than all the pastors there that week, would be forced to consider the question—and find an answer—of what a church leader should do when his country is torn apart by unscrupulous, violent leaders.

The very morning—25th January, 1971—that Festo was due to preach his sermon, he woke early, and drowsily switched on his little travelling shortwave radio. The headlines brought him bolt upright in bed: there had been a military coup in Uganda. Major General (Big Daddy) Idi Amin Dada had seized control of the country. President Milton Obote, in Singapore on a Commonwealth Conference, could return to Uganda only at certain risk to his life.

As the day wore on, the BBC World Service filled in some details: the coup had been carried out in the very early hours by a small section of the army, the Malire Battalion. After some gunfire, the ponderous voice of an NCO had come on to Radio Uganda to announce that the army, under Amin, had taken over the government. He read out a list of eighteen points of justification for this action. (The truth was that Amin had already stolen the army's loyalty away from Obote and with Obote out of the country, this was an ideal time to act. For years Amin had made good use of his ethnic links with the southern Sudanese: whole corps had been quietly absorbed into the

Ugandan Army units along with thousands of Nubians. Such soldiers gave their loyalty to Amin, not to Obote, nor to the people of Uganda.)

Within minutes the streets of Kampala had been full of crowds, stamping on Obote's picture and hailing Amin's action with joy. Celebrations were still in full swing by the time Festo flew into Entebbe. Amin was touring the country accompanied by his cabinet and senior officers. The people were wildly excited to hear his promises: that the body of the exiled Kabaka would be brought back from Britain; that sixty political prisoners (including five former cabinet ministers) would be released; that free elections would be held as soon as possible, with all parties, including Obote's, to participate. The Church of Uganda warmly welcomed all these changes, and Festo joined in giving thanksgiving to God for the passing of Obote. It was a widely-held Christian belief in Uganda at this time that Amin had been raised up by God as a sort of Cyrus of Persia—a pagan who would nonetheless deliver them from the evil of another pagan ruler—in this case, Obote.

International reaction to the coup was mixed. President Nyerere of Tanzania, where Obote was soon to take refuge, was furious. He broadcast: 'This is an act of treason to the whole course of African progress!' But Kenya under Jomo Kenyatta was pleased: her capitalistic economy found Obote's socialism anathema (in the years to come she would long provide Amin's economic lifeline in East Africa). Great Britain, Israel and the United States also welcomed Amin, for a complex mixture of political and economic reasons. Other countries, including France, India, Pakistan, West Germany, Japan and Italy would also find economic advantage in helping him in the coming years. Later even the Soviet Union and Libya would find Amin's rule of such advantage that they supported it.

Meanwhile, for the first few weeks, Amin's popularity soared in Uganda. Rich Buganda businessmen, military officers and top politicians smelt advantage and money for themselves in the new regime. Amin also said the things that ensured the warm support of the Church of Uganda. For one thing, in February Archbishop Erica Sabiti told Festo in amazement that Amin, a Muslim, had urged all Ugandans to be faithful in worship at their church or mosque. He had actually thumped the Archbishop on the back: 'Archbishop, I want your help and advice. If you see anything going wrong, come to me at once!' Festo told a friend: 'We were astonished and pleased!' Later that month in a newsletter overseas he continued, 'The country is much more at ease since the coup! We can only thank the Lord, who put his hand over our country.'[1]

Festo attended the great funeral in Namirembe Cathedral when the Kabaka's body was finally brought safely back to Uganda. He and everyone else was in a euphoric state, especially the Baganda Christians. Then, while Amin built the (later infamous) 'State Research Bureau'—a three storey pink stucco office building next to his plush Kampala residence, Festo turned his attention to the development of an African Enterprise team for East Africa.

Michael Cassidy flew up to Uganda and Festo introduced him to various people he had tagged as ideal members for the first Eastern African Evangelistic Enterprise Board and team. Archbishop Sabiti had agreed to act as Chairman of the Board. Men for the teamwork included Zebulon Kabaza, Festo's former classmate from Mbarara days; then there was John Wilson, a Ugandan sales manager and director of Caltex (Ug.) Ltd; Matt Nyagwaswa of Mwanza, Tanzania, with whom Festo had preached in the USA, was another. There was a big meeting held at Limuru conference centre outside Nairobi.

Festo and Michael Cassidy arrived with high hopes of forming an East Africa AEE Board which would be based in Nairobi, as well as a team that would consist of Christians from all the East African countries. However, Festo and Cassidy soon learned to their cost that it was one thing to share hymn-singing and testifying at conventions with brethren throughout East Africa, and quite another thing to attempt to organise them into a coherent, organised team. Festo's oft-reiterated line that the evangelism of East Africa was too crucial to be left to individuals, and so 'We must have a team that will always carry on the work!' went unheeded. The Kenyans were full of suspicions about an organisation being set up among them so that a limited number of brethren could do the evangelistic work they had always done—and be paid for it! The idea of salaried full-time evangelists struck them as bizarre. There was also probably a good deal of resentment that Festo, as a Ugandan, would be the head of such a team over the Kenyans. In any event, there was a 'fair degree of obstruction', which Cassidy found 'terribly tiresome and trying'.

In the end, it was obvious a single board of African Enterprise for East Africa would simply not happen. It was decided to simply launch a Ugandan board that year, headed by Festo, and a Tanzanian board.

This meant that the first East African AEE base had to be in increasingly destabilised Kampala. Because of Archbishop Sabiti's support for the work, it proved possible to have a room in the Provincial Offices of the Church of Uganda situated on Namirembe Hill, just below the cathedral. No more space was needed: it was obvious AEE was to have small beginnings in Uganda. What *was* needed was someone to run the office and administration. Festo approached Lilian Clarke, who after thirty years in the Ruanda Mission, was due to retire that year, and not looking forward to it. Somewhat tentatively Festo suggested: 'There is an open door here for you, if you want it.' Lilian gladly accepted, believing that an East African AEE team was 'a very, very sensible idea'. It was arranged that after leave in England, she should return to Kampala in 1972 as executive secretary.

So Festo launched the Uganda AEE that spring from the room in the Provincial Office, with the sole help of Zebulon Kabaza. (Wilson was not free to leave his job, Matt was in Tanzania with the Ministry of Education, but would help with the Tanzanian AEE where he could.) The first aim was simple enough: simply to make AEE known: 'No one in East Africa had ever heard of it!'

Certainly there was an urgent need for a strategy of evangelism in East Africa. Church leaders throughout Uganda, Rwanda and Burundi had been discussing the 'new and demanding challenges' facing the African Church: 'That the age of foreign missions in Africa is now over is a fact ... We must stir ourselves up to realise that the age of home mission in Africa is dawning.'[2]

This was precisely Festo's vision for AEE. He agreed with Michael that the main effort should be made following 'the drift to the towns and the gradual urbanisation' ... this was the Africa 'of the future ... Here live the politicians, the pace-makers of African life and the managers of Africa's future economy. This is the world of challenge to the Christian Church ...'[3] Michael Cassidy had high hopes that year. 'I coveted seeing Festo in the city-wide campaigns we would hold across Africa.' He was disappointed when Festo had to refuse several because of other engagements in Europe and the USA.

Meanwhile, as early as March it was widely known—though quietly talked about—that Amin had given his military extra-ordinary powers of arrest. There were rumours that many men of the Langi and Acholi tribes, serving in the military and the police, had been killed. No one seemed immune from the purges: even the revered judge of the Uganda Supreme Court had 'disappeared'. Soon several more of the country's intelli-gent, capable leaders did as well. Others fled Uganda.

For the pink stucco State Research Bureau was now active, with a staff of SRB 'agents'—thugs and killer squads aided by a vast array of electronic equipment: computers, radio communi-cations gear and phone-tapping systems. Ugly rumours of beatings and murders spread.

Around Easter Festo went to Ghana, to lead a Scripture Union house party. The political turmoil he had left behind was very much on his mind. But, as always for Festo, everything began or ended at the cross, and it was from here he seems to have tried to make sense of Amin:

> The cross speaks of life in conflict with death, life defeating death ... The cross is ... God moving in love to meet violent men and women, himself facing violence and suffering for us ... Your faith was born in violence. The Christian is not scared when nations are upset, when the whole world is shaking. Your faith was born on Calvary— it can stand anything. It is an all-weather faith.[4]

It needed to be in Uganda that year. By May there were mass killings within the military and police. 6,000 would die by July. Ugandans were replaced by Kakwa, southern Sudanese and Nubian recruits. The church and its leaders—Festo among them—joined in reminding people to look to their faith for strength, and to pray.

For Festo, there was only one taste of the more positive side of African politics that year—when he went to Dodoma for the first pastors' conference held in the country, and discovered that the President of Tanzania, Julius Nyerere, was also coming because he wanted to speak to the pastors. Nyerere—a Roman Catholic—said he wanted an African socialism which was not atheistic. He welcomed the church, its ministry and contributions, in the communal villages he envisaged. Nyerere went on to say he wanted for Tanzania a socialism which accepted God and Christ. Festo was much moved by the speech.

Back in Uganda after a series of missions and conferences from America to Europe, Festo also squeezed in several missions in Uganda itself, including one at Makerere University. (The students congratulated themselves at having got him as guest speaker—by now every time news went out that Festo would be in Kampala on such and such a date, the Christians fought each other in persuading him to come to them for a mission.)

Unfortunately, the growing fear of Amin did not serve to reunite the Christians of the 'reawakened' movement to the rest of the Church of Uganda. To Festo's dismay, that autumn the 'reawakened' ones broke off completely from the Church of Uganda. (Within a few years the movement would have dwindled away.)

As a member of the Kigezi Diocesan Council, Festo was embroiled in another church row that year. The two Buganda dioceses argued with the rest of the dioceses over whether or not to make the capital, Kampala, a separate diocese to be headed by the Archbishop. One diocese threatened to secede altogether from the Church of Uganda. Another simply refused to discuss the proposed changes to the constitution at all.

To everyone's utter amazement, Amin suddenly intervened. He declared he did not want a divided church in his country, and called all bishops and diocesan councils to a meeting at Kampala's conference centre to settle the matter once and for all. Festo later described it:

> For two days we sat and looked at one another, and the differences remained. But on 28th November, the Lord gave us a message from

Philippians. We saw that we were men going up, each one thinking about his reputation and demanding his rights. But that day we caught a vision of the man-coming-down; Jesus, 'who, though he was in the form of God, emptied himself, taking the form of a servant ...'(Phil 2:6, 7).

What a change he made! In the presence of 'him who came down', our dear Archbishop, Erica Sabiti, and each of the nine diocesan bishops, went down in confession of the sins which had contributed to the divisions in the Church and a great melting by the Holy Spirit came upon us all.[5]

President Amin in the months and years to come would laughingly remind the bishops that he had 'saved the church'.

Meanwhile, through Festo's strenuous efforts, the African Enterprise team in East Africa was slowly becoming known. A faint pattern for its ministry began to emerge. The work would be on international, interdenominational, inter-racial, non-political lines. The make-up of any one particular evangelistic team for a mission would vary: alongside the core AEE staff would be evangelists seconded for that particular outreach. (Very few were ordained.) The missions would usually begin when an invitation came from a group of churches in a given area, asking AEE for their expertise in holding an evangelistic outreach. After lengthy talks the AEE team would then link up with the local churches for the outreach. Festo attended as many AEE missions as he could, other engagements permitting.

Not all the missions were in East Africa. As the team became known, invitations arrived from Holland, Norway, West Germany, the United States, and other countries. These churches in turn helped support the work going on in East Africa.

AEE continued to suffer its fair share of hiccups. (Teamwork is never easy even among people of the same background and culture.) Between the South African and East African team members apartheid was always in the background, misunderstandings and tensions could erupt all too easily. A superhuman effort had to be made at times.

In these early days of AEE for East Africa, Michael Cassidy and Festo teamed up for many missions in Africa, but especially overseas, in an effort to get the East African team as well launched as possible. Michael Cassidy was able to introduce Festo to many new contacts, as Festo for his part was able to use his extensive contacts to widen AEE's horizons.

Teamwork also gave both busy men an opportunity to get to know one another better. Though both were gifted evangelists and preachers, their personalities were very different. Where Michael Cassidy was intense, conscientious and meticulous with regard to the organisational side of things, Festo didn't go in for details, having more of an easy-going approach. He was content to let other team members do the hard footwork to make the mission run smoothly, only asking for a day's warning for meetings.

Then too Michael Cassidy was amenable to team life, and willing to abide team decisions. Festo decidedly did not like to be over-ruled. When crossed, 'he did not cope at all well', and those involved spoke of 'painful encounters'. This was in all likelihood due to his seniority in age and experience over the others, as well as the many years of having been his own boss. Working now within the confines of a team was a painful adjustment. With hindsight, Michael Cassidy noted 'with surprise' that 'Festo never once apologised to me for anything in all the years together'.

In line with this, Michael Cassidy found Festo was 'better at preaching brokenness and openness than doing it'. In fact, Cassidy found it hard to 'get really close'. This was undoubtedly due to Michael Cassidy's South African background, with all the implied tensions of apartheid. Festo was a proud black African, and loathed the apartheid system. So the early years of close contact with South Africans—even devout Christians—was at times difficult for him. As Michael Cassidy put it:

> He was not spontaneously open and transparent with me. But I found if I shared something openly, it would sometimes elicit a similar response from him. But he never voluntarily made himself vulnerable. He could be quite self-protective.

The men also varied in their reactions to the stress of missions where thousands of people were involved. Inevitably, the media was there as well with TV cameras, radio reporters, microphones, and bevies of reporters. Michael, more sensitive and self-doubting, admired Festo's 'astonishing' self-assurance. 'At times when I'd be scared to death of a situation, Festo would appear as cool as a cucumber. No nervousness, no hesitation.' Cassidy put this down to 'a deep personal security within himself'.

The two evangelists also preached differently. As they carried the main burden of preaching on any mission, both spent more time in preparation and needed more solitude in which to do so than the other members of the team. Michael would fully prepare his sermons, writing them out after much hard work and prayer. Festo, thoroughly mentally prepared, would rely, at the very most, on his notes. His approach was more bold, strong and relaxed. Cassidy recalls:

> It surprised me—he would extemporise to such an amazing degree. One verse would trigger off an astonishing flow of material and insights. It was brilliant. He was so steeped in theology and the Bible, plus the anointing of the Holy Spirit.
>
> Many of us have other dimensions to our lives than our ministries, but for Festo, that was it: evangelism was the air he breathed, the food he ate.

During these early years of AEE joint team missions, the two preached in revival 'tandem' fashion many times, Cassidy marvelling at Festo's 'amazing flexibility—he would take up wherever I left off and carry the message forward to a natural climax'.

Off duty on the tours, Michael Cassidy soon realised that Festo shared his love of reading and had learned to grab every spare moment during the mission to steep himself in theology, picking up insights as he went. 'He was always into some deep theological work—especially anything on the cross.'

> I can't tell you how many times I was astonished to see what Festo was reading—often dense German theology. Most of us took three or four books along, none of which we read. But Festo usually had just one book with him, well scored, and open on his hotel desk which he was thoroughly absorbing. I admired this tremendously.

Such wide reading was done with a definite purpose. Festo explained once to friends, 'The gospel cannot be preached apart from what the people who hear it are themselves struggling with.' Therefore he was determined that, whatever he said, his message would 'really speak to the situation in which we are today'. Hence the modern theology and philosophy. 'He really got in to the heavies,' said Cassidy, 'and this no doubt provided an ever-deepening base to his popular ministry.'

When it came to reading the Bible, Festo was 'in many ways more of a Hebrew than a Greek', found Cassidy. For whereas the Greeks were attracted by the passionless contemplation of truth, the Hebrews were passionately involved, seeing truth as action.

> The Hebrews saw things in pictures. They wrote about them in pictures ... they saw the world as something dynamic, speaking ...
>
> Festo had the amazing capacity to see the Word of God at both the immediate level and also the subterranean, picture level. He always saw the picture beyond. For example, in the story of Zaccheus coming down from the tree, Festo told of our need to 'come down', to humble ourselves if we are to find Jesus. And when he told the story of the disciples rowing on the lake in the storm, he found in it parallels to 'our struggle with life, being battered without Jesus'.
>
> He was extremely vivid—you could see your own life and spiritual walk in terms of a vivid picture there in the Bible, which he had just expounded so beautifully.

As for the different translations of the Bible, Festo deliberately changed his every two years or so, finding the clean, unmarked pages 'a great stimulus'. New translations were 'fascinating—I wanted to hear what they were going to say to me!' However, his favourite version remained the AV or King James Version, which had been his basic Bible for years and years. 'I was steeped in that ... although sections of it were in arcane language, certain expressions were very powerful, which new translations did not bring out as clearly.' He also liked the RSV. The NEB he found 'too English', and the Good News 'tended to play down certain things'.

Of course, both men missed their families, though Mera—the children grown—now travelled with Festo whenever possible. But whereas Michael Cassidy was careful to safeguard his family life, he did marvel at Festo's obviously happy marriage, despite an 'extraordinary degree of absenteeism'. Once when Mera admitted to having had to 'repent of bitterness' at being left alone so much during former years, a colleague of Cassidy's only comment was, 'Yes, but has Festo repented?' Yet the Kivengeres' marriage was undeniably very happy.

However, Festo was aware of the dangers. As he told friends: 'People are crowding, you are preaching ... the tendency is to get steeped in your preparation and forget that your wife is being increasingly isolated ... to give her time means to push away your wonderful books and notes ...'

In giving Mera time, Festo had sometimes to make quite an effort to switch his attention from international evangelism to simple domestic life. And while he could cope with the strains and stresses of constant travel and major public appearances without losing his poise, he once confided to a friend, in a somewhat bewildered way: 'I so often lose my peace when I go out shopping with my wife!'

One of the earliest meetings of the South African and East African AEE teams was held in Glion, Switzerland. It had been planned to provide a chance for fellowship; it turned into very rough going. Cassidy recalls: 'We were all in a very heavy mood. There was great distrust between the South African and East African teams due to the stereotypes and presuppositions which dominated the thinking of all.' At one point, 'it really did look as though the ceiling was going to fall in'. Next morning, it was Festo's turn to open a session. He began with a testimony. A couple of hours before, he said, he had been praying and expressing his love for Christ. Suddenly he had heard an unmistakable inner voice say: 'I know you love me, but do you love Michael?' Festo went on to admit that he had had to confess to a lack of love, and that the Lord had then poured love in.

The Revd Dr Don Jacobs, a leader in AEE recalled,

Having given us his witness, Festo crossed the room and embraced Michael before all of us. This was a moment which had about it the aura of eternity. The fellowship between the South African and East African teams was built upon that little walk of ten steps that Festo took toward Michael. Michael, of course, responded in the spirit, and here was great joy as the Holy Spirit melted the barriers which were separating these teams.

By late 1971 Amin had consolidated his grip on Uganda. His army, now half southern Sudanese and Nubian, had no loyalty to the Ugandan population, and for many, working in Amin's army, police or spy networks was a 'golden chance of driving a car ... extorting money or picking up people'. State Research Bureau agents favoured flowered shirts, bell-bottom trousers, sunglasses, platform shoes, and latest model cars. They were 'notorious for tossing their victims into trunks of their cars, and speeding off. Invariably, the victims were never seen alive again.'[6]

But as the terror increased, so too was there an immense rekindling of interest in spiritual things. Festo later told friends: 'We saw people coming to fellowship meetings who had been absent a long time. ... We read God's Word with an urgency of needing to know what he wanted us to do in our situation.' Throughout Uganda, Christians in villages and cities sought God for 'strength to keep going, and to share his love with others, despite widespread fear'.[7]

January 1972 arrived—the first anniversary of Amin's coup. Festo was again out of the country, this time on a preaching tour in Indonesia, where the church had been experiencing widespread revival since the early 1960s (since, in fact, about the time Festo had first visited there with the Ugandan evangelist William Nagenda and the English evangelist Roy Hession in 1963). The churches by now were bursting with enthusiasm and Festo, always a great people lover, responded with joy to the 'deep love for Christ'. 'It has been a great beginning of 1972 for us,' Festo wrote to a friend.

There were in fact many reported instances of the Indonesian Church experiencing the miraculous at this time—most usually in the form of visions. Festo accepted that this might indeed be happening. He wrote later:

> When the Lord began to bless Indonesia he had to use unusual manifestations and miraculous experiences so that the Muslim, who finds it difficult to be convinced about Christians, would be assured it was true. When a Muslim is confronted by a vision, there is nothing to argue about.

But, inevitably, excesses and misunderstanding had crept in. Festo was not surprised: 'Because we are human, we tend to pick up certain attractive things in the movement of the Spirit of God, and give them prominence at the expense of the real work he does in the hearts of his people.'

One incident in particular which had occurred on the island of Timor had provoked a scandal. It had all started with reports that at a certain Holy Communion service in a church in Timor the prayers of the Christians had resulted in water being changed into wine. Great rejoicing had followed, and the news had spread rapidly. Of course there were then many attempts to repeat the miracle. All of them ended in vain. At one such attempt, however, the transformation had been faked—and found out. Scandal had erupted. When Festo arrived in the midst of it all, his counsel had been sought.

He kept what he had to say loving and simple. 'Brother, how many times in the New Testament did water turn into wine?'

'Once.'

'Then why try to do it twice?'

A friend later reported: 'Little by little some of the hard lessons learned in East Africa were [thus] shared with the Christians of Indonesia.' Festo would certainly challenge people who spoke of *having had* a revival, those who believed that when the miraculous manifestations had subsided, that was it. As always, his insistence was, 'But *real* revival is Jesus Christ himself! Don't think the manifestations were given to feed you! They shook you up, so you could go to the Bread of Life himself.'

From Indonesia the next port of call was the Solomon Islands—his hosts, the South Seas Evangelical Church. When he arrived early that February the enthusiasm was such that on his arrival from the airport he was given 'precisely twenty minutes to freshen up' before being whisked off to the church to preach. 'The singing was so powerful that I thought the roof would almost be blown off!' Festo nearly didn't preach. 'The Holy Spirit was preaching. Why bother with a preacher? Anyway, I did say a few things, and I got excited too, because the Spirit of God blessed me through them ...' He spent three weeks in the Solomon Islands, preaching three times a day. Congregations averaged 2,500.

Here again, the very success of the revival had generated some confusions and excesses. Festo strongly advised the church leaders to follow the example of the revivalists within Uganda, and stay within the mainstream church, and not split away. 'Having experienced revival in Africa for years, Festo's help was invaluable,' missionary George Strachan wrote home to England. 'I had never heard anyone speak so much of Christ before. He understood all sides. He explained that ministering in revival is a very dangerous time. People are fired up, divisions easily arise.'

Festo wrote to a friend at the time: 'In the end it is the patient, ever-loving, ever-caring Jesus who matters. In HIM incomplete lives are continually made complete, by the agent of the Holy Spirit, who made us God's children.'

Unfortunately, the exhilaration of the trip could not last long. Back in Uganda that February, Festo was greeted by horrific rumours of further mass slaughters. So it was all the more bizarre when Amin suddenly gave Festo and several others permission to accompany the chief army chaplain, Bishop Wani, to preach at army barracks throughout the country. He even supplied them with an army Land Rover. Festo and his colleagues hastily accepted the offer and set out, only to be further astonished when they found that Amin had ordered that all his army personnel attend because 'these men are coming to tell you about the love of God. This is not for a particular group. All men must come.' So Muslims, Catholics, Protestants, and non-religious men came, even their wives. The commandants at each barracks greeted Wani, Festo and their colleagues with 'Here are the officers and men: you can preach to them as long as you want.'

Festo, for one, needed no further encouragement. 'For a whole month we saw the glorious working of the Spirit. Some of these soldiers we saw in tears ...'

Despite the worsening political scene, and indeed the horrific civil war which erupted in Burundi that April, life had to go on somehow. Festo concentrated on the enormous task of building and developing AEE. With opportunities for mission at every turn, the name and reputation of AEE was slowly beginning to capture people's interest. Lilian Clarke returned from furlough to find the AEE office buzzing with activity ... and soon set to work to achieve some order. The mailing list of supporters worldwide was growing: from England to the States to Australia to West Germany, all Festo's popular stamping grounds. Closer to home, Festo even appealed for help to the rich Bahima cattle owners of Ankole and Kigezi.

Then in late May of 1972 came news that was to change the rest of Festo's life. On 30th May the fourth diocesan council for the diocese of Kigezi had met. Bishop Dick Lyth had announced that he believed his work was done in Uganda, and that he would be retiring that autumn. The diocesan council was appalled and tried to dissuade him. One member described his choked feeling in graphic if not idiomatic English: 'There is a football in my throat.' Nevertheless, Lyth remained adamant: Kigezi must now look for a new bishop.

Lyth would be a hard act for anyone to follow. Under his gifted leadership, Kigezi had come a long way, and he was greatly loved. His background training for the job had been ideal: as well as being the son-in-law of one of the original founders of the Ruanda Mission, Dr Stanley Smith, Lyth had been a missionary, a wartime army officer and then a District Officer in the Sudan for many years, before going for ordination and ministry in Uganda. As the first ever bishop of the newly created Kigezi diocese, he had been an inspired choice—English (and therefore above tribal suspicion), a brilliant administrator (building firm foundations for the running of the diocese) and concerned for mission (thousands had been converted). He had also launched the Christian Rural Service (which would spread in time throughout Uganda) which trained men and then sent them into villages to found literacy classes, build roads, and teach basic hygiene. He had stressed stewardship in giving, and the diocese had responded.

Within a few days the diocese was buzzing with the news of Lyth's impending retirement, and the choice of the next bishop. There was a common consensus that he should be a Ugandan and from there it was a short step as to which Ugandan: Festo Kivengere. As a friend put it: 'We knew his gifts of vision and message would be to the good of the diocese.'

In fact, many people had earmarked him since before even his ordination. There was the time in April 1966, when Lyth was being chosen, and he had written in a letter to Festo: 'The church in Kigezi had been wanting their own bishop ... and though of course they have always had you ultimately in mind ...'

Certainly the diocese badly needed a strong popular leader in whom as many as possible had confidence. In addition to the inevitable tensions due to tribalism, the man would have to guide a diocese in the face of widespread terror which now existed. Christians throughout Kigezi's thirty-six parishes prayed for the future bishop.

Soon an informal delegation from members of the diocesan synod and council approached Festo and Mera, and asked Festo to pray about becoming their next bishop. Festo was deeply touched. In a letter to a friend he wrote: 'One feels so unworthy for such a regard. It is Christ's love alone that has made us worthy of such consideration from his children.' Festo was immediately receptive to the idea, recognising that he did indeed have the popular groundswell of support needed. Nevertheless, his early reaction to the idea was one of 'Yes, but!' He would under no circumstances abandon his calling to be an evangelist. If he was ever to be Bishop of Kigezi, it would have to be in *addition* to his international commitments in evangelism. He made this quite clear to the delegation.

He was perhaps not quite so straightforward with AEE at this time. He did not warn Michael Cassidy that he was becoming a serious candidate for the job. Most likely because he could guess his reaction all too well. Privately by now it seems he had determined that, if called, he could do both.

Discussions continued throughout Kigezi diocese. The common people had no trouble in accepting Festo's ultimatum about evangelism if he was to be their bishop. The church in Kigezi had been founded within the lifetime of many of them by evangelists, and evangelism was considered a duty and privilege of everyone. (Indeed, a prospective bishop who said he would give up all personal evangelism would have seemed even stranger.) Undoubtedly most of the people did not appreciate the demands on a bishop if he was successfully to pastor his diocese. Even so, in Africa the traditional custom was that the people wait upon the pleasure of the leader for their needs, and do not consider their leaders as public servants. That Festo's travels would mean he would have little time to serve the diocese did not weigh against him in their minds then. At this point they simply wanted their favourite, most popular preacher: Festo. That he was an evangelist of international standing only enhanced him.

So, common feeling soon crystalised along the following lines: 'If you want to be an evangelist while bishop, fine. When you go away on safari, all we ask is that when you return, you tell us what God is doing.' It had echoes of the travelling teams in the early days of the revival. The vast majority of people thought this marvellous. Not everyone agreed with them, of course. A good few—probably those with administrative burdens of their own—had doubts as to Festo's ability to take on such an enormous workload, impossible for anyone. They feared the diocese must inevitably suffer.

Soon the electoral college of Kigezi diocese met. Their task was to finalise the two names to be put forward to Archbishop Erica Sabiti and the House of Bishops—a first choice and a second choice. But as with Bishop Lyth's appointment in 1966, by unanimous decision they sent forward only one name: Festo Kivengere. Bishop Lyth, as current bishop, had to endorse this. He did so willingly. The House of Bishops were left the simple choice: accept or refuse Festo. According to the Provincial Constitution, they had three months in which to make up their minds. In the end they would take a matter of days.

The news of the House of Bishops' decision was broken by the Archbishop. Festo Kivengere was to be the new bishop of Kigezi diocese. The news spread like wildfire throughout Kigezi, but unfortunately they had to celebrate without Festo: he was abroad on a mission. Lyth was delighted that at last Kigezi diocese should be in the hands of a Kigezi man.

There were eddies of criticism at the choice, but these were drowned out in the general joy.

When Festo and Mera got back to Kigezi, they went to meet the diocesan synod. They talked. Festo later described it: 'They were most gracious and said they knew I was called to serve God in many places in the world, and they wanted me to feel free to do this with their blessing. It was a very touching invitation and my wife and I felt it was of God.' (The four daughters were delighted for their father, but little affected, as they were studying or working in Europe by now.)

When the news broke at AEE, it took their collective breath away. They were, quite simply, appalled. Michael Cassidy explained: 'A team such as we had in South Africa, and such as was being birthed by Festo, was more than a full time job. One was endlessly stretched and pressured just coping with that alone.' He felt that while making Festo bishop 'was a great honour', it was also, so far as AEE was concerned 'almost incomprehensible'.

Complete dismay settled like a cloud on the heads of Michael Cassidy and Don Jacobs and the rest of the team, both in Africa and the States. 'We simply could not see how the dear man was going to cope.' Michael feared an early collapse of the East African division of AEE, heartbreaking after all that Festo had done to get it established and actually growing. But with a diocese to administer, it seemed a very real possibility now. The idea that Festo being a diocesan bishop would in itself open many doors for AEE seemed irrelevant to Michael Cassidy at this time: he simply wished with all his heart that Sabiti had not chosen Festo. (Indeed, he could never bring himself to ask Festo to what extent he had acquiesced in the initial suggestions as to his appointment.)

Another friend who saw problems ahead was Leslie Brown, first Archbishop of Uganda, and now retired and back in England. He wrote:

> Festo, you will remember our conversation when you first came to me about ordination. I said there were different ministries in the church, and of my understanding that the work of a pastor and even more so the work of a bishop is related to a particular group of people of whom you are pastor. Now I don't know whether you are going to carry on with your work of worldwide evangelism now that you are to become a bishop, but I do beg you to make sure that *your own diocese* really come to know you as a father in God and as their pastor.

For Bishop Brown and other English clergy did have their doubts as to the wisdom of the appointment. Brown warned Festo: 'It remains a question whether you should be bishop unless you be a bishop. It is not a rank, but a role in the church, very specific and very demanding.' Festo did not reply to this part of the letter.

That July, as Bishop-designate of Kigezi, Festo was a guest speaker at a convention of special significance for him personally: the Keswick Convention in Cumbria, England. He began his first address to the convention:

> Let me share with you that it is not an easy experience for me to address the Keswick Convention ... You see, I am a product of missionaries, most of whom heard their call to the mission field at this convention; therefore I am aware of my inadequacy to speak from this platform.

Festo had been invited to the convention at the suggestion of its General Secretary, Canon A. Houghton, who had preached with Festo in Kampala during the 1968 Keswick Convention tour, and been much moved by his messages. Keswick gave a warm welcome to Festo and Mera that summer: tolerant of his running over time in preaching; touched by his expository preaching on Christ; moved by poignant stories of the suffering in Uganda; and excited by the thought that here was a Bishop-designate converted through the efforts of missionaries called to Uganda at the Keswick Convention generations ago.

A highlight of the convention for Festo was meeting up again with John Stott, whose path he had crossed before. If John admired and noted down his turn of phrase: 'You've only got to take the throne of your personality and sit yourself on it, and you see at once that you are conspicuously too small for it;' Festo in his turn was electrified by Stott's Bible Readings: 'He put me to shame!' he confessed later to friends with rueful humour. 'I would listen to him in the morning, and all neat and clear. I would scratch my little head and come on to speak that evening with my little bits and pieces hanging out all over! Whatever could I do!' Festo would confide to friends that such a discrepancy between their ministries could 'have made John a little bit too high for me ... ', but was grateful this was not the case, thankful that John 'had a great love'. Indeed, as their ministries continued to cross down the years, Festo found that John's teaching and example taught him 'lessons of grace and discipline' for which Festo was 'deeply grateful'.

Though Uganda and Amin were far away, Festo's messages that summer were coloured by the ordeal his people and church were going through. Typical of him, he did not expound specific political solutions—none of which he or anyone else would have had a hope of implementing anyway. Instead, he looked to his faith not for comfort so much as for brisk courage.

For example, in a service rounding off Keswick's 'holiday week' he declared that whereas other faiths have stemmed largely from speculation or philosophy, 'Your faith,' he cried, 'was born in blood and sweat outside the city.' And that, he went on, was what anchored God's servants to reality, helping them face present cost and often danger. 'You live in a revolutionary world,' he said. 'That's nothing new! We in Africa know all about revolution, and we shall see plenty more of it. There's nothing about it that should deter the Christian revolutionary!'

Outside the meetings, Festo and Mera blended quietly into the houseparties. 'He wasn't the life-and-soul-of-the-party type,' found Alan Neech, 'but his demeanour and ever-ready smile and cheerfulness meant for stimulating conversation' —though not along the lines of grumbling about the vagrancies of the weather—for Festo's mind was only always on the wider canvas: world evangelism, Amin. Small talk came hard to him.

Soon after Keswick there was a ten day mission back in Dodoma, Tanzania, which attracted 20,000 people and had the support of all the churches. There would have been even more Christians, but those coming from Uganda were stopped, arrested and imprisoned at Makinbi by a government suspicious of collusion with the Tanzanians. (It took the Archbishop's pleading on their behalf to get them out of prison.) Meanwhile, President Nyerere of Tanzania had accepted the convention's invitation to come and greet them. Festo welcomed him to the platform, and afterwards responded to his commendation of their commitment and belief on behalf of the convention.

Back in Europe, Festo went to Germany, to the little town of Grossalmerode, at the invitation of Reinhold Abraham, a former diocesan youth worker in Kigezi and now a member of Missionswerk Frohe Botschaft. He spoke at a Bible week and afterwards was introduced to the founder and head of the mission, Wolfgang Heiner, who in turn made sure he met several strategically important church leaders in the country, including Pralat Roth, the assistant bishop of the diocese of Evangelische Kirche Kurhessen-Waldeck. The groundwork was laid for future invitations to evangelistic conventions.

The end of August found Festo in California, sharing a series of AEE missions with Michael Cassidy. The co-operation of a black African and white South African caused a 'certain amount of excitement' among Christian leaders interested in supporting the work AEE did in Africa: for them it was a sure sign of God's grace at work. Before flying out of Los Angeles Festo joined the platform for a press conference to help launch the Lausanne Congress for World Evangelization—planned for 1974. (He was already one of the 164 convenors for the Congress, and then found himself a member of its planning committee, and also billed as one of the top ten major speakers coming from all over the world.) The press conference, held at the Airport Marina Hotel, was chaired and launched by Billy Graham, Bishop A. W. Goodwin Hudson, Bishop A. Jack Dain, the Revd Akira Hatori and Samuel Escobar. Their aim then in 1972 was to draw the attention of American Christians to the need for a congress that would not only stress the need for world evangelisation, but make the Third World representatives the major beneficiaries. Festo knew as well as anyone that if the congress was ever to be a success, it needed the financial support of American Christians. As the American introductory leaflet 'Let the Earth Hear His Voice' had pointed out: 'Over seventy-five per cent of the Christian money in the world is in the hands of the believers in our country,' and went on to express the belief that these 'God-given material blessings' were meant to be used to 'share spiritual blessings with the disadvantaged of the world'. It was an argument Festo would make great use of in future years on behalf of the Ugandans.

Festo returned to Uganda in early September to find that Amin had ordered the expulsion of more than 50,000 British Asians, effectively Uganda's middle, commercial class. It caused an international outcry, but made good sense to many Ugandans at the time: they were jealous of the Asians' success. The Church of Uganda, however, was upset by the callousness of Amin's action, and indeed as Festo spent much of September in Uganda he grew more and more alarmed by Amin's increasing violence and destruction, and astonished by his occasional bizarre attempts at friendliness towards the church.

For instance, in mid-September the largest-ever pastors' conference was held in Uganda; sponsored by World Vision. To everyone's surprise, Amin attended one of the meetings—telling Festo and the other leaders, 'You are my eyes and my right hand and I need your advice!' This they found 'difficult to swallow', because, 'We knew of so many brutal murders and disappearance of fellow countrymen through what appeared to be by government action.'[8]

This was by now the era of Amin's wild speeches, which won so much notoriety in the world's press: defence of the Palestinians' attack at the Munich Olympics; praise for Hitler's extermination of six million Jews; proposing that all Israelis move to Britain. 'There were times,' Festo told friends, 'when we heard Amin begin to speak on the radio and we held our hearts, not knowing what would come next.'[9]

Even so, no one was prepared for the shock of 18th September, when pro-Obote guerillas in Tanzania launched an invasion of Uganda. (The invasion was Nyerere's response to a plot he had discovered in August, that Amin intended to invade *him*.) It was a disaster. Plans went awry, were leaked, and Obote's guerillas, led by one Yoweri Museveni, failed. Amin's army threw the invaders out and calm was only achieved by the Mogadishu Agreement that October. Festo and the other Ugandans

> sensed that, from the time of the invasion, the President's whole attitude changed. As his sense of insecurity grew, the method of widespread murder also increased. Many Christians were attacked because they happened to have been involved in the former government—specially those who had been in high positions. Many lost their lives, and others escaped out of the country.

But Festo would always stress that many Christians had found a supernatural peace, 'in spite of the fact that when the husband and father left home in the morning, they had no idea whether he would return that day or not. This is when faith is tested and comes out singing.'[10]

In the midst of it all, the plans for Festo's consecration in

Kampala on 5th November and his enthronement in Kabale on 3rd December went ahead. This was when Festo wrote to Bishop Maxwell Wiggins in Dodoma and invited him and his wife Margaret to come. He was keen that Maxwell should preach at the consecration. But when the Revd Yona Okoth, then Provincial Secretary (later Archbishop) tried to get this permission, it was refused.

Meanwhile, thousands of people in Kigezi were planning as to how they could get up to Namirembe Cathedral for the big day. Many buses and cars were hired and filled to overflowing, arriving in Kampala the day before. Guests filled up the hotels and spilled over into Christians' homes throughout the city, competing for beds with hundreds of others who had flown in from all over the world, including bishops, evangelists and retired missionaries.

The three-and-a-half hour service, which began ten am, was packed. Every single seat in the vastness of Namirembe Cathedral was taken. Some resourceful missionaries, still determined to see the service, wedged themselves on to the pulpit steps.

When Archbishop Erica Sabiti consecrated Festo as the new Bishop of Kigezi, it was a momentous step: Africa had another one of its own in charge of a diocese.

Friends and family crowded round to embrace and congratulate Festo after the service. Hundreds strolled down to the Archbishop's compound for an outdoor party of chicken, beans, matoke and soda pop. Festo and Mera spent the night, like most everyone else, in Kampala, before setting off next morning at the head of a great rejoicing convoy for Kigezi. Thousands more Christians were waiting for them at the border of Kigezi's high hills.

In Kabale, Bishop Lyth prepared to hand the diocese over to Festo. It was with some trepidation as well as joy.

I reminded him that, though a man might be ordained and, after serving a curacy in a parish, might be led on to minister in schools, prisons, hospitals, industry, etc, a man was consecrated as bishop to be the pastor of his flock, and it was his duty and responsibility to give himself fully and unstintingly to the care of that flock. It has to be said in honesty that Festo failed largely to do this, and inevitably caused resentment among his fellow bishops and many of his diocesan clergy and people.

As he said good-bye, Lyth again reminded Festo that the diocese needed a bishop who would be a *pastor* to them. Bishop Festo avoided a direct reply, and Lyth understood: 'I knew in my heart that Festo was an evangelist, not a shepherd.' He and Nora would pray long for Festo and the diocese, urging the people in a farewell letter 'to show the same love and co-operation to Bishop and Mrs Kivengere that you have shown to us'.

3rd December, the date of Festo's enthronement at St Peter's Cathedral, Kabale, approached. Kabale was inundated with visitors—the missionaries' cars rushing back and forth to the airport as thousands poured in from all over the diocese, together with hundreds of foreign guests, including prominent evangelists, bishops from Europe, USA, East Africa, Australia and the UK. Gifts arrived, among them a set of exquisite episcopal vestments from the Episcopalian diocese of Pittsburgh.

By early in the morning of 3rd December nearly 11,000 people had gathered in the outdoor amphitheatre on Rugarama Hill just below the cathedral. They prayed and sang hymns. 'I can hardly tell you how happy everyone was, how we praised God,' recalls one there that day.

The doors of St Peter's opened at nine-thirty am. A capacity crowd of 1,500 poured in, eager for the ten am start.

Amidst great rejoicing and 'oohs' Bishop Lyth presented Bishop Festo with his bishop's staff and mitre, and led him to the bishop's throne. The canons showed him formally around the cathedral that he had known so well since his teenage years.

Bishop Festo was careful to keep the splendour of the robes and ceremony in proportion. He quoted a dear friend, Yohana Omari, who, when made the first Archbishop of Tanzania, had said: 'I want to be like the little donkey our Lord chose to ride on to enter Jerusalem. They laid their robes on it and shouted, but the shouting was all for the Lord Jesus, whom he was carrying.'

Addressing himself specifically to the diocese, he publicly thanked God for Richard and Nora Lyth, and promised to continue the good work already established, to preach the gospel, and to work for harmony between clergy and laity as a basis of development. The church, he said, was properly concerned with many things, from planning to development, but preaching the gospel was the most important, and as such would take first place in his diocese.

Jubilation and festivities occupied the rest of the day, as 11,000 people partied in the warm sunshine.

Next day it was down to work, as Bishop Festo chaired his first diocesan council meeting. Their final warm farewells were made to Bishop Lyth and then Bishop Festo addressed the council. He first thanked them for their love and confidence in him. He was conversant with diocesan policy on evangelism, development, education and basic health care, and stressed that this was excellent. In the years ahead he hoped only that it would expand and continue.

Letters of congratulation had poured in from all over the world—so many that Festo turned to Lilian Clarke for help. 'Whatever you reply will be all right with me!' he assured her.

Within a week on 10th December, Bishop Festo had held his first two ordinations: J. W. Kahangirwe and S. K. Tunewesigre. Four more he ordained to the diaconate. He made minor changes to his diocesan staff, promoting his old friend and evangelist colleague Ernest Shalita from education to diocesan secretary.

As 1972 drew to an end, Bishop Festo spent many hours in prayer seeking God's will in the new ministry he had begun. There was the pastoral care of the diocese, its development. But no one could ignore the maelstrom of hate, violence and terror that had engulfed the country. By now about 90,000 people had been murdered, 'there was hardly a prominent family left in Uganda which had not experienced the brutal killing of one of its members'. As a Christian leader at national level what would God have him say to comfort and strengthen the people in such desperate need?

The answer he was to reach would provide the overall keynote for the rest of his ministry. A clue lay in a simple story he already loved to recite:

One day a little girl sat watching her mother working in the kitchen. She asked her mummy, 'What does God do all day long?' For a while, her mother was stumped, but then she said, 'Darling, I'll tell you what God does all day long. He spends his whole day mending broken things.'[11]

There were literally millions of broken lives all over Uganda, smashed by hatred and violence. Trying to mend them, bringing them Christ's healing love and forgiveness seemed an impossible task. But as Bishop Festo prayed, he became convinced that this was the vision for his future ministry. Reconciliation.

CHAPTER SIXTEEN

AMIN'S SHADOW LENGTHENS

1973–1974

Bishop Festo takes over Kigezi diocese; faces up to Amin; public executions; AEE expands; Lausanne Congress; worldwide preaching; violence in Uganda increases.

FESTO KIVENGERE tackled his new role as Bishop of Kigezi with all of the evangelist's urgent approach to life. That winter he had 'a kind of dancing fire within him' a missionary friend recalls as he and Mera, from their new, spacious bungalow on Rugarama Hill, threw themselves into the new job. From the outset, Bishop Festo had a clear vision for the five-year-old diocese. Briefly, it was as follows:

First, that the diocese should continue to expand its programme of evangelism with all possible speed. Bishop Festo would commit himself to as many Kigezi missions as possible in the coming years. It is worth noting that Bishop Festo never encountered the conflict of some African Christians, who rejected what the early missionaries had taught—that the religions of Africa were no more than a mass of superstitions, taboos and magic. Instead they believed African theologians *could* glean from the vastness of African religions many valuable truths.

But Bishop Festo never looked back to traditional African religion or beliefs as aids by which to build an 'African Christianity'. He never saw the Christianity that the missionaries had brought to Kigezi as English and therefore needing reinterpretation. Rather, he believed that the Holy Spirit, in reaching out to Uganda, had sent the English Christians so that they might bear witness to Christ. The English were just the conductors of the gospel, in no way the owners of it. As Festo wrote: '... it is God's work ... when Christ becomes a living, risen Lord in the life of a believer ...' And when this happened, the believer didn't think about whether it was an African Christianity or an English Christianity. Rather, he thought about what Christ personally wanted of him:

> Go back to a village a week after a man comes to the Lord. The whole village knows . . . He has paid his debts . . . He has gone to people he hated and said, 'I'm sorry.' He's now telling them what Christ means to him. He has carried his new belief into his business practices. It isn't something he sits on as a comfortable experience. Christ was at the centre. And the word was not just read; it was obeyed.[1]

Of course, when an African theologian argued that the African Church should be speaking the language of Africa, Bishop Festo would be entirely in agreement. As Bishop, he encouraged his Kigezi musicians to compose their own Christian songs; communion bread and wine should be what was locally available. And when it came to preaching, whether at Makerere University, the slums of Kampala, or the remote rural villages of North Kigezi, there was simply no other preacher in Africa that could pull the crowds as Bishop Festo could.

His utter assurance of an eternal hope came across when that January of 1973 one of Bishop Festo's closest fellow evangelists and best loved friends, William Nagenda, died. Bishop Festo preached at his funeral at Buloba near Kampala, which was attended by 4,000 people. 'Death, to William, is finding all the answers he never found before ... He has pulled up his tent. He has moved the camp. He has entered into the permanent residence!'

Bishop Festo's second priority for the diocese was that of development (in which he would be enormously successful). Development, in education and medical care, had become the magic word in Africa at this time.

'In this way Festo endeavoured—and to a great extent succeeded—in raising the standard of Christianity in the diocese. Increasingly we pastors were able to properly study the Bible and teach the people.' Bishop Festo's education of his clergy became a great hallmark of his time as Bishop. He would actively pursue scholarships in America for his men—numerous were provided by the Billy Graham Association. (Kigezi, one of Uganda's smallest dioceses, would end up with more trained clergy than any other diocese—thirty graduate pastors by the mid-1980s.)

One example was Edward Bakaitwako, one of Bishop Festo's very first ordinands. Not only did Bishop Festo secure him a place at Trinity Seminary in Chicago, but at the airport suddenly produced a present: the 'long johns' or thermal underwear he himself had worn in Pittsburgh years before. 'You'll need these,' he advised—and was proved right.

More education for the laity was a big hope of both Bishop Festo and Mera; but in early 1973 no specific plans were in hand.

As far as other developments were concerned, in the years to come Bishop Festo would woo—and win—for Kigezi a number of western doctors, nurses, agriculturalists, secretaries, teachers, and engineers, as well as vehicles and equipment for them to do their job.

To finance such plans, Bishop Festo would turn firstly to the diocese itself, and stress responsible stewardship. (The revival's impact had been terrific, and though no cash crops were grown, giving was already very high.) Bishop Festo adopted Lyth's Financial Regulations Handbook, which set down how church money should be spent. He also expanded the stewardship teaching courses for clergy. Such money raised would be used both in the maintenance of the existing churches and the creation of new parishes, and also to finance a mammoth project dear to the heart of Kigezi: the building of a new cathedral for Kabale.

Next, Bishop Festo determined to continue to tap the resources of generous western Christians and Christian organisations. He never saw it as a threat to true African Christian independence (indeed, woe betide anyone who tried to dictate to him what he was to do within his own diocese—their offer was unequivocally dropped), but as brothers in Christ, 'strengthening our weak hands'.

Of course, it was not up to Bishop Festo to make decisions for the diocese on his own. He would have to work through the diocesan councils, boards and synods. Here his gift for leadership came into its own.

The secret of his success as Bishop lay with his personal qualities. A missionary found 'his obvious charisma made him a leading figure in whatever group he joined'. Tedd Smith, pianist with the Billy Graham Crusades agreed: 'He always came across as an intelligent, caring, deeply spiritual human being with a great sense of humour. His presence somehow carried with it a sense of order, calm and respect.'

This was partly due to his obvious holiness, which both warmed and disarmed people. 'He was never one of those harsh leaders,' a fellow clergy explains: 'Festo was full of the love of the Lord.' Another adds: 'He could inspire us to faith in God because his own was so obvious.' His love for Christ was not kept for public use either: time and again private letters reflect a deep spiritual walk: Christ is referred to with love and gratitude and was obviously a dearly-loved daily companion. 'He always had a pertinent word from the Lord, whatever the circumstances.' He was 'a transparent, approachable Christian man', a missionary found. 'He never seemed proud of any achievements—his had not altered his essential humility.'

Such personal holiness ensured his reputation for unquestionable integrity. 'He practised what he preached.' Adds one: 'This gave him extraordinary authority and power.' Another says: 'We had heard many glowing sermons from many mediocre clergy—but Festo's words matched his life.' Just one example was in his marriage: people took to heart his sermons about love and giving because they saw the quality of the relationship it had yielded in Mera and Festo's marriage.

Thirdly, Bishop Festo obviously loved people: this made him irresistible as Bishop. Though never a great one for small talk, or a gifted pastoral counsellor, neither the 'hail-fellow-well-met' breed (at first acquaintance he could seem rather reticent), once a firm contact had been established, Bishop Festo was generous in his friendship. He had a great capacity for enjoying the company of others. His love gave him a sensitivity that charmed people. For example, a poor family in Kigezi were delighted when he agreed to marry their daughter for them, overwhelmed when at the party afterwards he ignored the small table set for him and sat companionably on a bench with the other guests, eating the food with his fingers as they did. Then there was the young English doctor who decided to spend a year in his diocese, much to her parents' consternation. Then they met Bishop Festo at a church in England: immediately he hugged them and said, 'Thank you for your daughter.' His warmth won them over completely, and the girl had no more parental opposition.

Fourthly, a vital ingredient was Bishop Festo's self-confidence and poise. He had an unconsciously aristocratic, dignified bearing: he was not the grandson of a king for nothing. Such self-confidence inspired confidence in others. As a senior clergyman put it: 'You felt that nothing could go amiss for long once he knew of it.' For Bishop Festo was willing to take responsibility, and to make decisions. Indeed, once made, it took a lot to change him—criticism was brushed off—he knew his own mind. This helped especially when it came to fighting that scourge of Africa: tribalism. In his appointments to key posts throughout the diocese he would utterly ignore the tribe from which a person came when making a decision. The clergy were at times irritated and appalled at this (especially those who came from the prominent tribes), but also impressed. As one explained: 'When Bishop Festo reminded us that in Christ there was no Gentile or Jew, it made a deep impression because he was living it out. Festo knew no difference between a muhima or a mukiga or a munyaruanda—his tribe was the Christian tribe.'

Bishop Festo also revealed himself to be a shrewd judge of character and capabilities—perhaps a legacy from his years in the classroom. He would prove to have a knack for choosing the right man for the right job. Whenever possible he would discuss the appointment with the person concerned (not normally done among African bishops).

Bishop Festo would be greatly loved for one other hallmark of his leadership: his belief in other people's capabilities, and his enthusiasm for developing them. Far from expecting everything to collapse if he went away, his line was more: 'I have clergy and lay people who are behind me and who know their jobs. So my presence does not mean much—I work with a team.' A former missionary recalls, 'It was characteristic for him to inspire us with a vision, and then leave us to get on with working it out!'

(Though he would always be diligent in keeping abreast with diocesan news from cattle farms to buildings. 'I don't know how he does it,' admitted a colleague.) 'He trusted us,' recalls one team member with gratitude. But it must be admitted that it worked in theory better than in practice, because there were times down the years when some people's decisions would be revoked by Bishop Festo on his return—a source of frustration all round. It led to some reluctance to make any decision at all. But his team still loved working for him. As one missionary put it: 'We felt bereft when he was not there.'

As for discipline, it was firm but fair—with every chance given for a man to redeem himself. It was very much a case of hate the sin and love the sinner. For example, the few clergy who committed immorality or who were dishonest were summoned to the Bishop at once and faced with dismissal: but only if they refused to change their ways.

Indeed, Bishop Festo's patience with people and his optimism that even the worst could and possibly might change with God's help, became something of a byword. It also attracted criticism, in that it made him slow to act where clergy were making constant errors. Others, however, loved him for such clemency: 'It was the way Jesus dealt with fallible people.'

For example, there was a difficult pastor with drinking and emotional problems who was driving everyone mad. Bishop Festo was begged to dismiss him, but he refused. He argued that the man was doing the best he could, and 'Jesus died for this man'. The diocesan secretary at the time, Ernest Shalita, recalls: 'Festo would sort out the mess the man made time and again.' Finally, Bishop Festo entrusted the man to Shalita's care, confiding, 'There are those who think we should send him away, but I think we should bring him close to ourselves.' Only after months of failure did Bishop Festo reluctantly defrock the man.

Ernest was there the morning it happened, and was with Bishop Festo in his office as the man left and wandered out into the road. Bishop Festo watched him from the window and suddenly said: 'That man is going to perish.' He rushed out after the miscreant and summoned him back. A very minor job in the diocese was found for him. Shalita recalls: 'In all my time with Festo, that was one morning I shall never forget. His great love for the sinner, his determination that no one should be allowed to fail ultimately and perish became a real challenge to my own life.'

In cases of deliberate deceit, as in the case of the clergyman who was caught with his hands in the Sunday collection, Bishop Festo was prompt to protect the parishioners: the man was immediately defrocked. But when the man left the diocese and repented, Bishop Festo gave his approval to the man's subsequent reinstatement in another diocese. Ernest found:

> there were many such cases. Where once the man had acknowledged his sin and repented, Festo welcomed them back. Even when they fell time and again and the rest of us doubted they meant to change at all, Festo didn't give them up.

But neither did Bishop Festo like discussing their shortcomings with all and sundry. Everyone was strongly encouraged to mind their own business. Clergy who went to the Bishop in search of a sympathetic ear while they moaned about the shortcomings of their fellow clergy were brought up smartly. 'Go and tell him this,' the Bishop would reply briskly. 'Sort yourselves out, or come back to me together with him.' The clergy found this very disconcerting. One ruefully admits: 'This certainly controlled any backbiting!'

On the opposite side of the coin, of course, Bishop Festo's faith in people could blind him to laziness and wastefulness. So alien were they to Bishop Festo's own nature, that he found it hard to remember to watch out for them in other people's. For example, with perhaps more realism, Bishop Lyth had kept a keen eye on his clergy with regard to their efficiency. Timekeeping was insisted on, reports to be written promptly, minutes done soon after the meeting concerned. With his years in colonial administration, Lyth had developed a weather eye for the pitfalls men encounter when setting out on administration for the first time. With the admonition, 'It is God's time, and you must be responsible with it,' he had sent many a cleric off with a flea in his ear.

Bishop Festo's line, on the other hand, was to take their willingness to work hard for granted, on the grounds that 'if you're saved, you'll want to do God's work and so you won't cheat God's time ... so automatically you'll do some sort of planning.' (It was probably as well for the diocese that Lyth's training had come first.)

But Bishop Festo's greatest advantage—and Kigezi's blessing—during this time of Uganda's turmoil, was that he was a born optimist. 'He always *but always* bounced back.' Crises and obstacles were challenges. 'We quickly came to rely on his vitality and imagination for ideas as to how to get round a problem.' He could see 'the opportunities ahead after the storm'. Certainly one thing became crystal clear early on: Bishop Festo would not be one to hang about. His line was constantly: 'If something is right, go ahead with it quickly—don't miss any opportunities!' This stark urgency was soon transmitted to the diocese and things began to happen so fast that Kigezi acquired a nickname in Uganda as 'the rocket diocese'.

'With a rocketing bishop' would not have been incorrect, either. Bishop Festo spent his days in the diocese in an episcopal blur: at the diocese office in Kabale in a whirl of diocesan boards, councils, and endless individual pastoral concerns; then out on the long, mountainous roads to visit the parishes. Always infamous for his speeding (in fact, some brethren had 'challenged' him on this the time they learned he had done the trip from Kampala to Kabale in four hours), Bishop Festo found himself a chauffeur, Kashari, who also knew a thing or two about acceleration. The Bishop was soon thundering along to confirmations and other engagements at a speed which brought people in villages passed running to their doorways to gape in astonishment.

A missionary observes: 'Living as fully as one possibly can, and with a controlled urgency, had become a way of life.' His energy and stamina were by now legendary.

But in Uganda in 1972 no bishop, however busy in his diocese, could long forget the lengthening shadows of terror spreading out from Kampala.

In early February there was a new wave of killings in Kampala. It soon leaked out that Amin and his advisers had drawn up a list of something like 2,000 people they wanted dead: and they were not wasting any time in working through the names. Most of the people on the list were prominent professors, businessmen, church leaders, government officials and others. Ten squads of assassins, largely Nubians of the notorious SRB, set off to hunt down the victims. A Ugandan writing later, described the terror of such arrests:

> The Nubian assassins, dressed in their 'uniform' of sunglasses, flowered shirts and bell-bottomed trousers, entered an office or home in broad daylight. They called out the name of their victim, and humiliated him in front of employees and family members. The terrified man was then tied up and dragged away to the boot of a waiting vehicle. His screams for help meant nothing. No one dared to lend a hand.[2]

Such victims were then subjected to the horrors of the SRB. Lucky were those who managed to die quickly—these were very few. Prisoners were hammered to death, or had their flesh carved off them with bayonets—and were made to eat that flesh. Some were immersed in deep pits of freezing water and fed only enough to prolong their agonising death. Others had arms, legs and genitals cut off, and were left in the dirt to bleed to death.

Kampala was degenerating into a charnel house. Dozens of bodies were rotting in the streets. Many smart government cars parked downtown had human legs protruding from their boots. The violence achieved one thing: Amin's power was now absolute. He quickly pressed his advantage, dismissing his entire cabinet and replacing civilian ministers with Muslim army men. He disarmed the legal Uganda army and gave the Nubian mercenaries the keys to the armoury. Any pretence of a civilian government in Uganda was put aside.

About this time Amin announced on radio that a number of men had been arrested for subversive activities. The military tribunal had decided that each of the men should be shot in their own home communities as a warning to everyone else.

Three of the men were from Kigezi diocese. Bishop Festo was in Kampala when the announcement was made. In an act of tremendous personal courage which he was always to shrug off as merely his duty, he telephoned Amin on a private line and requested a face to face interview.

Amin said Festo could come to see him. Festo went.

He chose his words with care, and after the formalities, plunged in:

> Your Excellency, I am troubled about the announcement of the public executions of the men who have been arrested. You have often said that you hear God, and God created human life in his own image, and therefore I plead that these men be given a chance to defend themselves.
>
> You see this little boy of yours, sir? God will give him as long as he needs to grow into a man. So when you think of taking away life, first give it as long as possible before you take it away.[3]

Bishop Festo later reported: 'The President was not angry, and listened carefully. He didn't promise anything would be changed, but I left with some hope.' Nevertheless, the executions of the three men from Kabale were booked for 19th February. People were commanded to come to the stadium at Kabale to witness their death by firing squad. A silent crowd of about 3,000 turned up on the morning.

Bishop Festo obtained permission from the authorities to speak to the men before they died. He was delighted to find they were Christians and not afraid of death.

Bishop Festo's desperate risk of confronting Amin was to be the first of several stark encounters (very few of which Bishop Festo ever divulged). 'Festo was so courageous,' recall colleagues. 'As the arrests continued, he kept going back to Amin to face him with the enormity of what he was doing.' In doing so Bishop Festo became a hero to Kigezi diocese (which spent days and nights in prayer and nail-biting anxiety over his safety), and the spokesman for the House of Bishops, who sent letters of protest to Amin via Festo. On one occasion Bishop Festo even went on national TV to read a protest document from all the bishops, chiding Amin.

Bishop Festo would always believe that ideally the church and state relationship need not be one of automatic enmity. Ideally, their shared common concerns: the moral, material development of a healthy society should make them allies in many things. But Uganda in 1972 was light years away from such an ideal. And if the church remained silent, the people would have no voice at all.

Meanwhile, the work of African Enterprise called to him. The AEE team had been faltering as Bishop Festo adjusted to his new commitments, and certainly Bishop Festo blamed them least of all. As Michael Cassidy said, 'The ambiguous situation that his being a bishop had put on the team had not been lost on him.' For example, early that year there arose a crisis in the team over leadership. The International Board was firm in wanting Bishop Festo to remain 'head' at any cost, but Festo was 'anxious not to be caught in a power struggle'.

Michael Cassidy and another leader of AEE, Keith Jesson of the Pasadena Board, were both in Nairobi at the time. They flew to Entebbe, and prayed and argued their way through countless troubles with passport control. 'We knew the whole future of the East African AEE was in the balance.' They finally got through—only to have a long distressing session with the AEE team, which preserved Bishop Festo's leadership only at the cost of some hurt feelings. Then Michael Cassidy was thrown out of Uganda the next day by irritable authorities, but such an unpleasant end to an unpleasant trip did have a silver lining: it was indirectly responsible for bringing John Wilson, the Kampala businessman whose wife had been reluctant for him to go into full-time ministry, on to the full-time AEE staff. She was so indignant at Cassidy's treatment that it made up her mind: 'If our leaders can do that to a man like Michael Cassidy then it is time for you to go to AEE.' It would prove a major appointment for AEE. Wilson was a brilliant people man, encourager, initiator and diplomat. AEE's ministry in Middle East missions would come about through him, and in later years, he would act as Bishop Festo's deputy—relieving him of many speaking engagements when diocesan duties pressed.

Certainly Bishop Festo himself was very keen to continue as leader of the East African AEE team 'His zeal for AEE never flagged,' says Lilian Clarke, who by now was running an efficient AEE office in Kampala. Another colleague adds: 'Festo felt that God had equipped him, as indeed he had, to do that work.' 'Festo's first calling was always evangelism,' explains another.

And the aims of the AEE staff remained the same: to 'be servants' of the church in East Africa and further afield. The team was prepared to assist local African churches and groups of churches in evangelism, as well as to respond to invitations to missions from Christians all over the world. And that spring the invitations poured in. Fortunately, the team had grown with the work. Bishop Festo, Zebulon Kabaza and Lilian Clarke had been or soon would be joined by Titus Lwebandiza and Methuselah (Matt) Nyagwaswa, both based in Tanzania, John Wilson and James Katarikawe of Uganda and Daniel Serwanga based in Kenya. Meanwhile, Wolfgang Heiner of West Germany was busy helping to bring the teams to Europe, while invitations arrived from Australasia, India, the States, and throughout Africa.

And it was soon apparent that having Festo as Bishop would work to AEE's advantage. A friend recalls: 'From then on, worldwide, churches, people and Christian organisations would reason: "Here's a man coming as an evangelist, but he is also a bishop of the Anglican Church. Therefore he and AEE must be taken very seriously."'

In country after country, important doors in the Episcopal and Anglican world began to swing open for AEE teams. 'And of course once Festo was through them, he no longer needed his status to commend him. His own deep spirituality, great knowledge of the Scriptures and obedience to the Holy Spirit meant that he was at once accepted as a voice from God.'

But his admittance as a bishop raised some questions in people's minds; as one put it: 'Being a bishop is not a rank but a specific, demanding role. It requires you to be in the diocese! Not gallavanting about the world, for whatever worthy cause.' To be fair to Bishop Festo, he was only doing what he had warned the diocese he would do—continue his evangelism. Moreover, he would continue to go where he felt God led him—for if some weren't happy with an evangelising bishop, still others, mainly the AEE Board, were wishing he would evangelise more in Africa than in Europe, Oceania and the States. Michael Cassidy, for one, had hoped that Bishop Festo would join him in his specific vision of pinpointing the cities of Africa. While Bishop Festo would give some time to missions in Africa, he was also firm in continuing his commitments abroad.

This would frustrate Michael Cassidy.

There were many times when we wanted his invaluable help for a mission here in Africa, but he was off in Montreal or Helsinki. I knew that there was only one Festo, and he was the man Africa responded to. But Festo would give, relatively speaking, so little of all his time and energy to Africa beyond Uganda. I felt saddened by it, and it was a pity that he wasn't able to give more time to a wider ministry on the African continent.

But I may have been selfish in wanting this. Colleagues kept reminding me that the cities of Africa were more my calling than Festo's. They would say: 'Festo's call is to Uganda and to the world, and you should rest content with that.'

Festo himself urged, 'You *must* release me from your vision. God has given me a broader vision.'

Certainly Cassidy was the first to say that 'the East African revival message needed to be heard in churches worldwide'. And Bishop Festo was Africa's one great internationalist—the only one with the truly genuine worldwide ministry.

'So probably Bishop Festo's calling was proper in the divine economy.'

Insistent invitations poured in: come to Canada, Norway, Holland, Finland, the Caribbean, the States (Virginia, New York, New Mexico, Pennsylvania, etc), Australia, and speak to us: in our churches, conferences, missions, rallies. Bishop Festo juggled such invitations with those pouring in from the Sudan, Ethiopia, Kenya, Nigeria—again to name but a few—from churches and Christian groups keen to hold missions, keen to have the encouragement of such a leading statesman of the world church. Lilian Clarke marshalled the invitations into some kind of order, and kept a stern eye on the comings and goings in the office diary.

The first of the little books of Bishop Festo's messages was produced in Ghana in 1973 after his ministry there—*When God Moves In Renewal* (Asempa Publishers: Accra, 1973).

During April and May Bishop Festo had a chance to become better acquainted with his diocese, and they with him, when he chaired his first diocesan synod. He did not try and dominate the meeting, but did keep a firm hold on the agenda, so that everyone who wanted to contribute to the debates was given a chance to have their say. People talked and talked—and Bishop

Festo let them—much to their delight. Then in winding up the debate 'out of all the points we had raised, he guided us to the best solutions'. The conclusions were applauded, but just as much the process. 'It was much appreciated by Africans that even those in disagreement can have a full say.'

Items on the agenda had included the definite decisions to appoint an assistant bishop, and to divide the diocese into three archdeaconries, and so decentralise power. Both ideas were Bishop Festo's, and he had had to do a lot of persuading to get them approved.

On one item there was no disagreement: that a new Kabale Cathedral should be built. The building then in use had been built in 1927 and was not in good shape. A collection of funds for a new cathedral had been going on since the 1950s (Festo had donated some of his teacher's salary to it) but no building plans had as yet been drawn up. But as Kigezi's morale under their first African bishop soared they decided they needed a *huge* cathedral (never mind the problems of getting any building materials at all under Amin).

By the summer of 1973 Amin had killed an estimated ninety thousand people. The boatman at Owen Falls north of Kampala had a full-time job on his hands removing corpses from the water.

The economy was also in a shambles. The vast Asian wealth, carefully nurtured for years, had been squandered in the space of a few months. Machinery in factories went wrong and was not repaired. Large dairy farms had been given to butchers— who slaughtered all the milking cows. Salt, sugar, bread, cheese, cars and household goods were harder and harder to find. Increasingly, anyone with any leadership know-how or ability was using all their wits not to help run the country but to get out of it at all costs.

Despite such turmoil, the Ugandan Christians held their Keswick Convention in Kampala that July. One of the convention speakers, Gottfried Osei-Mensah, was refused entry at the airport and only Festo's going to the Minister of the Interior got him through, after a three-hour argument. Gottfried, emerging exhausted from the fray, reflected that Festo was becoming very English in his knack of understatement: 'I'm terribly sorry about that, the situation here is getting bad.' The Keswick was hardly expected to be a carefree event in a dying city, but that week it was touched by another sorrow—William Nagenda's wife, widowed only a few months before, took ill and died. Festo preached at what turned Keswick into a memorial service.

In all the church was magnificent under Amin. Stories poured in: at King's College, Budo, at Bweranyangi Girls' School and in the other high schools, young people pushed forward to become Christians 'in a way not seen for a good few years'. One Sunday in north Kigezi 8,000 people streamed from villages to the foot of a hillside where Bishop Festo and the diocesan authorities had announced a gathering. 'We were permitted to participate that day in a mighty outpouring of God's blessing, and hundreds came to the Lord, young and old.'[4]

Also—the Roman Catholic bishop told his people that when Festo was in an area preaching, 'they should go and hear the Gospel'.

By the time of his first clergy conference at Rugarama hill that September, Festo had begun to woo some of his old revival friends out of their teaching jobs into the ministry. 'Your diocese needs you full time.'

He was also arranging clergy conferences (many more would follow through the years) on everything from encouraging greater spirituality to improving clergy marriages. He was determined that his clergy should have as much chance as possible to continue to learn and grow themselves.

Both on pre-ordination retreats and in individual pastoral interviews it seems that for many young men, Festo became almost an adopted father figure, replacing the father/chief figure they would have looked to otherwise. Says one: 'He told me very many helpful things—just what I needed at the time. Nobody had ever talked like this to me before.'

Late September found Festo in Europe again. By October he was talking to ministers and evangelists in St Louis Missouri, who were taking a course at a Billy Graham Crusade School of Evangelism. One young evangelist from Britain, Eric Delve, would be deeply moved by what he said about ministering in Uganda. For Festo was still haunted by the public executions that February, and asked the school how they would have coped.

'You are facing men who are going to die. Where are all your fine illustrations now, preacher? Where are your proof texts?' He added sadly: 'I tell you I looked at mine and none of them made any sense.

'So I said to Jesus, "Lord, none of this makes sense. What on earth am I going to say to these young men?" And Jesus said to me: "Festo, tell them about me, I will make sense."'

And he recalled, 'When I got to the jail, the young men were already converted! They said to me with joy, "Bishop, go home and tell our parents that we are going home to Jesus."' Festo gave his class of young evangelists 'a lovely smile'. 'So I just sat back and had a good time.'

Delve said, 'The impact of that story was never to be forgotten. Time and again when I have been in difficult situations, I have remembered those words: "Tell them about me, I will make sense."'

Festo returned to Uganda late in the year about the time the Soviets were moving in—with their first military mission to Amin.

Throughout December 1973 Festo was immersed in diocesan work back in Kabale, and in taking the ordination retreat for six deacons and three priests. Already his first year as Bishop was completed.

1974 was a year of atrocities, barbarism and chaos. Amin, who loved military pageantry and weapons, gave himself the title of 'field marshal' and paraded around in army fatigues, adorned with rows of self-awarded medals. Meanwhile, his military elite continued to plunder the land. Society had been turned upside down—and was now ruled by a police state (headed by the State Research Bureau, Amin's corps of body-guards) made up of mainly minority Muslims and non-Ugandan mercenaries. They continued to arrest and kill. Thirty Italians at Owen Falls Damn Station soon resigned due to constant sighting of floating corpses.

Once again, January and February held missions in Europe and America for Festo, but before he left, on 3rd February, he installed a new dean in St Peter's Cathedral, Kabale—the Revd Canon William Rukirande. Rukirande, from a village near Kabale, had just finished a diploma in theology from Mukono and was serving as chaplain to Kigezi High School. Festo would soon have other ideas for William Rukirande.

Also that month, Festo and Mera shared with the diocese a 'dream' they had concerning the secondary education for the girls of Kigezi. A school was needed urgently: in 1974 there were 1,846 girls in Primary Seven but only 100 secondary school places for them. Now a building at Muyebe, about six miles from Kabale, was soon to be vacated, and Festo and Mera desperately wanted to grab the opportunity to found a secondary girls' school. The diocese began to get excited: though there was no money, many assumed that Festo would just ask the Americans and money and teachers would pour in. (In the event, this was not true at all, but those founding the school did not regret it: 'We learned to trust God instead.')

Then in March Amin suddenly announced on national radio that there was only one Christian Church in Uganda—the Roman Catholics. 'The Church of Uganda (Protestant),' he said, 'only came into being because the priests and bishops wanted to marry.'

The announcement, out of the blue, didn't make any kind of sense at all, no one could think of a motive. Nevertheless, the bishops did not feel they could let it pass without an answer, as the statement had also appeared in all the papers.

This was closely followed by a bizarre rumour of Festo's death, which began when some people saw a car wrecked on a road that looked very much like Festo's car. The driver's mutilated body lay beside it: putting two and two together, they assumed Festo had been taken and killed. The news spread rapidly.

When it reached the Archbishop in Kampala, he immediately phoned Mera in Kabale. Brother Erica asked, 'Where is Festo? Is he all right?'

'Festo is far back in the country, holding meetings.'

'Mera, dear, we may have some very sad news for you.'

He shared the report, which sounded very authentic by then. 'Imagine how Mera felt that night and the next day, when I didn't get home until late at night! But what a reunion that was!'[5]

After that, Mera was glad to pack Festo off to Japan on an

AEE tour. But before he left, in April, the Diocesan Council gave formal approval that the girls' school, now nicknamed the 'Bishop's Dream', should go ahead. A name was chosen: Bishop's Girls' School Muyebe. Liz Trail, already leaving Kigezi High School that June, and with over seven years with the Ruanda Mission, was formally appointed headmistress. Plans were made to start building. Volunteers, prayer and donations flooded in. Festo wrote an appeal letter for beds, teachers and income.

Then Festo was off to Japan with Zebulon Kabaza. The invitation to go to the Church of Hokkaido had come from the CMS, who wanted to support the few struggling Japanese Christians in this their centenary year. Bishop Festo and Zebulon preached at churches and various small groups. 'They are precious people indeed,' was Festo's later comment to AEE. He had been touched by the Japanese church's commitment amid the vast pagan majority of Japan.

In June the two Ugandans flew on to West Germany and joined an AEE team mission where 2,000 young people were eager to hear the famous Uganda bishop preach. A snippet from a personal letter Festo wrote that morning reveals that up until the last minute not even the famous bishop himself was quite sure what they would get: 'I shall be speaking to them this afternoon on Africa! What? I do not know ... But I have his peace—I know he has a message for them.'

It was a theme that often cropped up in his speaking. Later that summer in Leysin, he commented, 'I am nothing but a bishop. The important one is the Lord who takes hold of insignificant people to make them something that glorifies him.'

And then in July came the Lausanne Congress for World Evangelization, which aimed at doing just that: helping 'insignificant people' become effective witnesses to 'glorify him'.

Bishop Festo and David Cohen, a leading Australian churchman (and later international head of Scripture Union) flew up from East Africa and arrived at Lausanne to find nearly 4,000 participants and guest observers from 150 countries (and every continent), representing 130 Christian denominations and groups, housed at hotels and pensions throughout the city. The majestic Palais de Beaulieu was the venue for the morning and evening plenary sessions: 3,700 headsets for simultaneous translation into six languages. A vast ten-day programme (10th to 25th July) offered 120 different items in a mix of plenary sessions and small working groups to the evangelists, missionaries, pastors, cross-cultural Christian workers, young evangelical leaders and representatives of Third World nations. Billy Graham and a group of senior international clergy and evangelists hoped the Congress would become a concerted, worldwide evangelical statement countering the prevailing mood of the world church at the time. It would be an attempt to put evangelism back on the agenda.

For in 1974 many (especially in the Third World) were calling for a moratorium on missions: 'Missionaries go home . . .' was a familiar cry. The World Council of Churches supported this, claiming that the day of missions was over: they were a colonial anachronism. At the 1973 WCC conference in Bangkok on World Mission and Evangelism, the theme 'salvation today' had been defined on political lines; the freedom of Vietnam from the US; the freedom of Angola from Portugal.

Lausanne would prove to be a significant milestone for evangelicals from all over the world. It gave them a chance to formulate and express their own beliefs about modern day world evangelism. In the 'Lausanne Covenant' salvation and mission were defined biblically. Social justice (in the past a weak point for evangelicals) was accepted as the biblical Christian response. Evangelism throughout the world was seen as vital: extensive research had revealed that a staggering two-thirds of mankind had not heard the gospel; many were in 'unreached people groups'—separated by culture, not geography.

Festo had been in on the Congress from its inception. As mentioned previously, he was one of the 164 convenors for the Lausanne Congress, a member of its planning committee, among the 142 church leaders who had signed the 'official congress call', and had been billed as one of the top ten headline speakers. With his robust enthusiasm he was keen for a 'biblical declaration on evangelism' to show to the WCC Assembly of 1975 as a statement of evangelical conviction.

Lausanne was full of friends and colleagues for Festo, from Billy Graham the Honorary Chairman, and Bishop A. Jack Dain, Anglican Bishop of Sydney and Congress Executive

Chairman, to international church leaders like John Stott, Don Hoke, Gottfried Osei-Mensah, Warwick Olson (later international chairman of AEE), Dr Paul White, a former missionary to East Africa and Michael Cassidy. He was hailed with delight by members of the Billy Graham Association: Cliff Barrows, the Programme and Music Director, considered him a 'friend and beloved brother'.

Festo was booked to give the last of the plenary papers on 'The Cross and World Evangelism', as well as a testimony to the Congress. He was also one of three to testify to a rally after Billy Graham had spoken.

The Laustade Rally at the Olympic Stadium had attracted a crowd of 45,000 stoical Swiss. Festo's impish humour won him a great laugh when he said that after his conversion 'I got excited and wanted to tell every African about it ... Now, I'm an Anglican bishop, and we bishops don't usually get excited, we are as careful as you Swiss people.'

And as far as moratoriums on mission went, Festo made his own position clear: 'I am not ashamed to say that I am a product of missionaries. Bless them, they were compelled by the love of God ...' But it was with his plenary paper on 'The Cross and World Evangelism' that he 'had Billy Graham and those thousands of others of church leaders in the palm of his hand', according to a senior clergyman. Another senior evangelist adds: 'It bordered on oratory.' A Tanzanian found 'he came out as one of the best world leaders'. Like Billy Graham, he had that rare ability to relate to many different cultures. An English clergyman was left with the 'vivid impression of the revival joy and fellowship in Christ'.

Here, where evangelist merged into theologian, was perhaps the secret of all Festo's tremendous stamina and continued power in his ministry. For, as one church leader had put it, 'if you're merely operating at a methodological level, you eventually wear out.' Not so Festo, whose evangelism had always sprung straight from his entire faith: Christ's redemptive, reconciling love for all mankind. His paper was delivered with passionate force, with 'freedom and movement, and much fluency'. With a complete assurance and urgency he was speaking on the subject dearest to his heart.

Such a powerful delivery and message brought him a wave of adulation, including public thanks from Billy Graham: '... wonderful job ... touched everyone ... one of the greatest [messages on the cross] I've ever heard. Certainly the Lord used you to prepare the hearts of the people ...' Though Festo smiled graciously, he did not soak up the praise heaped on him by admirers after the meeting. As a colleague noted: 'When people gushed, there was no kind of response from Festo. I don't remember him ever encouraging a fawning kind of relationship.' Instead, there was 'a vague distancing', according to one, 'a certain almost aristocratic separateness about him'. 'He never indulged in ego trips.'

By the time the Congress closed on 25th July the East African delegation had unanimously decided that AEE should from now on be the 'major organ of evangelism in Uganda'[6]—a major achievement and cause of celebration for Michael Cassidy and Festo. (Certainly the Lausanne Congress also helped AEE to redefine and renew its purposes for evangelism of East Africa—from reaching out to the pockets of still unreached tribes, to intensifying evangelism in schools and universities, to continuing revival crusades and conventions in city, town and village. They felt confident of success: Africa had after all been singled out as the continent where Christianity was growing faster than anywhere else in the world.)

The Lausanne Continuation Committee was set up to act as a link for missionaries and national church leaders. Festo was appointed as the representative for Africa.

Shortly after Lausanne, it was a scramble back to Uganda where everyone seemed to be screaming for his attention. Some in the diocese felt the first faint stirrings of frustration at having such a peripatetic bishop, especially when in a few short weeks he was off again, this time back to Europe, beginning with a CMS preaching tour of England with Eustace Ruhindi, a senior clergyman from Kigezi diocese, and Zebulon Kaboza. In Bristol more than 1,200 people turned out on a freezing wet night. 'Poor English people!' Festo wrote home. 'They had to listen to three whole sermons—twenty-five minutes or so each! Accents included! But in spite of all this, the presence of the Lord was felt, and we had great liberty.'

Their popularity was also evident at Cambridge, where the congregation was queueing up to twenty minutes before the service began, just to be sure to get inside.

Then it was on to the Christian Lawyers Fellowship of the Law Society in London, then the Swanwick Conference Centre in Derbyshire, and on to Northern Ireland, where he was preaching three times a day, and where at Ballymena a church gave a large cheque to his girls' school. Then on to Dublin, before he held some more missions in West Germany in late November. He only got back to Kampala on 6th December, just in time to prepare hurriedly for his third ordination retreat. People were delighted to hear news of the trip, but some did grumble. Why was their bishop preaching in comfortable Europe when Uganda needed him in its agony? AEE staff were also frustrated that he was not preaching more in the cities of Africa, but Festo immersed himself in diocesan duties, determined to clear his desk for the AEE missions planned for the new year in Ghana, Ethiopia and a possibility of New Mexico.

CHAPTER SEVENTEEN

GROWING MINISTRY ... GROWING TERROR

1975–1976

International preaching; Bishop Festo appoints a suffragan bishop; Amin visits Kigezi; Eurofest; fourth Kabale Convention; Central America tour; World Council of Churches Assembly; AEE grows; Christoval; pleads for the ordination of women; PACLA.

BISHOP FESTO RETURNED from the mission to Ghana near the end of February 1975 for a meeting of the House of Bishops, where, among other things, it was decided that Kigezi was indeed to have an assistant bishop. They also approved Bishop Festo's choice of the Dean of St Peter's, Kabale, William Rukirande.

That month also saw a rare event: a joint Christian service at Kabale stadium with the Roman Catholics. The Catholic bishop was fond of Festo, and linked up with him later that year to lead a march of faith around Kabale. As an English clergyman explained,

> Bishop Festo's stress on the unifying effect of the love of God ... made him a special sort of ecumenist, relating readily to Roman Catholics and others not normally associated with evangelical fellowship, yet without thereby losing contact with his more traditional evangelical friends who could not doubt the depth of his own personal walk with the Lord.

April was an historic month in Kigezi. First, the long-awaited 'Bishop's Dream', the Bishop's Secondary School for Girls at Muyebe was, against all the odds, opening. Somehow, there were teachers, and equipment. Bishop Festo led the service of thanksgiving and celebration.

Then in April the new Archbishop of Uganda, Rwanda and Burundi and Boga-Zaire, Janani Luwum, arrived for the consecration of William Rukirande. It was an auspicious occasion: not only had many of Uganda's bishops made the long trek down to Kabale for the service, but so, astonishingly, had Amin and many of his officials. Bishop Festo lent William a set of his own episcopal robes and an episcopal ring, before coolly preparing a sermon to preach before one of Africa's worst tyrants.

St Peter's Cathedral was packed on the day. 'Your Excellency,' he began, 'on behalf of the Christians of this diocese, I would like to take this opportunity to extend our heartfelt and warm welcome to you ...' He attributed Amin's visit to that of showing 'your concern for things spiritual in the affairs of our nation', and continued, 'Our country needs citizens whose hearts are united by the love of God.' Some of Amin's speeches had expressed 'concern' over 'overcharging ... bribery ... too much force ... This is very encouraging to us all,' said Bishop Festo. But 'your enforcement of the laws may restrain men, but it leaves them unchanged ... Only the power of God's love can change men completely, from bad men to good men ... Therefore, the Government and the church are God's instruments to enable people to live together in peace.' This was both Festo's political ideal and dearest hope for the future of Uganda—both Government and church working together for the good of the nation. He would stress again and again that no government could do it on its own—development would only make men 'clever animals'; the 'church's ministry in the nation is to make men and women human'.

Festo picked on the good things Amin had said in various speeches—such as the clergy being his 'right hand', and his alleged desire that all Ugandans have 'a piece of land where they can grow food and build a house and live in it safely' and addressed Amin as if he had meant them—they were 'the greatest treasure you can give to us, and we pray that you will fulfil it by God's help'. Sadly, of course, Amin never would.

The service over, and Amin's helicopter gone, next day Bishop Festo and Bishop William met to work out the details of their joint leadership of Kigezi. Rukirande would concentrate on pastoral care and teaching, as well as relieving Bishop Festo of some of the confirmation tours, which included hundreds of people in a four- to five-hour service.

Summertime meant convention time, and that year the calendar fairly bristled with such meetings. In July Bishop Festo and Mera flew to the UK for the annual Keswick Convention, stopping off in London to visit friends, among them Richard Bewes, now Rector of Emmanuel Church, Northwood, Middlesex and about to take over the leadership of the English branch of African Evangelistic Enterprise for them. Bishop Festo urged the Northwood congregation never to forget their riches in Christ—especially as they were Anglican.

> We tend to make precious things lose their preciousness through traditionalising them too much. Tradition perhaps is one of the greatest killers of reality, and again and again we have to ask the blessed Holy Spirit to bring his light afresh ... particularly when tradition has become thick through the centuries, so much so that sometimes we starve spiritually in the midst of God's plenty. And that is pathetic, isn't it?

From Middlesex, it was on to Cumbria, where after the strains of a spring in Uganda, Bishop Festo and Mera basked in the warm friendship of the Keswick Convention. It had a huge attendance as Billy Graham was among the speakers.

Festo spoke several times: 'Africa is a continent that is rampant with bitterness everywhere, racial bitterness, tribal bitterness, political bitterness.' He did not let the church off lightly, either: denominational bitterness—'I hate you because you are not as evangelical as I am'—we do that without even using those crude words. Festo deplored it: 'We are doing exactly what the Pharisees were doing in the Temple. Jesus never gives anyone among us permission to keep another person at arms' length. Never, even if he is in rags and tatters. Under rags and tatters is a man or woman for whom Christ died.'

No sooner was Keswick over than Eurofest loomed that July: a major European youth event in Brussels aimed at 8,000 young people all over Europe. The Revd John Stott, the Revd Richard Bewes, not to mention singers Cliff Richard and Garth Hewitt were coming from England, while Billy Graham and his team were organising the evening evangelistic rallies.

Bishop Festo and the Argentinian evangelist Luis Palau had been invited to take the Bible readings at the morning session at the vast Palais du Centennaire, on alternate mornings. Their addresses were visually amplified on to large screens, and translated simultaneously into six different languages. Luis Palau was looking forward to meeting Festo. 'For many years I had wanted the chance'—he had read much on the East African revival and it had 'blessed' his life. He was not disappointed at Brussels. Meeting Bishop Festo moved Luis Palau deeply. '... The revival impact on his life: the established confidence the Bishop always displayed in his living, was so restful and authoritative.'

Festo put to good use his African ability to communicate in pictures. He told the 8,000 teenagers: 'The love of Jesus is your spiritual shock-absorber. If you have not this love, you are like an old, old, car!' And he urged them to share this love, this faith: 'God has a long queue of people waiting to meet you.'

Now the Americans were running Eurofest, and therefore had contrived a very organised schedule, with every minute neatly accounted for. One morning Bishop Festo launched into his Bible study, got enthusiastic over one passage and then carried away completely. The red warning light on the pulpit flashed urgently to stop him, but to no avail: in grasping the pulpit, he had accidentally covered it.

Richard Bewes, platform chairman, could see the Americans on the platform beginning to twitch. The minutes ticked by. They stared at Festo's back in anguish, trying to make him *feel* their urgency. One finally leaned over and pleaded with Richard to 'have a word with Festo'. Bewes gaped helplessly: Bishop Festo was in full flow before 8,000 people. 'I can't!' he hissed. More minutes went by. The Americans were by now in torment. '*The programme! We've got to get on with the programme!*'

Desperately, Richard Bewes devised a plan. After all, the platform was very high off the ground, and edged with huge floral displays ... these would provide some cover, at least. So he slipped off his chair and, on his stomach, wriggled slowly across to the pulpit. If the congregation didn't see him, neither did Festo—not until Bewes reached out a hand, grabbed his ankle and squeaked 'STOP!' Bishop Festo froze in astonishment.

Then he rallied: 'The Lord bless you!' and left the pulpit, leaving Bewes supine on the platform in relief. He stood up without thinking a moment later and many in the audience blinked in astonishment: where had he come from?

A few days after Eurofest ended, the fourth Kabale Convention got underway. Nothing could have kept Festo and Mera away: the ten-yearly gatherings were great landmarks in the spiritual history of Kigezi diocese. It had been at the first convention in 1945 that they had been called to Tanzania. Festo had chosen the theme this time: 'Christ's love reconciles us'— very 'timely for Uganda and Africa' he said, in the face of so much turmoil, hatred and fear.

Preparations for the catering for and boarding of several thousand people had been in hand for months, but even basic necessities were all but impossible to get hold of. In the end the lorries to transport the extra food were to come from a most unexpected source: the Muslim governor of the southern province, Bashirr Juma. Bishop Festo managed it, though he hadn't had that on his mind when he went to see the governor shortly before the convention got underway. He had heard that the governor, encouraged by Amin's anti-Christian policies, had been speaking against him as the Anglican bishop of the diocese. He begged, and was granted an interview, where he made his position clear. Reading from the first part of Romans 13, he assured the governor that his faith decreed that he submit to the secular authorities over him. On the other hand, he slipped in a challenge: 'This word tells also what is your responsibility, to govern under God's authority for the very good of the people.' By the end of two hours the governor realised he had nothing to fear from the Christian bishop, and indeed went so far as to offer what help he could towards the convention. That was where the lorries came in, plus an even bigger surprise: he agreed to Bishop Festo's request (which must have startled many brethren) that he come and open the convention (at which he went as far as to quote from the New Testament).

More than 7,000 people attended from Kigezi, Ankole and all Uganda, from Kenya, Burundi, Rwanda, Zaire, USA, Canada, England, West Germany, Norway, Switzerland, and even Japan. Numbers swelled to over 15,000 for the weekend. AEE was represented—nearly seven of their staff evangelists were fully busy ministering. Other guests included nearly all Uganda's bishops.

Friends and colleagues describe Bishop Festo as being very 'high' for the whole of the convention. 'He was in his element'— this despite the palpable fear that hung in the air: Amin's spies were known to be in the crowd.

Bishop Festo's international ministry was not confined to the spoken word, for it was in this year, 1975, that Dorothy Smoker prepared a small book of Festo's messages (taken from those in the Swahili monthly mission periodical *Outlook*) called *Love Unlimited* (Regal Press: Glendale, CA, 1975). This was to be translated and distributed widely in Dutch, German, French, Spanish, Portuguese, Japanese, Ghanaian English, Zulu and English.

After the Kabale Convention came the Uganda Keswick Convention at the end of the same month. Festo and Mera, on their way to England, stopped off in Kampala for the opening Sunday, where Festo joined James and Zeb and other members of the Convention Committee in preaching at churches and chapels in the area.

Then it was on to London, where Festo had urgent business on the Lausanne Executive Committee. A few days later they flew on to Switzerland where Lausanne Cathedral was celebrating its 700th anniversary. Festo was to strike up a warm acquaintance with the two pastors of the Cathedral, of the official Church of Switzerland: *L'eglise evangelique et reformée du canton de Vaud*. One said later, 'I have been in many evangelistic campaigns, but this is the very first time that one has deeply touched my heart.'

To illustrate 'liberated to live in the right relationship with your family', Festo used a favourite example: he compared a family to a piano keyboard:

There must be harmony to make listeners happy! ... There is no harmony if they play themselves. You need an artiste ... He does not strike the keys with a stick. He has a gentle touch. But at his touch each key must go down. If it does not obey the artiste's will, he can't play, because the key refuses to bend.

Festo warned that if anyone in the family tries to play the keyboard, 'it only creates confusion. There is only One Person qualified to play the keys of life. ... There is harmony in the family when Jesus is the player ... How many notes do you need to bring disharmony? Only one! ... '

And when he spoke to a group of church leaders in Lausanne, he reminded them:

> It is one thing to know the truth, but something else to let the Spirit operate. ... Saul of Tarsus was ... so legalistic you could not get near him. He needed a spiritual operation ... How did the Holy Spirit do that? One instrument ... two pieces of wood in the form of a cross ... nails ... a body utterly helpless. ... God shows us there love bleeding ... It is very expensive love, very deep, universal. That is the knife God used on the heart of that Jew ... Now here is man who can go anywhere with this wonderful love. 'The love of Christ compels me.' His only motive, the engine which drives him, is the love of Christ. No wonder there are tired pastors. Their motor is: *my* theology, *my* experience, *my* service. When the experience goes down, there is a dead engine.

Bishop Festo's joy in the *grace* of God was once well illustrated by a brief encounter with a puzzled nun after a meeting. She confided: 'I have given my life to help Ugandans and to teach them about Jesus. But I don't seem to have the same joy as I see in you. What is wrong with me?'

Bishop Festo replied, 'Sister, why compare yourself with me? I think you are more holy than I am—I have never given up half of what you have ...'

'Then why do you look so happy, and I so miserable?'

'I will make a guess. You want your joy in the Lord to depend on what you do for God, and my joy depends entirely on what he keeps doing for me. Look at what Christ did—and does—for you, and you will rejoice. That is the sinner's joy.'

The nun began to laugh. She walked away singing. 'She had discovered,' guessed Bishop Festo, 'the secret of the Prodigal Son—which the older brother never knew.'

9th October marked Uganda's thirteenth anniversary of independence. Festo and Mera were back in Kabale in time to attend the celebrations at the stadium—but in truth there was little enough to be joyful about: Festo was heartsick at what was happening to his beloved country; Amin paraded about with a shimmering chestful of self-awarded military medals, while thousands of innocent civilians died at his soldiers' hands.

The diocese was crying out for attention, but a previously-booked preaching tour of Central America called, and in a few weeks, Bishop Festo had met up with Keith Jesson in New York and as soon as Michael Cassidy and one of his team, Ebenezer arrived, they flew south to Guatemala City and then on to Managua, Nicaragua's capital to link up with the Anglican bishop there, Bishop Aynesworth. While Festo never made any but the most basic reports of his missions, Michael Cassidy was an inveterate scribbler, and extracts from his ministry tour report of the trip reveal humorous behind-the-scene incidents that put the lie to any idea that international preaching must always be glamorous. For example, after a short split to cover different meetings, Michael Cassidy and Ebenezer were to meet up again with Festo and Keith back at Managua, and then fly on to Costa Rica to a series of more meetings. It seemed such a simple idea at the time ... 'But,' wrote Michael:

> as we were coming in to land, there we saw the runway surrounded with fire engines. This is not exactly calculated to give one a comfortable sensation. However, after landing we gathered from the pilot that this was not for our plane, but for the plane which had been due to bring Festo and Keith from Bluefields! Apparently its landing gear had jammed ...
>
> We got into the airport and were astonished to find Keith and Festo who had just flown in on a military plane specially chartered for them—the plane due to pick them up had indeed been unable to land even at Bluefields because of the landing gear problems, and had flown on to Managua ... However, the military plane bringing Festo and Keith had begun to run out of petrol and they had to land in a little forest strip for more fuel. They were cooped up with a whole lot of turkeys and chickens and had been required to hold their suitcases on their laps. Imagine a Baptist layman and an Anglican bishop in a tiny plane surrounded by chickens and turkeys and laden down beneath their own suitcases. The picture tests one's doctrines of man, nature and grace to the limits!

But the day had only just begun. From Managua they caught the plane for San Jose in Costa Rica, but the weather was too

bad to land. They circled the airport for an hour. Then the pilot
gave up and flew back to Managua—where they sat in the plane
on the runway for an hour trying to guess what was going to
happen next. They flew back to San Jose. Again they couldn't
land. Again they circled. Then the pilot suddenly headed for
Panama, 'as if anyone on our plane wanted to go to Panama!'
Nevertheless—there they were in Panama, 'midnight local time,
the airport in chaos'. They got to sleep in a local hotel by two
am—only to be summoned back to the airport at four-thirty ...
for another three-hour wait. 'You can imagine our fragile state
...' Finally another—successful—attempt on San Jose. They
landed and sped to town to meet up with the Anglican bishop—
the whole purpose of their visit. But he never turned up. So it
was back to the airport for the noon flight. They got there in
time to watch it being carted off the runway by tractors. They
were due in Limon, Costa Rica that night for a crusade—and
miraculously enough, in the end they made it—preached to a
crowd of 2,500 and 'a number responded to the invitation'.

During the days that followed there was more frustration—
but this time not with travel à la Latin America. Instead, it was
all too familiar throughout the world. The meetings were
'almost wrecked by the length of the programme and the rather
shaky quality of the music ...'. They had all long ago realised
that 'proper programming of evangelistic meetings is something
very few people can do well', but even so, Festo and Michael
Cassidy were frustrated that 'none of the critical evaluation we
had made of last night's meeting was followed through, all the
same mistakes, and more, were made'. It was with relief that
both evangelists found they still had 'great liberty in preaching'
when their turn finally came.

One of the reasons behind such chaos was that all the local
clergy 'were struggling to get on to the programme'. At a seven
am clergy breakfast meeting next day, Bishop Festo gently
tackled them on it by a 'brilliant word' on the way Jesus had
dealt with the disciples who were arguing over who was the
greatest—'he simply responded by washing their feet'. It
was hoped the point had got across. In any event, the Latin
Americans seem to have enjoyed their visit. As one said, 'They
were men of God and had hearts full of love. And our people

went crazy about them!' The team was touched by the warm welcome, but flew home in a rather exhausted state.

Only a few days later, in November, both Bishop Festo and Michael Cassidy headed for Nairobi and the World Council of Churches Assembly, whose theme that year was 'Jesus Christ Frees and Unites'. Like the Lausanne Congress, it drew several thousand delegates from all over the world: Asians, Africans, Europeans, Americans. Like Lausanne, it encompassed a large number of denominations: Baptist rubbed shoulders with Anglican bishop. But here the resemblance ended: here was no theologically homogenous gathering, but instead 'unbelievable theological pluralism', according to one astonished guest. Charismatic evangelicals holding prayer meetings in tongues brushed shoulders with liberal politically motivated Christians, a few of whom even advocated political violence as a means of achieving their aims. The whole spectrum of views held by people who professed Christ was there.

The Assembly threw up several key questions, among them two posed in the paper given by the Moderator of the Central Committee, Dr M. Thomas, an Indian theologian, and which many of the evangelicals considered to be 'crunch questions for the WCC at this time'.

They were: 'How can the struggles and conflicts to bring human dignity to the poor and the oppressed, even the power politics which opposes institutionalised violence with counter violence, be kept within the spiritual framework of ultimate power of the crucified Christ in the ultimate goal of reconciliation of all people in Christ?'

And: 'How can the church participate in political ideologies, structures, and processes in our nations in a manner which will communicate this awareness? ... We need a theology of political engagement that will help Christians and churches in such participation, a theology that will clarify the dialectical relations between faith and ideology in the light of the *cross* and the resurrection.'

It was precisely the problem that Festo had been facing in Amin's Uganda. But while agreeing that the Gospel should be applied to their situation, the evangelicals and the WCC kept hitting a major difficulty: were they talking in fact about two radically different versions of the gospel? Both parties claimed to put themselves under the authority of Scripture—i.e. the problems of hermeneutics had arisen. This led numbers of evangelicals there to conclude that in the end it was not 'two different but complementary understandings of faith' but rather: 'two incompatible positions which are as different as night and day, error and truth, chalk and cheese, a man-centred or a god-centred faith, a biblical hermeneutic, or a cavalier and selective approach to Scripture which makes it say whatever one likes'— as one leading evangelical described it.

Certainly the different approaches led to different outcomes. John Stott observed to a friend that while the year before he had to plead for a greater social concern at Lausanne, here he found he was pleading for evangelism not to fall off the agenda. Bishop Festo found the lack of stress on evangelism 'immensely disturbing', but perhaps not surprising, in view of the fact the WCC's theological position on salvation was basically universalist, while the evangelicals believed in the need for personal, individual salvation. He was worried by the suspicion that liberal theology was leading to political liberation becoming synonymous with salvation.

Which, of course, brought one back to the cross of Christ. Bishop Festo was the main speaker at the mass rally on the Sunday, and, as at Lausanne, he again focused on the cross— stressing the need for personal salvation. Individuals had to find Jesus if any peace and harmony were to come to wider society. His message was backed up by leading evangelical churchmen in other sessions and papers and committees.

December again found Festo and Mera in Kabale, preparing the deacons for their ordination to the priesthood. It also gave Festo a chance to meet the twenty-four-year-old girl that CMS had sent out that October to be his secretary. (Having a trained, experienced English secretary greatly facilitated life for Bishop Festo and other Ugandan bishops: such women would be beyond any accusation of ever acting out of tribalistic motives, and could be totally discreet.) Judith Trickett, from Yorkshire, had been a missionary in training at Selly Oak College in Birmingham when one night she went along as a counsellor at a one-off mission at the cathedral. Bishop Festo preached, she was 'very impressed', one thing led to another, and that October she arrived in Kabale. The diocesan staff made her very welcome, though explained she was on her own, as 'Bishop was away for a while'. 'This was to become a very familiar way of life!' She decided she would begin by tidying the Bishop's office and getting her own office set up. Thereupon the diocese staff took her to the diocese office on Rugarama Hill, and said, 'This is the Bishop's office—and this little outer room is your office.' Judith was glad of the information: as otherwise she would not have guessed: there was nothing there but concrete walls, floor and ceiling. 'No desk, no chair, no nothing!'

Bishop Festo did not have time to meet her until the day before Christmas Eve, when she had a message to go and see him up at the bungalow. She felt 'welcomed' by his warmth and courtesy, and intrigued that he called her 'Judi'—no one else ever had or did. 'But to him I would always be "Judi".' He said he would send down his files, so she returned to the office. 'The next thing I knew was a huge suitcase was coming down the hill on a boy's head.' With a dawning horror, she began to realise just how unorganised things had been until now: it was crammed full of hundreds of documents dating back to Lyth's time three years before, and dozens of letters, none of them yet opened. Judith went through them, and found some addressed in her own hand. 'I had written saying, "Please, Bishop, what shall I bring?" I opened them now and read them, and sure enough that was what I'd said!'

Judith's office was already swamped with paper when 'a filing cabinet came down on somebody else's head'. It too went back to 1972—thousands of bits of paper all relating to the diocese and all needing sorting and filing and dealing with. 'Festo had been too busy preaching.' This was true enough, and didn't change: apart from a brief handshake at the door of the cathedral on Christmas morning, Judith did not see him again until late February.

Such absenteeism irritated many people, for inevitably it caused disruptions and delays in the running of the diocese. One clergyman found: 'Bishop Festo was very nice to work with, only he was always out!' People began to write bitter, anonymous letters complaining about it. Some of the bishops of

Uganda's other dioceses became forthright in their belief that as Bishop he *belonged in Kigezi*. Perhaps it frustrated the *muzungu*, or whites, most of all—with their higher expectations of efficiency, and belief that bishops were there to *serve* their diocese. (In Africa, traditionally those in authority often kept people waiting for months.) But the vast majority loved Festo for what he was, were indeed proud of having a world evangelist as bishop, and wanted him on any terms. Phrases like: 'We want him, but we don't want to be selfish ...' 'We want him *here*, but we want him *there*—he's a fruit of our revival!' crop up again and again.

Meanwhile, the end of January 1976 found Bishop Festo in Nairobi for key four-day AEE team meetings. The work was thriving: new staff were joining—including James Katarikawe, who had helped out on a part-time basis now for some time. A vet in Tanzania, Titus Lwebandiza, had recently decided to take early retirement so that he could concentrate on developing the Tanzania AEE branch. In London, the AEE support prayer groups had come under the wing of Richard Bewes, and were growing.

Then it was on to Accra in February, for a mission to the University of Ghana where the students jammed the hall, sitting on the floor. Following this visit, another booklet of Bishop Festo's talks was edited and printed in Ghana. *The Spirit Is Moving* was produced by Africa Christian Press: Achimota, 1976.

Meanwhile, the Lausanne Continuation Committee was hard at work. Festo had flown out to Mexico City for the first major meeting with men such as the Revd Gottfried Osei-Mensah, who was appointed full-time Executive Secretary, and Dr John Stott, chairman of the Theology Working Group. The Committee's first job was to give itself a brief—and soon a heated debate was underway. The Americans wanted to stick solely to evangelism. John Stott declared that this would be to betray the Covenant, which had pledged involvement in political and social issues as well. Billy Graham made a pragmatic observation while he agreed that evangelical social involvement was important, he doubted that evangelicals throughout the world would ever unite on anything but evangelism. But Stott argued that if it were not attempted, many younger evangelical leaders would be deeply disillusioned. Bishop Festo kept a low profile. Stott guessed him to be 'a little bit in the middle. I think I knew him well enough to say he was really on my side, for he did have a social conscience, and saw the need ... but he was very much a man of peace, and did not like these confrontations.'

Festo returned to Kabale in late February to find a mountain of letters and papers waiting for his attention, and an endless queue of people outside his office, anxious to see him. He drew 'Judi' into his office, shut the door, and addressed himself to the paperwork—scanning the letters and then dictating replies at enormous speed, oblivious to her occasional sneeze—and then mad scramble to catch up again. As well as diocesan matters, there were one or two offers of western aid: Bishop Festo welcomed such offers cautiously—some came with strings attached and he would not be told what to do in his own diocese.

Judith soon learned to keep a sharp eye out for anyone in the waiting area trying to sneak by her and get to the Bishop. On mornings when he arrived at the office and was overwhelmed by people, she even developed the habit of presently going outside and physically leading him in and away. But when he eventually emerged for lunch she could not save him: people would literally run across the compound to be near him, and cluster around. One would start to talk, pause for breath, and another would plunge in. One clergyman found the solution was to 'grab Festo and speak very quickly. If I blink, someone else has got him!'

Bishop Festo also needed to meet with Bishop William. Tensions had arisen between the two: though in theory their roles were different, with Bishop William to concentrate on teaching, confirming, preaching and pastoral counselling, while Bishop Festo looked after the executive management of Kigezi; in practice, the lines blurred. They hit upon a solution they could fall back on at need in the years to come: 'We "sat together" (as the East Africans say) we talked it out, and we repented.' Both would be ready to admit 'This was not easy! But Jesus was with us. It was his work, and he helped us.'

As for Sundays, Bishop Festo was not always preaching. On the rare free mornings he would nip onto his VW combi and thunder down the hill to St Peter's in time for the morning service. His arrival caused much whispering and smiles, and his habit of note-taking during the sermons would badly rattle the dean or whoever was preaching that morning—reluctant to find himself without warning having to preach before the diocesan bishop—a world renowned preacher.

By that February, Amin had given control of the army and cabinet completely into the hands of his own supporters. Under Amin, they continued to plunder and pillage and kill. No one could do anything—but Bishop Festo was among the handful who even continued to try. With quite astonishing courage, he acted on his belief that the church must be willing to stand for justice, regardless of consequences. On one occasion he drove to the Parliament, leaving Mera in the car and telling her only that he had to see somebody (she later wept when he confessed who); when he entered the building, the man on duty was too frightened even to tell Amin he was there. Festo persuaded him to dial through and took the phone himself to ask for the audience. Curiously enough, Amin continued to see him: Bishop Festo's calm, distinguished manner seemed to soothe him; but still it was like stepping into the ring with an enraged bull who might or might not charge immediately.

Yet somehow, in this trial by fire, Festo had come into his own. It was almost as if all the periphery things in his life had been burnt away. Friends and colleagues speak of him at this time as 'more vibrant than ever'; 'more full of energy for the Gospel'; 'more bouncy than ever'; 'Festo's great courage, based on his deep love for Uganda, was seen especially in those dark days.' A daughter says, 'I remember Daddy as someone who never had a worry about anything,' though Festo confessed later that this was not so as the downfall of Uganda made him heartsick.

But Festo's line was 'A living church cannot be destroyed by fire or by guns'; and though he believed Amin's barbarities had pushed Uganda 'back a century', he still felt that 'Jesus never said "Blessed are those who are bitter in hatred towards others" ... It became increasingly clear to me that my duty as a believer in Jesus was to communicate to my fellow human beings God's life-restoring love in his son Jesus Christ.' But the bitterness he had to conquer first was to be in his own heart.

Early that spring Festo was able to spend some more time in the diocese, where he made time to visit his new Bishop's Girls' School in Muyebe. The headmistress, Liz Trail, was taking a geography lesson when he arrived, and seizing a map, asked him to show her pupils where he had been recently. The pencil jabbed quickly: 'Here, here, here, here, here—oh, and here, here, here, here ...' the class dissolved in laughter, and Liz had a new nickname for her coded letters home. Amin was already 'McGregor' after the farmer in Beatrix Potter's stories; Festo was now 'WT'—world traveller. But Bishop Festo's travels did not seem to have harmed the diocese: by now 250,000 of the 650,000 inhabitants of Kigezi were Anglican; cared for by two bishops, five archdeacons, fifty-five ordained pastors, 713 church teachers and eight missionaries.

With the onset of early summer, Festo and Mera packed their bags and prepared to fly north to Europe, like migrating birds. Convention time was upon them again, meetings where Bishop Festo would prove so popular that yet more invitations to 'come back for longer missions at our church' would pour in from churches throughout Europe that autumn.

For Whitsun week Bishop Festo was booked as one of the speakers at the Christoval in Essen—it drew more than 13,000 young people from Germany, Austria and German-speaking Switzerland. Colleagues were amused to see that a bodyguard of orange-shirted German youth insisted on escorting Festo to and from the platform to stop him from being mobbed by autograph hunters and handshakers. On the Sunday Billy Graham and Festo shared the platform—and an 'African bear hug', to the delight of the youngsters.

Soon it was on to Basel, and another three day convention for several thousand young people. After that, the Kivengeres headed north to Norway, for meetings in cities including Kristiansand and Oslo and Trondheim. In Trondheim his sermon was broadcast from the famous old cathedral on national radio—an honour never 'done before'.

Then it was south to Switzerland in early July, for another large outreach, this time involving Billy Graham and Stanley Mooneyham of World Vision and the popular convention speaker, George Duncan. Here Festo learned with amazement of the Israeli's famous raid on Entebbe to free a planeload of people hijacked by Palestinian commandos.

Then the Kivengeres made a quick hop back to Africa for meetings in Kampala, Burundi and Zaire (to install the Bishop of Bukavu) and then a few days in Rwanda for a pastors' meeting. Then it was back north—this time to Northern Ireland for a worldwide missionary convention. Other similar overseas missions, conferences and outreaches followed, but by September Bishop Festo and Mera were again in Kampala for the Uganda Bishops' Conference.

Archbishop Janani Luwum was in the chair for the last time (within months he would be murdered by Amin). A missionary attending the conference as a translator recalls: 'Here I became aware of Festo's forward thinking on issues like the ordination of women, communion wine, and also his directness with the very few unholy and politically-minded bishops.' For certainly, the ordination of women was the subject of one lively debate. Luwum had already given his go-ahead, and Festo was eager to start straight away. Others were cautious: 'Should we not wait for the Church of England?'

Festo's retort was prompt: 'If you wait for the Church of England you wait until doomsday!'

A bishop replied, 'Well, okay, let's write a paper on the subject.'

Festo snorted in derision. 'If you write a paper on it, you'll produce something for the archives which will gather dust for ever.'

A colleague recalls: 'Festo was always refreshingly direct and straight! He was at home in the cut and thrust of debate, and knew his own mind. When one or two bishops would go for him, he would go straight back for them too.' In the end, it was sixteen three against ordaining women immediately. So the matter was referred for debate to the diocesan synods and the provincial assembly, several years ahead.

Then there was the discussion on communion wine. Many bishops were still paying enormous prices to have it imported. Festo thought this absurd, and advocated banana juice, coloured if some preferred it so. 'He was for anything that would work, that was in the line of progress and in local culture.' In practical matters, he was very much for the African solution: 'He was not at all wedded to English Anglicanism!'

Festo had firm friends among the bishops; he also had firm enemies. 'He was not liked by everyone. He was too direct. He kicked too many of their sacred cows.' Any hint of political ambition or compromise would be certain of a stern response. Then, too, there was also the problem of jealousy. The other bishops did not forget that he of all their number was really at home in the western sophistication, counted as friends leading figures such as Billy Graham, had lived in America, and had the financial support and friendship of wealthy Americans and Europeans for his diocese and for AEE. Festo did all he could not to stir up any jealousy, and was generous with what he had, but that made some resent even his generosity. His frequent absences from his diocese gave them a target for their anger, and for this he was bitterly criticised, even though by all measurable means his diocese was in fact better run than most, with higher giving, and more confirmations.

The conference over, Bishop Festo was off to Ethiopia to an International Pastors' Conference organised by World Vision. From there he flew on to New York, where the Trinity Episcopal Church in Wall Street (Lower Manhattan) was holding a crusade. Bishop Festo spoke to 'crowds' at noon at the lunch-time services each day, and then again at a series of evening meetings, held in Greenwich Village. His buoyancy and love won him great popularity with the Americans. 'Words are totally inadequate to describe the gratitude I feel for all that you did for the people of our church and for me personally,' one pastor told him.

The Rector of Trinity, the Revd Ray Parks, had had Festo as a visiting preacher before, but this time was delighted how well the week's meeting had gone down with the wider 'Wall Street Community'. Bishop Festo was also a 'primary influence' in Trinity's decision to give priority to the church in Africa in its grants programme of one million dollars a year. (Trinity was often said to be the wealthiest church in the world.) Parks considered Bishop Festo 'a modern day St Paul in his missionary zeal and worldwide travels'.

While in New York, Bishop Festo also made time to visit Dr

Stephen Olford, President of Encounter Ministries, and his wife, Heather, both good friends of the Kivengeres. Such quiet, private times Dr Olford would find 'most meaningful':

> It was one thing to preach with him and to hear him preach, but quite another experience to relax quietly in a sitting room and just talk about Jesus. Here was a couple who were not interested in discussing cars, television programmes, clothes or trivia; their one 'magnificent obsession' was the Lord Jesus Christ.

Dr Olford had grown up in Africa, which helped him appreciate that the African doesn't

> speak in terms of propositions; they communicate in terms of pictures. There is a vividness and concreteness about their theology. There were times when the Lord Jesus became so real, in the living room or kitchen or wherever we were sitting, that we almost turned to the first vacant chair to hear him speak to us.

Dr Olford once asked Festo what he considered to be the two most used words in the revival.

> Straightaway Festo said 'brokenness' and 'walking in the light'. 'Brokenness,' Festo told me, was 'willingness to repent when sin interrupted fellowship with God, or with one another.' 'Walking in the light' was virtually living in obedience and in the fulness of the Holy Spirit. Failure to walk in the light, Festo continued, was 'to be hiding in the bushes.'

This had amused Olford, 'But the more we came to think about it, the more we realised that this is the whole picture of Genesis 3. Once Adam and Eve ceased to walk in the light they ended up in the bushes with fear and shame.'

November found Bishop Festo back in Uganda, where he and Mera visited the Makerere University Mission. Charity, now a student here, shared the daughterly anxiety that her dad might preach for too long; but, as the year before, she found her non-church-going fellow students pressing eagerly into the hall to hear him.

December brought the long-awaited PACLA conference—the Pan African Christian Leadership Assembly of 800 delegates from forty-seven countries which took place in Nairobi. Mera went along gladly, looking forward to seeing their daughter

Joy between sessions: Joy was married now and living in Nairobi.

The idea for PACLA had emerged from the South African Congress on Mission and Evangelism in 1973. It was felt that an assembly bringing the rising Christian leadership across Africa together would be an invaluable strategic move. Christianity was growing so fast, and amid such turbulent cultural and political changes, that the church in Africa would benefit from a chance to face the challenges of the continent together. The assembly would give leaders a chance to meet and form friendships with each other throughout the continent, thus increasing mutual trust and communication.

From its earliest inception, however, Michael Cassidy and others (among them, the Ghanaian and ex-pastor of Nairobi Baptist Church, Gottfried Osei-Mensah [PACLA Chairman], John Gatu, the General Secretary of the Presbyterian Church of East Africa and Vice-Chairman of the All Africa Council of Churches and John Mpaayei, the Bible Society Director) had taken the enormous responsibility of bringing it to birth— Bishop Festo, never a willing paperwork man, was simply too overcommitted already between AEE missions and administration and the oversight of Kigezi.

By late 1975 the Nairobi ad hoc committee for PACLA had widened to include the Archbishop of Kenya, Festo Olang, Dr Don Smith (Director of Daystar Communications), Bishop David Gitari (Bishop of Mount Kenya East), Dr Ken Tracey (Director of World Vision) and leaders from twenty-five African countries.

It was perhaps one of the most difficult assemblies AEE ever organised. As well as basic problems with even getting letters to and from different countries, and finance, there were two obstacles of theology and politics—either of which could have blown all attempts sky-high. Theologically, PACLA had decided to renounce all tags in the naive belief that this would soothe everyone. Not a bit of it. Instead, Michael Cassidy and his colleagues instantly became the target for dark suspicion from *both* those Christians in the wider ecumenical church, identified as the All Africa Conference of Churches, and those in the evangelical 'camp', the Association of Evangelicals of Africa and

Madagascar (AEAM), each watchful for any 'hidden agenda' and competition from PACLA in their own spheres of influence. Festo dictated dozens of letters of reassurance in support of Michael Cassidy and Gottfried Osei-Mensah. Just one, to a stern evangelical who thought he smelled heresy, ran:

> I am a firm believer in John 12:12, 'When I am lifted up from the earth I shall draw all men unto myself.' As long as the drawing is to Jesus Christ I am not ashamed to invite all men, from every persuasion, to meet under the sound of the Gospel. The essence of evangelical truth is not in the neat expressions used in the Creeds, but the essence is the Lord Jesus Christ and him crucified ... Those who claim to be strict conservative evangelicals will come to the Cross that they may be melted afresh, those who were too loose in their liberalism will come to the Cross that they may be spiritually renewed and perhaps tightened ... PACLA is ... an assembly with one simple aim: to bring God's people together to face the challenge of living for Christ on the continent of Africa together.[1]

Only heroic efforts and fathomless patience and prayer kept PACLA on the rails and the delegates arriving on 9th December, 1976 for the ten day assembly.

There were any number of papers given on what leadership in the church of Africa meant and what it should mean. But Bishop Festo laid his finger on the most basic vital fact of all: that of the need for the leaders to be *worthy* of leading such a vast church through such turbulent times. And with this regard, he believed that PACLA might help enable 'Africa's Christian leaders to develop and grow spiritually so that they could better fulfil their demanding calling'. It was such a keynote address, and so revealing of his own views of leadership, that it is worth quoting in some detail.

Festo based his point of departure on PACLA's theme verse from Ephesians 4:15: 'Growing up in all ways into him.' He reminded his listeners that no growth or transformation can take place without pain, and:

> In fact, a great battle rages between the flesh and the Spirit. One drags life downwards into deterioration ... And the other, the Spirit, draws life ever more deeply into Christ. These two forces meet head-on in the open battlefield of our daily lives, especially in our relationships with each other in the church and in Christian work.

And the main problem was one he had seen the world over:

Our self-centredness, which produces jealousy, hatred and suspicion. In such an atmosphere there can hardly be growth. Characters degenerate and we find it very difficult to find spiritual unity, for the atmosphere is dry and poisoned. Disunity and disharmony reign supreme. Broken relationships are the rule of the day. And right relationships become rare. Right creeds, neat dogmas, and long-overworked theological expressions replace vital relationship with one another and with Jesus as the Head from whom the healthy streams of Living Water flow.

And sadly, the results, worldwide, were the same:

Togetherness is feared. ... The vision is filled with self. And the community becomes either a threat to our security, or a cumbersome imposition to be resented, fought or ignored!

Bishop Festo then challenged each person in the assembly to 'vacate' his 'secure borders' and learn together to become spiritual adults, to conform to the image of Christ.

The point of our compass must forever point *to Christ,* or we shall be over-baked in one aspect of our Christian life, and under-cooked in another. For instance, a Christian can be overgrown in sound doctrine and stunted in kindness. Or he can be fully grown in religious zeal but sadly lacking in love. Or well-advanced in outward moral life but sadly backward in simple good manners. In other words, we can easily find ourselves failing to grow '*in all ways*' into Christ. Such unbalanced growth is grotesque and unchristian. And it will inhibit the advance of the Gospel on our continent unless we set it right.

And then he returned to a well-loved theme:

The most effective remedy at this point, is the spirit of love. You see, love is the key mark of those who are truly in Christ. Not doctrine or denominational affiliation. It is the *love of God* poured into the believer's heart by the Holy Spirit which is the unmistakable mark of spiritual growth. ... In communion with him by the Holy Spirit, our starved humanity bursts into fuller life. We cannot tell how it has come about! But we know we are different! And in a most unusual way, unusual to our natural way of doing things, we find ourselves wanting and enjoying things we never did before. We feel we cannot do otherwise. It comes from within and we do not know why!

Festo was rarely openly critical of other Christians' spirituality, but at times he did sadly reflect on some of the shortcomings he had found in church circles around the world. Self-righteous orthodoxy without love grieved him especially. He would recall the New Testament story of the Pharisees dragging out the woman caught in adultery and preparing to stone her.

> There was beautiful orthodoxy in what they were doing, but *no love* ... it was a religion without mercy. Jesus didn't want to condemn her, he wanted to renew her. ...
>
> We need a spirit-filled Church, which means a Church whose centre is not doctrine ... Christians think that when the doctrine is right, they are right. They are not right. They can have the most sound doctrines and be the most sleeping churches. ...

It was a message that would touch many deeply, especially when Bishop Festo later introduced Michael Cassidy to the assembly and explained that their joint ministry—of a black Ugandan and a white South African—had been possible only through their discovery of each other in the reconciling love of Christ.

PACLA ran over two Sundays. On the first, Billy Graham preached to the enormous open air rally, Bishop Festo translating his message into Swahili. On the second, Africa responded with its own 'Mr Evangelist': Festo Kivengere '*the* evangelist for us Africans', as one delegate put it. Another adds bluntly: 'Both Billy and Festo are similar in that their power comes from an anointing of the Holy Spirit. Their actual sermons have the same content as everyone else's!'

CHAPTER EIGHTEEN

FLIGHT FROM UGANDA
1977

Festo preaches against Amin's oppression; raid on the Archbishop; bishops write protest letter; Amin summons bishops; threatens them; Janani Luwum detained and murdered; Festo and Mera flee for their lives.

ON 30TH JANUARY 1877 the first CMS missionaries to Uganda, Wilson and Shergold-Smith, had arrived and contacted the Kabaka Mutesa, triggering off a series of events that led, through martyrdoms and exiles, to the founding of the Church of Uganda. That same weekend, 100 years later, the Archbishop and Bishop Festo set in train a number of events which led to the martyrdom of the Archbishop and the exile of Bishop Festo ... and through their witness the church would grow stronger, more certain, and more resilient in its faith.

Bishop Festo had begun the year with preaching engagements in New York and Britain. He arrived back in Uganda mid-month, eager to make the acquaintance of his very first grand-child, a girl, just born to Peace in Kampala. Then he and Mera went on to Kabale. He was to preach at the consecration of Yorum Bamunoba, who was about to become the first Bishop of the newly formed diocese of West Ankole (next door neighbours of Kigezi diocese and until 1978 a part of Ankole diocese).

It was a major religious and civic occasion: an estimated 30,000 people made their way by foot, by bicycle, by lorry, by car from all over the diocese and Uganda. There were government leaders, army and police chiefs, religious leaders, and security men by the carload. Slowly the crowds converged on

Bweranyangi, the new diocesan centre at Bushenyi, and were seated under a vast canopy of banana leaves.

Bishop Festo and the others had determined that day that 'everyone was going to hear the gospel, even the security men hiding in the bushes'. Hence, the three sets of microphones were 'so clear that you could hear every word half a mile away'.[1] What Festo had to say would be far from popular when news of the consecration was reported to Amin. But by the end of 1976, he had discovered that 'living in danger, when the Lord Jesus is the focus of your life, can be liberating. For one thing, you are no longer imprisoned by your own security, because there is none.'[2] And he, along with the Christians in Kabale and throughout the diocese had, in prayer and meditation, asked 'the Lord to show us, in the situation that was upon us, how we could demonstrate his glory'.[3] Practically, of course, a bishop could *do* little to stop the carnage, but he could proclaim the truth; despite the fact that 'when we stand where our Lord stood in this world, representing his Light and Truth, we are an embarrassment and a threat to the darkness. We are likely to be hated and called 'a subversive community'.[4] Moreover, 'it became clear to us, through the Scriptures, that our resistance was to be that of overcoming evil with good'.[5]

So that day Bishop Festo took as his text Acts 20:24, 28:

> But I do not account my life of any value nor as precious to myself, if only I may accomplish my course and the ministry which I received from the Lord Jesus, to testify to the gospel of the grace of God ... Take heed to yourselves and to all the flock, in which the Holy Spirit has made you overseers, to care for the church of the Lord which he obtained with his own blood.

Bishop Festo's words that day seemed prophetic. They rang in people's ears for a long time afterwards: 'Don't guard your own life ... it is precious in so far as it is useful to preach the gospel.'

Then suddenly Bishop Festo paused and said: 'Now I'm going to speak directly to government authorities. Remember, all authority comes from God. ... How are you using your authority? ... to crush men's faces into the dust?'[6]

Festo, quite obviously supported by the Archbishop, went on to condemn the use of force and exploitation of Ugandan by

Ugandan. 'Friends told me when it was all over that I was quite passionate.'[7] Missionaries from Kabale were 'terrified the security men would arrest him there and then'. One warned Archbishop Janani afterwards: 'You and Festo must choose your words more carefully!' All wondered what *they* would tell the President when he asked what had been said at Bweranyangi'.[8] But the Muslim governor got up, walked over to Bishop Festo, and deliberately shook his hand in thanks.

If Archbishop Janani and Bishop Festo had wanted any reassurance that their message had at least got through to Amin, they were not disappointed.

Soon the situation 'heated up considerably'. On Saturday, 5th February, Archbishop Janani was awakened at one-thirty by three armed men who tricked their way into his house and accused him of harbouring illegal guns. Archbishop Janani replied,

> I was called by God to serve Uganda, Rwanda, Burundi and Boga-Zaire. There are no arms here. Our house is God's house. We pray for the President. We pray for the security forces. We preach the Gospel. That is our work, not keeping arms to overthrow the government.[9]

After a long search, the raiders left. That same night, in the diocese of Bukedi, way over on the Kenyan border, Bishop Yona Okoth was also visited by armed raiders.

Next morning, when news of the raids broke, everyone was stunned. A raid on the *Archbishop*? 'Suddenly it became clear that no man was safe.'[10] Cardinal Nsubuga of the Roman Catholics suggested to Luwum that a joint meeting of all the bishops be held to draft a joint letter to the government, underlining once more their stand against the anarchy in Uganda. That same day telegrams went out to Anglican bishops all over Uganda, urgently summoning them to Kampala.

Bishop Festo was about to begin an AEE mission in Kabale itself. When the telegram arrived, he jumped into his car and sped to Kampala. The bishops, meeting on Namirembe Hill, were outraged. Too long, they decided, had they meekly submitted to Amin's atrocities. Too long they had hinted and politely asked for moderation. Festo argued passionately:

'The President and his Muslim entourage have thrown the people of Uganda to the ground over and over again. Each time they have meekly risen to their feet without recounting any of their past suffering.' No more. The bishops resolved to write an outspoken memorandum to the President, expressing their grievances at the way the country was being run.[11] A drafting committee was set up to write the memorandum. Festo was on it. 'Every phrase must pierce the heart,' he urged.[12] But it would be, 'in effect, the Archbishop's death warrant'.

When done, it covered three pages of typed A4.

Addressing Amin as His Excellency Al-Haji, Field Marshal Dr Idi Amin Dada, VC, DSO, MC, it 'made clear our view of how far things had got out of control', and how Ugandan citizens had 'become insecure, afraid and disturbed'.

The bishops said they were 'deeply disturbed' at the raids on the bishops: 'In the history of our country such an incident in the church has never before occurred.' And they wanted Amin to know of their 'shock and protest'. They reminded Amin of his statements that religious leaders had his 'respect' and that to search the Archbishop 'at gun point deep in the night leaves us without words. The gun whose muzzle has been pressed against the Archbishop's stomach, the gun which has been used to search the Bishop of Bukedi's house is a gun which is being pointed at every Christian in the Church ...'.

The bishops also objected to the pressure being put on Christians to become Muslim, to the attacks of the uneducated on the educated and a 'braindrain' destroying any progress, and the widespread violence. The bishops were quite specific. 'Too much power has been given to members of State Research, who arrest and kill at will innocent civilians.'

Further, they reproached Amin for making himself 'more and more inaccessible' to the Archbishop, a 'gap' which had brought 'estrangement and alienation' between Amin and all Christians. They complained that Uganda was no longer its own master, but under influence of Palestinians, Sudanese, Somalis and Russians, who had 'not the welfare of this country ... at their heart'.

As for bishops preaching bloodshed, as Amin had said in his Christmas Day broadcast, 'We were shocked ... we waited ... to be called by Your Excellency to clarify such a serious situation, but all in vain.'

The bishops stressed: 'We are ready to come to you whenever there are serious matters that concern the Church and the nation, you've only got to call us.' By Wednesday the bishops decided that this time they wanted a personal audience with Amin. They would go together in force. But for this, the eight bishops so far in Kampala were not enough. Cars were hastily despatched, and by Thursday afternoon, 10th February, fifteen of the Church of Uganda bishops were there (two were out of the country, and one assistant bishop stayed in his diocese).

At this point it became clear that it would be an Anglican initiative: the Roman Catholics felt that the memorandum was too centred on Anglican grievances for them to sign it, but Cardinal Nsubuga offered to write a covering letter supporting the memorandum.

The church memorandum was typed and duplicated many times, and all copies signed personally by Archbishop Janani Luwum and the fifteen bishops present in Kampala. Then a message was sent requesting an audience.

Friday passed. Saturday arrived. Still no word from Amin. About half the bishops, mindful of Sunday duties approaching, decided to go home. Half remained in Kampala, including Bishop Festo. Sunday passed.

Monday 14th February. At last, some response, but Amin sent for Luwum to come alone. He was to go to the State House in Entebbe. He went. There, Amin angrily accused Janani of plotting with Obote to overthrow the government. He gave as evidence a story that children had discovered cases of arms near the Luwums' house. (No children or arms were ever produced as evidence.) But all the same, that night the same groundless allegations were broadcast nationally on Radio Uganda, and the TV, and next day in the official newspaper, *Voice of Uganda*.

Luwum strenuously denied the charges, and handed the memorandum to the President.

Back home, on Tuesday 15th February, after talks with Festo and the others, Janani drew up a letter carefully refuting Amin's allegations. He intended to make the letter public. But by then events moved too swiftly for him even to get it to Amin.

For late that same afternoon, word reached the bishops, who were meeting at the provincial office on Namirembe Hill that President Amin had called a meeting for nine-thirty am the following morning, Wednesday 16th February, at the International Conference Centre in Kampala. Amin, it seemed, wanted to address all the government officials, members of the armed forces, ambassadors and religious leaders.

Bishop Festo and the others immediately decided that Archbishop Luwum should not go alone. A car hastily set off to drive through the night and collect all the Church of Uganda bishops on the eastern side of Uganda, and bring them back to Kampala.

So it was early in the morning of Wednesday, 16th February, that the Archbishop of Uganda, Rwanda, Burundi and Boga-Zaire, accompanied by Bishop Festo and Bishop Wani, arrived at the spacious grounds of the Nile Mansions Hotel, beside the huge conference centre. Four other bishops came in an accompanying car. Amin was ready for them: he had summoned a 'vast assembly' of support: about a thousand troops, large groups of governors, administrators, heads of departments, diplomats, and the nation's religious leaders. But there was another surprise waiting for the Anglican bishops: an accusatory display of suitcases full of Chinese automatic weapons, thousands of rounds of ammunition, hundreds of hand grenades. 'Like a stranger in an alien land, they felt themselves hemmed in by evil on every side.'[13] Festo later told a friend, 'You could see the hatred in the men's eyes.'

Proceedings were protracted while the sun blazed in a scorching sky. The bishops were sweltering in their heavy clothes but forbidden to move into the shade. It was soon apparent that a staged trial was underway, with the Vice-President in charge. He ordered that a long memorandum be read out. It was allegedly written by the deposed President Obote, still in exile in Tanzania. It suggested various ways of mobilising an opposition to Amin's regime. One was that arms could be smuggled into Uganda through the help of the Anglican bishop Yona Okoth on Kenya's border, who could then arrange for them to be sent on to the Archbishop in Kampala.

Bishop Festo was standing next to Janani Luwum. When his name was mentioned, he merely shook his head in silent denial. He whispered to Festo: 'They are going to kill me.' Then he added, 'I am not afraid.'[14]

The Vice-President made a speech. His line was that church leaders had been acting as if they were above the law, and had been meddling in government affairs. He ended in the demand, 'What shall we do with them?'

On cue, the hundreds of troops shouted back, 'Kill them! Kill them!'

The Vice-President continued, 'Put up your hands, all you who want them shot in public.' Every hand went up.

'Put up your hands, all of you who don't want them to be shot.' Not a hand was ventured.

Bishop Festo and his companions braced themselves for immediate arrest, and maybe even a public shooting. Then the Vice-President backtracked. 'No, they will be given a fair trial by military tribunal.' And at two pm the crowd was dismissed. But the leaders, religious, government, senior military officers and diplomats were told to go on over to the conference centre. The bishops were swiftly conducted that way as well, but taken to a side room along with the Muslim mufti. A security officer guarded them.

The minutes passed. In the background they could hear applause and shouts. But no one came. The minutes crawled on. It was clear they were virtually prisoners. They sat quietly, no private conversation possible.[15]

Then—surprisingly—came an order of dismissal. The guard said 'Now you can go home.'

But suddenly came fresh orders: 'You, Luwum, are wanted in that room by the President.' It was three-thirty pm. 'He wants to discuss something.'

Festo later told journalists, 'I suggested to Bishop Silvanus Wani, as Dean of the Province (he was later Archbishop) that he should accompany the Archbishop to meet the President. He went with him to the door, but was then ordered away by the security men, who said the President only needed the Archbishop.'

So Janani turned and smiled at his bishops. 'I can see the hand of the Lord in this,' he said, and walked away meekly between the armed soldiers. It was his farewell; they never saw him again.

So a car load of bishops set off back for the Archbishop's house. But Festo and Silvanus went 'and sat by our car and waited'. As Festo later told the story in his first interview with the British press:

> At ten to five Bishop Wani went to find out what was going on. He was told the Archbishop was still in 'serious discussions' with the President. He wasn't satisfied and eventually spoke to the Chief of Staff of the Armed Forces who told him he thought the Archbishop was still talking with either the President or the Vice-President in the Nile Hotel. We waited for a short while and then went to the soldiers who were guarding the Nile Hotel and asked where the Archbishop was and why he was not coming out. We were told he was still talking with the President. They said we could go home; they would bring him in another car. We said, 'No, we are not interested in another car. His car is sitting there. We came with him, it would be embarrassing to go without him.'
>
> In the end at about five-thirty we were ordered by the officers to get away because they didn't like us walking there. We were dressed in our bishops cassocks and we were the only ones left. The Archbishop's Mercedes-Benz was the only car there—except for a government car parked just in front of it. We had an argument with the security men and one of the officers came up and said, 'This is an order! Get in your car and go!'
>
> We talked with him and told him how embarrassing it was to go back without our Archbishop. He said: 'Don't you think that we too are God's people?'
>
> We said we didn't know—we hoped so. But it was very bad for us to go back without our Archbishop. He went away and then two military policemen came with guns and forced us to get into the car and go.
>
> As we sat in the car, Bishop Wani said to them, 'I hope you will bring our Archbishop.' They said: 'Yes, sir.'

Reluctantly, Bishop Festo and Bishop Silvanus drove off to the Archbishop's house to rejoin the other bishops.

Helpless, they turned to prayer, but Mary Luwum grew hysterical, and demanded to go and see her husband. So Festo and Silvanus accompanied her and the provincial secretary by car back to the Nile Hotel to see if she could be allowed to see her husband. 'But we only got as far as the gates. The security men with their guns almost shot the driver, so we went back to the Archbishop's house.'

At six-thirty pm that evening the government radio announced the arrest of the Archbishop and the two government ministers, Erinayo Oryema (Minister of Land and Water Resources) and Charles Oboth-Ofumbi (Minister of Internal Affairs) who had also fallen out of favour with Amin. This news shocked all Uganda. It was a terrible night. Festo paced his room at the Namirembe Guest Home.

Next morning, Thursday 17th February, early, Festo joined the other five bishops at the provincial headquarters. They prayed and were discussing how they should get Luwum released.

At nine am a woman in tears burst in, waving a copy of the *Voice of Uganda*. In banner headlines it screamed: 'Archbishop and two ministers die in motor accident.'

Their hearts froze. They snatched the paper for news, but the story it told was bizarre: that the prisoners had attacked their driver and in the ensuing struggle the jeep had crashed and overturned somewhere between the Nile Hotel and the Research Centre a quarter of a mile away. There was even a photograph of the smash up—but it showed vehicles which were known to have crashed two weeks earlier, and been awaiting repairs in a nearby garage.

Festo said later 'No one in Uganda, not even a child at school, could believe that. We all knew without a shadow of a doubt that the Archbishop had been shot.'[16]

> I went with two other bishops to the hospital to claim the Archbishop's body so that we could prepare for a funeral. When we got there we found most of the nurses and doctors in tears. We tried to see the superintendent of the hospital, but could only speak to his deputy. He was signing a document, and we noticed his hand was trembling. He had a security man behind him, and we knew what that meant. We waited for an hour and were eventually taken to the mortuary where we were told the bodies were.

But they were not allowed in. 'It was guarded at gunpoint, and had been since six pm the previous evening—the very hour the Archbishop had been shot.'

Later that day one of the bishops spoke to a nurse who worked at the hospital. She said she had seen 'the Archbishop's body with two bullet holes in his chest and blood in his mouth'.

Meanwhile that afternoon Bishop Festo and Bishop Silvanus went to see the Minister of Health to claim the body, but without success. 'When we got back to our provincial headquarters, a Christian soldier came and told us he had seen the shooting and the running of a vehicle over the bodies of three men.' The rumour was that 'they were trying to make Luwum sign a confession, which he would not do'. We were also told that he was praying aloud for his captors when he died. Bishop Festo talked with eyewitnesses 'who claim they saw him shot, and to others who saw the bodies in the morgue with bullet wounds'. Evidence seemed to say that Luwum was shot at six o'clock either at the Nile Hotel or at the Nake Nakaseko 'torture house'.

'We continued to press the authorities to let us have the Archbishop's body. The Minister of Health told us he hoped we would be able to take the body—after the government investigation.' The day wore on. Meanwhile, of course, the news of the tragedy had become public knowledge. And with it, an awed hush settled over Kampala. Festo comforted Margaret Ford, the Archbishop's secretary. 'Let's pray,' he said, and began, 'O Loving Father, help us to forgive the men who murdered Janani.'[17] The Christians in the Anglican compound stayed close together that night, mindful of Festo's comment, 'We lost Janani because we allowed him to be isolated.'[18]

Friday, 18th February dawned. The bishops were told that the matter now rested with the military.

We contacted the Military Secretary, who told us that the bodies had been ordered to be taken to their respective villages for private burial.

We said that the Archbishop could not be buried like that. Constitutionally, and in accordance with our religion, he must be buried alongside his cathedral. If you can't bring the body, we said, give us permission and we'll go and get it ourselves.

The Secretary consulted the Minister, and then later we were told that the whole matter of the Archbishop's body was in the hands of the President—'and don't you ask any more about it'.[19]

By this time reports were flying around that Bishop Festo too had been murdered.

'People met me in the street and wept when they saw me, because they thought I was dead.' And by Saturday, 19th February, several high level persons had indeed passed on a warning that Festo was now at the head of Amin's death list. Festo and Mera decided there was no further point in staying in Kampala. There would be no funeral to bury Luwum. He told friends, 'If we are to be taken and killed, I want it to be in my own diocese.'

But before they left, the phone began ringing. First it was Dr Leighton Ford, the American evangelist and son-in-law of Billy Graham, who had had a strong inner conviction he should ring. He got through easily, and assured Festo, 'Many people are not only praying for you, but are aware of your situation and are very concerned for your safety. I thought it possible that someone might be listening in and that it would be good if it were known in Uganda that people in other parts of the world were watching to see what would happen to Festo.'

T. W. Wilson, another associate of Billy Graham, also rang. So did W. Stanley Mooneyham, head of World Vision. After a guarded talk, he decided to ring back a quarter of an hour later—but got no answer. This immediately rekindled his great concern. 'Had they been taken? There was no way to know. For the next forty-eight hours it was as if they had dropped off the face of the earth.'

In reality, Festo and Mera had been on their way out of the door when Mooneyham's first call came through. Long before he rang back, Festo and Mera were in a car, 'going like the clappers' through the streets of Kampala and headed for the long, long road for Kabale. Later Bishop William Rukirande passed them on his way to Kampala. They didn't stop, but the look on their faces as they passed shook him. What *had* happened in Kampala? Festo later recalled,

> When we arrived ... Kabale was full of security men. We were told that my house had been watched and checked three times already that day. I knew that if I stepped inside, either I would be under house arrest—as good as executed—or they might wait until after I had preached on Sunday and then arrest me.

Events had moved too fast for Festo and Mera. For the moment they were irresolute over this new problem, unsure what to do. Their friends, overjoyed and amazed to find them still alive, free and unharmed, insistently urged them to fly at once. 'One bishop's death this week is enough for us,' they said. 'Remember Peter! With the help of God's angel he escaped Herod's captivity and moved on to serve God elsewhere. Go now!'

Briefly, Festo and Mera prayed together. 'Then my wife and I decided to take our chance and get out. We didn't wait to unpack our suitcases, and we didn't stop to take anything from our home.' They left everything: clothes, personal possessions, thousands of sermon notes, hundreds of books, rooms of furniture.

That same night soldiers called on one house nearby where one of Festo's clergymen, Yosia Bany was. They accused him of being Bishop Festo. When he finally dissuaded them of this, they rounded on him and tried to get him to say Festo had brought him guns to fight Amin. When he absolutely denied this, they took him to the Nakasero State Research Prison and tortured him.

Meanwhile, a young couple left their five youngsters to drive Festo and Mera off into the darkness. Once the Land Rover nearly drove into a roadblock set for them by security personnel. They were redirected just in time by Christians waiting for them on the highway. They went on. But the terrain was rugged, and the route unfamiliar, and they got lost. Later they nearly drove over a cliff. Still later they reached the remote village of Kacerere, one of the most remote of Festo's 1,000 parishes, where the road ran out. From here on the way forward was on foot. Mera was suffering from bronchitis and a fever and was encumbered by a long skirt. Five miles to go to the Rwanda border. But friendly parishioners, quietly awakened, guided them. Festo later told a friend: 'You will never know fear until you are running at night for your life in your own country.' For two and a half hours they climbed. As dawn broke about six am on Sunday, 20th February, they at last reached the Ugandan–Rwanda border, 9,000 feet up in remote mountains. 'I'll never forget that experience,' Festo told friends later.

The young man who was our guide said 'Now, you just go on, walk about three more steps.' We did. It was no marked border, but he knew the territory well. He said, 'Now you are in Rwanda. You can breathe.' I looked at him and said, 'We've been breathing all the time.' He replied, 'Now you can breathe a little freer!'

Their relief was tempered only by their utter exhaustion. But they sat on a big rock and held 'a little praise service' just the same. 'As the sun came up, we remembered that verse "But for you who fear my name the sun of righteousness shall rise, with healing in its wings"'(Mal 4:2). They cried to God. Then it was on into the Rwandan forest, while in far away Kampala 4,500 Christians defied Government threats and set off for the cathedral to remember their Archbishop, singing the Martyr's Song over and over again. In Kabale, the Christians packed out the cathedral, and tensely waited for any news. They finally decided that no news was good news: surely they would have heard had Festo and Mera been captured.

Only a little further into Rwanda Festo and Mera encountered an African businessman with a car—the only vehicle for miles around. The anonymous stranger offered them a lift to Kigali, Rwanda's capital eighty miles away. A pastor there knew the Kivengeres and they decided to seek his help.

Hours later, they were dropped off at the pastor's front door. As Festo told the story, 'This dear brother had just finished his morning prayers, and he had been praying particularly for us.' He had heard all the disturbing reports on the radio, and feared Festo and Mera might well have been taken by the security men and imprisoned—or worse. Then he went to the front door to see who had driven up. When Festo and Mera got out of the car and waved cheerily, 'he almost had a heart attack!'

CHAPTER NINETEEN

EXILE

1977–1979

Coming to terms with bitterness; helping the other exiles; preaching worldwide.

A FEW DAYS' REST, and then the pastor tackled the ticklish problem of getting Festo and Mera out of the country. At Kigali Airport immigration control demanded to know why it was their passports had not got the proper stamp. 'You are illegal immigrants!' The fate for such was deportation back to Uganda. Festo was silent, for once at a total loss for words. The pastor stepped forward, thinking quickly. 'Ah, you see,' he said confidently, 'he came out on a Sunday.'

'What are you talking about? He has come from Uganda, but there is no stamp! Why?'

'I've just told you. He came out on a Sunday.'

The official gave it up then, assuming the pastor was trying to say that on such a lax day the control had not been manned. 'Clergy!' he muttered as he stamped and regularised their passports. He scribbled with chalk on their suitcases and the two refugees were cleared for Nairobi.

Not that Nairobi itself was any too safe, and Festo and Mera avoided the Wilsons' house: their close relationship through AEE was too well known. Instead, Gottfried and Audrey Osei-Mensah made room for them in their big Baptist manse on the outskirts of the town—which had the additional attraction of being near a police station should any trouble occur. Festo and Mera were still shaken by their experience, and very concerned for those they had left behind. When soon several more Ugandan bishops fled to Nairobi, Audrey found, 'We had days when our sitting room was full of anxious bishops, praying and discussing what to do.'

Those bishops in Nairobi were right to fear for Uganda. In the wake of Luwum's death, sixteen more men, mostly top civil servants, were soon arrested and accused of plotting with the Archbishop. Twelve would be sentenced to death. In addition, a mass persecution had begun: diplomatic sources later reported that between February and May that year about 10,000 Acholi and Langi were arrested and murdered; it was the worst series of massacres since 1972–73. Many hundreds of Christians would also die—six young actors who had been preparing a play on the early martyrs for the centenary celebrations were themselves martyred and dumped in a field near Kampala.

Soon Mera decided to stay on in Nairobi—she was going to try to persuade Charity, still in Kampala sitting final exams for her degree, to join her. Festo flew on to Europe, making a brief stopover in Rome. By now it was a Sunday late in February, and he attended the English speaking church in the city that morning. When the scheduled preacher did not turn up, he was asked, as a visiting clergyman, if he would like to share a few words. ...

It was his first opportunity to speak in public since his exile. As it dawned on his congregation who he was, where he was from, and what he had just been through, they were electrified. Here was a man who 'had just stepped out of world headlines'!

It was soon on to the States, and Pasadena, California. It was decided that the Kivengeres should use Pasadena as their base. Generous friends arranged for a flat in a quiet suburb of Pasadena to be lent to the Kivengeres. Meanwhile, reporters from a host of newspapers and radio stations were eager to talk to Bishop Festo and he found himself interviewed extensively about Luwum, Amin and the sorry state of Uganda. The press conferences and interviews inevitably tended to cover the same territory.

One question was usually a direct 'Was the Archbishop involved in a military plot?' Bishop Festo would scoff at the idea: 'We have never believed in arms. Our duty, as the salt of the earth, was to tell the government about the things that were going wrong. ...' He absolutely denied that Luwum had ever had any contact with President Obote or with any other overthrow plot. 'He died because he spoke the truth and the truth embarrassed those who practised evil.'

Many journalists were tempted to interpret the Archbishop's death as just the worst example yet of a growing campaign by a Muslim President against the Christian majority. Festo disagreed. 'Muslims in Uganda often attend our meetings, I and other Christians have spoken in their mosques. *This whole business has nothing to do with any Muslim–Christian conflict.*'

Other press reports had emphasised the tribal aspect of killings. Amin, a Kakwa, seemed to direct his venom primarily against the Christian Langi and Acholi tribes. Bishop Kivengere agreed that tribal loyalties played a big part in Ugandan life, but would not commit himself further. As far as Amin personally was concerned, journalists were eager to hear Bishop Festo's impression; he had met the man so often. Was Amin 'even sane'? was a favourite question. But Bishop Festo was not prepared to say. '... I'm not a doctor, and can't analyse his character. In my view he is a military man who has tried to rule with too much force and in so doing has himself become a victim of that force.'[1]

Neither would Bishop Festo put all the blame for Uganda's sufferings on Amin only. 'President Amin has now created machinery which it has become impossible for him to control.'

Why had Bishop Festo fled when other bishops had stayed with their diocese? Festo explained that:

the authorities were looking for trouble makers. I think I was more of a threat because of my way of speaking—and I wouldn't say every bishop should speak as I speak ... I considered it my duty as a preacher of the Gospel to speak against the brutality, torture, dehumanisation of every kind, politically, economically and socially. ... My intention was never to overthrow the government, but to speak against these things in order that the government might rule the people better.[2]

And he rejected criticism from Kenyan bishops against the Church of Uganda for not making enough of a fuss against Amin following Luwum's death. 'The Church spoke out in such a way that it lost its Archbishop. Having spoken out, the Church must get on with its job of strengthening the Christians.'[3]

Bishop Festo would not make any predictions as to the future other than 'My hope is that the day will come when I am called back again to Uganda'—then with a glimpse of his impish humour, 'Not that I was expelled by President Amin. He just couldn't guarantee my safety!' Certainly there was 'going to be a struggle until President Amin and his government ... realise that the gun cannot rule. I believe if they do not change their ways, the words of my Lord Jesus are applicable: "He who lives by the sword will perish by the sword."'[4]

And it was not for the church to seek revenge. 'We don't believe you can heal the community with a gun. There are other forces God can use to overthrow governments. I don't believe the church can ever take up the sword to fight and still have a ministry of healing.'[5]

Festo was given extensive media coverage. In March when he spoke publicly for the first time in the USA at the Episcopal Church Centre, the *New York Daily News* reported with interest that he, 'second after Luwum in Uganda's Episcopal Church', and 'often called Africa's Billy Graham', said that rather than simply condemn Amin, '... I am condemning evil because evil is bigger than Amin ...' Indeed, Amin was a man 'we loved, we have prayed for him ...'.[6]

A few days later, speaking to an overflowing congregation of 1,200 at La Canada Presbyterian Church on the west coast of the States, he urged that it was the job of the Americans to protest to the United Nations. The *Los Angeles Times* (14th March) did a story quoting him as saying that 'Christians should shout louder against the forces of destruction'.

Back east, in Washington DC, the *Washington Post* (25th March) gave his account of Luwum's death many column inches, quoting him as saying that, 'the good name of our country can only come back when the law replaces the gun', and calling for America's help in 'exerting international pressure'.

Indeed, with this end in view, Revd Dr Don Jacobs, an old friend and occasional AEE evangelist, executive director of the Mennonite Christian Leadership Foundation, set up a number of appointments with a variety of senators and congressmen so Festo could alert them about what was going on in Uganda.

Festo and I went from one office to another and gave briefings. He did not make any suggestions as to exactly what the US Government should do in the light of Uganda's distress. I recall vividly that as I walked out of a few of the offices I was approached by staff persons asking me whether this was Festo's campaign to replace Idi Amin.

One asked me straight 'Is Bishop Festo planning to become Uganda's Bishop Makarios?'

After a couple of days of this, I finally confided to Festo what was being said in the corridors. Hearing this, he laughed and laughed. He then picked up his Bible, tucked it under his arm, walked a step or two and said, 'This is my politics, the word of God, and I have no ambition greater than to preach that mighty word.'

I had the opportunity of sharing that response with a few of the persons we had interviewed, to their astonishment and delight.

Meanwhile fears were growing for the safety of his daughters Charity and Peace, who were still living in Kampala. Charity, along with a group of university students, had already been detained once by soldiers, and made to walk on their knees over sharp stones until they bled. After that, Peace had removed her from the Hall of Residence at Makerere University, and took her home to live with her and her husband, Stephen Lwanga. Peace's changed last name helped protect her, but Charity now taking her finals for her degree at Makerere University, was still in an exposed position. When some friends told Charity that several young men had been hanging about the campus, asking people to describe what she looked like, she realised the SRB was after her, and fled to Nairobi and Mera.

Mera grew frantic in her pleas that Peace also should leave. Every time Festo gave an interview to the BBC or an American radio reporter about Amin and Uganda, she would round on him furiously: 'If Peace is killed it will be *your* fault!'

In London that spring Festo also took seriously the increasing warning from responsible sources that Amin had assassins looking for him. He grew a beard, bought a large peaked hat and a shapeless coat, and his disguise was so successful that it deceived even those who knew him best—his own daughters. Joy and Hope walked right by him at Victoria Train Station, and at first dismissed him as 'some creep' when he approached them.

While in London Bishop Festo had long meetings with the UK

AEE Board, and other church leaders, to review the situation. There were thousands of Ugandan refugees, in desperate need. The AEE board decided to begin to contact people they thought might be in a position to lend a hand. This was the beginning of RETURN—'Relief, Education and Training of Ugandan Refugees Now'. The project was Bishop Festo's 'message in action: that we should be our brother's keeper', a friend explained later. 'The shortened form turned out to be quite prophetic!' After a chat with Bishop Festo, David Owen, then Foreign Minister in the Labour Government, promised to help find jobs for some senior Ugandans.

Easter 1977 was approaching. By now Bishop Festo had travelled over ten thousand miles and preached to thousands of people. He had talked to any number of colleagues, friends and reporters. It was an exhausting schedule but on top of that, reaction to his own experiences and bereavements was setting in. Although his external line was always firmly that of love and forgiveness, he was after all still in exile, reliant on the goodwill of others for everything; his friend murdered, his home in danger of pillage, his daughters nearly arrested. A bitterness and hardness that he didn't even admit to himself stole over him. He was tired, heartsick, and discouraged at times. Even his optimism could see no solution. Friends asked him how they should pray. 'Just say,' he began once 'Oh God, Uganda ...' and trailed off. 'That will be enough for the moment.'

On Good Friday he was alone. He walked up London's teeming Regent Street to the 'BBC Church', All Souls', Langham Place (next to Broadcasting House)—an old favourite since his student days in the late 1950s. He quietly slipped in to join the congregation for the three hour service of meditation upon the crucifixion. It was the first time for weeks that he had had the opportunity of attending a church as a private, individual Christian to worship, to pray and to reflect, rather than to minister. Gradually his thoughts settled themselves. He began to wait on God in prayer.

The congregation were quietly invited to reflect on the death of Jesus and how it should affect their lives now. The crucifixion story was read out, and the words, 'Father, forgive them, for they do not know what they are doing.'

Festo began to meditate on the words and 'immediately there was, as it were, a great searchlight in my heart. Amin came into the picture and the Lord said, "You owe Amin forgiveness."' Festo was shocked, very shocked. Sitting in All Souls, he felt stunned beyond words.

'But Lord,' he stammered, 'I don't hate this man.'

The Lord said, 'Wait a minute. You have been growing hard towards him. Your attitude has been stiffening. Amin is not the loser. You are, Festo. Your hardness will only lead to your own spiritual loss. It will take away your ability to communicate the love of God, which is the essence of your ministry and testimony.'[7]

It was quite a shock. Then the Lord said, 'You think it's hard to forgive him? Suppose when the soldiers were putting nails into my hands, one of them had been President Amin. Would I have said, 'Father forgive them, all except Amin?'

It was enough for Festo. In silence he bowed his head. In what he would always consider the high point of his spiritual pilgrimage, he sought the grace that could grant him this level of love and forgiveness. When it came, it was 'fresh air for my tired soul. I knew I had seen the Lord and been released; love filled my heart.'[8] He 'hurried to tell Mera about it'.

Two days later, on Easter Sunday, he preached his first sermon in Britain since leaving Uganda. It was at the Anglican church of Emmanuel, Northwood, whose vicar, Richard Bewes, was now head of AEE for UK. First he humorously but absolutely denied recent reports of his own murder, though they had been so many that 'I am beginning to taste the meaning of resurrection!'

And he passed on something of what he had discovered:

Resurrection is not for upright people. It's for brokenhearted people, the defeated and shattered. ... Before Christ died and rose again, suffering was meaningless, empty, a shattering experience which made life bitter. Then Jesus died in suffering and pain, and he covered suffering with love—victorious, holy love. This kind of love will never be conquered!

It was the secret of what he had found. And it was the same with the Church of Uganda. He read the congregation a letter a friend had just sent him: 'It is exciting. People are being born again. Since the Archbishop died, it seems a new life is beginning.' 'Janani,' said Festo, 'was like a grain of wheat which fell into the ground. A harvest is being produced. This is the pattern of Calvary and Easter.'

All the same, Festo would firmly reject any idea that persecution itself could ever improve a person as a 'very dangerous' idea. 'You can't explain a man's life as having been improved by persecution unless he says so himself. What I *can* tell you is that there are lives which shine out for Jesus in persecution.'[9]

Before Festo left London he attended the memorial service for Luwum at Westminster Abbey. Bishop Leslie Brown, former Archbishop of Uganda, was to preach. Bishop Festo was the only Ugandan bishop who could attend. In a quiet lunch at the House of Lords with Bishop Leslie his mood 'was one of great hope—God was still there and could work even though Amin was firmly in power at that time. There was no sense of defeat.'

In May came news that Bishop Silvanus Wani, had been consecrated the third Archbishop of Uganda, Rwanda, Burundi and Boga-Zaire. Other news came too: that same month Kigezi diocesan synod decided not to go ahead with the division of Kigezi diocese into Bishop Festo's diocese of Kigezi and a new one of North Kigezi. (With 30,000 confirmations in 1976 alone, the number of Christians in Kigezi was so vast as to warrant two bishops.) Some from North Kigezi were frustrated at the delay, but deeply moved and ashamed when a man stood up in the synod and quoted Jesus' words to his disciples: '"Can you not wait with me even one hour?" Our Bishop is in exile! How can we carve up his diocese at a time like this?'

Meanwhile, Bishop William had been made 'acting bishop', and was inundated with pastoral work. There were so many bereaved families—it was a 'long haul' to get them on the road to forgiving the murderers of their loved ones.

As for the Kigezi house, a pastor, Ishmael Bugaiga, his wife Nora and their two sons had been moved in to keep an eye on things. But Festo and Mera weren't told until much later that twice soldiers had arrived and threatened torture and death unless they were given the goods and news of Festo's whereabouts. Bravely the Bugaigas stayed on, their only defence to paint in large white letters 'Property of the Kigezi Diocese' on all the house's contents (many signs were still there ten years later). They hoped this would convince the soldiers that the property was public and not private, and therefore not worth killing them for.

Meanwhile in America, Mera was homesick and lonely and worried about her daughters. She stayed in the flat most of the time, wondering if she would ever see Uganda and her loved ones again. Sue Jesson and other friends tried to cheer her up.

Festo, however, was very much at home in Pasadena, where the American AEE board was based and where he had friends at many of the local churches. Soon he was hectically busy with AEE's new work: that of helping the thousands upon thousands of Ugandan refugees who were scattered worldwide. The African Enterprise board realised with dawning fright quite how big Bishop Festo's vision for the refugees had become. 'He was tearing from one country to another, trying to help hundreds of Ugandans,' Michael Cassidy recalled. The AEE board wondered if they could cope: 'We were really still in short trousers! Handling the administration of the finances of (eventually) several thousand Ugandans worldwide would push us into the long trouser league of organisations!' His constant travels and public appearances on their behalf had his American friends concerned about his own safety. Several urged him to accept a twenty-four-hour professional bodyguard—a notion that Festo politely but firmly vetoed. He argued that it was too much trouble, 'and anyway, when my time comes to go to heaven, whether it is a bullet or a heart attack, doesn't make much difference'.

In May of 1977, Bishop Festo asked the Australian branch of AEE to help RETURN; which they willingly did.

On 3rd June, 1977, the day that the first Ugandan martyrs were remembered, he was in New York where he met up with three other Uganda bishops in exile: Bishop Yona Okoth, Bishop Melkizedek Otim, and Bishop Benoni Ogwal, at the Episcopal Church Centre in New York. The Ugandan bishops, in a joint statement, thanked the Church of England, Episcopal Church, Anglican Church of Canada and the Church of Kenya and called on Ugandans everywhere to help refugees with relief, resettlement, and continuing pastoral and social support.

Meanwhile, Dorothy Smoker and Bishop Festo had worked

Festo preaching at Emmanuel Church, Pittsburgh, late 1970s.

on a book about his experience entitled *I Love Idi Amin* (Fleming H. Revell Company: New Jersey, USA, 1977). The title was not turning out to be popular. In a letter to a doubtful Lilian, Festo admitted that '*I Love Idi Amin* sounds rather emotional or sensational', but:

> I would rather have that than *Victory in Uganda*—this sounds militaristic. The other is my testimony, for as a Christian I am not ashamed of loving Idi Amin, even if I hate his destructive actions.
>
> It is certainly going to arouse key questions, and even doubts, in many hearts of my brethren, but I feel I am not wounding consciences by loving my persecutor, without playing down his crimes—which I expose in my testimony. I trust it is speaking the truth in love, that of a suffering church loving its enemy.

The little book would become something of a Christian bestseller, and have considerable influence in many languages.

As to the *why* behind Uganda's sufferings, Bishop Festo always argued that there was no easy answer.

> I fear interpreting things which happen as God's judgement or God's approval. I would rather say that the sufferings are lessons of life ... If you waited for a righteous country which *deserved* God's favour, the whole world would be in hell.
>
> Events which overtake countries like Uganda are human errors, human selfishness, and therefore are lessons to be learned by those citizens and the leaders of the country.

Festo's travels continued that summer, including a trip to Norway, where Sigmund Aske, now a member of AEE council, translated for him at a series of large conferences. Festo even preached at the famous cathedral at Trondheim—and was broadcast live on national radio. In Bergen Festo gave a Christian union at the university a short political lesson: 'Revolution,' he said, 'is a phenomenon that goes in a circle. You decide that what is in your way is the man ahead of you. So you eliminate him. Then someone else comes along. They decide that *you* are in *their* way. So they eliminate you ... then *they* in turn get in someone *else's* way ... Violence creates violence. This is a fact of history.'

Festo's stand of love and non-violence against murderous tyranny was of course in sharp contrast to that of the Christian theologian and pastor Bonhoeffer and the Christian group who had attempted to assassinate Hitler during World War Two. Festo was quizzed on this on 20th July, the anniversary of Bonhoeffer's attempt, by journalists at a press conference at the offices of the German Evangelical Churches in Frankfurt and Main. (He was in Germany on a preaching tour with Wolfgang Heiner, a German evangelist and an ally of AEE.)

'Could you imagine Christians in Uganda being involved in an attempt upon Idi Amin's life?' queried the journalist.

Festo replied:

> I don't want to charge Bonhoeffer and the Christians who were involved in this attempt, but for me and for us in Uganda, it is clear: God doesn't need our bullets. If he wants to stop Idi Amin, he can send him a heart attack or something else. Our experience in the past was that after an attempt like that, Idi Amin has killed many persons whom he thought might have been involved. A bullet can kill, but a bullet cannot heal.

He said much the same that August in Britain when he appeared as guest speaker at the UK Southwold Holiday Conference. 'Praise God for my exile. I had to forgive Amin. I sent a message to him. I am just learning to forgive. If I don't love him, I am the loser.'

But he knew how hard this could be. 'Pray for my brothers and sisters in Uganda exposed to the temptation of hating, retaliating ...' For Bishop Festo accepted that most people were after instant change, and

> they say that if you use violence — knock out the tyrannical oppressor with a bullet, perhaps—you'll bring about quick change. But the Lord was aiming at a redemptive change, one capable of moulding a new community, a new outlook, a new value of life ... The new, revolutionary way was *healing* the person. ...

In September Festo flew to North Carolina where Billy Graham had invited him to talk about Luwum's death and his flight from Uganda at the Billy Graham Western Carolina Crusade at the Asheville Civic Center Arena in Asheville. (This was practically Billy's backyard—only ten to fifteen miles from his home in Montreat.) A video made of the crusade was broadcast throughout the States later that year, and on into early 1978.

On it, Festo was as undefeated as ever: 'When a man stands for Jesus, and ... dies saying so, that is not a tragedy, that is glory. My Archbishop gloriously went home ... in the footprints of the Master.' As for the centenary of the Ugandan Church, the Archbishop has 'sealed the 100th year with his blood'.

That October Festo was back in Norway—he had been chosen as one of four winners of the first International Freedom Prize. The award was given by Liberatas Norway, a pioneering organisation 'championing freedom', together with similar organisations in eight other western countries. A cable to the astonished, incredulous, pleased and fairly embarrassed Festo, had informed him that he had been chosen for 'his influence as a religious leader, and for his fearless stand in speaking out for religious and human freedom in Uganda'. Bishop Festo shared the award that year with Justice Lewis Powell of the US Supreme Court, Mr Andre Sinyavski, a leading Russian dissident author, and the signatories of the Charter 77 document in Czechoslovakia. The president of the Norwegian Parliament awarded the prizes at a special ceremony on 12th October.

The same autumn, Bishop Festo was also awarded the Distinguished Public Service Award of Messiah College, Grantham, Pennsylvania.

Christmas in exile was hard, but it was a fate to be shared with thousands of Ugandans that year. Festo provided those he met with 'Christmas presents'—carrier bags full of expensive trousers, shirts, jackets and shoes that generous Americans at churches throughout the States had pressed on him.

In January of 1978 Amin celebrated the seventh year of his 'life presidency' by declaring to the world that there were no violations of human rights in Uganda—it was all nasty people telling nasty lies (in which he included the International Commission of Jurists, Amnesty International, the Commonwealth heads of Government, and the Roman Catholic bishops of Eastern Africa, all of whom had scathingly condemned the 'unprecedented violation' of human rights in Uganda). The year would not fulfil Amin's promise: throughout 1978 the killings continued.

For Festo, 1978's diary was again full to overflowing with preaching engagements, conferences, conventions. In January an

AEE mission in Panama drew 5,000 people to rallies in three cities. Bishop Festo and Michael Cassidy preached. Among those who responded were US citizens, Caribbeans, Indians and a 'surprising' number of Spanish-speaking Catholics.

There was also a week in Bermuda for the Lausanne Continuation Committee—where a good selection of the evangelical leadership of the world prayed and strategised for the future. A member recalls: 'Both Festo and Michael spoke in a very informal but dynamic fashion showing forth their faithfulness and their energies for saving the people of Africa.'

February's engagements included an unusual challenge that Festo admitted to friends had at first 'scared me to death': he had to address the North American Congress of the Laity—1,000 Christian leaders with former US President Gerald Ford in the chair. It wasn't the people that worried him: it was the topic he had been given: 'Creativity and Transcendence'. 'What a subject! So how was I to approach it?' As the days slipped by, he would rummage for the Congress programme and eye it with alarm: 'Bishop Festo Kivengere: Creativity and Transcendence.'

Finally, in his reading Festo came across the description of Christ in Colossians 1:16, 17:

> In him all things were created, in heaven and on earth, visible and invisible, whether thrones or dominions or principalities or authorities—all things were created through him and for him. He is before all things, and in him all things hold together.

That was it! Transcendence was there—and so was Christ. 'Of course *then* my worries are finished, my hang-ups are gone and now I am dealing *with the Lord*.' He would tell the Congress that, 'It is Christ, the powerful basis for creativity and relationships that the world needs. Apart from him, human creativity becomes chaotic!' It was to make 'a strikingly African contribution', according to one who attended, and draw a comment from an eminent doctor: 'I want you to know I was among those who stood, tears running down my cheeks, after your talk.'

Then in late February Bishop Festo was off to Nairobi for a crucial East African Team Meeting. Top of the agenda came the work of RETURN, the administration of which was an enormous challenge. By now AEE were financing, placing and maintaining 700–1,100 refugee students on university campuses the world over—and faced with the prospect of four more years of it. AEE had also found people bringing them children whose parents had been killed or lost: so far they had placed 200 such children in special Kenyan orphanages. Such a workload made the meeting a key one, and Bruce Bare, chairman of the US board of AEE flew in along with Keith Jesson (Executive Secretary of the Pasadena Office) who brought news that in Australia an AEE committee had just been launched to help the refugees. Bishop Festo flew to Sydney, Melbourne, Adelaide, Canberra and Brisbane to help get the appeal started. Wolfgang Heiner (the AEE man in Germany), Michael Cassidy and Malcolm of the South Africa AEE team were also there.

The team members from Uganda brought sad news of sky-rocketing inflation, rampant poverty (there would have been mass starvation except that Uganda is so fertile that people could grow their own vegetables quite easily). Petrol was scarce and prohibitively expensive, with black market corruption everywhere. Soldiers had tried to close one church by threatening to kill people who attended it—but after an initial success, the people had 'repented of their fear' and now 'the church was full again'.

Bishop Festo, who had just flown in from America, reported on 'the extraordinary range of opportunities for missions coming from the Episcopal church'. He had already taken five missions since he had gone into exile, including one in the midwest whose Bishop was known for reserve and restraint. But, say eye witnesses, 'The day Festo came to the cathedral to speak to all these pastors, the bishop came too. When Festo was done, the bishop literally jumped off the platform, rushed over to Festo and gave him a great hug.'

Since then, fifteen more invitations from dioceses across the States had come in. They all wanted Bishop Festo. Interest was increasing from US TV stations as well. One TV team flew out to Nairobi to do a lengthy interview on the Ugandan refugee situation and the RETURN ministry, and it was shown on stations throughout the States.

Laboriously the AEE team meeting sifted through a mass of

'major invitations' from no fewer than twenty-six countries, over half outside Africa. It was dawning on them that AEE had, as Michael Cassidy said, 'almost overnight become not simply a continental ministry, but one caught up almost willy nilly with the Lord's workings in the wider world'. (Bishop Festo was accepting his exile cheerfully, reasoning 'The timing I leave in God's hands. I'm sure he has a job for me to do for the moment outside my country.')

One of the highlights of the year was a two week AEE team visit to Egypt that spring which took in Protestant churches in Cairo, Assuit and the port of Alexandria. The team was quite a cosmopolitan crew. Bishop Festo teamed up with Michael Cassidy and Malcolm Graham (South Africa AEE), John Wilson (Kenya) Matt Nyagwaswa (Tanzania), Don Jacobs (USA AEE board member) plus Wolfgang Heiner (AEE representative in Germany). But the mission did not begin smoothly. Before they even left Nairobi they were warned by certain US authorities of a possible threat to Festo's security in Egypt. But when Abd-el Masih Istafanous, 'spark plug' of the mission, pooh-poohed it, Festo went ahead.

But in Cairo there were yet more warnings that Amin probably had agents who had followed the team to Egypt, and were waiting an opportunity to assassinate Festo. As the news came from various US government sources, the team took it seriously, and Festo was persuaded to remain in the hotel while the team began its preaching commitments.

That night Michael Cassidy decided to 'ask the Lord if he had some little word about Festo's situation which I could sleep on'.

I opened my Bible and found it directly at Psalm 91: 'He who dwells in the shelter of the Most High, who abides in the shadow of the Almighty, will say to the Lord, "My refuge and my fortress" (v 1) . . . For he will deliver you (v 3) . . . no evil shall befall you . . . (v 10) . . . For he will give his angels charge of you to guard you in all your ways (v 11) . . . Because he cleaves to me in love, I will deliver him; I will protect him, because he knows my name' (v 14).

I immediately felt this was the word from the Lord. I got out of bed and tottered into Festo's room. I shared it with him and both of us this morning, along with the other guys as well, feel we should move forward and not have Festo leave the country at this moment. . . .

So that morning Festo joined the rest of the team as they left the hotel and plunged into the heat, chaotic traffic and teeming streets lined with kiosks and bazaars. They fanned out to preach in packed churches all over the city, from Presbyterian to Pentecostal to Coptic to Evangelical.

Everywhere the team was greeted with warmth and smiles of 'Yooo aarr well-cum' and agreed, 'Slowly we are losing our hearts to these dear Egyptians.'

If the team found the Egyptians refreshingly different, the same was also true of the Egyptians, who smilingly nicknamed Michael Cassidy and Don Jacobs 'the milk of the gospel', and Festo, Matt and John Wilson 'the chocolate'.

From Cairo the team boarded the train for Assuit in Upper Egypt, and Michael wrote home: 'We have just been served coffee which is the nearest thing imaginable to solid coffee beans dampened with a little hydrochloric acid. Festo took one sip and burst out laughing.'

Traffic in Assuit turned out to be as chaotic as Cairo. Festo, in the back seat, cheerfully told a terrified Michael Cassidy, sitting up front, he would be a good shock-absorber for him if there was a crash.

Again there were packed churches with up to 1,500 inside, and 500 more waiting outside. The team spoke to pastors from all over Upper Egypt by day and to evangelistic rallies of nearly 2,000 by night, where Festo and Michael most often preached in tandem. Both were 'overwhelmed' after the meeting by the crowds, both inside the church, and out, eager to shake hands. The Egyptians' 'love and appreciation overflowed and our hearts were touched beyond words'.

Festo kept saying, 'Michael, this whole thing is impossible to take in: right here in the heart of Islam, this incredible crowd and these amazing believers.' Local Christians agreed they had never seen such crowds either.

Certainly Festo did not let any worries about assassins' bullets worry him as he preached in church after church. When he tackled 'The Minister's Power'—and got on to the Holy Spirit, he 'took wings'. On 'The Minister and his Family', Festo 'was at his lyrical best', noted Cassidy. 'His message was pure genius—penetrating and also at times very amusing.'

Then it was on to the Mediterranean port of Alexandria, where again thousands came to hear the team. By the time the team flew out of Cairo into a midnight starry sky above the pyramids, over 23,000 people had been addressed. 'We had a good feeling of mission accomplished.'

As May was merging into June, Bishop Festo and Mera (she travelled with him often now) joined forces with Michael Cassidy and Matt Nyagwaswa (Tanzania AEE) for a mission in the suburbs of Sydney, Australia, 'Bridge 1978'. The mission, aimed at preparing the ground for the following year's Billy Graham Crusade, was also a success in raising interest and cash for AEE's work among the Ugandan refugees. Michael Cassidy and Festo preached in tandem to crowds of up to 1,500. The Archbishop of Sydney and Primate of All Australia, Sir Marcus Loane, lent his support to AEE RETURN.

The Australian Broadcasting Commission were so intrigued by a Ugandan bishop both forgiving Idi Amin (his book had attracted a great deal of attention) and raising money to help the people Amin had made refugees, that they decided to broadcast his sermon at the Blakehurst Anglican Church, giving him fifteen minutes to address their 500,000 viewers.

The nation's National Press Club at Canberra were likewise intrigued and took the unusual step of inviting Bishop Festo (neither a politician nor leading notable) to talk to them. Warwick Olson, for years a media man (his company, Pilgrim International, had set up the AEE branch in Australia) was astounded at their response: a 'standing ovation'. Festo answered their questions on Amin in depth and humorously. 'They said they'd have him back anytime.'

Other TV appearances followed, and Warwick Olson estimated that by the time Festo flew on to New Zealand with the AEE team, some seven million may have heard him. 'The greatest media exposure of my life!' an amazed Bishop Festo told friends, though, as always, they noted that 'there was never any sign that he was keen to see what the papers said about him'. Certainly, it was a great boost to the AEE launch—already thousands of donors and hundreds of thousands of dollars. In a time of private prayer and fellowship, Festo and Michael agreed that they were 'rather astonished at the way the work seems to be developing . . .'.

Later that summer in August, soon after Australia, Festo caught a flight to England, where the 1978 Lambeth Conference for Anglican bishops the world over was being held in Canterbury. Festo got to Canterbury in time to preach at a pre-Lambeth Renewal Conference where one of his listeners was Bishop William Frey, Bishop of Colorado. Bishop Festo preached on a line from a chorus, 'Spirit of the living God, fall afresh on me.'

Frey recalls,

As so often happens, the group, which counted most of the better known figures in the renewal movement in the Anglican Church, had been talking all afternoon on some fairly heady topics. Festo was able to bring us all back to earth and enable us to focus more clearly on just who and what we really were.

One of the highlights for Festo at the conference was the opportunity to meet up again with his fellow bishops from Uganda. But even in England he had to be careful: Amin had sent along an enormous 'press corps' to watch the bishops, and watch them they did, despite the frosty reception they received from everyone else at the conference.

But time and opportunities were found for Bishop Festo to slip away with his special friends—among them Bishop William, his suffragan, and Bishop Yustase Ruhindi. Sadly, there was some tension between some of the bishops in exile, and those who had come straight from Uganda. But most of the bishops forgave Festo Kivengere his freedom as 'in the end he did a lot more for Ugandans in exile than he would have been able to do had he stayed in the diocese'.

The plight of the Ugandan bishops aroused the concern and pity of all, including Dr Robert Runcie, then Bishop of St Albans and later Archbishop of Canterbury. It was here that he first met Festo and was impressed that 'Festo was outstandingly articulate and quite uncompromised by politics ... Festo was not a political animal ... but he was someone who had all-round respect.'

As another attender of the conference, a missionary doing translation work, recalls, 'Festo was always the evangelist; his drive for it came across constantly.' For instance, in a debate on the best way forward in Christian contact with the Muslims, he grew impatient with liberals' proposals stressing 'dialogue' and 'listening'. So he plunged in, 'May I say something?'

Archbishop Coggan stopped him with: 'Bishop Festo, do you wish to speak to the amendment, or to the amendment to the amendment?'

Bishop Festo brushed away the cobwebs of procedure. 'I've just got something to say!'—and went on to point out that it was fine to talk to Muslims, as long as Christians always were at liberty to put their belief in the lordship of Christ. This, as always, was his heart's joy.

More international missions followed Lambeth, among them one in Montreal that September, which culminated in 4,000 people packing into Montreal's Roman Catholic Church of Notre Dame to hear Bishop Festo preach. Shortly after that, it was back to Africa, for a major AEE mission involving most of the churches in Nairobi. The schedule was 'a real blinder'—102 mission meetings in twelve days, culminating in a mass rally of 15,000 at Uhuru Park. Nairobi's churches and Christian organisations had been preparing for it for months, and despite the occasional administrative hitch (such as the afternoon Festo and Michael went off 'cock-a-hoop to storm a township for Christ' at what they expected to be a large rally. They arrived to find a pastor and two young girls waiting for them. After the shock, they found it funny and 'rather salutary—does something for the soul!')

The mission was a great success—contacting over 40,000 people; 3,000 came forward for counselling, including 500 prisoners at a prison Festo visited. Particularly encouraging to Festo and Michael was the warmth with which senior government officials welcomed the mission, including the Mayor of Nairobi, the Minister of State for the President's Office, the Minister of Agriculture and Miss Margaret Kenyatta, the late President's sister (who told Festo firmly after one meeting: 'You people must keep preaching to us! You see, some of our hearts are so tight closed').

Despite the pressure on Festo from all the hordes of Ugandan refugees (who daily swarmed the Kenyan AEE headquarters, and whose relief supplies themselves gave headaches—where to put forty-five tons of clothes from Holland?) he was at his lyrical best in the pulpit. This was especially so the morning he and Michael addressed the prestigious Mayor's Prayer Breakfast— the first of its kind in Kenya. Festo told the story of Zaccheus the tax collector, and gave 'a positively masterly and scintillating word painting' according to one colleague. 'It was in some ways the most brilliant sermon I ever heard him preach,' adds another.

Festo's skill lay in his ability to retell the first century stories in a twentieth century context. When talking of Zaccheus the local receiver of revenue, 'the tax department of Nairobi was there before us in living colour'; and he always brought the nuances and implications of a story to life 'with incredible vividness'.

The Mayor of Nairobi chuckled afterwards: 'Can *that* be the same story I read in my Bible?' and urged Festo to consider coming to speak at a major civic gathering he was planning.

The mission was a particularly busy time for Festo, who had a 'mad schedule'. This included flying to Holland for a mass Youth Rally on the Saturday evening (10,000 went, and Dutch TV covered it nationally) before flying back overnight to preach in Nairobi at the mission's closing rally at Uhuru Park on the Sunday afternoon. 'Once the Dutch got their clutches on him they were not about to let him off the hook!'

For the Sunday rally in Nairobi, Festo and Michael preached in tandem. John 7:37: 'If anyone thirst, let him come to me and drink' had been 'swimming in my mind', as Festo would often say, and so Michael launched him off with the beginning of the story of the Samaritan woman at the well. Hundreds responded.

That evening, after such a stressful time, Festo and Michael were due to fly to the UK, but first there was dinner with all of the mission crew 'in a rip-roaring mood and the joyful thankful-ness that we all felt in our heart to the Lord was quite irrepressible'!

CHAPTER TWENTY

FORGIVING THE UNFORGIVABLE
1980–1981

Amin falls to Tanzanian invasion; Bishop Festo and Mera return; reconciliation and reconstruction; political turmoil; Bishop Festo visits South Africa; Obote returns; Kigezi diocese divided; epidemics threaten Uganda; British tour 'From Uganda with Love'; Cross of St Augustine.

THE YEAR 1979 BEGAN with Bishop Festo and Mera, in common with thousands of exiled Ugandans the world over, daily tuning into the headlines for news of the war at home. Amin, faced with increasing internal threat to his regime including from the army, had tried to divert attention by invading Tanzania. Ugandan troops and aircraft had attacked in October 1978. Events moved quickly. It was soon apparent that the invasion was floundering. Thousands of Amin's troops deserted, leaving such a vast array of weapons that the Tanzanians had trouble carting them away. Other Ugandans slipped across the border to join up with the exiled Uganda National Liberation Army.

Within weeks, Amin's army had been routed. But President Nyerere of Tanzania in turn decided to invade Uganda. The hope was that this would provoke a popular uprising against Amin. On 24th and 25th February Nyerere's army ransacked the two southern strongholds of Amin's army: Masaka and Mbarara. Here he paused—and waited in vain for the people to revolt. They were too cowed and terrified. Yet there were dozens of little scribbled notes pinned to trees for the Tanzanian army: 'Don't leave us.'

Tension mounted to almost unbearable level for exiled Ugandans. Bishop Festo, in Nairobi for the annual AEE inter-team meetings, hastily urged that they launch yet a further appeal: whatever happened now, Uganda would be needing aid desperately. (By April £140,000 would have been raised.)

In Dar es Salaam, Nyerere, in conference with exiled leading Ugandans such as the deposed former president, Obote, as well as Yusufu Lule and Yoweri Museveni, planned the next stage of the invasion. Tanzanian and UNLA troops marched east and west. Amin's troops scattered before them. Within weeks the invading joint armies had met at Mpigi, within artillery range of Entebbe and Kampala, where Amin was making a last desperate stand.

Here again Nyerere ordered a pause. It was clear now that Kampala could be taken, and Amin's regime destroyed. But what then? Nyerere, whom Bishop Festo was to describe as the 'most unusual and unselfish leader on the African continent' decided that he would have to install an interim government until Uganda could have a chance to hold free elections.

To organise this, the Moshi Unity Conference was held on 24th March. Bishop Festo, along with other leading exiled Ugandans, flew to Dar es Salaam to take council over Uganda's future. He was among those who approved the choice of Yusufu Lule, an elderly Muganda and former Makerere University Lecturer, as the new president. Lule, a Muslim convert to Christianity, had worked closely with him on RETURN in helping exiled Ugandans. Bishop Festo himself was approached with offers of high government office in the new Uganda, but refused with a smile—his work, he stressed, was that of a minister of the gospel.

On Monday 9th April, 1978 Amin fled Kampala with the help of Libyan friends.

On 10th April Tanzanian troops took Kampala. It was more a victory parade than a foreign occupation: the men and women cheered, drums beat and many climbed aboard the Tanzanian tanks as they rolled through the ravaged city. Amin's regime was over; the country was now under Uganda National Liberation Front (UNLF) control. International and internal support was immediate. Soon after, Lule was sworn in as the new, interim president.

With the fall of Amin, Bishop Festo dropped everything in his busy diary and prepared to return to Uganda. From Dar es Salaam he flew to the UK, where he abruptly cancelled an extensive month long AEE mission that churches all over Britain had been planning for months in conjunction with the Ruanda Mission. Congregations from Birmingham to Cambridge, London to Merseyside lost thousands of pounds, but Bishop Festo hardly paid attention. (It was left to the Ruanda Mission to soothe the widespread frustration.) 'Helping to heal the wounds of my country' had become Bishop Festo's dearest wish and firm resolve that spring of 1979. But first, at a press conference in London in mid-April, he was publicly grateful to Nyerere who 'out of his poverty' had still invaded Uganda to save the people from Amin—a 'tremendous burden' which, 'now lifted, sends people into a kind of ecstasy'!

The biggest, most far-reaching phase of Bishop Festo's ministry was about to begin. It would absorb him for the rest of his life. If a man can be said to have his 'hour' in life, Bishop Festo's hour had certainly come. At President Lule's invitation, he led the call for national reconciliation. Also, with his access to international aid through his leadership of AEE, he was asked by President Lule to be the first chairman of Uganda's and the Church of Uganda's National Committee on Relief and Rehabilitation. He would draw millions of pounds of aid into the country for the physical relief of the impoverished citizens—no matter of what race or faith. His was an evangelical social conscience *par excellence*.

Bishop Festo's faith in Christ gave him an optimism, energy and wisdom which would become infectious. Thousands would soon catch his vision of a Uganda reconciled to its hideous past, forgiving the evil, and bent on building anew with hope in God. President Lule and his other government ministers would time and again support his calls for reconciliation in order that Ugandans might 'redirect their energies towards creativity, not destruction'.

But to begin with, from London Bishop Festo flew on to Pasadena, both to pick up Mera and to help organise the transport of the first shipment of aid to Uganda from AEE, World Vision, and many other Christian relief organisations.

Bishop Festo also sent off a flurry of Western Union mailgrams to Uganda, among them one to the Archbishop, Silvanus Wani: 'Praise to God for Uganda's resurrection from destruction. Mera and I will soon be with you. Psalm 126.' And also one to his assistant bishop, William Rukirande: 'Alleluia Christ is risen. Uganda is risen. Mera and I will soon be with you second week of May. Psalm 126.'

Psalm 126 had become *his* psalm. Its words summed up his feelings on returning from exile.

Bishop Festo, Mera and several other Ugandan bishops landed at Entebbe airport in a gentle drizzle of rain on Friday 11th May, 1979. An international welcoming committee was waiting to greet them, including the President of Uganda, Yusufu Lule; the Archbishop of Uganda, Rwanda, Burundi and Boga-Zaire, Silvanus Wani; the Roman Catholic Bishop of Kabale; John Wilson and other team members of AEE, along with reporters from *Time, Newsweek*, CBS, a Dutch TV film crew, Dr Stanley Mooneyham of World Vision, and his own TV film crew (who filmed Bishop Festo's homecoming *Return to Uganda*), as well as many other friends and well wishers. As Bishop Festo disembarked, the crowds shouted and cried their welcome—his return had become a symbol for them that Amin had truly gone for ever.

With a large umbrella over him, and a large microphone in front of him, Festo stammered a greeting, choking back tears:

It is a great, great joy—I can't put it into words—to feel in Uganda the fresh air of liberty, to look around, no guns at one's back ... Jesus Christ using ordinary people like Tanzanians and Ugandans has brought this liberation—I simply have no words except to say, 'Praise God!'

... the hope of coming back never died. We waited for the return *every evening* listening on the radio. I feel absolutely in another world.

... it is true we have ... very deep wounds, deep sufferings, but Uganda is not destroyed... This country is a country of the resurrection and we are going to come and tell Ugandans to recover from frustrations, intimidations, hiding their heads, and say it is a new day!

But first the 'wonderful healing love of Jesus Christ' was the 'only antidote to the poison' of the Amin regime, and was badly needed as 'you can't reconstruct without reconciliation'!

Reconciliation. Relief. Reconstruction. In the months ahead Bishop Festo would laughingly call them 'the three Rs' of AEE.

After the rapturous welcome at the airport, it was on to a formal reception at the State House near Entebbe airport. President Lule repeated his 'great satisfaction' in having them back, but warned that 'the Uganda you find is not the Uganda you left ... [there is] no respect for life, no respect for individual property ... the type of behaviour we used to know ...' had disappeared.

'The churches have a very important role to play in the rehabilitation of our society. Therefore in welcoming you back, I should like to stress the important role you have to play in helping us to solve these very complicated problems.' Bishop Festo assured him: 'We are taking your challenge very deeply ... Without reconciliation, reconstruction would be waiting for the next round of destruction.'

On their way on into Kampala though, it was difficult to see what could possibly be left to destroy ... Bishop Festo and Mera stared out the windows in horror, heartsick at the sight of blasted buildings, torn streets, everything a shambles, people dressed in rags, with haunted eyes. The State Research Bureau had been opened, revealing rotting corpses, torture chambers, and arsenals. And in the streets, anarchy continued. The UNLA soldiers were not disciplined, and their drinking and carousing was leading to yet more violence and looting.

Still, it *was* Uganda, their beloved country, and it was marvellous just to be back. The car swept them up Namirembe Hill to the cathedral, which was packed with thousands of Christians, who clapped with joy as Festo and Mera and the other bishops entered. Only once before in the history of Namirembe Cathedral had a congregation clapped for anyone's arrival: and that had been the king, the Kabaka, on his return from exile.

Next morning, Saturday, 12th May, Festo and Mera set out for Kabale, accompanied by a large entourage of friends, clergy, the World Vision and Dutch film crews and AEE team members. Across the equator the cars went, wending their way south on perilous roads, stopping only to see the former archbishop, Erica Sabiti, now retired, for a tearful reunion.

At the border of the high hills of Kigezi district a crowd of 6,000 from the local neighbourhood (conditions made travel over any distance impossible) was eagerly awaiting them. Bands played. Choirs sang. School children cheered. When Festo and Mera stepped out of the car, large garlands of flowers were flung about their necks in a 'tremendous demonstration of love'.

Bishop Festo and Mera could hardly describe that moment. 'We were—well—the crowd was too big and they all came, and we were mobbed with love. ... I spoke, but I broke down. I couldn't speak. It was too much,' Festo told a friend later.

Now two motorcycles led the triumphant procession as they travelled the last twenty-four miles. At the entrance to Kabale, 10,000 more people were waiting.

> We were completely overwhelmed. My car was almost lifted into the air! We spoke there and it was very difficult, because every time we tried to speak, words failed, and we had lumps in our throat. People were pulling my arms, and it was wonderful to feel them.

By the road on the way up Rugarama Hill were 2,000 more well-wishers. Lining the road to the cathedral were hundreds more. They waved and waved. The cathedral was packed out, with more than 3,000 people singing and cheering.

Bishop Festo was formally welcomed back to his diocese by Bishop William, who led him by the hand back to his bishop's throne in St Peter's. Government officials and district commissioners smiled a warm welcome. The congregation sang and prayed and then 'I gave a greeting, not a preaching, reminding the people it is a time for reconstruction and love, rather than retaliation and revenge.'

Going to their own home afterwards was 'a traumatic experience', as they had left in such fear. Now the house was crowded with friends, singing a welcome. A feast was held in their honour that night at Kigezi High School. Then Festo and Mera slept, exhausted, as thousands of Christians stayed on and spent the night outside under the stars, around a huge fire in the compound, singing and praying.

Twenty-five thousand arrived for church the next morning (though only 3,000 could get into the cathedral). There would have been more except that only the local Christians could

I was asked how I would react if I were handed a gun and President Amin were sitting opposite me. The only reply that I could give was that I would hand the gun to the President and say: 'I think this is your weapon. It is not mine. My weapon is love.'

BISHOP FESTO KIVENGERE
Exiled Bishop of Kigezi
and international evangel

Poster advertising Festo coming to preach at a mission. His stand on Idi Amin was attracting a lot of attention. Late 1970s.

Festo returning to Entebbe airport in May 1979, after two years of exile.

actually get to Kabale. Bishop Festo processed with all his clergy and the Bishop of Western Ankole, at whose consecration in January '79 the troubles leading to the exile had all begun. Then it was out to the amphitheatre, where he preached to the vast crowd for nearly two hours. He quoted the verse about going out in tears to sow, and returning with joy.

> We and other Ugandans left ... with seeds of suffering. Now we are coming back with the fruits of joy ... love, reconciliation and forgiveness. Not bitter, wanting retaliation or revenge ... Those seeds which would be poisonous for Uganda today ...

Bishop Festo broke down a number of times. Later he joined his congregation in dancing and singing the afternoon away.

If coming back to Uganda was a dream, the country itself was a nightmare.

One missionary reported:

> ... there are estimated to be half a million orphans. Some are starving and many are cold from lack of clothing... Hospitals are stripped of medicines ... with very few nurses and doctors left ... it is reported that Masaka and Mbarara look like Hiroshima, without a building standing ... farms have been destroyed, with cattle looted ... in the last eight years not one school has been built, not one hospital, not one road repaired. Everywhere there are shattered buildings, a shattered economy ... national credit for urgent purchasing needs from other countries is non-existent because of the enormous debts left by Amin.

The damage was worst in the east and the north, and in patches of the south west where the Tanzanians had invaded. Kigezi diocese was among those least affected by the past eight years as Amin's death squads had never reached this remote part of the country.

While the Tanzanian troops continued to hunt out segments of Amin's army which were still at large throughout the country, the UNLA troops themselves slipped out of control and Lule faced increasing political tensions that threatened to unseat him. AEE under Bishop Festo set itself to work night and day to organise the beginning of the reconstruction of Uganda. (At Archbishop Wani's request, AEE would appeal in both Australia and Britain on behalf of the Church of Uganda). Already tons of food, medicine, clothes and other relief had been arriving from AEE supporters throughout the world, sympathetic western governments, and any number of other relief organisations.

Within a week a basic strategy had emerged: a three year 'middle range rehabilitation programme' would be required, the first phase of which would simply concentrate on emergency relief: medicine, feeding programmes, clothing and blankets. Plane after plane landed at Entebbe, laden with butter, oil, fuel, hoes, soap, skimmed milk powder, grain, corned beef, blankets, cotton wool, chemicals, repair tools, refrigerators and generators, to name but a few. Relief trucks, donated to distribute it all, became a familiar, and most welcome, sight throughout the country.

Along with this immediate physical relief, Bishop Festo and his AEE team launched a programme for tackling the vast spiritual needs of the people. They decided to begin by 'helping the helpers', with pastoral 'refresher' conferences up and down the country. Festo would speak at as many as he could, other AEE team members at the rest. Several national TV and radio broadcasts on the theme of reconciliation and reconstruction were also made.

Festo spent several hectic, but extraordinarily happy weeks in Kigezi diocese itself, his priority being to go out among his people again. Festo and his chauffeur, John Kaisari, set off on a reunion tour (slower than of old due to the shocking condition of the roads). They visited every archdeaconry. Thousands of people walked miles to see him, delighted to have their Bishop back among them, and marvelling at his beard. (He had decided to keep it.)

By the middle of June, other commitments called Bishop Festo away, including an engagement to speak at an evangelistic rally at the *Kirchentag* in West Germany. Bishop Festo addressed an estimated 125,000 in a grassy park near Nuremburg.

But in late June came news that sent Bishop Festo rushing back to Uganda: another political crisis had rocked the country. The National Consultative Council, feeling Lule was trying to seize excessive power, had thrown him out. Soon a British-trained lawyer, Godfrey Binaisa, of the Ugandan National Liberation Front, was sworn in as President, but many times it seemed as if Uganda had no government whatsoever as wide-spread violence against helpless civilians continued.

Bishop Festo had been due to fly to South Africa and join up with Michael Cassidy and others for SACLA—the South African Christian Leadership Assembly (the follow up to PACLA of 1976). It was heartbreaking to miss such a unique event—6,000 South African Christians of all denominational and racial groups, as well as a series of joint preaching engagements with Michael Cassidy from Pretoria to Soweto, Cape Town, Port Elizabeth and Durban. But Bishop Festo wanted to be on hand to make representation, along with Uganda's other religious leaders, to what little government there was, and speak out on behalf of the otherwise silent people. (The church was the only institution to have survived the Amin years intact.)

In a public letter to Binaisa, the country's religious leaders (headed by the Archbishop of Uganda, Silvanus Wani; Emmanuel Cardinal Nsubuga, the Roman Catholic Archbishop of Kampala; Sheik Muluna, Chief Kadhi of Uganda, and the Bishop of the Orthodox Church), voiced the people's 'general sense of fear and dissatisfaction'. Not only did the continuing army indiscipline and killing 'smell of a return to military government', but they were concerned that the political parties had been suspended for two years—was the UNLF introducing a one-party system?

Binaisa invited Bishop Festo to represent all the religious leaders. As a fellow bishop said, 'The politicians might not always agree with Festo, but they always listened to what he said.' Binaisa and Festo talked privately for three and a half hours.

But by the end of July, as Nyerere withdrew another 25,000 Tanzanian troops from the country, Uganda was still nowhere near stabilising itself. Disease and malnutrition were rampant, towns wiped out. There was no agriculture, no transport ... the economy was out of control ... Bishop Festo met with the other bishops at Namirembe at the end of the month, gravely concerned.

Bishop Festo filled President Nyerere of Tanzania in on the perilous state of Uganda that August when his preaching commitments included an AEE mission to Dar es Salaam.

Nyerere and several cabinet ministers made time to attend the rallies, which were so packed out as to be 'beyond our expectations'.

September's diary opened with Festo in Switzerland, for several conventions. Then he flew on to the States to preach at venues as varied as Methodist churches in Glendale, California and Tulsa, Oklahoma, the National Presbyterian Church in Washington DC, the National Press Club, the Episcopal Cathedral in Denver, and the Church of the Resurrection in Dallas. Wherever he went, Bishop Festo repeated his conviction that forgiveness and reconciliation were the only possible way forward for Uganda. He also defended the position he had taken in his book *I Love Idi Amin*. People were accusing him of having no idea of what they had suffered in losing their loved ones, or in being tortured themselves. They accused Bishop Festo of simply condoning all the evil. Bishop Festo was not surprised, or self-defensive. As he told a friend: 'If you are going to be a bridge of reconciliation between warring parties, you must be prepared to be walked on by both sides.'

While Bishop Festo was the first to acknowledge he had been fortunate in suffering so comparatively little, he was arguing his case not on personal experience, but on theological grounds: Christ's crucifixion 'was not a passive acceptance, but rather ... the great love of God ... released to the world'.

... Having been captured by Calvary love, you and I have only one option—at the same time that we are hating and protesting against the evil, we love those who oppress us until they are set free from the bondage of oppressing ... Violence can never create. In the spirit of forgiveness, people love their enemies until they become brothers. Only those who love like that can change things. Even when they can't change the political situation, they can change the attitude, the destructive disposition which had invaded the community.

Back in Uganda that autumn, Bishop Festo found both good news and bad news awaiting him: overseas relief was pouring in at a phenomenal rate, but the three-year drought that affected a great swathe of Africa had finally brought wide-spread famine to the north of Uganda, especially Karamoja. The government had done nothing to help the people.

Festo preaching to the children of a Ugandan village, early 1980s.

Autumn 1982—still urging the Ugandans to reconciliation.

So as the new decade began, and Bishop Festo entered his sixtieth year, AEE under his leadership redoubled its efforts with regard to emergency relief in the north of the country. 'Relief,' stressed Bishop Festo, 'must embrace all.' Any bias on grounds of tribe or religion he utterly condemned as 'miserable and self-centred'. In fact, never had Bishop Festo been so busy. Yet his active mind and enormous energy thrived on the work. 'This past year has been the most thrilling of my ministry,' he told friends. After the exile, he was still revelling in the freedom to be able to try and do something to help Uganda.

Also in January 1980 Bishop Festo and Mera gathered his pastors from Kigezi diocese for a pastors' conference. Two hundred pastors and their wives were urged to look always to 'our unlimited resources in the Lord Jesus'. (Other conferences followed: Lango, Bukedi, Ruwenzori, Busoga, etc.) Bishop Festo divided his time between yet more preaching commitments all over Europe and the USA, AEE work for all Uganda, and the care and responsibilities of his own diocese.

To back up this work, Bishop Festo invited Dorothy and George Smoker to put together in a book his special messages for Uganda in its needy condition. The messages in *Hope for Uganda* (Evangel Publishing House: Nairobi, Kenya, 1980) had been given at Bishop Tucker Theological Seminary in Mukuno at Easter. The Smokers, feeling also the need for a definitive book on the East African revival from the participants' point of view, collected together an autobiographical book of Bishop Festo's own experiences as told in his messages. Thoroughly revised by the Bishop, *Revolutionary Love* was finally published in 1983 (CLC Publishing House: Pennsylvania, USA, 1983).

May arrived with little to celebrate. One year into liberation and the country was still on its knees: sugar cost $20 a kilo, soap $1.50. Corruption was endemic. Bishop Festo's greatest concern was by now for the children, who had never known anything but terror and disruption. He wrote to the USA supporters about them: 'This generation needs to be rehabilitated ...' He and the clergy of Uganda had the will, but lacked the means, so: 'We are asking you to strengthen our hands.'

May also saw the downfall of Binaisa. A military commission took over. Obote returned from Tanzania, soon to gain power. The people turned hopeful eyes to their new leadership.

June came and the famine tightened in Karamoja. Bishop Festo asked western supporters for continuing help, based on their Christian compassion. 'Whoever comes into the presence of Christ and sees the heart of God is immediately captive of his love. Let us love under all circumstances ...' At a large AEE mission in Mwanza, Tanzania, that same month, 10,000 turned out to hear him preach. Hundreds responded to his impassioned presentation of the gospel: the way in which he conveyed God's love struck a chord in people's hearts everywhere.

Then Bishop Festo rushed back to Kampala, where under the theme of 'New Man, New Church, New Nation', the 1,500 clergy of the entire Church of Uganda were to meet for the first time in eight years. Bishop Festo was one of the key speakers, and he saw the conference as crucial for spiritual renewal. He hoped it would be 'the springboard by which we can leap forward into the country and take the message of reconciliation and renewal so urgently needed in Uganda'. As was his way, Bishop Festo continued to paint arresting pictures from well-known Bible stories to back his point.

> If there is a Judas, love him. Do you know what Jesus did to Judas who betrayed him? He ... washed his feet as he did the other disciples. Although Judas did not change, he made a confession when he died: 'I am guilty because I rejected innocent love.' Jesus died for him. So can we not embrace our Judases?

In July Obote and his minister visited Kabale during a tour of the country, and Bishop Festo had a sermon ready for them.

> Forgiveness brings a new hope and encourages the guilty one to leave behind his guilt. As your brother in Christ, and your fellow Ugandan, I plead with you to open your hearts to one another, and release one another through forgiveness as Christ has forgiven you, and Uganda will be rebuilt, and morals will be renewed, and heart-wounds will be healed.

August included a trip to the States, where, among other engagements, Bishop Festo was a guest at Billy Graham's 'Grand Indiannapolis Crusade'. Here he presented Billy Graham with a portrait of Billy Graham, as a 'little token' to thank the Billy Graham Association for their generous aid to Ugandan student refugees.

Soon after, it was on to South Africa—Bishop Festo's first ever visit to that country. Michael Cassidy and Bishop Festo teamed up for an AEE-led mission which took them from Capetown to Durban to Pietermaritzburg to Soweto. They held morning seminars for hundreds of Christians, and evening rallies for much larger crowds. Not surprisingly, a black and white team, preaching in tandem, made an enormous impact. The dual ministry in 'the midst of racial tensions, student riots and school boycotts' fulfilled a twelve-year-old dream that had been seeded when Bishop Festo founded AEE in East Africa.

They found 'anger is rising day by day' in the townships, over apartheid policies, but Festo preached that 'guns and knives don't solve the problem'. 'Festo could say many things that I as a white South African could never say, and vice versa,' recalls Michael Cassidy. Highlights of the trip were rallies at two 'explosive' townships—Elsies River and Guguletu (where the churches were full to overflowing) and Stellenbosch University, an Afrikaner stronghold of the apartheid philosophy. Here 1,300 students turned out, as well as many members of faculty. 'It was wonderful for Festo, as a black, and me as an English-speaking South African, to stand before that student body and minister the love of Christ together,' Michael Cassidy wrote later. 'We believe firmly that unless South Africa experiences a mighty movement of the Spirit of God in terms of reconciliation, justice and evangelism, it must face the consequences of civil war and bloodshed ...'

Back in East Africa that September, Bishop Festo was delighted to share stories of his trip with over 1,000 pastors at the Kenya National Pastors' Conference, before returning to Uganda. Here the need created by the famine in Africa had taken precedence over all other relief work. More than half of the 350,000 people in northern Uganda were estimated to be in imminent danger of starving to death. Aid workers were horrified by the 'half-decayed skeletons with parchment paper skins from the heat' lying everywhere. Bishop Festo visited Karamoja for himself, and would 'never forget the experience'.

The little children who came and put their frail hands in mine ... I looked at the skeletal bones ... when they held my hands I felt the heartbeat of suffering humanity ... Emaciated men, women and children line the roadways, their eyes set back in their heads, bellies extended and arms and legs like matchsticks ... I was moved to tears. ...

October and November took Bishop Festo abroad again for a whole series of preaching engagements to the States, including meetings at St Andrew's Presbyterian Church, Newport Beach, California, St James' Episcopal Church, Batavia, New York, St Paul's Cathedral in Buffalo, St Paul's Episcopal Church in Indiannapolis. He was surprised and touched when the Lindsborg Medal of Honour was awarded him on a brief visit to Kansas. Then it was on to Holland to speak at a strategic 'world' conference for evangelical communicators. Before he returned to Uganda, Bishop Festo received another award, from the World Council of Churches in Geneva—the Edward Browning Achievement Award for spreading the gospel.

In December Obote was formally elected President of Uganda. Bishop Festo sent a letter of congratulations:

> We in the diocese of Kigezi wish you the best of success in leading our country, to restore our human dignity and rights, our freedom and security. We assure you of our loyal support in the noble undertaking of reconciling our people politically, or rehabilitating and rebuilding our beloved country.

Sadly, everyone's hopes would again be dashed by experience. In the weeks and months to come, nothing improved. Bishop Festo, so outspoken in his congratulations, was just as open in his criticism and again and again went to talk with Obote; telling him straight that the people did not see much difference between Amin and Obote's army. He repeatedly urged Obote to stop his soldiers massacring their own people. On one occasion he challenged the President about some of the brutal behaviour of soldiers towards defenceless people. The President replied: 'You criticise my soldiers, but you do not criticise these bandits against whom they are fighting.'

Festo rounded on him: 'Mr President, if they are *bandits,* they are not claiming to stand for the rule of law. Your soldiers *are* committed to defending the rule of law, and it matters very much that their behaviour should uphold it!' The economy lurched on: a bar of soap cost the equivalent of $40, a few eggs $7.

But Bishop Festo couldn't spend all his time in Kampala. He returned to Kabale and in late December went north to Kinyasano church to announce personally to the Christians there that they would soon have a new bishop based in Rukungiri: the diocesan headquarters of the new North Kigezi diocese.

1981 arrived, and Bishop Festo and the AEE team launched the second phase in their plan to remobilise the nation spiritually. After the pastors' conferences of 1980, 1981 was to be a year of widespread mission. Topping the agenda would be a city-wide mission in Kampala that summer, at which Bishop Festo would preach as well as John Wilson and James Katarikawe. Meanwhile, many village missions throughout the country got under way.

It was now forty years since Bishop Festo had himself become a Christian. Looking back, in a sermon, he summed up his experience in his clear picture language:

> Life is like ploughing a field ... Jesus never came to excuse anyone from pulling the plough of life ... I have a plough to pull in Uganda where I live. You have yours in the place where you are ... you may become weary ... The beauty of Jesus Christ is that he comes and he takes his place by your side ... Don't reject your plough. You don't need to change jobs, the problem is not with the plough or the field. You need that special instrument of grace to make the pulling easy ...
>
> I don't preach the gospel because it is my job. In fact, I would be utterly miserable if I refused to preach the gospel. It is natural for me, the excitement of my life.

And so his particular plough-pulling continued—a helter skelter schedule, well described by friends as 'convention, mission, diocese, convention, mission, diocese ... convention, mission, diocese!' It was a lifestyle that would have exhausted many a younger man with its never-ceasing travel, irregular hours, crises, meetings, and preaching, but Bishop Festo thrived on it. His daughter once said that 'if Dad stays in one place for more than two weeks, he begins to get restless ...'.

In late January of 1981 Bishop Festo was on the move again. He spoke with Gershon Mwiti of the Kenyan team at the bi-annual Wycliffe Translators' Conference in the Sudan before going on to Nairobi for a city-wide rally, 'Jesus '81', with

Michael Cassidy. Much of February and March were spent in
the USA on tour, raising funds for Uganda, and preaching at
rallies, missions and conventions.

During his trip in the States, a story broke which caused a
great furore in Anglican Communion worldwide: the Bishop of
Newark, New Jersey, the Rt Revd Jack Spong, had gone ahead
and ordained the first woman ever to the priesthood. Bishop
Festo was among those who applauded his action. With his
revivalist background, he had never seen ministry as having a
sacramental role: ordination was simply an outward sign that
you were set aside exclusively for ministry. So at the meeting of
the House of Bishops in Kampala in late February Bishop Festo
made an impassioned speech against the popular position that
women's ordination was 'okay—but not yet'. He argued that
the Lambeth Conference, having approved it in principle in
1978, should act on it. His arguments lay along the lines that
women as well as men should be able to use their teaching/
administrative/pastoral gifts for full-time use in the church,
and that their ministry to God's people was just as valid. He
grew impatient with views that only men were fit to lead the
church and that Jesus had always given a secondary position to
women. Bishop Festo demanded: Who was the first person ever
to proclaim that Jesus was risen from the dead? And if modern
women kept silent—from missionaries to the testifiers of the
revival background—where would the church be now?

(Mera put it more simply: 'God gave Jesus to a woman to be
looked after, so surely he'd entrust the care of parts of his
church to women. And what did the men think the women
would *do* that was so terrible?')

Bishop Festo also proposed that the whole question of ordaining women in Uganda be opened at the Provincial Assembly to
be held that August. (This was agreed, though then quietly
dropped from the agenda.)

The bishops in Uganda were in fact going through a difficult
time, with many tensions still to be resolved between those who
had stayed under Amin and those who had left—some felt,
deserting their flocks. Bishop Festo had never been particularly
popular in the House (though he had close friendships with
several of the bishops) and certainly his exile did not endear

him. Then too, his constant travels abroad earned him a great deal of criticism: 'He doesn't earn his diocesan bishop's salary.' His international preaching fame led to grumbling: 'empty barrels make a lot of noise', and now his work with AEE even drew accusations (all totally groundless) that he must be mis-appropriating the funds for his private benefit. ('It's "African *Enriching* Enterprise"',' sniffed his critics.) Many of the bishops were, quite simply, very jealous. And Festo's directness with them when he discovered any were playing politics or channel-ling aid money into buying themselves luxuries, did not increase his popularity. Finally, Kigezi's success as a diocese (though the smallest, it had the highest giving, and the most ordination candidates in the country after the Namirembe diocese)—did not help either. Bishop Festo was simply too successful in everything he did for many of the bishops not to feel a bit threatened.

In April 1981 the diocese of Kigezi was split into two. The first bishop of North Kigezi was to be Dr Yustasi Ruhindi. The big day was set for Palm Sunday. The Church of Uganda Newspaper, *New Century*, ran page after page of reports: how the Rt Revd Dr Dunstan Nsubuga, Dean of the Province (on behalf of the Archbishop Wani, who was ill) augurated the diocese; how Bishop Festo officially relinquished jurisdiction; how Ruhindi was enthroned. Then there were photographs of Bishop Festo hugging Bishop Yustasi, choirs singing, bands playing, and everyone cheering.

Back in his own diocese a couple of weeks later, Bishop Festo told his diocesan synod of his decision to ordain women. After lengthy discussion, synod backed him by 300–4 votes. This was the support Bishop Festo wanted. He wrote to the Archbishop and bishops of Uganda telling them he was going to go ahead and exercise his episcopal prerogative and ordain women, and inviting comments or objections based on the Bible or theology. Only one responded, though there were plenty of private grumblings that the Church of Uganda should wait for the Church of England ... When this was reported to Bishop Festo, he snorted 'If we do that, we'll wait forever!'

That spring also saw the last meeting under Bishop Festo's chairmanship of the Relief and Rehabilitation Committee. Under

Bishop Yoramu Bamunoba, the emphasis was to switch from emergency relief to reconstruction, and on another visit to Karamoja Bishop Festo was delighted to see children chasing each other, when 'last year they were all ghosts'. On the spiritual side of things, Bishop Festo and his AEE team planned to hold widespread missions drawing in 10,000 church leaders throughout the country.

May arrived, and the nation's disillusionment with Obote and his talk of helping 'the common man' grew. There was next to no rule of law and without civil order, violence flourished. The economy made daily life a misery for everyone. Bishop Festo got nowhere in his approaches to Obote, as he begged for some improvement. At the AEE Kabale Town Mission late that month, Bishop Festo stood before the crowd of 20,000 and reflected soberly: 'Everybody is thirsty for peace ... but many have practised the contrary ...'

Then it was on to Europe for preaching engagements that included a joint Protestant/Roman Catholic mission in Kassel, West Germany, before Bishop Festo returned to help launch phase two of AEE's plan in the spiritual rehabilitation of Uganda—a two-week city-wide mission to Kampala in June, involving most of the churches in the city. The city certainly needed any encouragement it could get; by now Nyerere had withdrawn all the Tanzanian troops, and the civilians were at the mercy of stray Amin troops, civilian looters, and UNLA soldiers.

Overseas engagements kept Bishop Festo from joining other Ugandan bishops on a trip to Zaire that summer, where the new Archbishop of Canterbury, Dr Robert Runcie, was attending the establishment of a new province. Dr Runcie spent some time with the Ugandan bishops, but missed Festo. So did Terry Waite, who had been in Uganda with the Church Army for many years, and an adviser to the first Ugandan Archbishop, Erica Sabiti. Terry, recalls Runcie, spoke of Festo in terms of 'affectionate respect'. 'Terry thought of Festo as something of a kindred independent spirit.' That was a tribute in itself, since Terry

> was always a little suspicious of evangelists, but not of Festo. He had a real admiration for his integrity, and energy; but he was amused

that he was absent from Zaire and immediately suspected that he was out of Uganda.

He was also a kindred spirit of Festo's since Terry suspected that he enjoyed ecclesiastical meetings and endless consultations as little as he himself did.

The Kampala Diocesan Mission in June drew thousands each day to lunchtime rallies at the city square near the banks and the high court. Bishop Festo preached every day and rejoiced along with the rest of the AEE team when hundreds of people responded to his evangelistic appeals. But on the final day, a Sunday, as he got out of the car to preach at the closing rally, he stepped awkwardly on to a broken kerb, and snapped the tendon at the back of his ankle. In spite of searing pain, he went on to preach a full message, to which 1,000 people responded. Then he counselled them before passing them on to individual counsellors ... it was nearly two hours after the accident before he sat down for the first time, and told his team he feared a sprain ... He went on to Nairobi for more meetings, where pain finally drove him to a doctor, who was horrified. 'What are you doing up?! That tendon is completely gone!' The ankle, horribly swollen and ominously hollow, was operated on and put in plaster ... for many months afterwards, Bishop Festo would have a limp, which made carrying luggage in and out of airports a painful business.

While recovering that summer and autumn, Bishop Festo and AEE found a new problem: measles, polio and TB epidemics were increasing in the country. After consultation, Bishop Festo launched an immunisation campaign, an extensive effort involving western medical teams, treating tens of thousands of children. Meanwhile, there was some good news on the rebuilding side: by now most RETURN students had completed their courses in foreign universities and colleges and were returning to Uganda. One became the Minister for Health. Bishop Festo was enormously proud of all the refugee students, calling them, 'Uganda's most valuable natural resource.' USA government officials agreed, publicly commending the programmes.

Meanwhile, that October brought yet another long AEE mission, this time organised by the Ruanda Mission in the UK. It was the fulfilment of the postponed mission of May 1979.

Bishop Festo with Bishop Misaeri Kauma and the Revd John Wilson flew to England to begin 'From Uganda with Love'. It was a knockout success from start to finish. From Devon to Cumbria, people packed cathedrals and crammed parish churches. The Archbishop of Canterbury, Dr Runcie, found the whole concept 'an imaginative move to bring the faith that inspired Uganda through the difficult Amin days and make it spark some of the faith that was called for in this country'.

Bishop Festo had suggested that 'From Uganda with Love' should begin with a visit to Dr Runcie at Lambeth Palace, a visit which gave Dr Runcie the chance to 'really meet Festo and begin to get to know him as a friend for the first time'. When Festo asked that Runcie give them his blessing, the Archbishop was touched: 'I was humbled by this and by the eager way in which they hoped for my encouragement.' Festo, as ever, was no rebel, and eager to work under the proper authorities.

For everyone, including Runcie, it was 'a memorable morning'. Runcie later recalled:

> We spent far longer than my programme had originally allowed. Terry was there and there was much talk of days together in Uganda. We went to the chapel and I led them in prayer. It was all very devout and orthodox. Yet their feelings were on the surface and they shared together in prayer.
>
> They all knelt down and I gave them a blessing for the work ahead and then we rose and spontaneously embraced each other. When we met on later occasions we were always likely to mention that sealing of our partnership in the Gospel.

At a press conference shortly afterwards, Runcie sprang a surprise on them: awarding all three the St Augustine's Cross, an award given only ever at the discretion of the Archbishop, for outstanding work on behalf of the Anglican communion worldwide. Bishop Festo was moved by the warmth and good will behind the generous gesture.

Then it was on to the United States and more preaching engagements. Bishop Festo's evangelism and his work in rehabilitation attracted a good deal of media attention. Dr Pat Robertson, head of Christian Broadcasting Network's 700 Club magazine chat show invited him as a guest, before an estimated twelve million viewers. Billy Graham welcomed his friend at a crusade in Houston. Then it was back to Uganda in time for the December confirmation tours in Kigezi diocese (which was growing at a phenomenal rate)—Bishop Festo confirmed 1,350 people in two weeks. Meanwhile, other progress. By Christmas, which he and Mera spent in Kabale, 30,000 children were being fed daily by AEE and the immunisation programme was in full swing.

CHAPTER TWENTY-ONE

MENDING BROKEN THINGS
1982–1985

Diocese of Kigezi growing; AEE expanding; Obote's troops cause havoc; international preaching engagements; Banyarwanda refugee crisis; Festo stands up to Obote; Bishop Festo ordains women; Amsterdam '83; new Archbishop chosen; Kabale Golden Jubilee Convention.

THE YEAR 1982 MARKED three important anniversaries: it was ten years since Bishop Festo had become a bishop. It was twenty years since Michael Cassidy had first founded African Evangelistic Enterprise. And it was twenty years since Uganda had gained its independence.

Ten years on, Kigezi diocese was certainly flourishing under Bishop Festo. That January, five new archdeaconries were formed, just to cope with the additional burden of pastoral oversight and administration. Although frustration remained that Bishop Festo could not spend all of his time in the diocese, his clergy loved him, and thrived under his guidance.

'Bishop told us always to put our people's need before our own,' recalls one. 'But he warned us that "You won't be able to love them as they need on your own. Look to Jesus; he will help you see their need."'

As for clergy needs, Bishop Festo would carefully delegate the work to them, and have periodic assessments of their progress. By all accounts he was always tolerant of honest failure. He would guide the clergymen to portions of Scripture that he thought might help, but add: 'We pastors, we must accept our weaknesses; we are not angels!'

One thing the diocese never had to worry about, and that was having a bishop who acted 'high and mighty' (though as an acknowledged elder statesman of the church, he had grown to accept a certain amount of deference wherever he went). But 'when he visited our villages, he talked to the simple people on their level,' recalls one clergyman. 'He never came across as one who thought of himself as anything special.' The reason was simple: 'I am a bishop by God's calling, not profession,' Bishop Festo told a conference that spring. And at the consecration of a bishop in western Kenya that year he spelt out what that implied for him. 'You are not loved because you are important, you are important because you are loved. Being a bishop can be like flying in an airplane—and if you go too high, you'll lose sight of your people.' As for all the fancy robes—'Who do we think we are?'—mischievously repeating a favourite story that in the Bible it was the donkey who had the robes put on him—'so he could carry Christ into Jerusalem'.

Bishop Festo was also very practical in his caring for the people of his diocese. His wife had his permission to give away his shirts, coats and other clothes whenever she came across 'a brother who had nothing', with the result that 'quite often I am searching my wardrobe for something that is gone'! And when goats and chickens were pressed upon him as presents, he gave them away in a parish where there was need.

The AEE ministry was also flourishing, both in South Africa and East Africa. Early that year Bishop Festo presided at the opening of a new headquarters for the East African team in Karen, a suburb of Nairobi. There were increasing demands on this 'handmaiden' of the church, from requests for missions all over the world, to help for massive relief projects within Uganda (including that year more extensive feeding programmes for the Karamajong, continuing education for children, and 'The Great Shoot Out' as a massive immunisation programme was cheerfully named which protected 180,000 children). 'Bishop Festo stirred the nation's conscience by showing what could be done,' said one Ugandan. Fortunately, support and prayer continued from Western countries; in the States, interest was so keen that in February the Pasadena office of AEE launched a radio ministry; fifteen-minute slots featuring taped messages by Festo on six radio stations in four states.

Twenty years into independence, Uganda was not such a thriving concern. The party ruling the country, Obote's Uganda's People Congress, had lost most of its popular support. The reason was simple; they were failing to rule. No one felt safe any more: army roadblocks were everywhere, often set up by men in stolen uniforms who robbed cars in broad daylight. Night-time looting was so widespread that whole suburbs were becoming deserted as people fled. Sunset fell in Kampala at seven pm. Offices closed at four-thirty pm so that everyone could be sure to be home by six pm.

The failing economy caused great suffering. In 1981 Uganda's currency had been devalued ten times while salaries had less than doubled. By 1982 the minimum wage for a month would buy a family enough bananas for perhaps three days. A blanket cost ten months' wages. A mattress cost a year's average salary.

In the face of the resulting widespread corruption and mismanagement of the country, Bishop Festo would find himself again and again in a quandary. While speaking on 'Christianity in a Changing World' to a large convention early that year, he explained it thus: '... I am not a politician, I have enough to keep me busy! But I cannot avoid being involved in politics'—he had to stand as the Christian conscience of the country in its reconstruction. And he went on to tell a story:

> When I was involved in RETURN, a man came up to me after a meeting in Tanzania and asked: 'Bishop, to where will you return these people? Amin is on the throne. First you must demolish Amin.' I said 'No, let's divide duties now. You demolish Amin and I'll take up the reconstruction—because I believe God called me for that.' And I think many Ugandans got involved in demolition, and we're still involved in reconstruction.

Meanwhile, Bishop Festo's diary for the year was similar to other years, dividing his time between increasing demands from all sides: a growing diocese, a growing AEE mission worldwide, and growing needs in reconstruction.

Indeed, a typical schedule would run something like: a series of meetings all over the USA, then on to Nairobi for AEE staff meetings, then on to Kampala for yet more meetings. Then drive furiously down to Kabale, get there at nine pm, and next day face a full agenda of diocesan committee meetings. The following day set off on a tour of confirmations that could include up to 1,000 candidates, and last for a whole week. Finish that, and that next day be on the way for a set of international conventions and missions, often lasting a month, at which he would preach daily.

'We kept looking for signs of a crack up,' admits one colleague. 'But Bishop Festo rarely showed any strain.' Part of the secret of Bishop Festo's legendary stamina and energy was undoubtedly in his singleness of purpose. Using the picture language he loved, he would sometimes compare a person's life to the ointment the woman poured over Jesus' feet in the gospel story (Matthew 26):

> Each one of us has a very special perfume which we can pour into special areas for him. Your life is your perfume. I am not talking about external little things, but the precious thing which is you ... He has a way of taking a life, even a marred, broken, difficult-to-get-along-with-life, and giving it what it would never have had apart from himself ... then if we come and pour the whole thing out on him, he smiles.[1]

Another part of the secret was in his rock-solid marriage. Mera was always a support. There is a saying in Africa: 'Women drive the carts from the back seat.' During these years Mera may not have *driven* the family cart, but she certainly kept it steady, and guided Festo when she thought he needed it. At times when he got carried away with enthusiasm over certain projects, she would tell him so. She also listened to his preaching with a critical ear.

'You spoilt that beautiful gospel message by shouting too much,' would be her only comment after a meeting where everyone else had praised him. Festo didn't always appreciate such honesty. 'Sometimes I don't find it easy to take instructions from her,' he later wrote. 'I want my own way.' But he knew that 'marriage is good in the ministry. The two work as a team, though that is never easy, as each of us prefers to go it alone.' In the end, he would tell friends, 'I will never be able to thank God enough for my wife, who has perhaps ministered more to me than anyone else. She knows my weaknesses, and has been a real, faithful and loving minister.'

They travelled together now almost constantly, she taking on the practical side of things and often rescuing her husband from his absent-minded habit of leaving things everywhere he went. (By now the Namirembe Guest House in Kampala had a special place for the things Bishop Festo left behind, from slippers and pyjamas to shaving gear.)

As for the continual stress, Bishop Festo would shrug it off.

> Life without tension is not worth the name ... Christianity survives better in exposure, not when it is protected ... It is those tensions which make life vibrate. You take the tension from the strings of a guitar, and see whether you will get the music ...

Following brief trips to the States, the UK and Kenya for AEE team meetings and other commitments, Bishop Festo returned to Uganda before setting off on a major mission to the Holy Land in April with other African Enterprise team members including Michael Cassidy and the Revd Dr Don Jacobs. The mission was a spin-off of the outstanding trip to Egypt in 1978, and involved Israeli and Arab Christians as well as missionaries in Haifa, Jerusalem and Tel Aviv. The enthusiasm of both lay and church clergy leaders for the mission was heart-warming to the hectically busy AEE team.

Other missions and conferences and conventions followed throughout the spring and summer. Bishop Festo flew here, there, everywhere and often back again: Tanzania, Kenya, the States, Zaire, Europe, Zaire, the UK, Rwanda. September found him in the States and then back in Britain.

Further commitments in the UK meant that Bishop Festo was not able to return to Uganda for the twentieth anniversary of independence on 9th October. Soon, however, came news that turned all thoughts of celebration to ashes for him anyway: Uganda had decided to begin expelling thousands of Banyarwanda—people of Rwandan descent—who had lived in Uganda for several generations. Mostly the Banyarwanda had settled widely in Ankole, where their houses were now being burnt, their property looted, their land and cattle given to others. Reasons for the persecution of these Banyarwandas were complex, but included jealousy—they had many thousands of cattle and much land, and politically most were Catholics, traditionally identified as the Democratic Party and not Obote's UPC.

Bishop Festo was appalled at the news, and immediately cancelled a mission he was about to lead in the Sudan. He rushed back to Kabale, furious to hear that the government authorities were even trying to prevent the Christians of Kigezi from aiding the hundreds of distressed refugees which had already streamed into Kabale. The authorities had also evicted the refugees from one of his own churches, and instead confined them in the open cold and mud of the local stadium.

Within two days Bishop Festo was pacing the offices of the Vice-President and the Minister of State in Kampala. The meeting he gained was 'not easy', for Festo was rebuked as a 'propagandist' for repeating the bad news, and insisting that it was true. Three days later he had a stern letter on Obote's desk, condemning the expulsion as 'a blot on the image of our country', declaring that he, and other church pastors were 'shocked, and grieved' with the suffering caused. 'This is a terrible spectacle in the history of Uganda, especially,' he added with heavy irony, 'for a civilised government which understands the value of human rights and human lives.'

Bishop Festo had already visited Kamwezi, where the Banyarwanda refugees had tried to cross the border and encountered the next blow fate had in store for them: as they had been born in Uganda, Rwanda would not take them. From eighty-year-old grannies to little children, Bishop Festo told Obote it was disgraceful they should be 'all bewildered on African soil'.

Bishop Festo then appealed to Obote to step in, punish the looters, and restore the people to their former homes, land and cattle. He warned of the damage otherwise on Uganda's international image. Restitution and justice were 'absolutely essential for our country'.

Bishop Festo faced an uphill struggle from the start. Obote was not persuaded. Neither, it soon transpired, were the Banyankole church goers, who stood to profit from the expulsions from stolen cattle and land. It was their influence which had silenced their own bishop, but they found, to their intense irritation, that they could not muzzle Bishop Festo, even though the people concerned were not of his diocese. 'He believed his duty as a church leader was to remind Obote of God's standards,' says a colleague.

Soon the refugees, unwanted in both Uganda and Rwanda, were dumped in camps of appalling squalor, with no facilities of any kind: no regular water, food, and no shelter. Disease spread rapidly. But it seemed that no one cared; even the world's press did not exert themselves as they had done for Amin's expulsion of the Asians.

So that autumn, indefatigably, Bishop Festo set about championing their cause. AEE was soon diverting substantial funds for food, blankets and medical aid to the refugees. Bishop Festo cancelled his overseas programmes and stayed put in Uganda. He made frequent visits to the various camps, especially Kitatumba, Rubaale and Kamwezi. Soon the refugees in the camps were greeting him with cries of delight: 'Our god father is coming! Our god father is coming!' Bishop Festo always took something, if only dried peas, for the people, but on one visit he brought very little—he was merely dropping by to see how they had liked the AEE lorry load of goods he had sent on the day before, via the Bishop of East Ankole.

When the people said, 'What lorry? What food?' Bishop Festo leapt back in the car and sped down the long miles to the Bishop's house. He woke him up in the middle of the night. The Bishop of East Ankole, half-awake, and deeply embarrassed, found it difficult to explain to a steely-eyed Festo how the lorry load of food had found its way into his own private stores. Whatever Bishop Festo said in the private interview that followed, the result was that the AEE food was in the camp next day, and no more food was delayed in getting through.

Meanwhile, many refugees were dying. Many more were very ill. Festo reported all this indignantly to Obote: 'Women are giving birth in the mud! They had no food, no protection! ... It was one of the saddest sights I have ever seen. We took some peas and a few clothes and tried to comfort them.'

Bishop Festo, along now with several other bishops, next pestered for meetings with the Vice-President and leaders of the town councils involved. He got nowhere. No one would accept responsibility. Everyone was evasive. So by November, Bishop

Festo was in Kampala, pushing to see Obote himself. Obote avoided him.

Finally, it was back to Kabale to do what he could: keep sending in hundreds of bags of peas, boxes of clothes, powdered milk ... And week after week Bishop Festo did the rounds—visiting the camps, embarrassing the authorities with news of what was going on in there, making his pleas for any humanitarian organisation to 'give any help they can'. (He later praised Oxfam and UNESCO for stepping in as well.) But in another long letter to Obote he wrote: 'The country gives the impression, even the church gives the impression, that everything is under control. As far as I can see, the only power which seems to be controlling the camps is that of imminent death.'

Still, he did what he could—as November faded into December, he took in teams of helpers, doctors and nurses. He compiled a list of who had died, their ages, and from what—mostly simple diseases aggravated by exposure to rain and cold. And he kept irritating everyone with distressing news and pleas for help—the Archbishop and the Bishops (many of whom helped), the Government, the Ministers of State. Soon the business community in Kabale, who had relations among the Banyan-kole, were thoroughly fed up with him. 'The Banyarwanda are not his people, it is none of his business,' was their argument. But no one quite dared say this openly to Bishop Festo. As for his feelings about many of them—these were all too clear in his Christmas message to Kigezi diocese that year:

> The recent events of displacing our fellow Ugandan citizens ... have demonstrated beyond any shadow of a doubt that our society is sick unto death ... We are all involved ... by our attitude toward their suffering. The silence of many toward the fate of these tens of thousands speaks louder than words against us.

January 1983 brought more grief. After a hasty trip to AEE Pasadena in the States, London and Nairobi for AEE council meetings, Bishop Festo returned to Uganda in February to continue his fight on behalf of the refugees. Obote finally agreed to see him—and at the meeting accused him of condemning him to the world's press. (The story was now attracting headlines.) 'It is not I who condemn you,' replied Festo. 'It is the camps.'

Under such pressure, the government said they would look into resettling the refugees until matters had been sorted out. Festo was relieved, but not impressed. He wrote in a letter to the Minister of Culture and Community Development that 'action must be of a *crisis nature*'—in a recent visit to Kakitumba, 'I saw dead children in the little grass huts waiting to be buried ... ! Mr Minister, that was too much of a human tragedy ... October to February is quite a long time for *an emergency*.'

February also brought grief—but of even more personal a nature. Festo Rwamunahe, Mera's brother, died of cancer. It was he who, on 5th October, 1941 had been converted, and whose testimony a few hours later had led to Festo's conversion. Mera and Festo attended the funeral on 14th February, which, though they would sorely miss his company, turned out in itself to be an occasion of triumph, for a man stood up and declared himself converted, then and there. Festo wrote to friends:

> We burst into a song of praise at the funeral! ... As I looked around, people were clapping and singing and rejoicing ... Is not that continuous revival—when a man who committed himself to the Lord in 1941 dies in 1983 and leads another man to the Lord at his funeral! Praise the Lord his Spirit never dies, he still turns people from darkness to light ...'

It was an encouragement to Festo, who grew frustrated at times with the Church of Uganda. But as he told friends that spring:

> The work of revival in the church continues—not without its ups and downs. But it has never been a smooth run for the Spirit to work in men's hearts. There are always pitfalls and dangers and roadblocks ... the church carries with it its tendencies to traditionalism and tradition and is not a very good team member with the Holy Spirit! But we praise God he never allows tradition to take the upper hand. He keeps breaking through ...

God's breakthroughs were what Bishop Festo and the AEE team had found both in missions from Kenya to Rwanda, and also in meetings for pastors in Uganda and Kenya—'In fact AEE work has mushroomed all over.' In March, Bishop Festo and Mera teamed up with others from AEE for missions to Bahrain, Jordan and Syria, their aim being, as Bishop Festo put it simply:

'To encourage our brothers and sisters and to proclaim the good news.'

One tradition that Bishop Festo was determined to break with that year was the all-male priesthood of the Church of Uganda. He had ordained women deacons as early as 1979, but now was determined to take the next step.

Late in 1982 he had written to the Archbishop, warning him of his intention. Though Bishop Festo did not want to do anything 'out of fellowship', he felt all the same 'rather frustrated' that it was now *nine* years since the Provincial Assembly had passed its Resolution to discuss the question of ordaining women to the priesthood.

Bishop Festo told friends, and the House of Bishops, that he had entered 1983 with 'a firm commitment' to ordain women. After all, the Lambeth Conference of 1978 had left the decision 'open to the discretion of the dioceses and their synods'. No Uganda bishop had raised any objections, so in February Bishop Festo had written to all his lady deacons, inviting them to come and see him to discuss their possible calling to the priesthood. (But his tentative plans to ordain some of them as early as that April did not in the end work out.) So in February, Judith, his secretary, at his request, booked all the women deacons in the diocese for lengthy interviews: Bishop Festo wanted to discover which of them felt that the priesthood was right for them.

By April he and Mera were back in America, where, among dozens of other commitments, the University of the South, in Sewanee, Tennessee, surprised and touched him with their decision to confer an honorary degree on him that May, and to have him speak at the Baccalaureate Service. After a few weeks back in Kigezi to catch up on diocesan work (many times dealing with paperwork until the early hours of the morning) and holding confirmation tours, Bishop Festo and Mera were off to Europe for a succession of conferences, among them the International Conference for Itinerant Evangelists, or 'Amsterdam '83', held that July. Convened by Billy Graham, it attracted 4,000 evangelists from all over the world. Billy Graham reminded them that any evangelist who is 'called by results will find his evangelism is likely to burst like a balloon. It is the Lord who brings the harvest. The evangelist is only called by the

Master to be proclaimer [of the gospel].' It was a point which Bishop Festo also stressed.

Soon Bishop Festo and Mera flew on to Utrecht, for a mission convention of about 16,000 people who were supporting mission work in Africa under the auspices of the Dutch Reformed League. The day before Festo was to address them, the Africa Secretary of the Reformed Mission League in the Netherlands, Kees F. de Blois, met up with him in the lounge of the Holiday Inn at Utrecht in order to go over the programme and brief Festo.

While talking, they were suddenly approached by a Scotsman who had been drinking heavily, and who was attracted by Festo, not only because of his clerical collar, but also because he was the only black person in the lounge.

Blois recalls:

The man started disrupting our conversation. Since we had important business to discuss, and I feared that this man was going to be a nuisance to the Bishop, I was about to ask the people at the reception to send somebody to throw the man out.

Festo decided to approach the matter differently. He decided to engage him in a conversation, and asked the man who he was. In his half-drunken condition, he identified himself as the son of a Presbyterian Church minister. He started quoting Scripture verses, which he said he had learned from his father when he was a young boy. Festo took him seriously and made the remark that the man must have had a wonderful father, who had taught him the truth of the Gospel. He then said he wished that the knowledge of the gospel stored in his head would go deep down and change and fill his heart. When Festo said this the man burst into tears.

When we finished our business meeting and Festo had left the hotel, the man waved Festo goodbye, still touched by this strange encounter. Festo told me: 'You see, the Holy Spirit is already at work!'

I felt a visitor in my own country! I would have missed the opportunity to be a witness to this man! Festo knew how to be an ambassador of Christ's love even in these awkward circumstances.

Then in mid-1983 a situation developed concerning the differing ministry developments of AEE teams in the South and Eastern areas of Africa. This led to spirited discussions during a meeting of AEE's International Council Meeting held in

Holland in early July of that year. During the following two months Bishop Festo considered whether it might be wise for the East African AEE teams to be formed into a separate organisation.

During a visit to the USA in late September, Bishop Festo asked Keith Jesson, then Director of AEE USA, to telephone the International Chairman, Warwick Olson, to advise him that AEE East Africa wished to withdraw from the AEE International partnership. Warwick Olson moved swiftly to deal with this crisis. He arranged for the main AEE Support Boards in Australia, USA and the UK to meet. He consulted the other AEE leadership by telephone and called an emergency meeting of the AEE Executive Committee to be held in California during the second week of October.

Prior to this meeting Warwick Olson flew from Australia to the USA for discussions with Bishop Festo and East African Co-ordinator Daniel Serwanga.

By the time the Executive Committee convened in California, Bishop Festo had drawn back from his proposed action of separation. Far from being an acrimonious or negative time, the meeting turned into a very positive three-day discussion about AEE's overall aims and objectives. Grievances were shared, and problems and misunderstandings discussed.

According to Warwick Olson, 'the group met in an attitude of prayer and openness and what resulted was the emergence of a more unified and powerful ministry partnership'.

Back in Uganda that September 1983, the House of Bishops met to choose a new Archbishop. Festo's name was on the lips of many. His work for the Ugandan Church had been outstanding and in many ways his stature was already that of the Archbishop, but he himself was non-committal on the subject. Part of him felt attracted to the opportunities the job would open up in renewing and rebuilding the church in Uganda; but if he was chosen, how could he continue such a heavy overseas ministry? It would be impossible.

In the event, the Bishop of Tororo, Dr Yona Okoth, was elected—the fifth Archbishop since Uganda's independence. It was not altogether a happy election, as many suspected there was some 'party politics' going on behind the scenes. In any event, Bishop Festo knew now that that particular door was not for him. He took it as a sign from God that his present ministry was the one he was to stick with, and plunged back into his AEE speaking engagements and diocesan work—which that autumn focused on yet further efforts to help the Banyarwanda, and to press ahead with the ordination of women.

Both met considerable opposition. As for the Banyarwanda, by now the charity of even the devout people of Kigezi diocese was strained, and some of the clergy later admitted to feeling: 'Why is the bishop doing this? These people are not his responsibility. They are simply going to die—all of them.' Criticism of Bishop Festo was rife among the business community of Kabale, for, by supporting the Banyarwanda, many felt he was taking action against the Banyankole, and also opposing what the Government was doing. Many in the diocese of East Ankole, where the trouble had begun, agreed. Festo paid no attention, and continued to press for the government to improve things.

Neither was Bishop Festo popular with the powers that be in the Church of Uganda that autumn. They objected to his plan to go ahead and ordain three women to the priesthood that December. Festo replied tartly that it was a bit late in the day. In a letter to Archbishop Silvanus Wani (who was still in office) that October he protested:

> In vain I have been waiting to hear from my fellow Bishops who said they were going to take up the issue with their synods. I feel the delay is unfair on my lady deacons and no reason whatever has been given to me to stop this next step. My synod is fully in agreement with priesting those lady deacons who deserve to be priested ...

So—he warned the diocesan bishops by letter that he would go ahead that December, flew to the States for several AEE missions in churches throughout America, and on his return, ordained on 11th December, 1983 three of his lady deacons to the priesthood—the first Anglican bishop in Africa ever to do so. The women, Margaret Byekwatso, Grace Ndyabahika and Deborah Micungwe had never once campaigned, or even asked, to become priests, although now they were, they shed tears of joy with their families and diocesan friends. In fact, the whole

Festo visiting a village in the 1970s.

Festo preaching at a refugee camp. Circa 1983.

diocese exulted at the packed service—over 9,000 turned out. The diocesan bishops elsewhere grumbled. Bishop Festo and Mera happily prepared for a family Christmas in Kabale.

Though it was not Bishop Festo who was consecrated Archbishop of Uganda-Rwanda, Burundi and Boga-Zaire on 29th January, 1984, one would have been hard-pressed by then to name any other Ugandan—or even African—Christian leader whose ministry was as internationally well-known as that of Bishop Festo.

By this time, whenever the Archbishop of Canterbury, Dr Robert Runcie, ran into Ugandan clergy, he 'always asked first about the Archbishop, and then about Festo. For me he embodied all that the Anglican Communion gets so richly "From Uganda with Love".' Runcie had decided that the 'common gossip' that Festo was *always* out of the country had been 'exaggerated'. 'There is no doubt that there were many calls on him, but when he was there he was a fine bishop, not only for his people but for the fellowship of bishops.'

As for Bishop Festo's activist nature, Dr Runcie concluded:

> ... he was relaxed about structures and probably did not spend a lot of his time reading the minutes of the Anglican Consultative Council and all the paper that landed on his desk from central authorities in London; but this should not be held as a judgement upon his ministry!

One Australian newspaper that spring summed it up well: 'Bishop Festo Kivengere is a genuinely charismatic personality ... People everywhere love the Ugandan bishop. When he exhorts them to action, as he invariably does, they want to co-operate ...' (Except, perhaps, Ugandan politicians!)

The impact he made was well illustrated that spring when he joined forces with other leading AEE team members including James Katarikawe, now the Ugandan team leader, for a month's tour of Australia (including Melbourne, Sydney, Perth, Wagga and Canberra) and a five day 'whistle stop' tour of New Zealand (from Wellington to Auckland).

Up to a month before he even arrived, newspapers in both countries were giving him many column inches. Their interest had been caught by the extensive support Australian Christians had given Bishop Festo in rebuilding the country through AEE, and then when they learned this bishop wanted reconciliation with the men who had so wronged Uganda, they were fascinated.

Bishop Festo and AEE team visited a bewildering variety of churches, halls, schools, rallies, rotary clubs and women's groups. When he told them that not only was reconciliation the only hope for Uganda, reconciliation was indeed necessary for everyone, he had touched an issue that was real to all of them, as most people live lives at odds with themselves, with God, and with others. The mission was called 'From Africa with Love', but Bishop Festo soon made it clear that if love brought reconciliation, it brought other things too: including a social conscience. Love was never a passive thing to Festo: it was active, seeking out the good of the loved one. And any lasting peace, he believed passionately, must also be based on justice. If Christians really loved their fellow men, they could not be content to let the innocent suffer. Hence the Bishop's involvement with Uganda's politicians: as he told newspaper after newspaper in Australia and New Zealand that March.

> I don't see how you can be a Christian and not be involved, though not necessarily by being a politician.
>
> From the angle of Christian faith, politics has gone wrong. It's selfish and oppressive. We need to challenge politicians from the standard of their responsibilities. I go to politicians as a minister and a Christian.

But Bishop Festo went on to stress that he believed it was very dangerous for 'the Church to organise itself politically to change powers. I don't see that in the New Testament. Indeed, the Lord refused to act that way, and said it wasn't how to do things.'

Certainly party politics never entered into it. He made this very clear when on his return to Uganda in March he found his clergy restless, and sent them a memo concerning the forthcoming elections promised by Obote the following year (1985).

'Political campaigning is not wrong. Christians are citizens of this country, and to be involved in politics is not a sin.'

Nevertheless,

Political campaigning must never be mixed with the church services because that is like trying to drink water mixed with soil. Even if the soil is very good, it is out of place when you put it in a glass of water. By separating political campaigning from church services, we are respecting the place of politics and the place of spiritual ministry.

For Bishop Festo was adamant that:

the church is where all Christians of different persuasions can meet on common ground. If we introduce party politics in the church, the church will be divided. 2 Corinthians 5:18, 19 says he gave us the ministry of 'reconciliation'. There is no campaigning there.

Within days of writing the letter, a tragedy occurred in Kabale when a bored soldier went on a senseless shooting spree and shot a pastor's son dead, and then shot off the right arm of Alice, a local nurse and devout Christian. Bishop Festo, who knew the families well, was appalled, and wrote to some friends in the USA, 'It was a dark day for this little town.'

But he added: 'But let me tell you the brighter side of it.' Alice, when he had visited her in hospital, opened her eyes and said, 'Bishop, I recognise you. The soldier has shot off my arm but he has not shot off my Lord.'

'I tell you, those words from a beautiful twenty-four-year-old girl who had had that horrible experience ... made me feel as if my Christianity was too superficial ...' For him, it was to be an outstanding example of the kind of love which could bring about the reconciliation of the country for which he daily prayed.

He then plunged in with his outspoken protests to Obote about it. As a friend once said, 'While Festo rarely lost his temper, he was not one to bottle up his feelings, and was certainly not afraid of showing anger when he felt it!'

So Festo wrote to Obote indignantly: 'My own so-called peaceful Kabale ... these people are innocent citizens!'

As for the Banyarwanda, 'It seems nothing has been done to alleviate suffering ... I can find no words to express my feelings ... , I admit, your Excellency, these are not comfortable things to bring to your notice. However, I consider it my duty ...'

The rest of the spring and summer took Bishop Festo and

various AEE team members on missions, conventions and conferences from the United States to Zimbabwe, to Egypt, to Europe, back to Uganda, then back to Zimbabwe. Canon James Katarikawe, a close friend, and leading AEE evangelist, was 'always amazed' at how quickly Bishop Festo got over jet lag. 'We would land at the airport, and he could go straight into town and preach without seeming tired.'

'He was good at relaxing, he could do so almost anywhere. Travel didn't unsettle him, or he'd have collapsed!'

But despite Bishop Festo's hectic schedule, the stranded Banyarwanda refugees still haunted him, and that autumn he again visited the camps, and took up the matter again with Obote:

> I seriously took your challenge on the language I used in my May letter which you called 'undiplomatic' for a Bishop to write. Let me take this chance to say that if I found any exaggerated statement I would not hesitate to repent and come to you and apologise. However, re-reading my letter I find it was a letter searching for words to express the tragedy of the loss of human life. That experience is not diplomatic in any way, your Excellency ...
>
> Maybe there is a difference in seeing the situation, for on your part you see situations from a political stand-point. On my part, on the other hand, I see situations from a pastoral stand-point. My expressions were out of deep pain ... Even my Lord Jesus who was patient, loving, far from being emotional, whenever he faced situations of that nature, he burst into expressions of which the New Testament is full.
>
> I hope I will have no occasion to write more letters of this kind as your Excellency is taking drastic measures to put the law above the gun ...

The reason behind Bishop Festo's concern, which was actually very dangerous for him to express openly, lay with his prayer life. As he once explained it:

> Prayer does not start with you, it is God concerned with his world ... He is the one urging you ... You will find yourself alongside Jesus in a garden of Gethsemane saying: 'My soul is very sorrowful, even to death', or 'My heart has been invaded with a kind of sorrow which is about to crush me' (Matthew 26: 38). It is only when men and women are crushed in love that they can be partners in the redeeming of the world.

Only bleeding hearts can heal bleeding wounds. In prayer you put your hand in the hand of the sufferer, and you share some of his suffering ... If you want comfort, you had better be afraid of prayer, because it is going to shock you into the place where the world is. It is going to open your mind, sensitise your personality, and widen your horizons.

Experiencing their suffering, you can whisper a prayer to the throne of grace and that prayer will not be only your prayer, it is the Holy Spirit praying through you for them. He never leaves the desperate to go through it alone.

But it wasn't just the government with whom Bishop Festo was at odds as 1984 drew to a close: an incident within the Church of Uganda had occurred which also made him angry: the Church's national newspaper, the *New Century*, had published a letter mildly critical of the Archbishop's enthronement, saying the security had been so tight and fierce (with savage police dogs) that many Christians could not even get there. For this, the provincial standing committee of the Church of Uganda, of which Okoth, the Archbishop, was Chairman, had forced the entire board and editor to resign, and had shut down the newspaper.

On New Year's Eve Bishop Festo sat down and dictated to Judith another one of his protest letters, this time sending a copy to the Archbishop, the board, the editor, all members of the provincial standing committee and the entire house of bishops in Uganda.

Addressing the letter to Okoth, he called the closure of the paper 'a blatant disregard of freedom of expression and press by our church', going on to insist that Christians have every right to criticise the leadership of their church, and to point out malpractice in church services as in anything else. The incident was 'shocking', the paper had been 'rudely throttled', and the low profile of Okoth and the bishops was a 'guilty silence'.

As the old year 1984 petered out, Bishop Festo knew there was hardly a government or church leader in Uganda with whom he was popular. But he was at peace with his conscience. If the leaders of the Church of Uganda shut down their own paper at the first hint of any public criticism, the vast majority of bishops in their turn seemed to be just as squeamish over publicly questioning any of Obote's actions, even though the economy was wildly out of control (the cost of living had recently risen by 400 per cent) and the army's mass killings and brutalities continued. Some people suspected several of the bishops owed their appointments to subtle party politics and were therefore, to some extent, Obote's men. Or they may have been—quite understandably—simply afraid. Whatever the reason, it seemed a curious silence to the group of leading churchmen from America and Europe which arrived in February 1985 for a Partners in Mission Consultation. The PIM 'external partners', as they were called, were headed by the American Episcopalian Bishop, Bishop C. Shannon Mallory, of El Camino Real diocese in California. He discussed with the bishops 'their priorities and needs, including everything from the physical amenities needed for even simple subsistence living to the spiritual fabric of the church and how to renew and reinvigorate that; missions leadership training, etc'. But again and again, Mallory recalls, the 'external partners' 'pressed for some significant mention of the human rights violations going on all around us at the time'.

> Indeed, if there were going to be a report about the life and priorities of the people of the Church of Uganda, we did not see how that could be complete without at least mentioning the terrible political and social hardship the people of Uganda were having to experience.
> ... Our dear Festo was a fiery prophet in the midst of that debate: calling passionately on the one hand for the spiritual renewal and reconciliation of the Church of Uganda, and at the same time boldly standing up (almost alone, it seemed) to speak out and condemn the political and military tyranny that was still going on in the country.
> We were so wonderfully encouraged and impressed by his leadership, which came down solidly on both aspects of life: the spiritual and the social/physical...

Of course, it was nothing new, for by now Festo

was famous for this kind of prophetic witness in his own home country. Nevertheless, it did come as a light in the midst of the darkness—Festo standing out as perhaps the most articulate and fiery witness of all of the leadership of the Church of Uganda, fearlessly denouncing evil, and yet doing it with such a gracious and caring manner about him—as we say, 'hating the sin but loving the sinner'.

The 'partners' went home, and in early March Archbishop Okoth paid an archepiscopal visit to Kabale. The day he arrived the story of Festo's letter of protest over the newspaper closing had been leaked to the national press of Uganda, who ran it as front page lead: it made for a rather formal and strained visit, though the political situation was by now deteriorating so rapidly that both men were far more concerned about that.

Despite the impending crisis, Bishop Festo felt obliged to leave the country for a few days in late March in order to join forces with Michael Cassidy to lead a major inter-church mission in Monrovia, Liberia. He and Michael and their teams had been invited to this key West African city by the Archbishop of the province, George Brown, and by the Bishop of Monrovia, Augustus ('Gus' to his friends) Marwieh. Despite a fair share of hiccups in the form of frequent power cuts, AEE team illness (Michael had suspected malaria) and chronic petrol shortage (making transport around the city a challenge), the team fanned out and in less than two weeks preached at a total of 400 meetings—including ones at the Presidential Mansion, Ministry of Justice, Ministry of Foreign Affairs, and the Military Barracks.

When thousands turned up for the rallies, and every church was packed, it seemed to earn one journalist's verdict as 'one of the most significant campaigns in AEE urban evangelism'. But, as usual, Bishop Festo and Michael Cassidy did not glory in their success. Both thanked God for the support of the Liberian women, who had prayed for the mission for months, and the goodwill of the churches throughout the city.

Bishop Festo preached to 10,000 at the closing rally at Antoinette Tubman Stadium, and once again, the attention he commanded could not be accounted for just by the simple words he used: 'There is no catastrophe on the cross. There is only salvation and healing. Liberia can be saved, Uganda can be saved, Amin can be saved, and you can be saved!' It was the spiritual authority that lay behind the words. The turmoils and upheavals had only made it grow with the years, his faith more certain than ever.

April took Bishop Festo on to yet more missions and speaking engagements in Germany, the UK and then the United States. In the UK he was back among old friends, including Michael

Green, then Rector of St Aldates, Oxford, and Richard Bewes, Rector of All Souls' Langham Place. Bewes invited him to speak to his evening service, where Bishop Festo told hundreds of students the latest sad news of Uganda, adding 'Africa is one big refugee camp.' The arresting little picture that it conjured up was vintage Festo. After the service, Bewes enquired 'Where do you get those luminous little phrases from?' Festo didn't know, but 'Sometimes I have something to say, and I ask myself, how am I going to say that in a way which will help people listen? Other times it just slips out.' He went on to preach at St Paul's Cathedral, Colchester Cathedral, Malmesbury Abbey, and more.

But what he had to say, as always, ranged far and wide and by no means concentrated on Uganda. For example, as it was now just after Easter, he chose the theme 'The Risen Lord in the midst of his people'—'. . . the really problematic people after the Resurrection were the very people who followed Jesus so closely—not the unbelieving Jews.' Doubt and fear were the key problems . . . the problem was therefore the church, the leaders, and not the ordinary people of the day. Today this was also true—it was the leaders of the church who often seemed to doubt the historical truth of the resurrection. Nevertheless, his remedy against theological liberalism was not to be judgemental but to emulate Jesus: 'How many times have we been patient with those weak ones who stumble and seem to be totally or partially unreliable?'

Soon it was on to California, where in addition to meetings in churches at Granda Hills, La Canada, Walnut Creek and the Bay Area, there was even a banquet laid on for him and AEE supporters in Pasadena. Such times of fellowship with old friends refreshed Festo, which was a good thing, for when he returned to Uganda in May, it was to a country at civil war. Museveni's National Resistance Movement was challenging Obote's Uganda National Liberation Army.

While he had no hesitation that the church should remind politicians of their moral responsibilities, Bishop Festo by early June was setting out clear guidelines for his clergy:

> I am by this letter reminding you all, and directing you all, to observe the following:
> 1 No church worker . . . in the Diocese of Kigezi is permitted to

participate actively in party politics, that is being an active member of a party, or working to promote a party member who is running for election, or using his church position to promote a particular party.

2 Any church worker who wants to be involved in politics should write to me resigning from his work, then he can freely engage in politics.

3 Party position should not be dragged into church positions, for instance the election of church wardens.

4 I will take very drastic action if I discover any church worker who is involved in politics as above.

Bishop Festo and Mera then joined the diocesan staff in trying to prepare for that summer's major event, the Kabale Golden Jubilee Convention, celebrating fifty years of revival, from when it first arrived in Kabale in 1935. Up to 30,000 people were expected, including guests from all round the world who had been touched by the East African revival. Local women had large gardens of peas, potatoes and other vegetables well under way in preparation of such a hoard of hungry mouths. Bishop Festo ordered some special drums and then made a special trip to East Ankole to ask for food. 'I will not leave until they have given twenty cows!' he joked as he set off—he came back with the good news that 'they have promised one hundred cows'! More in his line than cows and drums, he then joined in a mission to Kabale that was being held in preparation for the convention, preaching at the concluding rally of 4,000.

By late June he was in Kampala where he helped a close friend, the Bishop of Namirembe, Bishop Misaeri Kauma, and another leading evangelist, Yokana Mukasa, to launch the Greater Kampala Mission—a year long outreach to the capital on the part of all the churches in Kampala, including Pentecostalists and Catholics. The mission was partly to celebrate the 100th anniversary of Hannington's martyrdom, but mainly because everyone knew Kampala desperately needed spiritual direction.

A few days later Bishop Festo was off to Rwanda, where a big ministers' conference was being held in Butare, the university town, that July. Unfortunately, here again, all was not well: the Bishop of Butare was feuding with the Bishop of Kigali, to such an extent that their animosity was 'invading the spirit of the meeting' according to a missionary present at the time. The Methodist bishop in charge was thinking of going to try and deal with it, but after much prayer, Festo said quietly, 'No, they are in *my* church, I shall go to them.'

It was a great additional burden. While the team prayed, Festo talked far into the night with the two men on several occasions—all the time serving as the main speaker at the conference, and preaching in Kinyrwanda, a language he had not used for some time. When finally the two men were publicly united with each other on the last day of the conference, 'the place exploded in cheers and praise and glorious songs. Many, many people came forward for salvation after Festo's message that day!'

Then as July wore on, Bishop Festo headed for yet more missions, this time in Ethiopia and Malawi. By the end of the month he was in Mwanza, Tanzania, where he preached with Bishop Gresford Chitemo of Morogoro (in Tanzania); Bishop Ezekiel Birech, of the Africa Inland Church of Kenya, and Bishop-elect Matt Nyagwaswa. The mission attracted crowds of 30,000—and nowhere smaller than the vast CCM National Stadium at Kirumba would accommodate them. The highlight of the mission was planned to be the consecration and instalment of Nyagwaswa as the first Bishop of the Africa Inland Church in Tanzania, but for Bishop Festo other events would stand out even more. He tuned into the BBC World Service early on 27th July and found Uganda again in the headlines: there had been another military coup—a section of the army had joined rebels fighting the government and as they advanced on the capital, Obote fled the country. There was a short period of confused military rule and then in early 1986 Yoweri Museveni became President.

So disillusioned had Bishop Festo now become with Milton Obote that he could only greet this second ousting as good news. Museveni, after all, was light years away from being an Amin.

The next day, Bishop Festo flew home, via Kigali in Rwanda, as the road to Kampala was cut off by the Museveni's National Resistance Army (NRA). At least Obote's men could not get through, but then neither could anybody else. The Kabale Golden Jubilee Convention was cancelled at once.

Bishop Festo sat down to write out 'My assessment of the situation in Uganda after the coup d'etat.' He was the only Christian leader in the country attempting to help people understand and assess the rapid chain of events from a Christian perspective. His paper was widely circulated, and helped many hundreds of pastors and church people beyond his own diocese to make up their minds about Museveni. Because of his vital involvement as a non-political bishop in the politics of Uganda, it is worthwhile quoting the paper in depth—it was the nearest Bishop Festo ever came to setting out a Christian political philosophy. He wrote as 'a non-political observer' filled with 'concern'. He blamed the present troubles on past failure in 1979 'when many factions failed to get a unifying base for the political future of Uganda'. It was 'unfortunate' that people had assumed that if Amin went, 'his removal would bring a quick restoration of law and order, political freedom, social rehabilitation and a reliable government'.

Bishop Festo went on: 'While these are wonderful prospects, they just don't come from the air. There has to be a firmly established base and it wasn't there.'

And so in the meantime it was inevitable that 'political opportunism' took priority, which in turn 'inevitably' led to an increase in tribalism and regionalism.

Such a swing, Bishop Festo pointed out, brought 'consequences'—human rights and justice were disregarded, and corruption was widespread. 'There has been a superficial tendency to regard these external evils as if they were the cause of themselves, but they have fundamental causes.'

While Bishop Festo applauded the main reasons given by Museveni and his men who had led the coup—the restoration of peace to the country, the removal of tribalism as a base for government, and the establishment of a broad-based representative government, 'yet they cannot happen in a vacuum'.

Peace, said the Bishop, could not be established on 'a shaky foundation'—it must have first 'truth and justice'. Tribalism was 'a demonstration of insecurity' and to fight it there needed to be 'a credible security force for all citizens' under which they could be 'encouraged to work together as citizens of Uganda'.

Finally, Bishop Festo certainly agreed in principle with the 'repeated declarations of the need for "a Broad Based Government"', but in order ever to achieve it, 'power will have to be brought under the control of justice'.

And, 'Whatever government comes out to put the broken pieces together must be free of the threat of the gun and the gun must be under its control.'

Autumn came. After a hasty visit to AEE Nairobi to discuss with the wider AEE executive how the new government would affect the AEE ministry and relief work, Bishop Festo rushed back to his diocese for a three-week confirmation safari that would last nearly all of September. October too he spent mainly within the diocese, which was now being acutely hit by the shortages caused by the war: no petrol, paraffin, diesel, flour... The twenty-third anniversary of independence was on 9th October. Understandably, there were muted celebrations. Two days later the NRA swept into Kabale and cleared out the bank, so desperate were they for cash. On 29th October the church recalled the first martyrdoms 100 years before—but again, most celebrations were local.

Bishop Festo was on the road again in November: to Kenya, then to Dar es Salaam to lead a city wide mission with the AEE team. Then he headed north, to the UK, where among other meetings he was guest speaker at the Ruanda Missionary Conference. He chose a theme from what had become a great favourite of his, the prophet Nehemiah: 'Let us arise and build!' For his faith that this could be done was undiminished. 'One was always conscious that the Holy Spirit was speaking through him,' a missionary at the conference recalls.

By December Bishop Festo was back in Kabale for the ordination retreats and ordinations. On 17th December came news that Museveni had signed the peace agreement with other African countries. Just before Christmas, Bishop Festo and others from St Peter's visited the slums of Kabale to take clothes and presents to the children there. He had already founded a parish there, and even given the district a little school of its own..

'The harlots and drunks followed him about, wanting to be near him,' said a fellow clergyman, deeply touched.

Some of the Kivengere girls were able to come to Kabale for Christmas, but Bishop Festo did not enjoy the family reunion as thoroughly as he had expected: unusually for him, he was not feeling well. Colleagues had lately been astonished by flashes of irritability and even 'disturbing tirades' so totally out of character to him. They had put it down to stress and fatigue. But he had nagging headaches, and felt a bit below par. He too put it down to fatigue, and ignored the discomfort, not saying a word.

CHAPTER TWENTY-TWO

AN ELDER OF GOD'S PEOPLE
1986–1988

Museveni takes over Uganda; John Wilson shot; Bishop Festo falls ill.

JANUARY 1986, and Uganda was about to have yet another President. That month Museveni's National Resistance Army overthew the military government (UNLA). By the 25th he had officially taken control of the country. On the 29th he was sworn in as President.

Bishop Festo had long admired what Museveni was trying to do for the country, and that winter had come to believe that if anyone could save Uganda, perhaps Museveni could. Many Westerners agreed. As a senior English missionary, who had had long talks with Museveni, put it: 'Museveni is a deep thinking man, completely committed to "human rights", a Christian man who cares for his soldiers and for the simple people.'

Bishop Festo and the other senior Christians especially liked the fact that Museveni dressed in a simple private's uniform with the sleeves rolled up, and gave himself 'no fancy handles'— just plain *Mr* Museveni. Also, though it amazed people, 'he promised *nothing,* the first man to promise nothing!' But the people supported him all the same—they were 'now tired of cheering and dying, and so perhaps for the first time are listening, not to words but to actions'.

As he wrote to Billy Graham that spring:

We now have ... one country, under one government, with one President, and the war of guns is over, but there are tough wars to be won. The economy is still shattered, services are still broken, values are still twisted—the gospel is desperately needed in all this, but Mr Museveni with the support of the masses of Uganda, with one disciplined army, with a team of committed Ugandans to work with, is determined to bring about a creative change. Pray for him...

Bishop Festo's support for Museveni was based entirely on the fact that in him the Bishop believed Uganda at last had a leader with the good of the people and the country at heart. It was not that Kivengere decided to indulge in party politics, it was more that at such a desperate point in Uganda's history, he believed that here was at last a leader whose general aims the church could applaud.

So in late January, he once again wrote to all his clergy, urging them to support the National Resistance Movement. He believed this to be 'our responsibility as Christians in helping the movement for positive change in our country'.

He went on to stress that the clergy should certainly *not* 'stand back like spectators watching others actively engaged in bringing about the change we are looking for'. or 'jump to points of advantage in the movement in order to gain political power'.

Instead he urged his clergy 'to be actively involved in the "movement for positive change" in order to overcome the negative elements and attitudes'.

In their local communities, he urged, 'bring positive proposals for forming unsectarian, unfactional grass root village committees, the membership of which should not be based on religious affiliations or partisan background...' Further, their markets should not aim to exploit anyone; they should encourage 'positive trading which builds the wealth of the citizens...'. And socially, 'We must see people positively as our fellow human beings... Let us give each other another chance...' Politics, said Bishop Festo 'was made by man for man... Therefore ... let politics be the servant of the people—to unite them, protect their welfare...'

The National Resistance Movement, he concluded,

is not a political party; it is not the Democratic Party, not a Uganda People's Congress, nor UPM or CP. It is a movement of all the people who are working for a positive, creative change in Uganda. Join in the movement and contribute positively for a future with a hope for all of us and our children.

As a Christian servant of our Lord, I am not ashamed to make a contribution in the movement for a positive change to our wonderful country.

Bishop Festo's support for the NRM became widely known. Such was his influence that his words made headlines in the national newspapers, and several bishops and leaders of other denominations openly congratulated Museveni and pledged their support for what he was trying to achieve. It helped a little towards calming and stabilising the country. Ugandans were by now very weary of all governments.

Despite the fact that Uganda's troubles still threatened to be all-consuming, Bishop Festo's belief that faith should move men to social action also showed in the preparatory work he was doing for the forthcoming Lambeth Conference in 1988. Dr Runcie had invited Bishop Festo to be chairman of one of the four study sections of the conference, the one on Mission and Ministry, with the Rt Rev. David Sheppard, Bishop of Liverpool, as his vice-chairman. (Dr Runcie was 'delighted' that 'we had such a powerful team'.)

The two men had worked closely in drawing up a sheet of questions to send to all the bishops of the worldwide Anglican Communion as part of the preparatory process of responding to the Archbishop of Canterbury's invitation to 'bring our diocese with us to Lambeth'.

Bishop Sheppard recalls that two of the questions were 'very important' to Bishop Festo. One of these, which bore Bishop Festo's wording, was 'How can the experiences of renewal be turned outwards in service to the community rather than inward in sentimentality?' Bishop Sheppard later recalled:

> It was very important for him that great new experiences of Christ and his Holy Spirit should turn people outwards to serve God and people in the life of the world. He was very concerned at the amount of corruption in public life in Uganda. He told me that eighty per cent of the people of Uganda belong to the Anglican and Roman Catholic Churches, and was disappointed that so few took their faith into the places where decisions are made.

Bishop Festo also longed for a close co-operation between the bishops of the two churches in Uganda which could give them authority and strength in dealing with representatives of the State.

Another question which Bishop Festo contributed to the paper was to do with the 'ministry of the few and the ministry of the many'. Bishop Sheppard explained:

> It was very important to him that the 'ministry of the few'—those ordained as clergy and to other particular tasks—should not take away the proper ministry and calling of lay Christians. The great and important calling to be a priest was *not* for the few to take over all the tasks, but to enable and equip lay people to bear their proper ministry both in their daily life in the world and in the life of the Church.

When a video was made for circulation throughout the Anglican Communion to stir up prayer and reflection, Dr Runcie found Bishop Festo's contribution 'outstanding'. (Unfortunately, due to illness, Bishop Festo would soon resign his chairmanship of the Mission and Ministry section.)

By March Uganda was considered stable enough for the Greater Kampala Mission to be resumed, and Bishop Festo drove up to preach with John Wilson for a large rally at the City Square. For ever after he would be glad that he had done so. As he wrote to Billy Graham only a few weeks later:

> John was so full of the vision of preaching the gospel, and when I stood with him on the 9th of this month and proclaimed Jesus Christ and saw more than 120 people come to accept him it was a great joy. Little did I know..

Little did he know that six days later John, in front of his wife and father-in-law, would be dragged from his car on the streets of Kampala and shot by rampaging soldiers.

Festo was in Kabale when the news came through. He had worked with John for nearly fifteen years, and they were close friends. He was 'absolutely shattered', and wept for a friend destroyed in yet more senseless violence. The tragic news shocked friends and colleagues around the world. At the funeral at Namirembe Cathedral on 22nd March, Festo and Michael Cassidy both preached, Festo groping for words to express his grief: 'John was very close to me, to the extent that I feel a little bit lost,' he began. 'My expression of what I feel could be in the words of David for Jonathan: "I am distressed for you, my brother Jonathan ... your love to me was wonderful" (2 Samuel 1:26).' He paused and then: 'That is enough.'

But he went on to say that John's death was in reality 'a crossing over from death into life'. And he quoted his dear former friend and colleague, William Nagenda, who explained Christian death thus: 'When Satan gets angry with us he knocks us and we bounce on the ground like a tennis ball. When he gets more angry, he bounces us for the last time, but we bounce to heaven, and he doesn't see us again.'

'Heaven. I am longing to join him there,' continued Bishop Festo. 'One of these days in a car or through sickness, I will cross over and shake his hand. Of course they don't greet in heaven, but never mind, they praise God!'

He added later in his letter to Billy Graham, 'Pray for us of AEE as we try to fill the gap...'

Meanwhile, he did not know just how close he was to having his own longing to 'join John' answered. For his headaches, general malaise and flashes of bad temper had continued. When he got to the United States that April he went to a doctor for a full medical. But the doctor gave him a clean bill of health. Puzzled, but reassured, Festo and Mera flew on to Nairobi. But coming off the plane his feet just wouldn't negotiate the steps. He stumbled several times, and nearly fell down the staircase. Mera, deeply concerned, carted him straight off to a doctor in Nairobi. The doctor was also concerned, but did not have the equipment he needed to do a brain scan. So that same night he put Festo and Mera back on a plane, this time for London. He was taken to the Italian Hospital in London and tests began. By now his leg and arm were numb, and the paralysis was spreading.

Though AEE kept news of the Kivengeres' visit to London very quiet (not wanting to discourage too many guests), the news reached the keen ear of Terry Waite, then the Archbishop's envoy, stationed at Lambeth Palace. Dr Runcie recalls:

> Terry told me that the Bishop had been stricken with what seemed like a serious stroke. The news sounded bad... We decided immediately to go round to see him.
> I can remember we couldn't understand why he should be in the

Italian Hospital and Terry was already laughing away at the idea of
Festo falling into the hands of nuns of the Roman Catholic Church!
But they received us so warmly and we were shown into Festo's
room.

He was astonished and a broad grin immediately spread over his
face at the thought that we were so up-to-date that we had tracked
him down. Although he was still in part paralysed, he was so steady
and pleased to see us that this overtook all other emotions and I have
seldom met a man in that position who was so little eager to talk all
the time about himself. Though he did speak with faith and courage
of the operation which was awaiting him, his thoughts were very
much with his wife and his diocese. We prayed together and we
left—as others have often said—feeling that he had done far more
for us than we had done for him ... His spirits were never down.

On 19th May Festo was operated on for the removal of a
tumour at the base of his brain. 'The whole diocese was praying
for him!' recalls a clergyman and old friend, Stanley Kashillinga.
'We asked for a complete healing because we desperately needed
him back!' Friends around the world also prayed.

The operation was a success and within a week Festo and
Mera were in a nearby hotel for convalescence. But soon it was
apparent that Festo was not making the expected recovery.
Indeed, he grew weaker, and weaker. To Mera's alarm he was
barely able to make himself heard even when she put her ear to
his lips. Peace, in London from Geneva, rang him at the hotel.
'Hello Dad, how are you?' His response terrified her.

'Very, very faintly I heard him whisper "I'm fine."'

'I thought: "My God, he is dying!"and said, "I'll call back
later when Mum is there." I put down the phone and burst into
tears.'

Festo was within days of death with all the symptoms of an
advanced case of Parkinson's Disease, when the problem was
finally diagnosed: he had been given several medicines, and two
of them were violently reacting against each other. Once this
was remedied, improvement was rapid. When Peace again
visited him and Mera three weeks later, he was strolling about
on the grass outside the hotel. 'Oh praise the Lord, he's *much*
better now,' Mera told the many wellwishers who rang daily.

By the end of July, Festo was well enough to return to Kabale
with Mera, in time for the second attempt to hold the Kabale

Golden Jubilee Convention. But not to preach: that was strictly against doctor's orders.

The thought of Bishop Festo not preaching at a major convention brought home to the folk of the diocese just *how* ill he'd been. 'He must have been half-dead not to preach!' was the widely held opinion.

But he was very much alive, and furthermore, content. As he had already shared with friends in Nairobi, he believed he had learned something from God during his time in hospital, when he lay weak and helpless—a condition unheard of for him. He said:

> God gave me Psalm 131: 'O Lord, I am not proud or haughty. I don't think of myself better than others. I don't pretend to know it all. I am quiet now before the Lord, just as a child who is weaned from the breast. Yes, my begging has been stilled. O Israel, you too should quietly trust in the Lord—now and always.'

So for ten days while thousands gathered at the convention site, and the revival hymn *'Tukutendereza Jesu'* echoed throughout Kabale, Bishop Festo stayed quietly at home, resting, and welcoming the few visitors that were allowed to see him. He also gave a short welcome to the convention—slowly following Mera up on to the platform with the help of a walking stick.

Though he said, 'Praise God that we are here,' he also reminded them that, 'We have not come here to celebrate fifty years but to meet the living God!'

Bishop Festo also managed to attend the closing meeting of 20,000, when he took the salute of the Boys' Brigade (of which he was national president). There were so many people that one girl described it: 'No grass was showing—everywhere was people to people!' And they all cheered Bishop Festo: 'What a joy it was for everyone to see him again alive!'

Shortly after the convention, the Kivengeres left for a time of further convalescence in Nairobi. Prayers and good wishes followed them. As one prayer request charmingly put it: 'That God may speed up a full recovery of the Bishop and give him his usual strength to run around the world with the message of hope.'

Bishop Festo was resting in Nairobi about mid-September when the BBC World Service broadcast the news that Colonel Gaddafi, the Libyan Head of State, was paying a visit to Uganda. While there, he not only made very critical remarks about other countries, but used the occasion to try and stir up the Muslim community against the Church of Uganda, which he labelled as nothing more than 'a tool of colonialism'.

Bishop Festo again sat down with pen and paper to take up battle. In a press release entitled 'My reaction to the remarks of the Libyan Head of State when he visited my country', he condemned Gadaffi's statement and went on:

> Instead of encouraging the Muslim community to contribute positively to the construction of Uganda, he encouraged them to convert the non-Muslim into Islam, which is the normal attitude of any religious preacher in any place, but *not* the duty of a Head of State...

He went on to repudiate Gaddafi's statement that the church in Africa was a colonising community and that Christianity was not the true African faith; and added: 'The missionaries who brought Islam in Africa came with the Koran in one hand and a chain for binding slaves in the other.'

But

> if we dwell on digging up the bones of bad things in history the possibility of living in this world together will be nil. We in Uganda had our religious wars in the last century, we do not want any more of those wars here... Moslems and Christians in Uganda, having learnt their lesson now live together in peace.
>
> I see Moslems in my church listening to the message of God's love. And when I am asked by Moslems to address them I do not hesitate to do so. This does not mean that I want them all converted when I speak to them; but when they are convinced that it is God's message and they convert, they are free to use their choice without pressure. For instance, if a Christian becomes a Muslim we respect his decision and we do not follow him to kill him, for to us Christians killing a person because of his conviction is completely opposite to our faith. In fact any killing for us Christians is a curse and we do not believe in it.

His press release once again filled a yawning gap: no other church leader had said a word in protest. *The Telecast*, a

Kampala daily newspaper, lined up photographs of Kivengere and Gaddafi on the front page and, with no more than an introductory paragraph, ran the whole press release in full. *The Star*, Kampala's other newspaper, ran it as their lead story as well.

* * *

By October, Bishop Festo was improving rapidly. Peace was delighted to find him 'filling out, his face fresh'—though as absent minded as ever—losing his raincoat, pens, etc. She also found stacks of letters in his briefcase he had forgotten to post. 'How he managed to get around the world on his own was a mystery to me!' But manage he did, and on a brief trip to the States that month, told friends 'I had sensed in my heart that I was not going to die... I sensed the Lord still wanted me around. I do not know why, and for how long, but that is not my problem!'

He was eager to resume his preaching, and one of his very first engagements was late that month in Oslo, Norway, accompanied by Sigmund Aske, a Norwegian and AEE Board member. He was to preach at a large campaign rally on 'The Bible Open to All' arranged by the Bible Society in Norway, and held at Oslo's large Municipal Hall.

Aske recalls, 'We arrived in Oslo the day before and he was a bit nervous. It was the only time I ever saw Festo not sure of himself, but he was concerned that his health might not be up to it.' Things got further complicated when Festo and Aske climbed up on the platform to find two microphones, but no podium to lean the Bible and sermon notes on. So Festo put his papers down on the floor, stood up, took a deep breath, and plunged into his sermon. Aske, translating, soon realised this was not the sermon he knew Festo had prepared. 'He simply got his inspiration from the vast audience, and was speaking from his heart.' Soon Bishop Festo realised his strength *was* up to the challenge, and he became inspired. Aske began to struggle to keep up, when another fear hit him: he realised Bishop Festo had lost all sense of time—'and the programme was tight! After the service there was to be a torchlight parade by the Parliament to hand Bibles to top members of the Parliament!'

In the end, if the parade *was* a little delayed, nobody minded, and Aske was moved to see his friend's obvious joy in being back in his ministry. ('For me, *not* preaching is a complete misery,' Bishop Festo had confided to his friends.)

By November the doctors pronounced Bishop Festo completely healed and let him go back to the diocese, where he was greeted rapturously. His secretary found that if his hands shook sometimes, making it hard for him to sign letters, 'his mind was as fresh as ever', and he could dictate letters to Dr Runcie, Billy Graham and a little old lady in a nearby village (who was having trouble with her pastor) 'all in practically the same breath'.

In his Christmas letter to the diocese, he thanked everyone for 'your prayers when I was sick. The Lord has answered wonderfully and I have recovered beautifully and am now doing the work of the Lord as usual.'

But he was not as he had been. For the first time in his life, he began to look something approaching his age: sixty-six years old. After much prayer and discussion, he and Mera had come to some difficult decisions. He shared them with his diocesan council on 18th December: he intended to retire, perhaps at the end of the following year, and go back to his first and towering love, evangelism, pure and simple. He would become full-time leader of the East Africa AEE team (they were delighted at the prospect).

The diocesan council was appalled. Some panicked, and began to talk about getting the Bishop to sign some sort of document promising to stay on for at least another ten years. All of them pleaded with him to forget retirement:

'You say you've already been our bishop for fourteen years? That's nothing. That makes you only a teenager!' cried one, clutching at straws.

'Stay until the new cathedral is built!' begged another. (A mammoth project, all but impossible with building materials so scarce.)

'Who would be able to take over?' was the wail on everyone's lips. 'Will he evangelise? Launch projects? Bring in health care? Educate the clergy?'

Mera rang Peace in Geneva. 'They won't hear of us retiring!' Both she and Festo were deeply moved by such an obvious expression of love, and for the moment did not press the matter further. They would give people time to get used to the idea before fixing a date. Meanwhile, Bishop Festo was gathering momentum for his 1987 diary: it began the day after Christmas when he flew to Amsterdam for a large New Year convention.

This 'Mission '87', as it was called, included seminars, one of which Bishop Festo led on Liberation Theology. Although his revivalist background had stressed the 'spiritual side' of Christianity, having seen the suffering that injustice could cause, he had come to have a lot of sympathy for what the liberal theologians were saying.

To Bishop Festo, Liberation Theology was:

> a protest against repressive established status quos in the church, which has lost its spiritual sensitivity. In the church's desperate efforts to impress the political and social world it has borrowed heavily from the world and has lost its true identity as the salt of the earth and the light of the world.
>
> The church is like an army which, having advanced too far into the enemy territory with insufficient supplies has to depend on its enemy for sustenance—and so has lost its ability to advance into or retreat from enemy territory.

So Bishop Festo tended to blame any imbalances in Liberation Theology on the established church.

> Liberation theology was born out of frustration and disappointment in the established church. The Bible and the traditional liturgy were eulogised. They gave comfort to the members and sweetly sent them to sleep. The radical challenges of the Old Testament prophets on practical injustices, social discriminations, political oppressions, economic exploitations and many other evils have been ignored. These evils have spread like cancer without any challenge from the leaders. The church has increasingly become a party in all this, directly or indirectly. Opportunism in politics and social benefits strangled the protesting and rebuking voice. The suffering masses had none to highlight their cause—they became more and more dehumanised and sank deeper into their silent misery. This was the case in Latin America, predominantly [Catholic countries], and in the big cities of Western Europe and the USA. But the same situation does exist in our Third World situations.

Festo and Mera.

Festo in his diocesan office at Kabale—with globe beside him!

Festo with Anne Coomes, his biographer. March 1987.

When the tragic divide between what, according to the Old Testament and the New Testament, are the two sides of the same coin—*the Salvation of the lost souls of men* (liberating them from bondage to sin, and breaking their dehumanising chains of selfishness and greed) and *the concern for their social needs*—were cut asunder by the exaggerated extreme views of various schools of theology, the demands of our Lord were diluted or explained away in his name.

At this point in time it seems that the representatives of different schools of theology are beginning to listen to one another. It is my hope, and the hope of many of my brethren in Africa, that those who hold different views on certain aspects of serving God's people will learn from each other, and so enrich the ministry. It is grieving to the Lord that much energy is wasted in condemnation and criticism of one another instead of encouraging each other and so strengthening the body of Christ. '*Learn from me*' says our Lord, 'for I am gentle and lowly in heart, and you will find rest for your souls' (Matt 11:29).

Christ, Festo went on, spent his earthly ministry teaching, preaching and healing:

'He had compassion on the harassed and helpless crowd.' How often the Lord had compassion on the sick, the hungry, the weeping and the like! (Matt 15:32)

For me, the heart of spiritual liberation is Jesus and him crucified, risen and reigning among his people. But spiritual liberation never takes place in a spirit without the rest of what makes you and me human. It embraces the whole of me—my rights, dignity, property, security and freedom.

Mere *political and social liberation* do not go far enough. They need a greater dynamic to achieve a whole liberation for the whole person—spirit, body and soul. So the preaching of Christ, the healing and feeding of the body for which he died, and the enlightening of the mind, work in harmony to make man whole in Christ Jesus.

Back in Kabale in January, Bishop Festo was soon practising what he had preached, in tackling a new 'disturbing trend' which he discovered was spreading fast, at least in Kabale. This was the gross manipulation of a Ugandan legal procedure which had been originally set up to deal quickly with people who had kidnapped others 'with intent to murder'. Citizens had discovered that if they accused someone of this sort of kidnap attempt, then that person would be arrested, taken to court, and put in remand custody for a year or two (no bail granted) before the case was even heard. As a revenge on, say, political opponents under former regimes, it could hardly be matched, because even if in the end the accused was released, no action was ever taken against the accuser.

By mid-January Bishop Festo had issued a press release, angry at this 'blatant manipulation of justice to violate a citizen's rights', pointing out that 'this changes the law of Uganda ... it seems now to say a citizen is guilty until he can prove himself to be innocent'.

He pleaded that 'competent' government officials 'thoroughly investigate' each case and only arrest where evidence could be found. Also, as a deterrent, 'If the accused is found to be innocent, the accuser should pay damages for the trouble he has caused...'

He appealed to the government, coming up to the eve of its first anniversary in power (26th January, 1987), to 'rescue this country from chaos in the administering of justice'. And speaking of justice, Bishop Festo went on to write a letter to the Deputy Minister of Rehabilitation on behalf of the 500 Banyarwanda still stuck at Kakitumba Camp (since Museveni had come to power, the vast majority had been resettled).

Another long term African problem also raised its ugly head that month—tribalism. But this time the tensions were actually within the 'revived' Kabale Christian community. For Bishop Festo, to many people's dismay, had chosen a man from an insignificant family and a lesser tribe to be the new dean of the cathedral. He installed him on 18th January. Many clergy were upset, and let the new dean know that he had less than their full support. But no one dreamed of querying Bishop Festo's choice straight to his face. Not only was Bishop Festo increasingly briskly authoritative within the diocese, but he had made his position on ambition among the clergy widely known.

In a sermon preached only a few weeks before, he had said:

The mission of his [Christ's] entire life here on earth may be summed up in one expression: 'He came to serve in love.' When James and John desired high positions in the ministry—as a means to *serve better,* to *exert more influence,* to *carry more weight,* and *exercise more authority*—they approached him through their mother to make their request less obvious. But the Lord Jesus saw through the folly of their mistaken understanding *of what gives influence to service.* It is not the position of the one who serves, not the rank, but *the heart flooded with the love of God,* in Christ, by the Holy Spirit (Romans 5:5).

Soon AEE commitments again called Bishop Festo away from Kigezi—this time to Nairobi and then Harare for important AEE meetings. By mid-February Bishop Festo was back to Kampala for a week-long mission held at Namirembe Cathedral (the meetings were held in the afternoons—there was still gunfire in the streets by night and everyone wanted to be home and off the streets by six). The mission, though low-key compared to some, was still reported on national television and raised city-wide interest and sympathy.

Then it was back to Kabale for another assault on a mountain of diocesan paperwork (including a letter to Archbishop Runcie concerned about Terry Waite who had disappeared only a few weeks before), a crisis at the school, endless visitors, the installation of a clergyman, and a confirmation tour that had to be cancelled at the last minute when a government official was murdered and Bishop Festo raced back up the long road to Kampala.

In March, Bishop Festo teamed up with the Revd Dr Don Jacobs, a very dear friend and colleague, for a new venture. They were to tour China. Jacobs said later:

When Festo lifted up Christ in the Chinese churches and seminaries and spoke about the African experience, one could almost feel a spark jumping from the African church to the Chinese church. I felt as though I was tasting the first fruits of a rich and meaningful fellowship between African Christians and Chinese Christians.

In many ways, these two movements represent the most phenomenal stories in twentieth century Christianity, but the two churches have been unaware of one another. It would be hard to imagine another person filling this role as ably as Festo. The word which God gave him was Exodus 3, where Moses turned aside to see the strange sight: a bush which burned with fire but was not consumed. The Bishop related the church in Uganda to the church in China, both of which have been in white-hot furnaces of fire. But rather than all being consumed, God spoke out of the fire. On this China trip we heard the clear word of the Lord which promised ongoing life and joy for both the church in China and in Uganda.

Other preaching engagements in America, Britain and elsewhere followed that summer, including one at the Kirchentag in Frankfurt—a vast international gathering drawing together some 120,000 Christians of every conceivable variety.

On 9th October, Uganda marked its twenty-fifth anniversary of independence. It had been a quarter of a century since Bishop Festo and Lilian Clarke had driven to Kampala to see the celebrations surrounding the lowering of the British Flag for the last time on Kampala's Kololo Hill. Uganda was less enchanted now with the idea of self-government. 'What a Lousy Independence' cried a national newspaper's headline. Even under President Yoweri Museveni, who had stopped the mass killings and torture, there was still widespread unrest among tribal and political factions. Disease, malnutrition and the AIDS epidemic were rampant. The IMF and World Bank had been brought in that May just to save the country from complete collapse.

But as Bishop Festo had often said in his sermons, the whole tragic mess came back in the end to a spiritual malaise:

> Outside God's authority and therefore under the authority of other lords, life is—in the words of the late Professor W. Barclay—'walking civil war', whether in a home, at work, in society. ... Broken relationships, racial and ideological conflicts tear apart nations... Peaceful co-existence is an expedient phrase expressing human inability to solve their hostilities conclusively...

Poor Uganda could not even reach peaceful co-existence.

Bishop Festo spent a busy October mostly within the diocese, so busy that the question of retirement was postponed. Privately, many people in the diocese breathed a sigh of relief. Now that Bishop Festo had been back a year and was fit and well again, surely he would stay on for years to come.

Then in November, shortly after a week-long mission at Makerere University, Bishop Festo came back to Kabale and fell ill with an unexplained fever.

It landed him in bed for a few days and the general consensus was that he had contracted malaria. At least, the fever responded well to malarial drugs. But then he developed some considerable pain in his right knee. He was treated for that, though no one was quite sure what it was.

To Mera's dismay, he fell ill yet again within days. He was admitted to Kabale Hospital suffering from palpitations. When the doctors discovered he was also very anaemic, they gave him some blood and decided to transfer him at once to Nairobi, where he could receive far more specialised treatment, and have further tests. Because of the prevailing political situation between Uganda and Kenya, it was not possible to fly him direct from Kabale to Nairobi. So he was driven to Kigali, the capital of Rwanda, a few hours away. Here the Missionary Flying Doctor Service had obtained landing rights, and on Monday, 21st December, Bishop Festo and Mera were flown to Wilson Airport in Nairobi. He was collected by an ambulance and driven straight to hospital.

The doctors at Nairobi conducted an extensive medical examination. Before Christmas the results were back from the laboratory tests. The Nairobi physicians had found a bone marrow abnormality.

After talks with Bishop Festo, Mera, the Revd Daniel Serwanga (the AEE Regional Co-ordinator) and the Revd John Mpaayei, Chairman of the AEE Kenya Board, it was decided to send Bishop Festo on to St Thomas' Hospital in London for a review of the findings. The Nairobi doctors wanted them confirmed, and chemotherapy treatment given, if necessary. Leukaemia was a possibility.

On Tuesday, 29th December, 1987, Bishop Festo and his wife flew to London. AEE sent out a call for prayer.

By 12th January the London hospital was conducting more tests. On Thursday 14th, Bishop Festo returned for further treatment to Nairobi.

Two weeks later the doctors' worst fears were confirmed. On 9th February, 1988, AEE released the news: 'Bishop Festo Kivengere of Uganda is seriously ill. The doctors at Nairobi have diagnosed malignant leukaemia.'

The news was broken to the International Partnership Board of African Enterprise as they met in Malawi. Bishop Festo sent them a personal telex, but uppermost on his mind was concern for what would happen to the arrangements for the major evangelistic campaigns being planned around Africa.

On Tuesday, 9th February, Bishop Festo returned to his diocese, and shared with his secretary, Judith Trickett that the doctors had given him a month to live. She recalls:

Of course that made me cry, but he began to share with me what the Lord has meant to him over this last two months. What a precious time. (We were sitting in his little office in his house. He was in his pyjamas and dressing-gown but was fairly strong, able to walk unaided, speaking clearly.) He asked me to read from Philippians 1:20 and 21. He said those verses were so special to him. He said his one fear was that he would bring dishonour to the Lord before he died. His voice broke a little then. I assured him that the Lord, who had kept him all these years, would not allow Festo to waver at the end. That was the only time I saw him struggle—in case he brought dishonour to Jesus. Festo said during his illness, especially the days of 18th, 19th and 20th December the Lord was so close to him. The doors of heaven were open, but God enabled him to come back and see his diocese again.

On Friday 12th he attended the Diocesan Council which he had called. The sixty members of the Council attended, plus observers. The Bishop was able to walk in unaided from the car and down the aisle to the front of the Cathedral. (We hold such meetings in the Cathedral because it is a large building.) Bishop William opened in prayer. Then Festo asked us to sing Rock of Ages. He then prayed for us, and although his voice was weak he was OK. He then asked Canon Abraham Zaribugire to read from Acts 20:28ff. Then Festo thanked all members for their support and prayers over the years. He thanked the Council for asking him to stay an extra ten years but now the Lord had clearly shown, through illness, that he had to leave them now. He explained that diseases of the blood cannot be cured and therefore his time was limited. He retired from the Diocese as of that day, 12th February.

Mera then gave a word of testimony and challenge. None of us know when we will leav this world. Are we ready to meet the Lord? When a student goes to university he has to make choices. If he chooses to do history he doesn't do geography, if he choses to do medicine he doesn't do agriculture. So for us, during this life, we have choices to make. Are we choosing to go the way of Jesus, choosing to go to Heaven?

Bishop Festo closed in prayer, we sang *'Tukutendereza'*, he walked unaided to the car and went home.

Then on 18th February he wrote to all AEE Board Chairmen and National Team Leaders and Chairmen of the Support Boards in USA, UK, Australia, Canada and West Germany.

'Dear Brothers,' he began, 'our ministry has gone through its Gethsemanes and Calvarys most recently. First, my illness which came as a shock; then the added shock of losing our dear brother James Katarikawe' (who had died of cerebral malaria only weeks before).

All these things, as one Bible writer said, are beyond me, but they are not beyond my Lord. He still is in control and we must hand over the circumstances to the Master. He knows what he is doing. He has never made a mistake. What we do not see today, we shall see tomorrow. All that we pray is that the Lord will save us from panic and keep us under the control of his victorious love.

Since I was informed that mine is an incurable illness—unless the Lord himself reverses all that, and he can—I have been thinking about our AEE family and the future ministry. We are not shaken backwards; we are shaken forward. These kinds of experiences in the power of the Holy Spirit are springboards from which to jump forward, not deterrents to stop us from moving. ...

God puts his servants aside and then chooses his servants to take their places. This is normal and we must accept it ...

He suggested that Bishop Gresford Chitemo of Tanzania be made his Deputy for the East Africa AEE ministry. 'For me, Bishop Gresford has been a Timothy, and I praise God for him.'

Throughout the remaining days of February, the doctors in Nairobi continued to treat Bishop Festo with chemotherapy. Prayers were offered up by Christians all over the world. On Thursday 3rd March, a group of senior churchmen, under the leadership of the Archbishop of Kenya, anointed Festo and prayed for his healing. Michael Cassidy also flew up from South Africa to visit him about this time. 'It was a most moving, poignant meeting,' said Michael later.

We reflected together on all we had been through over the years and as we discussed the future, we felt tremendously close and in deep unity of purpose and spirit. In spite of the most fervent hopes and prayers of all of us, I myself suspected this might be our last time together.

So Cassidy had several photographs taken of Bishop Festo and himself 'for the purpose of especially remembering those moments'. (One would later stand in a place of honour in his study.)

Meanwhile, Mera practically lived at the hospital, taking the crisis, as did her daughters, with 'unbelievable calm and courage', as Festo proudly wrote to friends. Gradually the Bishop began to improve. By mid-March when he was tested again, the team of doctors, headed by Dr David Silverstein, were startled to discover that there was no longer any sign of leukaemia in his blood. Silverstein was puzzled as to what to make of it, explaining that patients with Bishop Festo's type of leukaemia rarely respond to chemotherapy. He went on to warn Mera and the family and AEE friends and diocesan staff that the treatment did not cure the disease, but caused remission. So although the symptoms were gone, the leukaemia could recur. When and where, no one could say.

Still the leukaemia *was* gone. AEE telexed the good news around the world on 17th March, and thousands of Christians praised God. Many decided that this was most probably a miraculous healing. Bishop Festo, although prepared for the worst, felt so much better that at that moment he believed, 'What has happened to me is a miracle. You are looking at Lazarus.' With his characteristic optimism and impatience for action, he took his daily walks, gained strength and yearned for the energy to get back to work, using 'the time God has now given' in full-time ministry with AEE. He looked forward 'to a great ministry not only in East Africa, but all over the world, for this kind of experience is not provincial...'.

A week or so later came another press release. More good news—there was still no trace of leukaemia. Bishop Festo gained strength daily. Meanwhile, he was as active mentally as he had always been, to the point where he was keeping two or three secretaries stretched just in taking his dictation and typing his letters for him, thanking friends for their prayers, but begging still to be remembered.

He then formally resigned from Kigezi diocese. He made

plans with the diocesan secretary for when he should return to Kabale and formally hand over the diocese. As for the new bishop, he encouraged the mournful Christians in Kigezi to look for a man with integrity, 'one who could be chosen of the Lord so that the people would be strengthened'. Bishop Festo even began to think of a major mission to Birmingham that July. April passed, and Bishop Festo grew stronger.

May arrived, and the recovery went on. Bishop Festo grew more active daily. He called a meeting of the Regional Steering Committee to discuss the future.

Then on 11th May he collapsed with internal bleeding and was rushed to the Intensive Care Unit of Nairobi Hospital. The leukaemia was back. By the following day the doctors had given him several blood transfusions and stopped the bleeding. He was moved to a general ward. AEE staff with Festo's blood type donated their blood, in order to secure sufficient quantities for future transfusions.

The doctors began a second course of chemotherapy, but warned that while it might cause a new remission of the disease, it was likely to be shorter than the first remission had been.

The AEE Regional Leadership went ahead and met at Limuru, outside Nairobi, but they hadn't the heart for much but prayer, wanting 'to hear what the Lord is saying in the present situation'.

Friends rallied round Mera and the children, who all continued to display a remarkable 'inner peace'.

Then, surprisingly, the leukaemia ebbed away again. Bishop Festo began to strengthen. By Tuesday 17th May the doctors decided he had made such a recovery that they would let him go back to the Kivengeres' Nairobi flat. Bishop Festo was jubilant.

Next day, Wednesday 18th May, Mera spent the morning with Festo at the hospital. They rejoiced together, and read Psalm 103 in their prayer time. Everything looked good. Bishop Festo's suitcase was packed for him to take home.

Midday came and went. Then suddenly Bishop Festo began to feel uncomfortable. Within minutes he had collapsed. Doctors rushed him into the Intensive Care Unit, where he soon lapsed into a coma. The greatest evangelist Africa has ever known died at five pm that afternoon.

Mera remained calm and in control but distraught AEE staff

in Nairobi sprang into action. A flurry of telexes went round the world with the sad news. Numerous telephone calls had to be made as AEE were determined that as many friends as possible heard the news at first-hand. Serwanga and his staff worked through most of the night. Radio Uganda broadcast the news at eight pm that evening.

Within hours AEE itself was engulfed in telexes and telephone calls of love and condolences as Christian friends and admirers of Bishop Festo shared their grief and recalled their memories. An AEE staff member said later: 'It was marvellous to discover just how well known and well loved our dear Bishop has been.'

This became increasingly obvious as the day approached for his funeral.

A Memorial Service was held on Tuesday, 24th May in All Saints' Cathedral, Nairobi. Thousands gathered to view the body—so important in African culture.

Mera had chosen 'Blessed Assurance, Jesus is Mine', as it was Bishop Festo's favourite hymn. Tribute after tribute was paid to him.

On Wednesday, 25th May, Bishop Festo's body was flown to Kampala, accompanied by the family and AEE staff and friends. They travelled on a twin engined Fokke Wolf plane of Uganda Airlines, brought out of retirement by the Uganda Government especially for the occasion.

Hundreds of people were waiting to meet the plane at Entebbe Airport. They sang their welcome.

Government officials then told astonished and delighted AEE staff that the funeral was to be a State Funeral—the highest honour Uganda could pay Bishop Festo. Meanwhile, Government authorities had arranged for Mera and the funeral entourage to meet up with AEE and other friends in the VIP lounge at the airport, then to proceed with minimum fuss to Kampala and Namirembe Cathedral. Museveni, in fact, provided a long motorcade preceded by an army vehicle, giving them clearance through the military roadblocks. The journey, recalled an AEE staff member, was 'full of singing, clapping, praising Ugandan Christians rejoicing together. It was a marvellous privilege. The body of the Bishop was back in Uganda and the people were glad.'

On Namirembe Hill, the Hill of Peace, there were hundreds waiting to say farewell to the best-loved bishop in Uganda. They sang and testified 'to what Jesus had done in their lives'.

The Archbishop of Uganda, the Bishop of Namirembe and the Kampala staff took care of Mera and the small group from Kenya.

On Thursday, 26th May the Memorial Service was held at Namirembe Cathedral. This was a four-hour service 'full of tributes and challenges from many, many speakers, including the Prime Minister of Uganda'.

Michael Cassidy preached, recalling with love his Ugandan colleague. Mera, usually so quiet, stood to share memories of her life with Bishop Festo, speaking 'with boldness of the living Lord in their lives'.

Then on 27th May it was on to Kabale. The Ugandan Government provided two ambulances for the body, in case one broke down on the appalling roads.

On the border of Ankole and Kigezi thousands of Christians waited for the return of their bishop. A thirty-car escort accompanied the body to Kabale in the late afternoon, while singing praises to God. Kabale was packed out for the coming funeral. There was not a spare room in hotel or guest house anywhere. That night AEE staff ended up on the floor of church halls, and even on the floor of Bishop Festo's old office. Others stayed up all night singing hymns.

Throughout the Saturday 20,000 people met in service after service. Bishop after bishop praised, prayed, preached and gave testimony. The entire cabinet of the Ugandan government was there for what became known as 'The Celebrations'. Bishop Gresford Chitemo, upon whom 'the mantle of Bishop Festo' had fallen in AEE for the immediate future, also preached, his 'quiet sincerity' endearing him to many.

The Cathedral remained open literally all the Saturday night, for singing and prayer. It closed at six am for a few hours so that it could be tidied and fresh flowers put in for the funeral, which began on the Sunday morning. President Yoweri Museveni and his wife Janet arrived by helicopter. President Museveni spoke of the Bishop with deep feeling, calling him 'a man of truth and a faithful servant of the gospel'. He also praised Bishop Festo for being a 'hard worker', a man 'who was never involved in double-dealing', a lover of Uganda, Africa, and the whole world.

The Revd Dr Don Jacobs, International Chairman of AEE, based his message on Isaiah 52:7, 'How beautiful ... are the feet of him who brings good tidings.' Jacobs said that Bishop Festo had travelled the earth representing Jesus, 'always travelling, always on the move ... but always speaking of Jesus. Bishop Festo had beautiful feet because he had the feet of Jesus.'

Mera also spoke and friends found her words of 'simple' testimony 'beautiful and challenging'.

Finally, at five pm Bishop Festo's body was laid in a grave in the grounds of St Peter's Cathedral, Kabale. Hundreds wept as, after further prayer and hymns, the National Police Band played the Last Post. The African Church was saying goodbye to its most effective, best-loved evangelist.

A friend later wrote:

So the services ended and the night came softly across the land, lit gently by an almost full equatorial moon. It brought a deep peace to us all. The body of Bishop Festo was resting in the ground. His spirit had joined the heavenly host around the Throne singing...

As the last AEE telex had said on 18th May:

Bishop Festo ... has been promoted to glory. He has kept the faith, finished the course, and inherited the crown. He has lifted up the name of Jesus. Physically we hurt, but spiritually we rejoice. We know that Festo has gone home.

Perhaps Bishop Festo's last message to the thousands of friends and well-wishers at St Peter's that night would have been the same as he had given one evening in Leysin, Switzerland, nearly twenty years before: 'Should you forget all my words, but should your attention have been fixed and centred on Jesus, my work is done.'

EPILOGUE

ON MONDAY, 30th May, 1988, the day after Bishop Festo's funeral, the Archbishop of Uganda, Yona Okoth, called a meeting of the Kigezi Diocesan Council. He explained that as Festo had died 'in office' (in Uganda a bishop, though retired, remains bishop of the diocese until his successor is appointed), the Archbishop was now the Bishop of Kigezi until a new bishop could be elected and consecrated. The following interregnum was very difficult for Kigezi diocese—many people had been so *sure* the remission of Bishop Festo's leukaemia was a total healing, that they could not accept that Bishop Festo was indeed now dead. For a time the diocese lost all energy and vision, and simply mourned its loss. Finally, fourteen months after Bishop Festo's death, in July 1989, the Assistant Bishop of Kigezi, the Rt Revd William Rukirande, was consecrated the new diocesan Bishop of Kigezi. Under him the diocese slowly began to pick up the threads of life once more.

The leadership of AEE for East Africa was out of Bishop Festo's hands several weeks before he died. He had asked his former (naughty) student and then fellow teacher from Dodoma days, Bishop Gresford Chitemo of Morogoro to move up from being Team Leader of the AEE in Tanzania to be the new Regional Team Leader of the Eastern African Region. The ministry has continued to flourish. A Bishop Festo Memorial Fund was launched by the London AEE office, to help finance the training of young African evangelists.

Mera Kivengere moved to Nairobi to be with her daughter Joy until September 1989, and then moved back to make Kabale her home once more.

Joy, her husband and daughter moved back to Kampala about the same time.

Charity has remained in Kampala, working with World Vision.

Hope is still in Kampala, working for the Government.

Peace has stayed on in Geneva, where her husband works for the World Health Organisation.

Judith Trickett, the Bishop's secretary, came back to England. At the time of writing she is a student at St John's College, Nottingham, preparing for ordination.

After Bishop Festo's death, memorial services were held in several countries. The author of this biography attended the one held in early July at All Souls', Langham Place, London. Bishop Dick Lyth, the first Bishop of Kigezi, was also there, and summed up the service well:

> It was wonderfully organised and there was a great spirit of praise amongst the big crowd. But I know Bishop Festo would have been saddened by the fact that it consisted almost entirely of a eulogy of him.
>
> His great testimony was of the grace of God daily reaching out to a weak and undeserving and sinful man; and whenever this testimony of his was diluted, the Calvary love and forgiveness of God was proportionately reduced. And Festo would have none of it.

NOTES

Chapter 2
1. *Ruanda Notes,* August 1931.
2. ibid
3. Joe Church, *Quest for the Highest* (Paternoster Press: Exeter, 1980) p. 90.
4. ibid, p. 91.
5. ibid, p. 99.

Chapter 3
1. Festo Kivengere with Dorothy Smoker, *Revolutionary Love* (Christian Literature Crusade and Kingsway, Eastbourne, 1985) p. 64.
2. Church, op cit, p. 8.

Chapter 5
1. Kivengere, *Revolutionary Love,* op cit, p. 9.
2. ibid
3. ibid
4. Sanna Morrison Barlow, *Light is Sown* (Moody Press: Chicago, 1956) p. 50, 51.
5. Kivengere, *Revolutionary Love,* op cit, p. 12.
6. Barlow, op cit, p. 51.
7. ibid
8. Kivengere, *Revolutionary Love,* op cit, p. 9.
9. ibid, p. 10.
10. ibid
11. ibid
12. ibid
13. ibid, p. 11.
14. ibid
15. Barlow, op cit, p. 51.

16. Festo Kivengere, *When God Moves,* Revised Edition (AEE: Pasadena, 1976) p. 9.
17. Kivengere, *Revolutionary Love,* op cit, p. 14.
18. ibid, p. 14.
19. ibid, p. 15.
20. ibid
21. ibid
22. ibid
23. ibid
24. David Porter, *Man of Africa* (Scripture Union: London, 1979) p. 20.
25. Kivengere, *Revolutionary Love,* op cit, p. 15.
26. ibid, p. 16.
27. Barlow, op cit, p. 52.
28. Kivengere, *God Moves,* op cit, p. 16.
29. ibid
30. Patricia St John, *Breath of Life* (The Norfolk Press: London, 1971) p. 154.
31. Kivengere, *Revolutionary Love,* op cit, p. 16.
32. ibid
33. Kivengere, *God Moves,* op cit, p. 17.
34. Kivengere, *Revolutionary Love,* op cit, p. 20.

Chapter 6
1. Kivengere, *God Moves,* op cit, p. 17.
2. ibid
3. ibid, p. 18.
4. Kivengere, *Revolutionary Love,* op cit, p. 28.
5. ibid, pp. 40, 41.
6. ibid, p. 41.
7. ibid, p. 33.

Chapter 7
1. St John, op cit, p. 9.
2. Porter, op cit, p. 34.
3. ibid, p. 36.
4. Church, op cit, p. 219.
5. St John, op cit, p. 158.
6. Kivengere, *Revolutionary Love,* op cit, p. 65.

Chapter 8
1. ibid, p. 66.

2. ibid
3. Church, op cit, p. 168.
4. Kivengere, *Revolutionary Love,* op cit, p. 66.
5. ibid
6. ibid
7. ibid
8. ibid
9. ibid, pp. 66, 67.
10. ibid
11. Mary Mance, *Uganda—Then and Now* (Adventures in Faith Series No. 10, CMS: London) p. 17.
12. Kivengere, *Revolutionary Love,* op cit, pp. 67, 68.
13. ibid, p. 68.
14. ibid
15. ibid
16. ibid, p. 69.

Chapter 9
1. Kivengere, *Revolutionary Love,* op cit, p. 75.
2. ibid, pp. 57, 58.
3. ibid, pp. 26, 27.

Chapter 10
1. Porter, op cit, pp. 38, 39.
2. Kivengere, *Revolutionary Love,* op cit, p. 70.

Chapter 11
1. Adrian Hastings, *A History of Christianity in Africa 1950–1975* (Cambridge University Press, 1979) p. 132.
2. Kivengere, *Revolutionary Love,* op cit, pp. 59, 60.
3. Hastings, op cit, p. 112.
4. Kivengere, *Revolutionary Love,* op cit, p. 75.
5. ibid, pp. 75, 76.

Chapter 12
1. Festo Kivengere, 'Who Are You' *Decision* (September, 1966) p. 7.
2. Kivengere, *Revolutionary Love,* op cit, pp. 70–72.
3. Leslie Brown, *Three Worlds: One Word: Account of a Mission* (Rex Collings: London, 1981) p. 169.

Chapter 13
1. His sister, *Mackay of Uganda* (Hodder & Stoughton: London, 1898) p. 210.
2. Stephen Olford, *Heart Cry for Revival* (EMI Books: Memphis) p. 132.
3. S. R. Karugire, *A Political History of Uganda* (Heineman Educational Books: Nairobi/London, 1980) p. 196.
4. Festo Kivengere and Dorothy Smoker, *Love Unlimited* (Regal Books: Ventura, California, 1975) p. 10.
5. Hastings, op cit, p. 139.

Chapter 14
1. Kivengere, *Revolutionary Love,* op cit, p. 61.
2. ibid, p. 34.
3. ibid, p. 62.
4. ibid
5. *New Day*, November 6, 1969.
6. Roy and Mrs Hession, *The Story of the Mbarara Convention,* 1969, p. 11.

Chapter 15
1. Festo Kivengere with Dorothy Smoker, *I Love Idi Amin* (Marshall Morgan and Scott: London, 1977) p. 18.
2. John Mbiti, *The Crisis of Mission in Africa* (Uganda Church Press: Mukono, 1971) p. 1.
3. *Christianity in Africa*, p. 56.
4. Kivengere, *God Moves,* op cit, p. 14.
5. Kivengere, *I Love Idi Amin,* op cit, p. 19.
6. Tony Avirgan and Martha Honey, *War in Uganda: The Legacy of Idi Amin* (Lawrence Hill: London, 1982) p. 8.
7. Kivengere, *I Love Idi Amin,* op cit, p. 18.
8. ibid, p. 22.
9. ibid
10. ibid, p. 23.
11. Kivengere, *Revolutionary Love,* op cit, p. 60.

Chapter 16
1. Olford, op cit, p. 131.
2. Kefa Sempangi and Barbara Thompson, *Reign of Terror, Reign of Love* (Aslan Lion Books, 1979) p. 87.
3. Kivengere, *I Love Idi Amin,* op cit, pp. 24, 25.
4. ibid, p. 27.

5. ibid, p. 29.
6. J. D. Douglas, *Let the Earth Hear His Voice:* International Congress on World Evangelisation (Worldwide Publications: Minneapolis) p. 1355.

Chapter 17
1. Michael Cassidy and Gottfried Osei-Mensah, *Together in One Place* (Evangel Publishing House: Nairobi, 1978) p. 27.

Chapter 18
1. Margaret Ford, *Janani: the Making of a Martyr* (Lakeland/ Marshall, Morgan and Scott: London, 1978) p. 78.
2. Kivengere, *Revolutionary Love,* op cit, p. 76.
3. ibid
4. ibid, p. 77.
5. ibid
6. John Capon, 'Exiled Bishop of the Martyred Church' *Crusade Magazine,* May 1977, p. 20.
7. ibid
8. Ford, op cit, p. 79.
9. Kivengere, *I Love Idi Amin,* op cit, p. 80.
10. Ford op cit, p. 81.
11. ibid, p. 82.
12. ibid
13. ibid, p. 86.
14. ibid
15. ibid
16. Capon, op cit, p. 20.
17. Ford, op cit, p. 90.
18. ibid
19. Capon, op cit, p. 20.

Chapter 19
1. Capon, op cit, p. 21.
2. ibid, p. 22.
3. ibid
4. ibid
5. ibid
6. *New York Daily News,* March 12, 1977.
7. Cassidy, *Together,* op cit, p. 218.
8. Kivengere, *I Love Idi Amin,* op cit, p. 62.
9. Kivengere, 'What Lessons for Africa?' (*Step:* vol. 3, no. 5) pp. 5–8.

Chapter 21
1. Festo Kivengere, *Outlook* vol. 19, no. 2, 1982, p. 1.

BIBLIOGRAPHY

Books

Anderson, W. B. *The Church in East Africa 1840–1974*. Central Tanganyika Press: 1977.

Allison, Oliver. *Through Fire and Water*. CMS.

Avirgan, Tony and Honey, Martha. *War in Uganda: The Legacy of Idi Amin*. Lawrence Hill: London, 1982.

Barlow, Sanna Morrison. *Light Is Sown*. Moody Press: Chicago.

Brown, Leslie. *Three Worlds: One Word: Account of a Mission*. Rex Collings: London, 1981.

Butler, William H. A. *Hill Ablaze*. Hodder and Stoughton: London, 1976.

Cassidy, Michael and Verlinden, Luc. *Facing the New Challenges—the Message of PACLA*. Evangel Publishing House: Kisumu, Kenya, 1978.

Cassidy, Michael. *I Will Heal Their Land; Papers of the South African Congress on Mission and Evangelism*. Africa Enterprise: Pietermaritzburg, 1974.

Cassidy, Michael. *Prisoners of Hope: The Story of South African Christians at a Crossroad*. Africa Enterprise: Pietermaritzburg, 1974.

Cassidy, Michael and Osei-Mensah, Gottfried. *Together In One Place: the Story of PACLA*. Evangel Publishing House: Kisumu, Kenya, 1978.

Church, Joe. *Awake Uganda! The Story of Blasio Kigozi and His Vision of Revival*. The Uganda Bookshop Press: 1957.

Church, Joe and colleagues of the Ruanda Mission. *Forgive Them: the Story of an African Martyr*. Hodder and Stoughton: London, 1966.

Church, Joe. *Jesus Satisfies: An Account of Revival in East Africa*. Revised Edition. Africa Christian Press: London, 1973.

Church, Joe. *Quest For The Highest: an Autobiographical Account of the East African Revival*. Paternoster Press: Exeter, 1981.

Cox, Thornton. *Traveller's Guide to East Africa*. Thornton Cox: Malta, 1970.

Dawson, E. C. *James Hannington: First Bishop of Eastern Equatorial Africa*. Seeley and Co Ltd: London, 1892.

Douglas, J. D. *Let The Earth Hear His Voice; International Congress on World Evangelisation*. Worldwide Publications: Minneapolis.

Faupel, John Francis. *African Holocaust: the Story of the Uganda Martyrs*. Geoffrey Chapman: London, 1962.

Fenton, Roy. *A Guide to Uganda*. Uganda Department of Information: Kampala, 1954.

Ford, Margaret. *Janani: the Making of a Martyr*. Lakeland/Marshall, Morgan and Scott: London, 1978.

Gleave, J. T. *Geography for Uganda Schools: Book One*. Evans Brothers Ltd: London, 1958.

Gluckman, Max. *Custom and Conflict in Africa*. Basil Blackwell: Oxford, 1955.

Hastings, Adrian. *A History of Christianity 1950–75*. African Studies Series: Cambridge University Press, 1979.

Hildebrandt, Jonathan. *History of the Church in Africa: a survey*. Africa Christian Press: London, 1981.

Ingham, Kenneth. *A History of East Africa*. Longmans: 1962.

Karugire, S. R. *A Political History of Uganda*. Heineman Educational Books: Nairobi/London, 1980.

Kavuma, P. *Crisis in Buganda*. Rex Collings: London, 1953.

Keswick Convention Council. *The Keswick Convention Week, 1972*. Marshall, Morgan and Scott: London, 1972.

Keswick Convention Council. *The Keswick Week, 1975: Centenary Year*. Marshall, Morgan and Scott: London, 1975.

Kivengere, Festo with Smoker, Dorothy. *Hope for Uganda and the World: the Secret Rehabilitation*. Evangel Publishing House: Nairobi, 1980.

Kivengere, Festo. *Jesus Our Reality.* Uganda Church Press: Mukono, Uganda, 1973.

Kivengere, Festo with Smoker, Dorothy. *I Love Idi Amin.* Marshall, Morgan and Scott: London, 1977.

Kivengere, Festo with Smoker, Dorothy. *Love Unlimited.* Regal Books (a division of Gospel Light Publications): Ventura, California, 1975.

Kivengere, Festo with Smoker, Dorothy. *Revolutionary Love.* Christian Literature Crusade: Fort Washington, Pennsylvania, 1983.

Kivengere, Festo. *The Spirit is Moving.* Revised Edition. Africa Christian Press: 1979.

Kivengere, Festo. *When God Moves.* Revised Edition. African Enterprise: Pasadena, 1976.

Mance, Mary. *Uganda—Then and Now.* Adventures of Faith Series No. 10. CMS, London.

Marsh, Z. A. and Kingsnorth, G. *Introduction to the History of East Africa.* Cambridge University Press: London, 1958.

Murray, Jocelyn. *Proclaim the Good News: A Short History of the Church Missionary Society.* Hodder Christian Paperbacks: London, 1985.

Okullu, J. Henry. *Church and Politics in East Africa.* Uzima Press: Nairobi.

Oliver, Roland. *The Missionary Factor in East Africa.* Longmans.

Oliver, Roland and Page, J. D. *A Short History of Africa.* Penguin African Library.

Parringer, Geoffrey. *Religion in Africa.* Penguin African Library.

Pirouet, Louise. *Black Evangelists: the Spread of Christianity in Uganda 1891–1914.* Rex Collings: London, 1978.

Pirouet, Louise. *Strong in the Faith: the Witness of the Uganda Martyrs.* Church of Uganda Literature Centre: Mukono, Uganda, 1969.

Price, Ena. *Those Who Say Yes.* The Highway Press: London, 1965.

St John, Patricia. *Breath of Life.* The Norfolk Press: 1971.

Sempangi, Kefa and Thompson, Barbara. *Reign of Terror,*

Reign of Love. Aslan Lion Books: 1979. (First published as. *A Distant Grief* by Regal Books, G/L Publications, USA.)

Stone, Elaine Murray. *Uganda: Fire and Blood.* Logos International: Plainfield, New Jersey, 1977.

Taylor, John V. *Guide to the Church in Uganda.*

Taylor, John V. *Processes of Growth in an African Church.* IMC Research Pamphlets No. 6. SCM Press Ltd: London, 1958.

Warren, Max. *Revival—An Enquiry.* SCM Press Ltd: London, 1954.

Welbourn, F. B. *East African Christian.* The Student's Library, Oxford University Press: London, 1965.

Wooding, Dan and Barnett, Ray. *Uganda Holocaust.* Pickering and Inglis: London, 1980.

Articles and Magazines

Capon, John. 'Exiled Bishop of the Martyred Church', *Crusade.* May 1977.

Kivengere, Festo. 'Who Are You?' *Decision.* September 1966: pp. 7 and 8.

Porter, David. *Man of Africa.* Scripture Union: London, 1979.

Purseglove, J. W. 'Uganda's Pearl Reclaimed: the Pioneer Kigezi Scheme', *East African Annual 1950–51*: p. 47.